ALPINES AND ROCK GARDEN PLANTS

ALPINES AND ROCK GARDEN PLANTS

A complete guide to care and cultivation

Richard Bird and John Kelly

WARD LOCK

To the memory of Roy Elliott, one of the greatest alpine gardeners

ACKNOWLEDGEMENTS

The publishers are grateful to the following for granting permission to reproduce the colour photographs: Duncan Lowe (pp. ii, iv, v & vi); Peter Stiles (p. iii); and G.S. & G.C. Phillips: all the remainder, except for p. xxiii.

All line drawings were drawn by Duncan Lowe.

A WARD LOCK BOOK

Ward Lock
Wellington House, 125 Strand
London WC2R 0BB

A Cassell Imprint

Copyright © Richard Bird & John Kelly 1992, 1994, 1998

First published 1992 as
The Complete Book of Alpine Gardening
Reprinted 1994 and 1995

This edition first published 1998

British Library Cataloguing in Publication Data
A catalogue record for this book is available from the British Library

ISBN 0-7063-7728-1

Distributed in Canada by
Cavendish Books Inc.,
Unit 5, 801 West 1st Street
North Vancouver, B.C.
Canada V7P 1A4

Text filmset by RGM Associates, Southport, PR8 4AS
Printed in Hong Kong

Contents

Preface

An increasing number of gardeners is becoming interested in alpines. This is partly because of the plants themselves but it is also partly because the style of gardening appeals to them.

The plants are very attractive and, whether seen on a rock garden, trough or show bench they always stop the passer-by in admiration. There are more alpine plants in cultivation than in any other area of gardening; in fact there are so many of them that no two gardens are ever alike in their contents. Although, of course, there are many hybrids and cultivars there are also plants that are very close to the wild originals, the majority being true species. This means that most have a simple elegance and true beauty that escapes the modern brash cultivars in other forms of cultivation.

Because of their wild origins and the fact that they come from regions that are so different from our gardens, alpine growers have to become much more involved with their charges than do other gardeners. Plants have to be provided with soil and positions in the garden that suit their individual needs. The more the gardener knows about the plants the more he or she will succeed. Many enthusiasts go regularly to the mountains each year just to see their favourite plants in their natural habitats so that they can both admire them and to see how they grow. Gardening at this level almost becomes a course in practical botany.

Of course not all growers go this far and much can be enjoyed at a more simple level. One of the advantages of alpine gardening is that it can be as extensive as the gardener requires. Some rock gardens can be several acres in extent, with streams running through them, while others are no more than the landscaped surface of a sink or trough. Alpine gardening is ideal for those who are elderly or infirm as their gardening can be scaled down to manageable size. Troughs or beds can be raised off the ground to give easy access, and tiring routines such as digging or weeding are virtually eliminated while the gardener is still in intimate contact with plants.

Some gardeners go further still and grow all their plants in pots, either in the controlled atmosphere of the alpine house or cold frame. Here each plant can be cossetted with detailed attention.

Although it is essentially a plantsman's form of gardening, where the plant is the most important thing, there are many different approaches to it which means that there is something in it for everyone.

In this book we have tried to distil our knowledge and experience in such a way that both the beginner and more advanced grower will discover much of interest and help. Ultimately there is only one way to learn about alpines – and that is by growing them, which we strongly urge you to do.

R.B. & J.K.

CHAPTER 1
Background to Alpines

What are alpines?

Over the years many definitions have been put forward as to what constitutes an alpine in the gardening sense. They can simply be considered as plants that grow on mountains, but then this omits those plants that grow in arctic regions at sea level. Another definition may be those plants that are covered in snow in winter but this forgets those crevice plants that hang on vertical rock faces as well as the many plants that grow in deserts and on the Mediterranean shores, in particular bulbs, that alpine gardeners love so much.

The other way of looking at the problem is to consider to what use the plants are put rather than where they come from, and here we begin to make progress. Alpine gardeners tend to grow low-growing plants (not necessarily small plants as some can be metres across) that are hardy enough to grow through a winter in the open garden or in an unheated greenhouse. The plants may have their origins anywhere in the world and at any altitude. They may be plants of the open mountainside or from woodlands and meadows lower down. In the garden they can be grown in rock gardens, scree beds, raised beds, sinks, troughs, peat beds, or in pots in alpine houses or frames. In other words, a working definition of an alpine is a low hardy plant grown by alpine gardeners.

Why grow alpines?

In many ways alpine gardening is the most stimulating and exciting form of gardening there is. In the first instance the range of plants that it is possible to grow is enormous. The majority of them are still very close to their wild counterparts and seed from species new to cultivation is being introduced all the time. This range means that it is rare to find any two alpine gardeners growing the same plants. It also means that alpine gardening never grows stale; there are always new plants to explore.

Exploration in its literal sense is also one of the attractions of alpine gardening. Many growers like to go to the mountains for their holiday to see the plants in the wild. In this way they not only have the pleasure of seeing the plants in their natural habitat but can also see the conditions in which they grow, which helps the gardener choose the right position and soils in his own garden for similar plants. In the past travel to the mountains was also to collect plants but this is now rightly condemned as we begin to realize the implications of such action.

Growing alpines involves a closer study of the plants than any other branch of gardening. There are, of course, many plants that are easy to grow but there are others that verge on the near impossible. This presents a challenge that ever stimulates the gardener. To achieve this, much time must be spent in studying the plants and working out the right conditions of growth. In many respects this level of activity approaches practical botany rather than gardening.

Needless to say, it is not essential to get as involved as this. A great deal of pleasure can be had from a simple rock garden but such is the subject that it can soon get into the gardener's blood and carry him to heights he did not realize he could achieve.

One way of showing this achievement is in the garden itself. A well-tended rock garden, particularly in spring, can be a sight to behold, but it is not only in the garden that the plants can be seen. Being small they are readily portable and they can easily be displayed at one or more of the many shows put on in every country by alpine societies. These are magnificent affairs and it is often the sight of the benches full of well-grown plants that inspires many people to grow them.

There are many other reasons for growing alpines. They take up little space and an alpine garden can be confined to an old sink or trough, making it possible for a person with no more than a balcony to have a garden. Raised beds can be constructed so that the elderly or people confined to wheelchairs are able to continue their gardening on a scale and at a level which suits them.

Last but not least is the beauty of the plants themselves. Because of the size of the plants, the gardener tends to be on a more intimate relationship with his charges and this reveals the full detail and fascination of the shapes, colours and textures. It is a magical world and one to which many people are turning in relief from the restlessness of the brash colours increasingly found in modern bedding and other forms of flower gardening.

Plants in the wild

As we have already seen, plants that are grown by alpine gardeners come from a wide range of places. The majority come from mountainous regions or lowland areas with the same climatic conditions. Some come from the high mountain tops where there is a short summer, allowing the plants to bloom briefly and seed before once again being covered in snow. Growth of these plants often starts before the snow melts and a band of flowers can be seen following the receding snow up the mountain. This immediate reaction of the plant gives it maximum time to get through its summer cycle.

What many gardeners do not appreciate is that these flowers are able to come into growth because in many cases the soil beneath the snow is not frozen, but kept fractionally above freezing by the deep insulating layer of snow. This is why some plants that come from high altitudes, where the winds are fierce and the winters cold, find that being exposed to the cold snaps in our relatively mild winters without the snow is too much to bear.

These high alpine plants tend to be short, partly because of the short growing season, partly because of the strong winds and partly because of the high levels of ultraviolet light at these altitudes. These factors have implications when they are grown in our lowland gardens as will be seen later.

On these high mountain areas the plants live in pockets of detritus or have roots that penetrate deeply into loose rock (screes) or into crevices. Their situations ensure that they have very free drainage. There are times when their roots may be immersed in water from snow-melt, but this is constantly moving water which is well aerated. In the garden, alpine plants must be given equivalent free-draining composts that do not allow for stagnant water to hang around the roots as this will spell death to nearly all of them.

It is not only water round the roots that many plants dislike. Many have adaptations to prevent too much water accumulating in their crowns. Some grow on their side in crevices, while others are covered in silvery hairs to give a waterproof protection to their leaves.

Another feature of the high alpines is that they tend to live individually and do not have the intense competition with which plants lower down have to contend. Plant a high alpine in an herbaceous border and it will not be long before it succumbs.

Further down the mountainside plants many live in woods or in the alpine meadows. Here they are able to stand more competition from trees and grasses as well as other flowering plants. The woodland flowers like the protection from sun and wind, and the conditions that the trees provide, such as the provision of humus in the form of dead leaves. These conditions can be copied in the garden as will be seen later in the book.

The meadow plants are much more lush than their mountain-top brethren. They have plenty of moisture running down the mountain side from the snow-melt. This water is also rich in minerals from dissolved rocks higher up. Food is provided in the form of rotting vegetation from the dead grasses and other plants as well as from detritus washed down the mountainside. These plants will require a different treatment in the garden to those growing higher up.

Outcrops of rock will provide homes for some of the higher mountain plants down amongst the meadows and even lower, sometimes right down to sea level.

Some plants grown by the alpine gardener – and here one is thinking mainly of bulbs – come from desert regions where the summers are very hot with the soil baked hard. Growth takes place in the wet season, either at the onset of winter or as it merges with spring. These conditions are difficult to achieve in the garden in an average English summer, but it is possible to grow many of these beautiful plants with the aid of some protection as will be shown.

Alpine plants come from all continents of the world; even areas such as Papua-New Guinea, which one associates with tropical vegetation, have a mountain of sufficient height to produce plants that are hardy in the British climate. Throughout these areas there is a great variety of soils varying from acidic to alkaline. Some plants have adapted to growing in one type and must be given these special conditions in the garden. Well-known examples of this are ericaceous plants, such as rhododendrons, which need acid conditions. However, travellers in the wild may sometimes be surprised to see these growing in limestone areas but in such cases there is usually a pocket of detritus which gives the rhododendron the soil it wants.

These then are some of the conditions in which alpine plants grow in the wild. Nearly the whole of this book is devoted to helping you create equivalent conditions in the garden.

Introduction of plants

Many thousands of different plants are grown throughout the world by alpine gardeners. With the exception of hybrids and cultivars that have been bred in cultivation, they have all been introduced from the wild at some time or other. Man has collected plants to decorate his gardens for many centuries and although a few alpines were introduced in this way, it was not until the nineteenth century and the evolution of the rock garden that they were collected in any systematic way.

The European Alps was one of the first areas to be explored and gradually, as demands grew for more exotic plants, collectors moved on to the Himalaya and beyond. Some areas like the Andes were not seriously visited until between the two World Wars and it is really only in very recent times that people such as John Watson have introduced new species in any quantity from this region to our gardens by way of seed.

In the past plants were introduced as seed, bulbs or as plants. The last were the most difficult as transportation was slow and the plant had to be kept alive for many months before it was in the hands of the nursery or the grower. Alpines are particularly difficult to transport as they like light airy conditions and are not really suitable to the glass Wardian cases in which plants were generally shipped back. What particularly exacerbated the situation was that many mountain ranges lie in hot regions and once the plants were down the mountain they had long periods of travel through tropical conditions. Seed and bulbs were a better option but they had to be collected when the plant was out of flower so the collector was not necessarily aware of whether he was collecting a good form or not. The way round this problem was to visit each area twice, marking the best plants on the first trip with a tag and then collecting seed on the second.

Collectors of the past were either commissioned by nurseries and seed firms to go out and collect plants or they were adventurers of private means with an interest in plants. Reginald Farrer was one of the latter. He collected first in Europe and then moved on to China and lastly to Burma where he died. As with all great collectors he discovered species new to science and had many plants named after him including *Gentiana farreri* and *Geranium farreri*.

Other famous collectors worked in the Far East in the early part of the century and many of our garden plants were introduced by them during these trips. The most famous collector of the era was E. H. Wilson, probably best known for his introduction of *Lilium regale* and *Lonicera nitida*. He introduced a wealth of plants but very few alpines, but his contemporaries George Forrest and Frank Kingdon-Ward introduced a large number of plants that are still grown in our gardens. Plants named specifically after the former include *Primula forrestii* and *Pleione forrestii*. Two of Kingdon-Ward's famous introductions were the blue poppy, *Meconopsis betonicifolia*, and *Primula florindae*, which he named after his first wife.

After the Second World War there was concentration on areas nearer to home when collectors such as Peter Davis, Paul Furse and John Watson explored the Near East, in particular Turkey. In the 1970s and 1980s attention again turned to the Far East, to the Himalaya and eventually, when it again became accessible, to China. During this period there was also an upsurge of interest in plants from New Zealand and many new and exciting plants were introduced from there, in particular by Graham Hutchins of County Park Nursery in Essex, UK. As mentioned earlier, John Watson made several trips to the southern end of the Andes, bringing back seed of many plants unknown in cultivation, the most famous of which was *Mimulus* 'Andean Nymph', which can be now found in most nurseries and garden centres.

Collectors of the past have brought back plants from the wild; indeed there were organized parties to the European Alps in particular, whose purpose was to collect material for their rock gardens. This is now to be deprecated. Collecting may not be the greatest of pressure on plants (development and pollution have far greater effects) but nonetheless every plant removed from the wild is one less plant to ensure future generations and there are numerous examples where over-collecting has wiped out species or significantly reduced their numbers. Most species are readily available in cultivation either from nurseries or seed exchanges, so there is little reason to dig up plants. A sad fact is that most plants that are dug up in the wild never make it back to the garden; they rot or die on the way confined in a sponge-bag or some other inappropriate container. Collect a few seeds by all means if there is a large enough population, but leave the other plants for this and future generations to enjoy.

History of alpine gardening

Unlike most other areas of horticulture, alpine gardening has a relatively short history. The first rock gardens were constructed more to show off the nature of the rock and the structures that could be made from them than as a home to a collection of plants. Thus before the beginning of the nineteenth century and, indeed, well into it grottoes and rocky landscapes were created, some miniature imitations of favourite mountains. Although some alpine plants were used, the main plantings were of conifers and ferns.

A few gardens had been designed especially for growing alpine plants and one of the first of these was in 1772 when such a garden was constructed in the Chelsea Physic Garden, but it was not until a century later that the botanic

gardens at Kew (1867) and Edinburgh (1871) built their first rock gardens. By then the movement was well under way with at least one nurseryman, James Backhouse of York, offering alpine plants and a construction service. William Robinson published his *Alpine Flowers for English Gardens* in 1870 and this added further impetus, until eventually the rock garden was becoming widespread in private gardens as well as in the botanical institutions and the large houses.

As well as the plunder of the wild for plants, these rock gardens required huge amounts of stone and as a result many limestone pavements in Yorkshire and elsewhere were ripped up. It took nearly a century before the implications of this were seen but now these unique natural phenomena are protected to prevent further destruction.

Another factor at this time was that the first attempts were made to make the rock gardens look like natural outcrops by paying attention to the geological formations of rocks. As we will see when the construction of rock gardens is discussed, this is still the approach favoured today.

During the early part of the twentieth century interest grew as more plants became available. Numerous books were published on the subject including several by Reginald Farrer whose influence on the movement was tremendous. Besides Farrer many other very influential men were appearing, Clarence Elliott at his Six Hills Nursery and Walter Ingwersen at Birch Farm Nursery being the most important. Although nurserymen, these and many others grew their plants out of sheer love rather than for financial gain and this has been a trend that has come down to the present day.

Alpine houses had been used since the nineteenth century to cultivate difficult plants. Indeed the first rock garden at the Chelsea Physic Garden had been built indoors but it was not until the early twentieth century that they became widespread. They soon evolved into their present design which allows plenty of air to pass through them.

By now the rock garden and the alpine house had evolved into the form that is still used today, but other events were taking place. In the early 1920s Clarence Elliott realized that many alpine plants could be grown to advantage in containers and he began to scour the country for old stone water troughs and sinks. Today this concept of growing alpines has continued and has been widened to include glazed sinks and fabricated containers.

By the 1920s and 1930s alpine gardening had more or less taken the form that we know it today. In the mid-1930s a group of enthusiasts got together and formed the Alpine Garden Society. Membership has continued to increase and by 1990 had reached 12 000, doing much to further interest in the subject.

After World War II many gardens were derelict through neglect but they were soon revived and enthusiasm rekindled. The approach is still basically the same as in the pre-war days except that the rock garden has gone somewhat out of fashion, with cultivation in raised beds and in pots taking preference. As the century closes there is a resurgence of interest in the rock garden as one of the best means of displaying alpine plants.

Modern technology has had little impact on alpine gardening except in some of the botanic gardens which have installed computerized alpine houses in which the temperature, ventilation, amount of sun, humidity, watering and security are all controlled by machines. Some have also installed specialized refrigerated plant to help simulate the alpine conditions. Very few individual growers have been able to go to these extremes.

In the open garden, even in botanic gardens, technology has had little effect, except possibly in that modern sprinkling systems make watering easier and more effective.

The modern grower, then, is still able to call on over a century of tradition that is as valid today as it has ever been.

PART I

ALPINES IN THE GARDEN

CHAPTER 2

Rock Gardens and Screes

Rock gardens are one of the most natural ways of displaying alpine plants. The rocks are not only reminiscent of the plants' native surroundings but they also set off the plants to their best advantage. If well sited and carefully constructed, the rock garden can be a very attractive feature of a garden, particularly in spring when the maximum number of plants are in flower. Another big advantage of a rock garden is that it can be designed in such a way as to give a number of different habitats: some in shade, some in full sun; some with a very gritty soil, while others might have peaty, moisture-retentive soils. This means that a large number of plants, each requiring different conditions, can be grown to their best advantage in a comparatively small area.

The arguments put forward against rock gardens are that they are expensive and that they are difficult to maintain. There is no doubt that the initial expense of the rock is high, particularly if you live in an area where there is no natural rock being quarried, but once it has been acquired it will last for ever, unlike peat and many other garden materials. It can also be used again if the garden is redesigned. As to the second argument, if well prepared in the first place, a rock garden should be no more difficult to maintain than any other method of growing alpines.

For a rock garden to work well a lot of thought must go into its siting, layout and construction. Do not rush out into the garden in a fit of enthusiasm and heap up a lot of sub-soil left over from the footings of a building or from the excavations of a pond and cover it with lumps of concrete. No matter how it is planted it will never look right even if the plants did manage to survive in the poor soil. Take time to consider all the following elements before thinking of starting. No matter how badly you draw (no-one else need look at it), doodle while you are thinking and try and get some visual idea of what you want to achieve.

Siting the rock garden

This is one of the most difficult aspects of making a rock garden and one of the most awkward to advise on as nearly every garden is different from the next. The siting must be right first time, otherwise tons of rock and earth have got to be dismantled and then reconstructed elsewhere.

There are a couple of basic rules that must be observed in all gardens. The rock garden should be sited in an open sunny position away from dripping trees and shrubs. It is possible to choose a site which only receives sun for part of the day but this will restrict the number of plants that can be grown. Most plants on a rock garden will tolerate the wind that an open position will bring but they do not like draughts that are produced by wind being funnelled between two buildings or other structures. This type of position should be avoided.

The second requirement is that it should not be located in a depression or other area in which water accumulates. In theory a rock garden is built above the surrounding ground and therefore should be immune to water at ground level, but of course water will move up through the soil by capillary action and only the very top of the structure will be dry enough to grow plants. The excess moisture will promote the growth of liverwort, moss and other weeds and the surrounding area will be trampled into a quagmire as you walk round it. If the ideal position for the rock garden lies in a wet area then drain that part, or, if necessary, the whole garden. Should the garden be on a slope then there will be no problem but if the garden is level then a soakaway should be constructed some way off by digging a hole about 180 cm (6 ft) deep by 90 cm or 120 cm (3 ft or 4 ft) wide and filling it with rubble. A drain (using either plastic drainage pipe or simply filling a trench with pea gravel) can be led from the site to the soakaway (Fig. 2.1).

Slopes make ideal sites, particularly if they

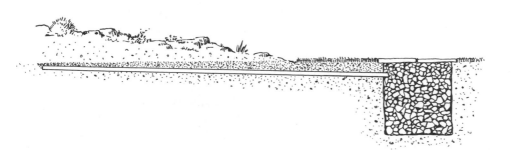

Fig. 2.1 Make certain that the site of the rock garden is well drained, using plastic drainage pipes or a trench filled with pea gravel leading to a soakaway.

Fig. 2.2a Frost rolling down a hill can be trapped by a hedge, forming a frost pocket.

face south. However the bottom of these can not only produce the problems of excess water as already mentioned, but can also cause frost pockets, where cold air rolls down the hill and gets trapped on the lower ground. Most alpine plants will take a large degree of cold, but frost hollows are also associated with damp air which is something that these plants are not keen on. Where possible avoid such positions. If the frost pocket is caused by the cold air trapped by a hedge going across the slope then a hole can be cut in the bottom of it to allow the air to pass on its way (Fig. 2.2). Alternatively, it might be possible that an inverted V-shaped hedge can be planted or a wall can be built up-hill of the rock garden to divert the cold air.

As long as the garden is naturally or artificially free-draining, it does not matter on what rock or soil the rock garden is built.

Other aspects of siting the rock garden relate to aesthetics and convenience. All other factors being equal, choose a site which will enhance the overall appearance of the garden.

Fig. 2.2b By removing part of the hedge or cutting a hole in its bottom, the frost can be drained away.

Choosing rock

In the choice of rock, consideration must be given to the delicate balance between aesthetics and the depth of the gardener's pocket.

Undoubtedly the best rock to choose is a local one. This will fit into the garden in a more natural way and should look at home. Limestone used in an area of naturally occurring sandstone can look out of place. Local stone will also be cheaper as it will not have to be carried so far. Not all such stones are suitable though. Some may crack up or split in

Fig 2.2c Alternatively a wall or hedge can be built higher up the slope to deflect the cold air.

15

the frosts, to be reduced to a heap of smaller pieces, and buying this type of rock can be a waste of money. Check before you buy but bear in mind that some sandstone is soft when it is first quarried and hardens when it is exposed to air.

The most commonly used stones for rock gardens in Britain are limestone and sandstone. Granite can be used but it has a very hard, unyielding look to it and somehow seems inappropriate for a small garden. Both the other two stones can be found in a range of colours. Sandstone often looks overbright when first quarried but will soon tone down. To some eyes the dark brown forms stained with iron can be too sombre, detracting from the appearance of the plants.

The great favourite of rock gardeners of the past was the water-worn limestone from Cumbria and Yorkshire. This was ripped from the ground, destroying many areas of natural rock garden. Fortunately this destruction has now ceased, but with it of course the supply of this wonderful stone. It is still possible to find it second-hand, but it is usually very expensive. The choice of limestone does restrict the number of plants that can be grown as the calcifuges (plants that cannot grow on alkaline soils) will have to be excluded.

There are some alpine growers who are lucky enough to have a free supply of rock, but for the most part it is one of the major expenditures. The problem is not so much the cost of the rock itself but the cost of the transportation to get it from the quarry to either the garden or to the intermediate point of purchase. If possible always buy rock direct from the quarry, rather than from a garden centre as this inevitably will be cheaper; and it is even cheaper still if you can arrange your own transport.

It is always best to go to the quarry and select the pieces of rock you want, otherwise you might get odd-shaped pieces, lumps that you cannot move, or a mass of small bits that are useless. The question of size is important: remember you have to move them, so unless you have access to a JCB, do not get carried away with the notion of large outcrops with huge pieces of stone.

Garden centres often offer alternatives to natural stone but these should be treated with caution. Synthetic stone tends to look what it is and the plastic imitation stone is only suitable for gnome playgrounds. Not only does the latter look horrible but it has none of the properties that a plant growing next to it requires, in particular a cool root-run and a sympathetic background. Also avoid lumps of concrete. Occasionally one sees this used to good effect but it needs a very skilful handling.

With the exception of lime-haters the plants will not care at all which rock is used. They will grow around anything, but always remember the dignity of the plant and the appearance of the garden and only use stone that is in keeping with both.

Soils

Whereas the stone on a rock garden is chosen for its appearance and with little reference to the plants, the soil must be chosen with the plants in mind, as it is from this that their health and vitality springs.

The most crucial thing about all soils and composts used for growing alpines is that it must be free-draining. In the mountains, as we have seen, plants may have their roots in running water for a short period when the snow is melting, but it is moving water. Their position and the abundance of sharp-draining stone ensures that the water quickly drains away. Having said that, deep down the cool rocks tend to retain a trace of moisture which is sufficient to maintain the plant throughout the summer.

Thus, the art of making soils or composts for alpine plants is to make it free-draining, to remove excess water, but at the same time to make it able to retain a little moisture to sustain the plants between waterings. Any good loamy garden soil will do as a basis; clay and other heavy soils should be avoided as they can only be adapted with a great deal of effort which often takes several years, but light, sandy soils can be modified by adding humus to them. If a good soil is not available in the garden then it will be necessary to import it.

To help drainage horticultural grit or gravel should be added to the soil. The amount will vary according to the natural amount of small stones already present. The composition is right when water from a watering-can passes straight through the mixture rather than sitting on top and draining away slowly.

To ensure that there is a degree of moisture retentiveness, humus should be added to the soil. In the past peat would have been the obvious material to use, but because of its profligate use by many gardeners, spreading it wastefully over their gardens, further use of this diminishing resource is now frowned upon in many quarters. However, in spite of its convenience, peat is not the best material as it breaks down too quickly, adding little to the soil as it does so. Leafmould is a much better material. Use of this does need a bit of planning as it is not instantly available. Leaves must be collected over a period of years and stored in a wire enclosure so that they break down and the leafmould is thus available when it is wanted (Fig. 2.3). Raiding the local woods is not a good idea as this is as environmentally damaging, if not more so, than using peat. Garden compost is another good source of humus as long as it is free of weed seed. Farmyard and other manures can be used but they must be very well rotted otherwise they are inclined to be too rich.

The three materials should be thoroughly mixed before construction begins. Some gardeners like to mix in some fertilizer at this stage but this is not necessary if organic material has been added. This will provide more than enough food for the plants. Too rich a mixture will produce plants that are out of character; alpines blown up to the size of cabbages are a revolting sight.

So far only the soil that will be used in the actual construction of the rock garden has been considered. There is, of course, the existing soil on which the structure will be built. The only criterion is that it must be free-draining. Again grit can be added but if there is even a suggestion that it could become waterlogged then a proper drainage system should be incorporated as described on p. 14.

One final important point must be made: the soil mix should be free of perennial weeds. If they have access to a large soil sterilizer, some gardeners sterilize the soil before it is used. This gets the rock garden off to a good start by removing all weeds and seed including annuals, but for most this is, unfortunately, out of the question. The alternative is to weed the area thoroughly from which the soil is to

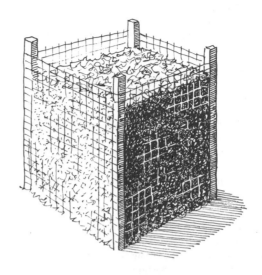

Fig. 2.3 A simple leafmould bin made of four stout posts and wire netting. In windy areas a top may also be required.

Fig. 2.4 The rock garden can consist of steep vertical bluffs with only small crevices for planting in.

come and then riddle the soil several times, pulling out any weeds that reappear. Once construction has taken place any annuals that appear should be removed before they seed.

Design

As construction proceeds the shapes of the stone will dictate the final appearance of the rock garden, but before work is started it is essential to have at least some idea of the overall design. Look at as many rock gardens as possible and make notes of any features you like. It is useful to make a sketch of the intended plan as it will make it easier when it comes to working out the layout on the ground.

Most gardeners' tastes tend towards making rock gardens look as natural as possible. There are several ways of doing this. The favourite way is to create an outcrop of rock that looks as though it is emerging from the ground or a bank. Other possibilities are to create a limestone pavement or, if there is space, a rocky gorge.

The outcrop is easier to design if the ground is sloping. The stone should be arranged in layers with fissures and crevices between them. Almost vertical bluffs can be formed where the only planting places are in the small gaps and crevices (Fig. 2.4). Alternatively the rocks can be stepped to form terraces on which planting on a larger scale can take place (Fig. 2.5). Some

parts should protrude further than others, creating areas of shade or places that are only reached by the sun at certain times of day. This helps provide a wide number of habitats, increasing the range of plants grown.

A similar plan can be followed on the flat ground, but here an artificial mound is created, often to give the impression of rock that has come to the surface by the action of the weather in wearing away the surrounding soil (Fig. 2.6). The same structural plan can be adopted as that for rock emerging from a bank, with vertical bluffs and terraces, but the rock may have to slope back more steeply into the ground. This matters not as the natural strata of rock can slope at any angle including vertical.

A limestone pavement is a horizontal area of stone, criss-crossed with fissures in which plants grow (Fig. 2.7). These occur naturally in areas where beds of limestone have been brought to the surface. Softer parts of this stone have been eroded away leaving what amounts to blocks of limestone with gaps between them. These gaps form a natural rock garden where many plants grow safe from the browsing of animals. Pavements of this type can be faithfully copied or used as a basis of the design for a path or terrace.

A similar idea is to create a dried-up river bed. In this case the stones can be more rounded with the spaces between filled with different sizes of pebbles and gravel to give the impression of a water-worn course (Fig. 2.8).

The gorge involves a lot of work as much soil has to be removed and built up on either side (Fig. 2.9). The sides are then covered in rock in the most natural way possible to give the impression that one is in a ravine. This can be spectacular particularly if constructed on a grand scale and on a winding plan. It provides a wonderful variety of habitats for plants. One essential thing about this type of structure is that it must not fill up with water, at least not stagnant water. It is possible to design it with a stream running through it, but if it just fills up with water that cannot run away then disaster looms over the project.

It is often difficult to know how to blend the rock garden into the rest of the garden. Many gardeners like to isolate it on a lawn, possibly with an area of gravel or path all round it to

Fig. 2.5 The rocks can be set back from each other to form terraces giving larger, flat spaces for planting.

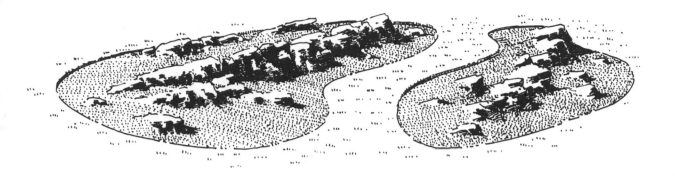

Fig. 2.6 On flat ground the rocks can be tilted to give the impression of strata of rock emerging from the ground.

Fig. 2.7 An alternative for flat ground is a limestone pavement with the plants emerging from the crevices between the closely packed rocks.

Fig. 2.8 In some areas smooth boulders, rocks, and pebbles are readily available. These can be used to create the effect of a dried up river bed.

Fig. 2.9 For the more ambitious a gorge can be created by excavating a wide trench and lining the sides with rock.

prevent the encroaching grass from getting a hold. Others like to place it in rough grass, this being more reminiscent of outcrops in mountain meadows, but, again, encroaching grass can become a menace if allowed to get amongst the rockwork.

Unless it is on a grand scale it cannot be placed directly next to other beds such as an herbaceous border, or worse still one full of gaudy bedding plants. One way round this is to plant low shrubs, such as dwarf rhododendrons or dwarf conifers, possibly on banks to give the impression that it is an outcrop amidst low scrub. This can then lead onto other, bigger borders thus blending in the whole.

Water can be incorporated into the design but this will be dealt with in a later chapter.

Construction

Before work starts on the actual construction it is essential to prepare the site. The two most important factors are freedom from weeds and good drainage.

The site must be thoroughly cleared of perennial weeds. Even the smallest piece left in the ground of, for example, couch grass (*Agropyron repens*) will grow up through the rock garden and cause a lot of trouble (Fig. 2.10). If there is time, clear the site at least six months before the construction begins so that any remaining weeds can be detected. There will of course be annual and perennial weed seed left in the soil but these should not present such a problem as they will be deeply covered.

Drainage has already been covered on p. 14,

but its importance should again be reiterated. If there is any doubt about the surface soil incorporate some gravel or crushed brick rubble into it making certain that there is a gully filled with rubble to lead any water away. The reason for this is that a hole filled with soil and drainage material could act as a sump and fill up with water from the surrounding area. Make certain that any water can escape otherwise the problem is compounded.

Before moving any stone consider carefully whether you are capable of doing it yourself or whether you need help. Rock is very heavy and it is very easy to cause internal injury as well as back problems. When moving two pieces of rock close together, watch out for your hands. They can easily get crushed between the two and the momentum of a heavy piece of stone against a static lump can do serious damage if a hand or finger gets in the way. Never take risks.

It is not necessary to lift rock (Fig. 2.11); it can generally be moved using levers and rollers. To move small pieces of stone, lift one end and roll it over, repeating until the destination is reached. In this way only a proportion of the weight of the rock is lifted. For moving heavier stones, use a long stout pole as a lever. The efficiency of the leverage can be improved if a small piece of stone is used as a fulcrum about which the pole rotates. Moving over longer distances can be facilitated by using trollies or sack-barrows, or by levering the rock onto rollers (round poles or short scaffold poles will do) and then by removing each one to the front as it comes out of the back as the rock progresses.

To get one rock on top of another, temporary ramps of small rock or earth can be constructed (Fig. 2.12). For larger rocks a mechanical digger can be employed. There are now narrow ones available for hire that can easily get into a back garden. This would certainly speed up the construction work and save a lot of aching backs.

To start with, keep the actual site clear of materials or there will be a constant need to move things. Arrange the stone in an arc or circle around the site with the best face pointing inwards. In this way it can all be seen at a glance and there is no need to be searching constantly through a pile of stone for the right

Fig. 2.10 It is essential to remove all perennial weeds before starting construction. Couch grass (*Agropyron repens*) is one of the worst offenders.

piece; the least number of times the stone is moved the better.

The whole structure should be a mixture of soil and stones. There is no point in making a heap of earth and dotting the stones around on it, even if an attempt is made to make it look natural. Any stone placed on top of loose earth will sink into it and the overall shape will be

Fig. 2.11 Large pieces of rock can be moved in a number of ways without having to lift them. Always beware of straining the back or crushing fingers.

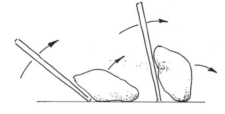

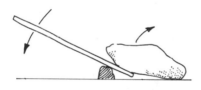

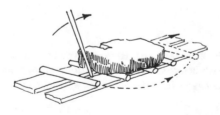

Following your rough sketch lay out the first layer of stones with the rock sloping slightly back towards the centre of the structure (Fig. 2.13). The reason for this is so that the rain will run back into the centre of the rock garden. If it slopes the other way there will be areas that could be permanently dry; at the same time the water falling over the front of the rock could erode away the soil beneath it. If there are visible strata lines on the stone make certain that they all run the same way (Fig. 2.14).

With a lever push the rocks as close to each other as possible, leaving the occasional natural looking crevice in which to place plants. Pack soil carefully around each stone, especially making certain that it is well rammed down on the under side of each stone so that it does not rock. Although you may not realize it at this stage, it is quite likely that you will jump from stone to stone while looking at or maintaining the rock garden and an unstable rock could be dangerous as well as making depressions beneath itself which would make ideal living spaces for slugs and snails.

You may be tempted to have as much stone as possible showing but it is better to have up to a third below ground, not only for stability but because it provides the plants with good root runs that they enjoy. These are not only cool but also hold a modicum of moisture which prevents the soil drying out completely.

The next layer of stone can be placed either on top of the first to make a bluff or further back if planting terraces are required. Since we are really constructing a habitat for plants rather than an imitation mountain to impress our friends, terraces are an important feature. The area behind the stones should be filled with the same soil mix and also a number of rocks, as mentioned above, to give support to the upper layers.

Pockets and terraces on the shadier side of some of the rocks can be filled with a soil mixture that contains more leafmould or other organic material. This will allow the growing of such plants as primulas that prefer a more moisture-retentive environment.

If the rock garden is on level ground with the back of the structure sloping down, then it is possible to roll the stones for the upper layers up this slope. On banks it will be necessary to build temporary ramps of earth to get the

lost. The core of the structure must consist of both stone and soil. There is no reason why this stone should be the same as that on the surface, it can even be lumps of concrete. This stone will help support the heavier ones on the surface as well as providing the plants with cool root runs.

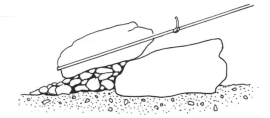

Fig. 2.12 Temporary ramps of smaller stones or earth can be used to roll or drag large stones on top of one another.

Fig. 2.13 Set the first layer of rock so that it leans back into the mound. This helps with stability as well as allowing rain water to run back into the centre of the rock garden.

stones to the required height. Scaffolding can be constructed and the stone rolled up planks of wood but this must be done with extreme care; in particular, make certain that the planks are well supported and that the rock does not accidentally fall over the edge causing painful injury.

Keep building up the layers until the top is reached. Once the rock garden has been completed it is ready to be top-dressed. This involves covering all the exposed soil with gravel or stone chippings to a depth of 2–2.5 cm ($\frac{3}{4}$–1 in) (Fig. 2.15). These should be chosen to match the type and colour of the rock; limestone chippings on a sandstone rock garden, for example, would look out of place. It is also possible to cover some areas with larger stones to form a scree bed (see p. 27). Some growers like to avoid limestone chippings as these make it difficult to grow calcifuges but others find that it makes little difference; it probably depends on the hardness of your local limestone.

There are several reasons for applying a top-dressing. It prevents the necks of the plants (one of the most vulnerable parts) from sitting in wet soil. It allows water to enter the soil without panning it. It acts as a mulch and keeps weed seed down, making them easier to remove if they do germinate. It helps prevent evaporation in summer and keeps the soil cool. Finally, it looks quite natural with the rocks and it sets the plants off to advantage.

Fig. 2.14 If there are any visible stratum lines on the rock, make certain that they all run the same way.

Planting

Opinion varies on when to plant. Some gardeners like to plant as construction progresses; others prefer to wait until it is finished; some even wait several months after completion so that everything has had a chance to settle and depressions can be topped up.

The advantage of planting as construction proceeds is that plants can be more easily inserted between rocks, particularly in vertical crevices. The plant is knocked out of its pot and the rootball squeezed gently between the

23

Fig. 2.15 When the rock garden is complete, top-dress with gravel or stone chippings, possibly covering some areas with large stones to form screes.

hands to make it oval in shape. This can then be inserted between rocks as they are levered together. Be certain that there is compost between the plant and the interior of the rock garden, otherwise the plant will be unable to get its roots down into the mass of soil (Fig. 2.16).

There are disadvantages to this method. If the rocks are in the wrong position and have to be moved again the plant can easily dry out as it too has to be taken from its position. It is impossible to water in as they are planted otherwise the construction area becomes a slippery mass of mud. Since the plants are put in individually, before the rock garden is complete, it is very difficult to get an overall picture of what the planting is going to look like and it may be necessary to move some plants at a later stage. Another factor which is often overlooked is that plants can easily be trampled on while struggling with lumps of stone for another part of the garden.

Planting after the rock garden is complete overcomes the objections in the last paragraph. If necessary one or two of the plants for the vertical crevices can be planted but the remainder can be left to a later stage. The problem of planting in these vertical crevices can be overcome by sowing seed directly into them instead. This can easily be done by placing some seed on the palm of one hand and blowing into the crack with a drinking straw.

Another advantage of planting after finishing the building work is that plants, still in their pots, can be dotted about the completed structure, giving some form of visual impression of how the finished planting will look (Fig. 2.17). This allows plenty of time to move plants around without having to keep digging them up.

It is important to put the plants in the positions that they would like best, exploiting the varying amounts of light and moisture that different aspects of the rock provide. As has already been mentioned, it is possible to vary the composition of the soil in different places around the rock garden to suit better the variety of plants you intend to plant.

Although top-dressing was mentioned under construction, it is often best left until after the planting has taken place. This allows any subsidence of the soil to be filled in and prevents soil and top-dressing getting mixed up during planting. If it is already in place then scrape it well back before digging a hole for the plant. A final word is to remind you not to plant during hot, very cold or very wet weather and water the plants in as soon as possible after planting.

The plants

The very construction of the rock garden, with its variety of habitats, means that a very wide range of alpine plants can be grown on it. For the beginner it is perhaps best that he or she sticks to the more easily grown plants. Fortunately these are as attractive (if not more attractive) than most of the more difficult ones, so none of the pleasures of alpine gardening will be lost in concentrating on them.

The beginner will find these easier plants less frustrating and more encouraging to grow and he will not only gain valuable experience in how to grow them but will also find that they are good plants on which to learn propagation and other techniques.

There are far too many plants that are suitable for the rock garden to list here, as virtually all the plants listed in the A–Z section

Fig. 2.16 (*Above*) Plants to go into crevices can be planted as the rock garden is being constructed. The roots must have good contact with the inner soil.

Fig. 2.17 (*Below*) A rough idea of how the bed will look when finished can be obtained by placing the plants, in their pots, roughly in position before planting.

are applicable. However, the beginner is encouraged to go and talk to the people at his nearest alpine nursery to ask for suggestions for plants that can be easily grown in his area.

Maintenance

Maintenance should not present too much of a problem if the preparation was thorough in the first place.

Remove any weeds on sight. Annuals should not present too much of a problem, particularly if the bed is well mulched with gravel, and with luck no perennial weeds should get into the garden. If they do, deal with them straight away. It is hopeless just pulling or scraping off the tops as they will continue to come back and spread. If the rock garden is still new it is possible that the weed is springing up from an

Fig. 2.18 Plants can be protected in winter from excessive rain by a firmly anchored sheet of glass.

old piece of root left in the soil-mix. By inserting a trowel into the soil to loosen it and then gently pulling the offending weed, all the root will come out. Once the weeds have established themselves then more drastic action is needed to prevent the whole area becoming infested. It is not really advisable to use weedkillers on a rock garden as alpines can be susceptible to even the slightest amount of drift or contact. The only way to cope is to grit your teeth and dismantle the affected part of the rock garden and search out every piece of root. Drastic action, but it will save a lot of time in the long run.

Take care to keep the rock garden tidy. Remove any dead stems and leaves. These not only look unsightly but can harbour slugs. This removal should be a continual process but should be complete by the onset of winter. If left until the spring there could well be problems in cutting off the dead parts as the plants may well be already into growth, giving a mixture of old and new shoots, which makes it difficult to trim neatly.

Another regular task is to ensure that there is sufficient moisture available to the plants. In areas with regular rainfall this is not a problem but in dry summers, or other periods of drought, plants must be watered. If there is no rain for ten days or so (even less in hot weather

or times of drying winds), water should be liberally applied. There is no point in dribbling a small amount onto the bed; at least 2.5 cm (1 in) should be applied, either by sprinkler over the whole rock garden or by can around individual plants. Organic material in the soil should be capable of retaining sufficient moisture for plants for several days. The rocks will also help store a certain amount, which tends to make the rock garden more efficient in this respect than a raised bed which will need more frequent watering.

In winter some plants need protection — not so much from the cold as from the damp. A sheet of glass, suitably anchored with wire or a piece of rock, will be sufficient (Fig. 2.18). If a number of plants requiring protection are planted near each other then a wooden frame covered in polythene can be made to cover the whole area. In either case, it is important to give free access to the air; any enclosed container, such as an upturned jar will create more problems than it solves and will probably kill the plant. These types of covers will also give a certain amount of protection from the cold. If there is any doubt as to a plant's hardiness it should be overwintered in an alpine house or cold frame.

With luck a rock garden will last for years without renewal. This does mean that the soil

Fig. 2.19 A notable feature of mountain ranges is the screes of broken stone that pour down the slopes.

will get tired: the nutrients will become used up and the humus will decay. There should be an attempt to replace this annually. However, the whole question of feeding plants does have its opponents. Alpines in the wild, in particular the high alpines, get little in the way of nutrients except from the small amount of decaying matter and minerals from the rocks around them. If over-fed with fertilizers in the garden they can become gross and overblown. Plants that are grown in pots have their soil regularly replaced and thus have their food supply replenished at the same time, but plants grown in the open do not have this privilege and to add to their problems, since the soil is free-draining, what food exists, is often leached away (washed out) with the water.

The answer then is to feed once a year with a slow-release fertilizer. Avoid high nitrogen types as these will promote excessive leaf growth which will make the plants out of character. The best way is to apply it sparingly in late winter, scattering over the surface, gently stirring it into the grit top-dressing; rain will take it down to where it is needed.

Humus is more of a problem. Again an annual sprinkling of crushed leafmould or peat can be incorporated into the top layer at the same time as the fertilizer, allowing the rain and worms to take it down further.

Once this has been done it is time to look at the top-dressing itself. Some places will have been worn thin where stones have been washed away or have naturally been incorporated into the soil. In other places, new planting or extraction of weeds will have mixed it in with the soil. Top up all these areas with the same type of gravel or chippings after any fertilizer or humus has been added.

If well maintained a rock garden should last for many years. Sometimes one area will become exhausted, or become infested with weed or an invasive plant that was planted by mistake. Rather than take the whole garden to pieces it should be possible to remove the soil in the area concerned and replace it with fresh.

Not only will parts of the rock garden become exhausted but some of the plants will as well. To maintain the vitality of the garden, old, tired plants should be removed and new ones planted. Sometimes newly planted plants have difficulty settling down in the position chosen for them and moving them to another might be of benefit. After a severe winter or drought some plants succumb and these will leave gaps to be filled. Although it is always sad to lose plants a look on the positive side shows that there is now space for another plant and space always seems to be at a premium in an alpine grower's garden.

Fig. 2.20 Screes can be imitated in a rock garden by allowing broken stone to flow between the larger pieces of rock.

Whenever plants are replaced or removed, take the opportunity to freshen up that part of the garden by adding new soil in and around the area being planted.

Screes

Anyone visiting the mountains cannot have failed to see slopes covered in loose stones and rock (Fig. 2.19). On the steeper parts of the mountain these are always on the move, at the foot of cliffs and on more level ground they become much more static. In both cases plants will be found growing on them. In the former the roots may be several metres uphill of the main part of the plant which has elongated as the scree has slipped. In the latter the roots are still likely to be long, plunging through the tumult of stones down to something that more resembles soil or possibly to a pocket of detritus caught in the stones.

Screes are made up of stone that has been broken and splintered by the action of the weather, in particular frost. In the garden they can be simulated by constructing an area of very free-draining compost and top-dressing it with stone. The make-up of the compost should be roughly 60% grit, gravel or chippings and 20% of both soil and leafmould.

Leaner mixes than this can be made with up to 80% being grit.

The most visually effective way is to incorporate it into the rock garden with the scree pouring down between the rocks (Fig. 2.20). A more formal way is to construct a raised bed (see p. 31) and fill it with a scree mix. Alternatively many growers make a scree bed on the flat or slightly sloping ground. Grit and leafmould is incorporated into the top layer of the soil and the whole is then covered with a mixture of gravel and larger stones. In some cases the latter may be rounded pebbles as one would find on the beach.

The siting of a scree bed is mainly a visual consideration of how it will best fit into the garden. However, it should be in the open and in full sun; scree beds in the shade are miserable affairs. It is no good having a very free-draining mixture for the plants to grow in if the bed is sitting in water. Make sure there is adequate drainage as discussed with regards to rock gardens on p. 14.

The plants normally grown in such a scree situation are the more difficult high alpines that need acute drainage. Many are cushion plants or those that form low-growing mats. When planting make certain that the roots of the plant come in contact with soil. If a realistic stony top-dressing is used, add extra compost between the rootball of the plant and the soil below. It is essential to ensure that the plant is well watered until it is established and able to search out its own moisture from below.

Maintenance is really no different from that of a rock garden (see p. 25) and as long as it is kept weed-free it should last for years.

Moraines are areas of rock and detritus dropped or pushed to one side by glaciers. Normally these specialized forms of screes are fed by a continuous flow of water from the glaciers and melting snow. This condition is difficult to simulate in the garden.

CHAPTER 3
Raised Beds

Not everybody has the space, finance or the desire to build a rock garden. There is, fortunately, a perfectly acceptable alternative in the form of a raised bed. This essentially consists of four walls enclosing a space which is filled with a well-drained compost (Fig. 3.1). This effectively lifts the surface of the bed above the surrounding ground making it not only free-draining, but also at a height which makes it both easy to attend and easy to appreciate the low-growing plants.

Many gardeners make a decorative feature of the raised bed. They incorporate it into the overall design of the garden, constructing it from sympathetic materials such as stone, and not only have plants on the top, sometimes cascading down the sides, but also have them planted in the vertical crevices of the wall. Others use it purely as a utilitarian device, construct it from any material that may come to hand and site it where it is most convenient, often near the alpine house or frames.

Siting
The siting of a raised bed is much the same as that of a rock garden. It should be in an open position away from overhanging trees and shrubs. Shade should be avoided unless it is specifically designed to grow shade-loving plants. Raised beds can be free-standing or they can be part of another structure. For example they can be built as retaining walls for a low bank or constructed using a building, such as a garage, as the fourth side. They can be sited in isolation on a lawn or can be built onto a paved terrace, sometimes as a double wall round its edge. Building it in one of these last two positions makes it easily accessible to people in wheelchairs; indeed, for the elderly and disabled it makes a very accessible alternative to the rock garden.

Materials
The structure can be of virtually any material. The most attractive in appearance is probably

Fig. 3.1 An easily built raised bed, landscaped with rocks, giving an ideal, well-drained habitat for many plants.

Fig. 3.2 Railway sleepers make an excellent wall for a raised bed. They are strong, rot-proof, warm and wide enough to sit or stand on when tending the plants.

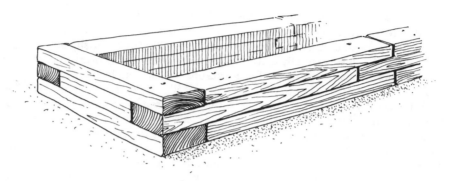

that using stones to create low dry-stone walls. These not only look attractive in themselves but give plenty of spaces for planting on their vertical faces. Brick or stone bonded with cement can be used, leaving occasional gaps in the mortar, in which to place plants. Not so attractive and of a more decidedly utilitarian design is the use of concrete blocks, or even concrete cast *in situ*.

Wood can also be used, either in the form of logs or planks. Both of these are likely to rot, suddenly releasing their contents in a minor avalanche. Wood can of course be treated with preservative but some, creosote in particular, should be avoided at all costs as they will kill the plants. Old railway sleepers make excellent raised beds (Fig. 3.2), their only disadvantage being the tar that can exude in hot weather. This is not so much a problem for the plants as for the gardener's trousers and shirts on which it inevitably seems to find its way. The very solidarity of railway sleepers makes them ideal as they give a wide edge to the bed that can be sat or stood upon while plants are being tended or discussed.

Size

A raised bed can be of any size the gardener likes. The minimum depth should be 25 cm (10 in). The maximum height should be 60 cm (2 ft). In anything deeper than this the soil will sink and will need constant topping up, which

is rather difficult if it is full of plants. It is possible to make deeper beds but there should be some way of supporting the soil so that it does not fill the whole depth of the bed. There need be no restriction on length, but the width must be carefully considered. It should be possible to reach the middle of the bed from either side, or reach right across it if it is only accessible from one side, so that it can be easily attended. It is possible to make wider ones and to use stepping stones to give access to the parts out of reach, but walking on a raised bed puts unnecessary stress on the structure.

Shape

A raised bed can be any shape that the gardener requires as long as the whole of the bed can be reached for maintenance. The convention is that they should be rectangular or square but this is often because they are the easiest shapes to construct. There is no reason why a bed should not be shaped to follow a contour or the edge of a terrace (Fig. 3.3). The shape can be dictated by the space available. R.B. has three triangular beds created at the ends of some cold frames that abut a path at 45°. Odd corners like this can be difficult to use as conventional low-level beds but come into their own as raised ones.

Regular-shaped beds have the advantage that if they are to be covered during the winter the frames are more easy to make and to fit.

Fig. 3.3 Raised beds can be any shape. They can be designed to follow the contours of a terrace, pathway or drive.

Construction

Any bed up to about 30 cm (1 ft) in height can be constructed without foundations. Anything above that, which is built of stone or brick, will be more stable with them. They are laid in the same way as for any wall. A trench is dug that is wider than the intended wall. A layer of hardcore about 10 cm (4 in) deep is placed in the bottom onto which is poured 10–15 cm (4–6 in) concrete. When this has set, the wall is built along the centre of it.

Dry stone walls are not easy to build, particularly if they are composed of irregular stones. The larger stones should be at the bottom and the wall should slope in slightly towards the centre of the bed (Fig. 3.4). It is easier to build a dry stone wall by filling it with the appropriate soil mix as it is constructed. This gives something solid for the wall to be built against, adding to its stability. If you are uncertain of your ability to construct a dry stone wall, it can be built using cement but make certain that none is showing in the gaps on the face of the wall.

Ordinary stone walls and brick walls should be built in the manner of any wall, except that small gaps should be left along the base for drainage (Fig. 3.5). Other gaps can be left higher up as planting holes. If the wall is over 30 cm (12 in), it will help the stability if piers are built every metre (yard) or so. These can be built on the inside sticking out into the bed. The beds should not be filled until the cement is dry. The bricks and stones are liable to stay moist as they will be in constant contact with

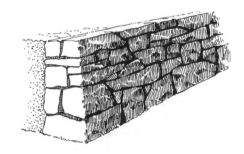

Fig. 3.4 Dry-stone walls make ideal supports for a raised bed. The stones should be laid so that the wall slopes slightly into the bed.

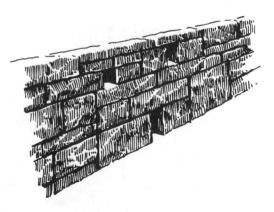

Fig. 3.5 Small gaps should be left in the wall so that excess water in the bed can drain away freely.

31

Fig. 3.6 Logs can make cheap walls for a raised bed as long as they are straight, so that there are not too many gaps in them through which compost can fall.

the soil mix inside. This means that they will be prone to shattering in any really cold weather. Therefore, it is advisable to use frost-proof bricks or stone that are not easily shattered. Choose bricks with a colour that will be sympathetic to its surroundings. Industrial bricks, for example, can be too harsh. It may be worth considering choosing colours that match the brickwork of the house or other structures.

Wood is not an ideal material for raised beds, but it can be cheap and often readily available. It is best suited to peat beds (see p. 49). This type of raised bed need not have any foundations but it will need some method of support. Railway sleepers are probably heavy enough for two, with one on top of the other, to need no vertical fixings other than a few long nails driven obliquely from one to another. Logs however will need parallel stakes driven into the ground between which they are

inserted to prevent the upper lengths from falling off. These stakes should be regularly checked as they are the first thing to rot, leading to a general collapse of the structure. Choose logs that are as straight as possible as any gaps between them will be a source of escape for the compost (Fig. 3.6). On the other hand these gaps make admirable planting holes. Planks need a batten nailed to the reverse to keep them in place. As already mentioned these rot very quickly and should be tannalized for longer lasting. It must be emphasized again that creosote should be avoided. Holes can be drilled or cut to provide drainage at ground level and higher up for planting.

Where space is short it is quite possible, with a bit of ingenuity, to make a taller raised bed with a raised base of slabs or corrugated iron, under which bags of compost and other material can be stored, one side of the structure being left open for access (Fig. 3.7).

Soil

The mixture that goes into the bed must be a similar one to that used on the rock garden. It must have sufficient drainage material to make it quick draining but at the same time contain humus to hold sufficient moisture for the plants' needs. As the basis for a filling, a good loam should be obtained. If it is not available from the garden then it must be brought in. If a lot is required, it is cheapest to buy it by the

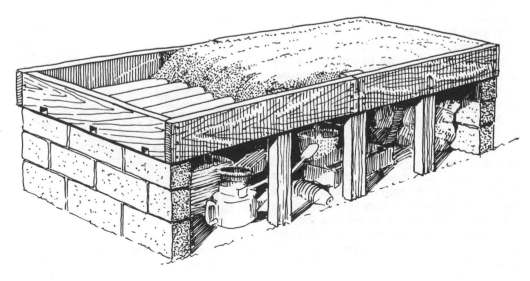

Fig. 3.7 Higher raised beds can be constructed which incorporate valuable storage space below the base.

A colourful corner of a well-furnished rock garden
in late spring.

Far right: A cluster of saxifrages in full bloom brings a delicate splash of colour to a small corner in a rock garden.

Right: An attractive group of saxifrages grown in pots that would normally be housed in either an alpine house or cold frame.

Below: Part of a rock garden, incorporating scree beds, in late spring, presenting a wide range of planting positions.

Above: A large, well-stocked trough made from natural stone.

Right: A lump of tufa with saxifrages, *Erinus alpinus* and a pulsatilla growing directly into it.

Far left: The corner of a raised bed in late spring.

Left: *Androsace alpina*, seen here in the Pennine Alps of North West Italy, is a delightful small plant that needs the protection of an alpine house.

Below: There are a number of anemones to grace the rock garden in spring. This is *Anemone baldensis*, named after Mt Baldo in the Italian Alps.

Aquilegia caerulea is a cheerful plant for the rock garden or scree bed. It often hybridizes with other aquilegias giving other colours.

lorry load; if only a small quantity is needed it can be bought by the sack either as sterilized loam or as John Innes No. 3 potting compost. It is not essential to have sterilized soil but if it is available it does reduce the number of weed seed and kill off any disease.

If garden soil is used it should be mixed in the proportions 1 part garden soil, 1 part leaf-mould or peat and 2 parts grit (all parts being by volume). If JI potting compost is used 1 part of compost should be mixed with 1 part of grit. The JI compost contains a certain amount of fertilizer and lime. The fertilizer should cause no problems but lime makes it unsuitable for calcifuges, such as ericaceous plants. The mix made from garden soil will contain no fertilizer but it will contain humus which will provide nutrition as it breaks down. The bed can be fed in future years as the soil becomes tired.

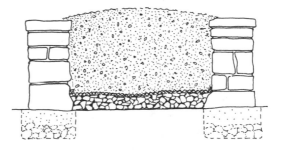

Fig. 3.8 A cross section through a raised bed showing the various layers. The compost should be heaped high when the bed is first constructed.

Filling the bed

As with all aspects of alpine gardening, drainage is of the utmost importance. We have already seen that drainage holes have been left in the walls and the compost contains a fair amount of grit. To help both of these function correctly a layer of broken clay pots, stones or rubble is first put on the base of the bed (Fig. 3.8). To ensure that the compost does not fall down into this layer and clog it up, a porous barrier should cover it. Traditionally this can be a layer of old or broken tiles, or possibly turf laid upside-down. A more modern material would be the sheets of plastic with drainage holes, used as a mulch or for standing pots on in a frame.

On top of this can be heaped the compost. Compress it as much as possible otherwise it will sink below the edge of the bed after the first shower of rain. The centre of the bed should be humped above the surrounding edge also to counteract this tendency to sink.

When filling the top of the bed, any rocks that are going to be used should be inserted. On a raised bed a few rocks not only improve its visual appearance but also provide the plants with some protection and cool root runs. In order that these rocks are stable at least half should be below ground. The easiest method is to insert the rocks as the bed is being filled with soil. The type of rock can be any the gardener chooses and need not be a local one. The lumps

Fig. 3.9 The top of the bed can be landscaped using rocks and gravel or chippings to form a miniature rock garden.

can be odd ones spread almost at random on the bed or they can be assembled in such a way as to present a miniature landscape (Fig. 3.9). This latter method is useful for providing habitats for plants that like to live in crevices. A good outcrop can be constructed, for example, from rock that fractures into slabs. Pieces of this can be inserted in the soil at about 45° to the horizontal and parallel to each other. Here saxifrages and some of the campanulas will be perfectly at home.

As with the rock garden it is possible to vary the soil composition in different parts of the bed so that plants that like a bit more moisture can be grown. For example, it may be desirable to grow some primulas in the semi-shade of the rocks and here it would be beneficial to include some more leafmould or peat into the mix. Whole beds can be constructed using a peaty mix but these are treated elsewhere (see p. 47).

When deep beds are built it is a waste of good compost if the whole bed is filled with it. There is no need to have more than 45–60 cm (18–24 in) at the most of compost and for many plants grown on raised beds 15 cm (12 in) will do. It is possible to construct beds that have their base raised above ground level by supporting a layer of paving stones or a sheet of corrugated iron on brick or concrete block pillars. An alternative is to fill the bottom of the bed with any old soil (including subsoil) providing drainage channels filled with rubble. Drainage material and the rest of the filling can then be placed on top of this.

Planting

If the impatience can be curbed it is best to leave the bed for a month or two to settle down before planting. The reason for this is that no matter how well the compost was packed into the bed, after a few showers it will sink. When this happens top up the bed so that it is level with the walls, again humping it slightly in the middle. The best planting time is either in the spring or autumn, but it can take place at any time as long as it is not too hot, cold or wet.

The range of plants that can be grown on a raised bed is very extensive. Those that prefer a well-drained soil, such as the high alpines, do best. Unless it is a big bed it is probably best to avoid using some of the larger, sprawling

plants or those that can overwhelm the bed with their vigour.

Once the bed has been planted it can be top-dressed with grit or stone chippings. This can be applied at an earlier stage but needs to be very carefully scraped to one side when the hole for a plant is made. Inevitably some soil gets mixed up with it and it can look messy, so it is probably best to wait until all or nearly all the planting is complete and then dress the whole bed. Water in the plants once they are in the ground. Any grit can be used; it is not so critical as with a rock garden as there is no structural rock to match. However, if rock has been used on the bed it is best to use a chipping that is in sympathy with it.

Maintenance

There is not a great deal of difference between maintaining a raised bed and looking after a rock garden. Regular routines should include removal of dead leaves and stems. The major pests are likely to be slugs and snails — in spite of the grit top-dressing — and removal of potential homes in the form of old leaves etc. is a simple preventive measure.

A raised bed can dry out very quickly especially in hot weather or drying winds so make certain that during the summer months in particular it is well watered. However, if water begins to lie in any part of the bed, then the soil has become compacted. Loosen the compost around the area and work in some grit to sharpen the drainage.

Some plants need winter protection from the rain and either sheets of glass can be used for individual plants or a special frame made to cover more than one plant. It is possible to keep all plants that need protection in one bed and cover the whole thing with a wooden frame covered in clear polythene (Fig. 3.10). Whatever method is used it is essential that it only shields the plants from the wet and does not prevent the free circulation of air. In windy areas, of course, these must be well anchored.

If well constructed a raised bed should not want any major attention spent on it. The soil will become tired but an annual feed in early spring of a balanced fertilizer should keep it productive. At the same time sieved leafmould or peat can be added. These can be applied by temporarily scraping back the top-dressing. It can also be spread on the grit, allowing the rain and worms to work it down into the top layer of soil. The top-dressing of grit or chippings is likely to need renovating every year with additional material added to replace that which has worked into the soil.

When putting in plants or replacing them once the top-dressing is in place, scrape the chippings well back from the planting area. Instead of piling the soil beside the hole place it in a bucket or large pot. When the plant is in position a little of this soil can then be replaced to help fill the hole. Experience shows this is the best method for preventing the soil and the top-dressing from becoming too mixed.

If replacing an old plant it is a good idea to dig out the old compost in the immediate area and replace it with fresh material. If one part of the bed seems to be lacking in vigour, again the compost can be removed and that area rejuvenated. In this way it is possible to keep the bed in active life for many years without the tedious necessity of replacing it all.

Fig. 3.10 Polythene lights can be constructed to give raised beds some protection, especially against rain, during the winter.

CHAPTER 4

Sinks and Troughs

One of the joys of alpine gardening is that it can be carried on at any scale. The gardener can construct a rock garden covering several acres if he so desires or he can restrict himself to a plot no more than 30 cm (1 ft) square (Fig. 4.1). Even in such a small area as this it is quite possible to grow quite a number of plants.

Clarence Elliott was the first to realize the potential of sinks and troughs for providing sites for these small gardens. The advantages are two-fold. Firstly the containers are small enough for the gardener to control the growing conditions, i.e. he can choose the composition of the soil and the degree of drainage present. They are easy to water and, if necessary, can easily be covered in time of excessive rain or extreme cold. Thus the sink makes an ideal home for plants that need that extra bit of attention and many difficult-to-grow plants have been successfully grown there.

Secondly they are small enough to be used in the smallest of gardens, even on a balcony if that is the only space available. This small size

Fig. 4.1 Sinks or troughs make ideal miniature rock gardens and will take a surprising number of plants.

also makes them ideal for the elderly and disabled as they are easy to tend and yet give the pleasure of creating a landscaped garden in miniature and growing quite a number of plants.

Natural sinks and troughs

In the 1920s, when Clarence Elliott introduced the idea of using sinks and troughs for growing alpines, there were still a lot of stone and slate containers of this sort to be found. Troughs were often discovered lying discarded in farms, having been superseded by galvanized ones, while rough stone sinks were being replaced by ceramic ones with a smooth white glaze.

They came in all shapes and sizes, usually hewn from local stone. The troughs had been put to a number of uses; water troughs, feeding troughs, troughs for catching blood in slaughter houses and so on. Joe Elliott (Clarence's son) still owns an enormous one which was once a Saxon coffin.

The rough stone made an ideal setting for the alpines which has never been bettered. Being old they had mellowed and had acquired a patina of age, much like the rocks of the alpines' native haunts.

Unfortunately, there is one big disadvantage with natural sinks and troughs: the supply has dried up. There was only a limited number around and most of these were soon snapped up. Occasionally old ones can still be found tucked away in an odd corner of a farm, but the most likely source is on the second-hand market where they demand incredible prices.

In the last couple of years or so, new troughs have put in an appearance at garden centres, a good idea but one not well executed so far.

Most natural sinks are ready for use when they are acquired as they already have a drainage hole in them. Some are on the shallow side and need to be built by utilizing suitable pieces of rock or stone. Troughs on the other hand were designed to hold water and therefore have no hole in the bottom. Many that are acquired second-hand are likely to have had holes drilled in them already but recently discovered ones may need to have one or two added. A trough that fills up with water every time it rains is useless for growing plants.

Home-made troughs

In recent years home-made troughs have become both an economic and attractive alternative to the real thing. They take two forms: adapting an existing sink to make it visually acceptable and making a new trough from a cement mixture that, when weathered, does not look too unlike rock.

The white glazed sinks that replaced the stone ones in so many cottages have themselves now been superseded by stainless steel. Most are deep and a good shape in which to grow alpines but their exterior appearance leaves much to be desired. Fortunately a technique has been developed which involves coating the outside of the sink with a cement mixture which, while not looking exactly like rock, softens the outline and colour of the sink to produce a finish that is a good setting for alpines. Thousands of these very serviceable sinks have been produced by amateur gardeners.

The magic mix that produces this finish is 'hypertufa'. It is a conventional mixture of sand and cement to which has been added sieved peat. This peat helps with the ageing process, producing a rock-like patina. It also gives the cement a more plastic quality which enables it to be carved or scored just before it hardens, thus allowing the maker to soften the hard lines of the sink giving it the appearance of worn hewn rock.

A glazed sink is prepared by thoroughly washing it to remove any dirt or grease. If possible it is best to place the sink in its desired final position (see p. 40) before proceeding any further as it will become very heavy after coating and virtually immovable once it has been filled. In either case prop it up off the ground on bricks, giving access to the bottom edge (and also making it easier to grip if it has to be moved).

Make up the hypertufa mixture which consists of equal parts by volume of cement, sand and peat. Add water until it reaches the consistency of a thick cream, the same as would be used for bricklaying. Cover this with a piece of damp sacking or paper to prevent it drying out too quickly.

Cover the outside of the sink with a layer of adhesive, such as Unibond. Continue this over the top and down about 8 cm (3 in) on the inside. Also make certain that it continues down under the bottom edge so that all visible parts of the trough will be covered. Apply the hypertufa mixture directly to the adhesive making certain that it is firmly stuck and that the whole of the outside of the sink is covered and as much of the inside as is likely to appear above the soil (Fig. 4.2).

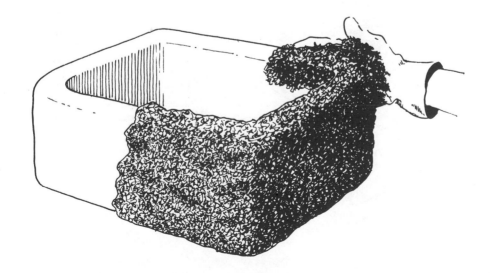

Fig. 4.2 The sink is covered with hypertufa, taking it over the rim to below the intended level of the compost.

Once the whole sink is covered, protect it with a damp sack so that it does not dry out too quickly and crack. Any hypertufa left over can be used for making artificial lumps of tufa.

When the cement is partly dry it will be possible to modify its surface shape and texture. It can be brushed to roughen it slightly and bring the sand to the surface, or it can be scored with various tools such as a wire brush, file or even a knife. Go carefully with this as it can easily be overdone; the idea is to make it look like real rock not like something attacked by a mad axeman. Often just a brush will be all that it needs to soften the outline and round the corners. Re-cover with damp sacking and allow to cure completely. Allow the completed sink to weather before filling with compost.

An alternative is to make a complete trough using the same mixture. The advantage of this is that you can tailor it to the size that best suits the position in which you want to put it. The disadvantage is that it takes more effort to make it.

There are two possible ways of constructing a trough. One uses wooden shuttering that can be used as many times as you like, the other uses temporary cardboard formers that can only be used once.

The basic idea is to build two wood boxes to go one inside the other with a gap between them of 4–5 cm (1½–2 in) (Fig. 4.3). The boxes should be demountable to facilitate their removal once the cement or hypertufa has set. The boxes can be made from any scrap, but if several troughs are to be made it pays to go to a bit of extra trouble and make them properly. The outer box need only be four sides; it can be simply stood on a wooden base or even on a sheet of polythene laid on a garage floor. The four pieces of wood can be screwed together or, if repeated use is expected, battens can be screwed to the shorter sides which are then attached to the longer sides with bolts and wing nuts. The inner box presents more of a problem as it has to be removed without disturbing the hardening walls. One way to do this is to stand the four pieces of wood in the required-size rectangle and nail pieces of wood diagonally across the top of each corner. Another way is to nail or screw fillets of wood down the inside of each corner. If the mixture is not too liquid a base for the inner box is not required, but it is easier if a wooden base is made. Be careful when making this: if it overlaps the outside of the inner walls at any point, it will be very difficult to get out. Extraction is

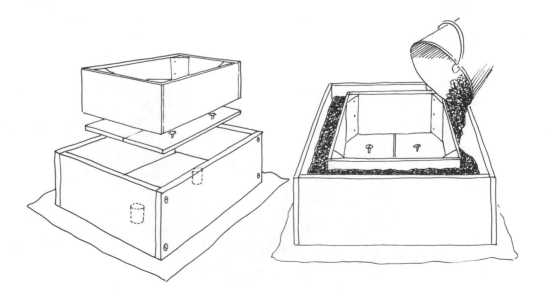

Fig. 4.3 Troughs can be made from cement or hypertufa using a demountable, re-usable mould.

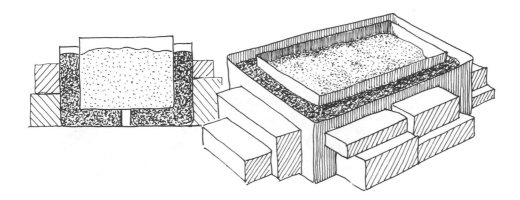

Fig. 4.4 A cheap alternative method is to use expendable cardboard boxes as formers for the trough.

more easily effected if the base is in two pieces, butted up to each other. Screws or nails in the base will make convenient gripping points to help removal.

The method of construction is to set up the outer box on its base and insert two wooden pegs, each 5 cm (2 in) long, on their end at points about a third and two-thirds the way down the length of the box. Once the cement has set these will be removed and will act as drainage holes. The base is then filled with a 5 cm (2 in) layer of either the hypertufa mix described earlier or a cement or concrete mix. The inner box is then placed in position standing on the layer of hypertufa and the two wooden pegs. The rest of the mixture is poured into the gap to form the walls. Make certain that the mix is tamped down and that there are no air pockets. Leave the trough for a couple of days, covered in a damp hessian sack and then carefully remove the wood of the outer box. It should still be soft enough to round off the edges with a brush or old file. The surface can be treated as described earlier, to make it resemble an old stone trough, but do not overdo it; simplicity has great virtues. Re-cover with the damp sack. After a few more days remove the inner box and leave until it is fully cured and then knock out the wooden drainage pegs.

To strengthen the trough, galvanized chicken wire can be inserted in the base and between the walls before the concrete is poured. This is a difficult task as none of the wire should appear at the surface. If there is no

intention to move the trough and if it is unlikely to receive knocks from wheelbarrows, this can be dispensed with.

The second method is a simpler version of the first but has the disadvantage that the formers cannot be used twice (Fig. 4.4). Find two cardboard boxes that fit inside one another with about a 5 cm (2 in) gap all round. Support the outside of the outer box with bricks or blocks so that it will not sag when filled with cement. Place two wooden pegs inside the larger as described above and fill with 5 cm (2 in) of the mixture. Place the inner box on top of this, ensuring equal spacing all round. Fill the gap with the mixture, filling the inner box at the same time with earth so that the walls do not collapse inwards, keeping the two levels roughly equal (the inner box can be filled with earth before the mix is added but if the cardboard is not too strong this will then bow outwards causing thin spots in the completed walls). Tamp the hypertufa down well making certain that there are no air pockets. Cover with damp hessian and leave for a couple of days. Tear off the cardboard and re-cover. When it has finally hardened remove the drainage pegs and leave to weather.

If the trough was made from hypertufa then it will age quite quickly. If it is made from cement or concrete then sour milk or a slurry of cow dung can be painted on the outside which will attract lichen and begin the ageing process.

By making the trough yourself you can make it to your own specifications. One modification

Fig. 4.5 A bigger feature can be made by removing paving slabs under and around a trough and planting the resulting space.

that might be worth thinking about is to make a hole in the side, either by inserting a wooden peg or boring it when the hypertufa is still quite soft. The point of this is to be able to give homes to plants that like to grow on their sides, for example, ramondas can be planted on the shady side of the trough. Be careful not to make too many holes or the strength of the trough will be impaired.

Although stone (or hypertufa) is by far the best medium for troughs some growers have successfully made them from other materials. Wood is an obvious alternative, but it must be treated to prevent rot as the bottom can so easily fall out. (Do not, however, treat it with creosote or you will never get alpines to grow in it.) I have seen some troughs that were polystyrene boxes covered with adhesive and then sprinkled with sand. These looked quite authentic and had the advantage that the polystyrene kept the contents warm in cold weather, but they do deteriorate quickly and are easily damaged, making the troughs look tatty.

There are a variety of other containers such as large plastic boxes and half barrels that can be used, but alpines tend to look out of place in these.

Siting the troughs

Unless you intend to grow shade-loving plants in the trough, it is best sited in an open position in full sun. To get the most pleasure out of them they should be sited in places that are regularly frequented such as on the edge of a path or drive. One of the best places is on a paved terrace, the advantage being that this will form a firm base. It is possible to make nice groupings of two or more troughs on a terrace, perhaps removing one or two paving stones so that the area around their base can be planted up at the same time (Fig. 4.5).

The area where they are sited need not be paved – many growers place them on lawns – but they do need firm bases. If sited on a lawn a paved or concrete base should be made, extending beyond the edges of the trough so that it is not repeatedly damaged by mowers. As long as there is a firm base for the plinth, the rest of the base can be covered with gravel or some other sympathetic material.

As has been already stated it is essential that the base on which the trough is placed should be stable. When full of compost a trough is extremely heavy and can cause a severe accident should it topple over onto somebody.

If possible it is best to raise the trough off the ground a little. This will ensure that the drainage works and prevent worms and weeds working their way in through the drainage holes. Four bricks will lift it a short way off the ground, but it is better if it can be a little higher than this (concrete blocks perhaps) as at this height leaves and other debris will easily collect underneath it, but will not be easy to remove. Again any plinth should be well made with no possibility of the trough being unstable or easily pushed over. It should be cemented onto properly constructed brick or concrete block piers. The plinth can be any height as long as it is safe. Extra height is most welcome for those confined to wheelchairs.

Filling

Once the troughs are filled they become very heavy so it is advisable to build any plinth and install the trough before it is filled with compost.

Make certain that there are drainage holes in the bottom and that they are not blocked up (Fig. 4.6). Some stone troughs may not have any and there will be the need to drill some. Ensure that if there is only one hole (such as in an old sink) it is at the lowest part of the trough; one end or the other might need lifting to ensure this. Cover the bottom of the trough with old broken pots or other drainage material to the depth of 4–5 cm (1½–2 in).

Next it is important to cover this with some material to prevent the compost falling into this layer and clogging it up. Traditionally inverted turfs were used (free of perennial weeds, of course) but now it is possible to use a polythene membrane that contains holes that will allow the water to percolate through but retain the compost.

On top of this is placed the compost. This is a mixture of 1 part (by volume) of loam, 1 part of leafmould or peat and 2 parts grit. To this can be added John Innes base fertilizer to make it up to the equivalent of JI No. 3 (see packet for quantities). Alternatively JI Potting Compost No. 3 itself can be used mixing it with an equal volume of grit.

The compost should be well pressed down and heaped up in the centre of the trough to allow for sinkage when it has weathered. The top of the trough can then be dressed with a 2.5 cm (1 in) layer of grit or stone chippings.

Most troughs look better if they also have some rocks added to them (Fig. 4.7). This is not only a decorative feature, but also provides the plants with a cool root-run, some protection from the sun and, for those planted in crevices, even more acute drainage. These rocks can be of any sort, perhaps some collected on holiday. It is quite good fun to have several troughs all with different types of rock, some jagged and fissured, others rounded or rugged.

The rocks should be well buried into the compost with only the top half or less showing

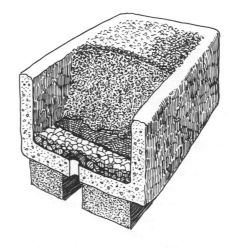

Fig. 4.6 A cross-section through a trough showing the method of filling it.

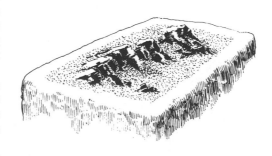

Fig. 4.7 A more interesting surface to the trough can be obtained by landscaping it with rocks and chippings.

above the surface. Again, top-dressing should be applied to the surface in between the rocks. It is best to use chippings that are in sympathy with the rocks and avoid, for example, limestone chippings with sandstone rocks.

Planting

In many respects it is better to allow the compost to settle before planting takes place so that any drop in level can be topped up before the plants are put into position. Having said that, it is probably a good idea to insert any plants that need to go between rocks or in crevices at the time of construction. Once the rocks are in position it will be far more difficult.

There are quite a range of small plants that will enjoy the free-drainage conditions that a trough will provide. As with its bigger relations, the rock garden and the raised bed, it is possible to provide pockets of differing compost to suit certain types of plants. Thus it is possible to increase the amount of moisture-retaining humus in some areas, particularly on the shady sides of rocks, so that a few plants such as primulas or gentians can be grown.

Avoid using plants that will grow too big or have rampant tendencies: small cushion plants or those that gently spread to form small mats are best. Variations can be made using small conifers and shrubs as well as a few trailing plants over the side. If holes have been left in the sides of home-made troughs then these can be planted with plants that like this position; for example, *Lewisia* can be planted on the shaded sides.

Maintenance

Little maintenance is required apart from tweaking out the odd weed as it occurs and snipping off dead stems and leaves. Regularly remove any leaves or other debris that collects beneath the trough as these will make ideal living quarters for slugs.

In the early spring a light sprinkling of a general fertilizer (at half the recommended rate) can be applied and washed in through the chippings. The latter should also be topped up if they have washed off or become mixed in with the compost.

If plants are replaced at any stage remove as much old compost as possible without disturbing the other plants and replace it with fresh. In this way the trough should remain vital for many years.

Sinks covered with hypertufa sometimes shed their covering and begin to look decidedly tatty. It is easy to become oblivious to this and ignore its dismal appearance. As soon as any falls off, do something about it; if you do not, water and frost are likely to get under the remaining parts and make the situation far worse. Clean off the affected area and remove any more loose debris, and then apply adhesive and a new layer of hypertufa.

CHAPTER 5

Tufa

Of all the rocks used in alpine gardening, tufa is one of the most fascinating. One of its many interesting qualities is that it absorbs water and this, plus the minerals it holds within it, is sufficient to sustain plants that will actually grow on its surface, with their roots burying deep inside the rock (Fig. 5.1).

Formation

As long as it is dry the rock is very light and usually surprises the gardener when he lifts his first lump. It is also very soft and can be easily bored with a drill or even a knife. Later, as it ages, it gets harder and more difficult to work. It is formed when water bearing various minerals, such as calcium and magnesium carbonates, passes through moss or some other vegetative material. The minerals are deposited on the living material rather like the scale on a kettle. The moss to avoid being smothered, grows another layer on the surface which in turn is covered with the minerals.

Thus layer upon layer of calcium and magnesium is built up until it forms a solid block. Solid is perhaps not quite the right word because there are many air gaps left between what were originally strands of moss. These air gaps are extremely important as it is these that absorb the moisture that keep the plants alive. Large deposits have built up (and are continuing to build up) in various countries and these have been exploited by alpine gardeners.

When it is freshly exposed tufa has a light creamy or sandy colour. This ages to a dull grey, pumice-like colour, as it is exposed to the air and weather. The surface texture is usually pitted with tiny cellular holes but there are variations on this including some which have rounded excrescences, which make the tufa appear to be bubbling over. It generally has a craggy appearance which makes it valuable for landscaping troughs and raised beds.

Fig. 5.1 A lump of tufa supporting a wide range of plants growing directly in it.

Purchasing tufa

Until recently it was only possible to buy tufa either direct from the quarries or from specialist nurseries, but increasingly it is being found in garden centres. Whether this increased availability will soon exhaust supplies making real tufa as rare as real troughs is something that the next few years will show.

Tufa is normally sold by weight so it is important to go and buy it after a dry spell as after wet weather more than half the weight of the tufa will be made up of water and there is no point in paying double the price. (It is reported that some canny nurserymen actually hose down their piles of tufa every so often to keep the weight up!).

If you can, go and select the tufa you require yourself. If there are quarries near you that supply it then these will offer the best value. They usually advertize in the various alpine gardening magazines so should not be too difficult to track down.

Have some idea before you go to buy the tufa what size lump or lumps you want. You will normally have the choice of pieces from very large lumps down to fine dust (the latter often being used by some alpine growers in specialist composts). There are no real criteria in choosing the tufa other than making certain that it is of a shape and texture that you like.

Unless you really want a large quantity or a particularly large lump it should be quite easy to bring away your purchases in the back of an ordinary car as the rock is so light. Avoid having it delivered if you can, as fresh tufa is quite brittle and what started out as an attractive shape can be somewhat modified by careless handling on the part of deliverymen.

Preparing the tufa

This is not a difficult material to use; indeed, it is very simple and once installed, needs virtually no attention for years.

Tufa should normally be placed in an open position in full sun. The north side of the lumps should provide enough shade for those plants that require it.

It obtains its moisture in two ways: from rain or overhead watering, and from the ground. Rain initially runs off the surface of the tufa and it requires a prolonged spell of rain or overhead watering to soak the block right through. The ground, however, yields a constant supply of water, as anyone with a house that has no damp course will know, and it is this that supplies the bulk of the moisture to

Fig. 5.2 An interesting feature for growing plants can be created by constructing a wall or cliff of tufa.

the centre of the block. Therefore when installing tufa it is essential that a substantial portion of the base is in contact with the earth, either the ground itself or the compost in a trough or raised bed. Having said that, I have seen enormous lumps of tufa hanging on chains and sitting on top of tall iron columns at Brno Arboretum which quite happily supports colonies of saxifrages. I suspect though, that there is a rigid watering regime to ensure that the blocks do not dry out.

The above was very decorative but presumably very time-consuming in watering. There are many other attractive uses for tufa. It can be placed in troughs or raised beds as already suggested, or it can be placed in isolation (or with other lumps of tufa) on a lawn or terrace, perhaps removing one or two paving stones and filling in the remaining space around the tufa with chippings or gravel. A prominent position such as at the top of some steps can be chosen but it must not be in a position where it can be knocked otherwise pieces are liable to be broken off. If it is placed in a grassy area, again it can be surrounded by chippings to prevent mowing machines getting too close. Several lumps of tufa associated with one or two troughs can make an attractive grouping.

Another feature that I have seen both in Britain and abroad is a tufa cliff (Fig. 5.2). The most celebrated one was built by Roy Elliott in his garden in the centre of Birmingham, UK. This comprised a raised bed about 7.6 m (25 ft) long by 90 cm (3 ft) wide and 45 cm (18 in) deep on which was piled large lumps of tufa to the height of about 1.80 m (6 ft), supported by a brick wall at the back of the bed. This needed about 6000 kg (6 tons) of tufa. The whole was protected by a cantilevered glass roof in the manner of a bus shelter. In this cliff of tufa with its minimum of shelter was grown an extraordinary collection of plants including a thriving colony of *Jankaea heldreichii*, a very difficult plant to grow. Being under cover, it needed regular watering.

Another remarkable cliff was built in the open, any plants that needed slight protection being planted under overhangs. It was dug into a hillside, with the walls almost vertical, rising straight out of the ground. An area the shape of a horseshoe had been excavated and had been lined with tufa to a height of about 2.5 m (8 ft).

This construction produced a vast number of facets offering many positions in varying degrees of sun and shade. This cliff again sported jankaeas and also fine specimens of the notoriously difficult *Eritrichium nanum*.

Moving back to humbler lumps of rock, having decided on its position and partly burying it in the earth the tufa is ready for planting. Holes can be drilled or scraped with an old chisel into the soft rock. These should be about 2.5 cm (1 in) in diameter and 5–7.5 cm (2–3 in) deep. They should slope slightly down into the rock.

Planting

Putting an established plant into tufa can be a bit of a problem. The easiest way is to select a young plant, wash off all the soil and wrap the roots in a damp paper tissue. This tube of roots can then be eased into the hole and the gap around it gently filled with compost (Fig. 5.3). The roots will soon grow away through the tissue. Alternatively the soil-free roots can be gently poked into the hole using a plant label or stick and again compost gently eased in around them. The compost and the surrounding area should be kept moist until the plant has established itself.

Instead of using grown plants it is often easier to use an 'Irishman's cutting', i.e. a shoot or a stem removed from a plant in the manner of a basal cutting but which already has a few of its own roots. Well-rooted cuttings that have been hardened off can also be used. An alternative is to sow one or two seeds direct into a small hole in the tufa.

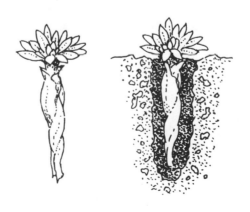

Fig. 5.3 Wrap the plant's roots in a small piece of damp tissue to help insertion into holes in the tufa.

The plants that do particularly well in tufa are high alpines that dislike competition and prefer a sharp drainage. Cushion plants such as saxifrages do well and so do many of the more trickier subjects such as *Campanula zoysii* and *Physoplexus comosa*. One fact that still puzzles many gardeners is that it is possible to grow some of the lime-hating plants in tufa in spite of calcium being one of its main constituent parts; various small calcifuge gentians, for example, can be grown in it.

Maintenance

Maintenance of a tufa garden is very easy. The main thing is to ensure that it receives adequate moisture. Sticking up in isolation, the wind and sun can quickly dry out the surface of the rock but as long as the ground beneath it carries sufficient moisture there will always be enough in the centre of the lump to supply the roots with their needs. Water will quickly run off the surface of the tufa, particularly if it is dry, so any watering should be prolonged. A good alternative is to bore a hole in the top and keep filling this up, covering it with a 'cork' carved from a small piece of tufa.

Weeding should not present a big problem. Occasionally weed seed will blow onto the rock and the resulting seedling will need removing. Similarly any self-sown plants that are not required should be removed at an early stage, before they become established.

In wet areas it may be necessary to cover the tufa with a sheet of glass or a polythene light. Never closely cover the tufa or plants will die; leave plenty of space for air to circulate. One of the biggest problems for tufa left in the open in the winter is that during harsh frost the water within the tufa can freeze. This expands and pushes off lumps of the rock, spoiling its shape and sometimes destroying it altogether. In really cold weather it can be advisable to give the rock some form of protection.

Tufa is a marvellous material that will give years of service with little attention and yet grow some of the most difficult of all alpines. It is relatively cheap to buy, particularly if bought dry.

CHAPTER 6

Peat Beds

Many non-gardeners think of alpines as coming from high mountains and being grown on rock gardens or what they conceive as other half-starved situations. The idea of peat gardens would probably never come into their calculations, but then they are very unlike other aspects of alpine gardening.

Alpine gardeners tend to be passionate about all types of plants and the barriers between the different types are of little interest to them. What is of interest is that plants should be properly grown and this involves creating habitats that most suit them. From this philosophy has derived the peat bed which is ideal for certain types of plant especially those that live further down the mountain in woodland or open moist conditions. It dramatically increases the number of plants the gardener can grow and is a feature well worth considering for any garden.

Basically a peat bed consists of a moisture-retentive compost that never dries out. In the past peat has been the main constituent, hence the name.

Siting

A peat bed is one of the most versatile of the alpine beds in that it can be situated virtually anywhere and has the advantage of being able to utilize an odd shady corner that is unsuited to any other purpose. Bearing in mind that most of the plants that will be grown in the bed will be woodlanders, then a shady position would seem the site but there are many plants that, while needing a moist compost, prefer to be in the sun. Another point to remember is that many woodland plants grow there because of the moisture that is ensured by the presence of deep damp leafmould, whereas out in the open the earth is dry. In other words it is the moisture they are seeking rather than the shade. This is borne out in practice in that many woodland plants will grow happily out in the open as long as the soil is not allowed to dry out.

However, most peat gardens are constructed in part shade, possibly under the dappled shade of trees or on the north side of a house or building. The ideal situation is where part of the bed is out in the sun; this gives the best opportunity for growing the greatest range of plants.

Avoid siting it under trees that make a dense shade such as conifers or beech. Another problem to look out for is tree roots. Some are extremely hungry and thirsty, horse chestnut being a good example, and will quickly send their roots into a newly constructed bed.

In a garden which provides no shade, or if the bed is needed in a part of the garden that is unshaded then small trees and bushes can be incorporated into planting to provide the shade. If the bed is utilitarian (i.e. just a home for plants rather than a decorative feature), then a framework bearing some form of shade netting can be constructed. If made properly this need not look too untidy and is certainly very functional.

The ground can be either flat or sloping, but in either case it should be well drained. Although the idea is to provide plants with a moisture-retentive soil, it is not intended that the soil should be soaking; indeed, very few plants will survive under waterlogged conditions. If the site is a wet one then the drainage should be improved by following the instructions given for the same problem in the construction of a rock garden (see p. 14).

Soil

There is no restriction as to the type of soil on which the peat bed can be built. Obviously it is more difficult on chalky soils than any others, as many of the plants that are grown in such beds are ericaceous, but this is a difficulty that can be overcome.

In the past peat has been the unquestioned main material in the construction of woodland-type beds. This use is mainly fostered by the easy availability of the peat rather than any inherent properties it might have. However, quite a number of growers, and they are usually good growers, have preferred to use leafmould as the basis of their compost and, growing pressures on the supply of peat apart, this is probably the best material to use.

Basically what one is trying to reproduce is the rich leafsoil conditions of the woodland floor. Any number of mixtures can be created to form this, perhaps depending on the local availability of materials. Leaves should be collected every year and stored in a wire netting cage until they have broken down into a loose fibrous mixture. This can be used in the first place to create the peat bed and in sub-sequent years to top up the humus levels. Avoid going to your nearest wood and pillaging it, as this depletes the resources available to the trees and woodland flora. A good mixture could be made from one part (by volume) of good loam, two parts of leafmould and one part of grit.

Peat itself breaks down quickly (and therefore needs constant renewal) and can produce very acid conditions. It is not particularly nutritious and certainly not anywhere as beneficial to plants as leafmould in this respect. A coarse grade should be purchased if it is decided to use it. It can either be used in the same proportions as the formula given for the leafmould, or, better still, substituting the 2 parts of leafmould with 1 of leafmould and 1 of peat.

Another possibility is a material that is becoming increasingly available: composted bark. This is much slower to break down than peat and is more nutritious. It also adds bulk to the soil which is something that peat never seems to achieve. Some people worry about honey fungus being introduced by the bark, but, unless the whole garden has been sterilized, chances are that it is there already and the introduction of composted bark is unlikely to increase the natural chances of trees and shrubs contracting the fungus. A good formula for this is 1 part (by volume) of good loam, 1 part leafmould, 1 part composted bark and 1 part grit.

It is possible to use other forms of humus as a substitute for leafmould including garden compost, hop waste and mushroom compost, although the last mentioned usually contains calcium so should not be used if the plan is to grow ericaceous plants such as rhododendrons or heathers. Avoid anything that is too rich. For example, rotted farmyard manure will produce plants that are totally out of character. A small amount of well-rotted manure can be added to a poor quality or tired loam to beef it up a bit but it should never become the main ingredient.

The function of the grit in all these mixtures is to prevent the compost holding too much water. It is particularly important if peat is used as this is notoriously difficult to re-wet once it has dried out. The presence of grit allows the water to percolate into the mixture and help with the process of re-wetting.

Construction

It is possible to build a peat bed into the ground so that the top is level with the surrounding ground, but it is more normal to build it up in the style of a raised bed. This can take the form of a flat bed or a series of terraces raising it up in the middle or towards the back. Terracing is easier to achieve if the site is a sloping one but it is by no means difficult to create two or three layers on a flat site.

The site should first be dug over and completely cleared of any weeds, particularly the perennial types. If necessary it should be left for a couple of months after this stage to ensure that all the weeds have been extracted. Digging over will not only present an opportunity to remove these weeds but the chance to open up the ground so that excess water can drain away. As has already been stated it is vital that the site should not be waterlogged and any drainage that is deemed necessary should be accomplished at this stage.

If there is the possibility of roots from nearby trees invading the bed it should be lined with a polythene drainage membrane, which will allow water to pass through but (in theory) prevent roots getting in. Eventually they will and the bed may have to be renewed.

On light sandy soil it is advisable to incorporate some humus into the base as this will help prevent the dry soil sucking out moisture from the bed above. On very dry soils a polythene drainage membrane between the native soil and the bed may be advantageous.

Chalky soils present their own problems,

especially if the intention is to grow ericaceous plants. Here the bed should be built above the soil so that the chalk cannot leach into the compost. Again it should be separated with a membrane. The chalk will eventually percolate up through into the compost and this will have to be replaced.

The walling is best achieved with peat blocks, logs making a perfectly acceptable alternative. Peat blocks were just becoming available again when the campaign against the use of peat started, so it is in no way certain that it will be possible to find them locally. The advantage of these is that they can be built up into a wall like ordinary bricks and then as the bed matures the roots of the plants bind them together forming a solid bank of peat which is not only attractive but a good place in which to grow plants. In theory, it should be possible to compress other organic material into blocks.

Before laying the blocks, they should be soaked in water for a couple of days and from this point they should never be allowed to dry out otherwise they will shrink leaving the wall unstable and plants with roots left hanging in the air where the gaps have formed. When thoroughly wetted, the blocks should be laid overlapping each other as in conventional brick laying (Fig. 6.1). Press them well together in order to make certain that the surfaces of the blocks come into good contact, leaving no air pockets. The wall should slope slightly in towards the bed to help with stability. Every so often one block should be laid end on so that it protrudes into the bed, acting as an anchor to the wall.

It is probably best to fill the bed with the compost as building proceeds, at least to fill in the area immediately behind the wall, as this will help to settle the blocks firmly against the bed.

Although there is no other material currently available that is the equivalent of peat blocks, a good alternative for building a wall is wooden logs. Large ones will make a wall in themselves but thinner ones can be stacked one on the other until the required height is reached. These will need some form of stake hammered into the ground on either side of them to keep the wall vertical. Try and choose logs or poles that are as straight as possible otherwise there will be gaps between them through which

Fig. 6.1 Lay blocks of peat in the same way as one would use house bricks. Soak in water before use.

Fig. 6.2 Logs set on end can be used to support the different levels of the peat bed.

compost will spill. It is a good thing to have a few irregularities as a few small gaps will make ideal planting holes on the vertical face.

Another possibility is to cut the wood into lengths and hammer it vertically into the ground, forming a sort of palisade to retain the bed (Fig. 6.2). This has a more formal look about it but certainly works efficiently.

Wood will rot, but by the time it does there is the possibility that the roots of the plants in the bed will have knitted everything together so that the exposed bank does not collapse. The

Fig. 6.3 To avoid compaction of the bed place stone or wood stepping stones at strategic intervals.

Fig. 6.4 Larger beds will need paths and steps for access. These should be of sympathetic materials, such as logs and chipped bark.

wood can be treated with preservative, but again I advise against the use of creosote which will kill most plants. Elm is a good wood to use if it is available because, unlike most other woods, if it is kept moist it will not rot. (It was once used for water pipes because of this property.)

Once the first wall has been constructed fill the bed with the soil mixture and press it well down. If there is time it is best to leave this until the weather has made it sink so that it can be topped up before building the next layer. Usually, however, there is an urge to get the job done, so compress as far as is possible the part around the area where the next wall is going to go. Build this, backfill the bed and so on until the final height and shape is completed.

Once the bed has been filled, it is finished by adding 4–5 cm (1½–2 in) of leafmould or crushed bark. This will help conserve moisture as well as helping to enrich the bed as it breaks down and is mixed with the top layer of soil by the worms. Bark can use up a lot of nitrogen as it breaks down so it is advisable to give the bed a slight sprinkling, at half the recommended dosage, of a general fertilizer before covering with the bark.

To avoid compaction it is advisable not to walk on the bed once it has been constructed. If it is too wide to reach all parts without treading on it, it is an easy matter to insert stepping stones at strategic points (Fig. 6.3). These will allow easy access for weeding as well as looking at the plants. They can be slabs of stone or roundels of wood cut from tree trunks. Be warned, however, the latter can become very slippery and should be covered with wire netting to provide the surface with a grip if there is the possibility of people falling over.

A large bed is likely to need steps and a path passing through it (Fig. 6.4). These should be made of sympathetic materials. The path can, for example, be edged with logs and covered with chipped bark. The risers of the steps can again be made from lengths of wood; alternatively they can be created out of roundels of wood as described above.

If there is no natural shade in the garden, or at least no shade where the desired site for the bed is to be situated, it is possible to create an artificial aid by building a framework over which greenhouse shading is stretched (Fig. 6.5). The framework should be at least 2 m (6.5 ft) above the bed to allow easy access. It should be strongly made as the net will catch the wind, putting a great deal of stress on the structure. Since the sun is not directly overhead all the time, the framework should extend beyond the edge of the bed so that plants on the extremities are not scorched on either side of midday.

The plastic netting should be left on only from mid spring until the autumn. If left on during winter it can become overburdened with snow and stretch, or, even worse, collapse.

Planting

There seems to me more enjoyment in the actual planting up of a peat bed than any other type of garden. I do not know why this should be but suspect it is something to do with smell and the wonderful leafy texture of the soil mixture as it slides through the fingers.

There are two areas of planting in a peat bed, the vertical walls and the main flat area of the bed. Plants can be inserted into the wall at the time of construction as this is easier at this stage than later as the wall can be upset by the insertion of a trowel (remember there is no 'mortar' in a peat wall to hold it together). Make certain that the roots are in contact with either the peat block or the soil mix behind it.

It can be easy to dig too big a hole and leave the roots dangling in mid air. (This is not so much of a problem in conventional planting as soil naturally falls into the hole; here the hole is horizontal and a conscious effort is required to make certain that all the hole is filled with compost.)

There is a wide range of plants that will cheerfully grow in these walls from ramondas and primulas to shrubby plants, such as vacciniums, which are useful in binding the wall with their roots.

The planting on the surface of the bed is undertaken in the conventional manner. If topdressing has taken place before planting, scrape back the leafmould or bark before making the hole. This is one area in alpine gardening where plants can be planted in drifts, if space allows. With plants such as epimediums, which have spreading tendencies, make certain that they are planted far enough apart not to swamp each other after the first year. Others that spread more slowly, such as trilliums, can be planted closer together so that it does not look too gappy.

If there is no natural shade for the bed it is possible to grow small trees and shrubs to provide shade for those plants that desire it.

An enormous range of plants are available for this kind of bed and they can transform what is an unproductive shady area into one of the most attractive in the garden.

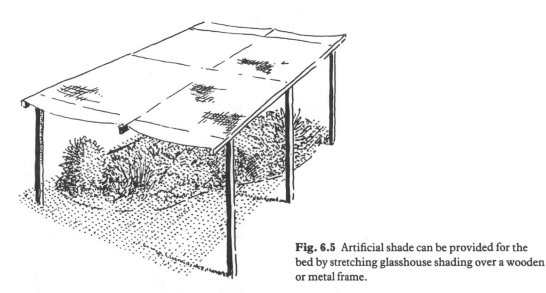

Fig. 6.5 Artificial shade can be provided for the bed by stretching glasshouse shading over a wooden or metal frame.

Maintenance

Plants grow well in peat beds, and so do weeds. It is essential to keep on top of them; a once-a-year blitz is likely to result in disaster. One of the disadvantages of using peat becomes apparent once weeding starts, great lumps are brought up adhering to the fine roots of the weeds and there can soon be more peat on the compost heap than in the bed if care is not taken. One way to prevent this is to remove the weeds when they are young and before too big a root ball has been built up.

Another way is to ensure that the bark mulch is topped up each year; this will make life considerably easier, both for the plants and the gardener. Top-dressing definitely helps to keep the weeds down. Once some of the spreading plants get going they tend to act as a ground cover and help to suppress weeds.

The bed should never be allowed to dry out, the peat wall being especially vulnerable. If the latter becomes dry it is very difficult to wet it again as the water runs off the surface. As the blocks dry they shrink, making the wall unstable and leaving plants with roots hanging in the air. A close eye should be kept on its condition and it should be watered with a sprinkler if necessary.

If the bed should sink (particularly likely in the first year), top up with the soil mix, particularly round the edges, as peat blocks left exposed above the soil level will dry out very quickly.

At least once a year leafmould or a top-dressing of bark should be given. This will not only maintain the vitality of the soil mix but help replace any removed with weeds and at the same time act as a mulch.

CHAPTER 7

Water Features

One of the most wonderful sounds in the mountains is the rushing and gurgling of water. Likewise in the garden, water can contribute greatly to the atmosphere, particularly if it is a natural stream. The biggest private rock garden that I have ever seen was about 0.5 hectares (1.25 acres) and had three natural streams running through it. It was a magnificent sight and yet did illustrate the dangers of natural streams in that the year before there had been a flash flood and half the rock garden had been moved further down the valley. Fortunately the owner was a resilient man and stoically rebuilt his garden.

Water in the garden can be stagnant in the form of ponds or moving as in streams, waterfalls and cascades. It does add another dimension to a rock garden or peat bed, but it is a lot of trouble and should be done properly if it is to be successful. Dried up concrete streams and ribbons of polythene do little for either the appearance of the garden or to the welfare of the plants. If there is any doubt that the gardener can build and maintain a system of waterways and pumps it is probably best not to attempt the project but channel energies into another aspect of the garden.

Pools

The simplest of water features in any garden is a pool. This does not have the magic of a stream but it does provide a reflective surface, animated with ripples and does supply conditions that many plants will enjoy. Unless it is being built on the grandest scale it is not difficult to build using polythene membranes, which if installed properly should prove watertight and of little trouble.

If the pool is to be built in a rock garden then it should be incorporated at the time that the latter is built, otherwise a lot of work will ensue in taking the structure apart and rebuilding it with the addition of the water. It is not such a problem with peat beds but again it does save work if it is considered at an early stage.

Fig. 7.1 Spread the butyl lining over the hole and, supporting it with bricks, fill it with water so that it sinks snugly into position.

The shape of the pool is entirely up to the gardener. Straight-sided pools look a bit out of place in the informal setting of a rock garden so it is more usual to have irregular shapes based roughly on an oval or ellipse. In profile the shape can be a semi-circle, but it is normally found that steps created along the edges facilitate planting.

A simple pool can be created by digging a hole to the required depth (making certain that the top edge is level all the way round) and shape, adding a layer of sand or newspapers to prevent any stones left in the soil penetrating the membrane, and then covering it with a butyl lining (Fig. 7.1). The lining should be larger than the pool and should be stretched horizontally over the hole and temporarily held in position with bricks placed around its edge. The membrane is now slowly filled from a hosepipe; it should sink into the pond and mould itself to shape under the weight of the water. Once full, excess liner round the edge of the pool can be covered by rocks or slabs of stone.

Fig. 7.2 Pools can be automatically topped up with water using a hidden cistern and ballcock connected with a horizontal pipe.

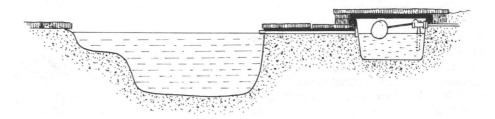

Fig. 7.3 Plants can be established both in the pool and at its margins in specially created boggy ground.

These simple ponds are easy to keep filled with water: they can simply be topped from a hosepipe connected to a mains water supply. Most water authorities allow ponds to be kept filled, even under drought conditions, if they contain pondlife. Check with your local water authority if in doubt.

Rainwater will contribute quite a lot of the required water, particularly if the gutters from nearby buildings are piped into it. Unfortunately this natural supply is not so easy to control and a storm producing 2.5 cm (1 in), or even 5 cm (2 in) in one go, can easily flood the pool, particularly if all the water from the roof of the house has been added to this. It may be considered prudent to provide an overflow pipe to prevent the pool overflowing and washing away part of the garden.

At its simplest, a part of the liner can be depressed to form a channel through which excess water can be led away. A more complicated but more satisfactory solution is to install an overflow pipe. It is possible to purchase special fittings that allow a pipe to be run through the membrane.

Static ponds, if lined properly do not lose a great deal of water and therefore the simple methods of topping up, mentioned above are usually sufficient. However, where cascades and streams are involved, water often gets splashed on the surrounding area and minor leaks are more likely to develop and here it may be necessary to provide an automatic device. This involves a small tank about the size of a WC cistern buried in the ground next to the pond (Fig. 7.2). This has an outflow pipe level with the water level of the pond and an incoming pipe, controlled by a ballcock, from the mains water supply. If the water in the pond drops, so does the level in the tank and the ballcock opens the supply from the mains, which runs until the levels have been restored. The tank should be well-buried (but accessible) or insulated and the outlet should be capable of being shut off so that the system can be safely closed down in winter to prevent it freezing. It is advisable to check with the water authority before installing an automatic system.

Bog gardens

For the pool to work properly it must obviously be watertight. However, there are problems with this; while an impermeable membrane (or layer of concrete) will keep the water in, it does mean that the surrounding area is kept dry and yet one of the purposes of having a pool is to be able to grow waterside plants that like a damp, even boggy position. If the only area for planting is in the pool itself then the choice of plants is restricted to a few floating plants, such as waterlilies (*Nymphaea*), or marginals that will grow in the water at the edge of the pond.

When designing the pool it is desirable to continue the lining beyond the edge of the water itself, and create an area of ground that varies from just moist to boggy so that a wide range of plants can be grown (Fig. 7.3). This

can be achieved in a number of ways. The membrane can be continued well beyond the pool, slowly rising so that it finishes above the water-level. This section is then filled with a peaty soil (see p. 47). The area nearest the pond will be permanently wet and the rest, above the waterline and furthest from the pond, will vary according to the amount of water it soaks up.

An alternative is to take the membrane up slightly above the water level over a ridge of soil or sand and then drop it down again to form a secondary, shallow pond. A layer 2.5 cm (1 in) of sharp sand or grit should be placed underneath the liner in this area and another layer on top of it. These are to facilitate drainage as the liner is punctured in a few places so that no stagnant water lies around. The shallow dish is now filled with a peaty soil. Every so often the main pond can be overfilled (blocking the overflow pipe if one has been installed) so that the water level rises and overflows into the boggy area. Excess water will slowly drain away leaving the peaty soil moist.

Moving water

The sight and sound of moving water in a garden adds another dimension to it. If a natural stream passes through the garden it is

Fig. 7.4 Water can fall directly from one pool to another or can be channelled between them by a series of cascades.

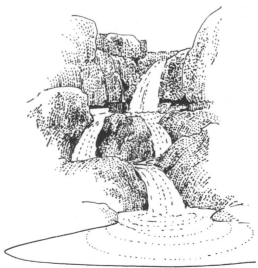

possible to build a peat bed, or even rock garden alongside it. Alternatively it might be possible to channel off some water into a separate stream to pass through the beds. The latter has the advantage in that it should be possible to control the flow thus ensuring that there are no floods to wash away the plants, soil and even rocks.

If there is no natural supply of water it is not too difficult a task these days to construct a stream that works on a close circuit with the water being pumped from the bottom of the system back to the top.

The various possible designs of a garden using moving water are too numerous to mention in this book, but a few ideas can be mentioned. The simplest is two pools one above the other in which the water trickles over the lip of one into the other (Fig. 7.4). The distance between the two can be extended, connecting them with a stream. Alternatively a system of cascades can be built where the water, instead of flowing smoothly down the stream, is constantly tumbling over a series of ledges or dams.

Complex structures are more easily constructed from concrete than butyl. The

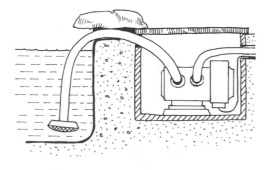

Fig. 7.5 A pump at the bottom of a waterfall can be hidden in an underground chamber with a pipe concealed by rocks leading into the pool.

number of twists and corners makes it difficult for the butyl to be laid without creases which inevitably seem to show. Many gardeners soon become blind to the sight of great creases of the black liner showing above the level of the water and disappearing half-heartedly beneath a few rocks; unfortunately to the visitor it is all too obvious and detracts from the quality of the garden. To a certain extent the edges can be disguised with rock, but these are often rough or contain sharp corners, causing them to penetrate the membrane, particularly if they are used as stepping stones.

Concrete is more complicated and strenuous to lay than butyl but it is strong and after a short time can blend in with the stonework giving a more natural appearance. Pools and stream beds are best lined with rubble before the addition of concrete. Vertical walls will need shuttering to prevent the concrete slumping before it has set. A waterproofing agent can be added to the concrete to increase its impermeability. Rocks embedded in the wet concrete are likely to weaken the structure and should therefore be added afterwards. Above the water line where strength is not so important rocks can be permanently incorporated into the design. However, this permanence might not be desirable as it does not allow rocks to be moved about if changes are desired.

Water can be circulated by the use of a pump. This can either be a submersible type which is placed underwater in the lowest part of the system, or a surface type which is kept on the bank with a pipe down into the water. The latter is more powerful and more easily disguised. A box or a chamber below ground can be constructed and the pipe led into the pond under a rock so that it cannot be seen (Fig. 7.5). Similarly the inlet at the top of the system can be disguised so that water appears to come from a spring in the rocks or wells up from below the surface of the pool.

The submersible pumps are cheaper but are not capable of moving such a large volume of water. These can be seen in a shallow pool and are not easy to disguise unless covered by overhanging rock. Their pipes can again be led out of the pool under rocks and allowed to enter the upper pool in the same manner as the surface pump mentioned above.

It is vital to remember that electricity and water are a lethal combination and if there is any doubt about the installation of the power supply to the pump a qualified electrician should be consulted.

There is not room in a book on alpines to go into all details of constructing water features and the reader is strongly recommended to consult a specialist book such as *The Complete Book of the Water Garden* by Philip Swindells and David Mason (Ward Lock).

Planting

With artificial pools that contain no soil, plants will have to be introduced into the water by first planting them into the special lattice pots that are sold for the purpose (Fig. 7.6). The soil should be a fibrous one and that suggested for the peat garden (see p. 47) should be suitable. Once planted the pots can be lowered onto the ledges round the edge of the pond for those requiring shallow water and into the middle for those requiring deeper conditions. It is possible to position plants by passing two strings through the top frets of the pot and then with one person on either side of the pond it is lowered into position and the strings withdrawn.

The edges of the ponds and streams can be filled with the same compost as was described for the peat garden (see p. 47) and plants such as primulas and mimulus can be planted directly into this. Some plants, again many primulas are a good example, will enjoy the buoyant air above a stream or pool and can be planted to great advantage in cracks in vertical rockwork overhanging the water.

Maintenance

A very important aspect of all maintenance work is to remember that if the pool is lined with butyl it can be easily punctured, so avoid walking on it. There must be a restrained use of a fork near the liner otherwise the inevitable will happen.

Fig. 7.6 Lattice pots make ideal containers for growing water plants as the roots can easily penetrate the sides.

It is essential to keep the weeds down as the conditions are very conducive to their growth and the area around the water can soon become overgrown unless regular attention is given.

The main problem in the pool itself is green algae. Oxygenating plants should be planted and the combination of these plus moving water should keep it at bay. If it does appear the options are limited, either it must be removed by hand at regular intervals or a proprietary chemical used.

Plants in baskets should be lifted every three years, divided and replanted in fresh compost.

Try to keep the pools clear of any debris and fallen leaves. The filters of the pumps will also need periodically clearing out. Every five years or so it will become necessary to empty the pool by siphoning off the water to a lower part of the garden (or if this is impossible, then emptied by bucket). Keep plants in buckets of water until the pond is refilled. Avoid puncturing the liner if there is one, when cleaning out the accumulated muck.

CHAPTER 8

Other Positions for Alpines

There are many other positions in a garden that can be used for growing alpines. Some of these may be part of the existing structure of the garden such as dry-stone walls or they may be a new feature.

Dry-stone walls

Dry-stone walls make a very good attempt at imitating vertical stone faces in the mountains (Fig. 8.1). The many cracks and crevices between stones make admirable homes for many plants. These fissures, particularly in the older walls, contain sufficient detritus, blown in over the years, to support the plants. In new walls, a gritty compost should be forced into one or two of the cracks to supply the questing roots with some nourishment. Many walls, of course, are retaining-walls and here there is a ready supply of soil into which the roots can reach.

In some areas gardeners are lucky in that stone walls are common features of the landscape and they may well already have one in or around their garden. Elsewhere they have to be built. Free-standing walls are not the easiest of walls to construct and are expensive, unless there is a plentiful supply of stone available. If there is a good supply of stone then the chances are that there will also be professional wallers in the area that can be called upon to carry out the necessary construction. There are books which the beginner can consult and courses on which he or she can go.

Smaller, low walls and retaining walls, however, may well be within the amateur's grasp (Fig. 8.2). A retaining wall should have a firm base and should lean slightly in towards the mass it is retaining. Every so often a long stone should be turned at right angles to the wall so that it goes back into the soil and acts as an anchor. The gap between the wall and the bank it is supporting can be filled with a gritty compost, such as would be used on a rock garden (see p. 16), if a large number of plants are expected to be grown on the face. Retaining walls can be built either as a dry-stone wall or as a bonded wall of stone or brick. There will be plenty of natural planting places in the first case, but in the latter holes will have to be left in the brick or stonework into which plants can be placed. This type of wall need not be confined to hold up banks, they can be constructed for raised beds as described on p. 31.

It is possible to force plants from pots or dug up from the ground into the gaps in the wall but it is not very easy to get them established.

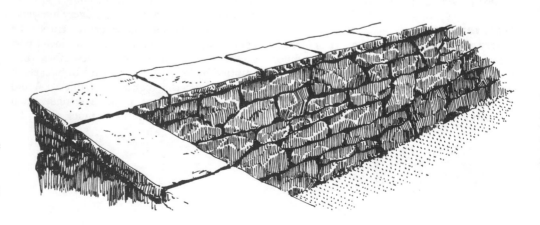

Fig. 8.1 Dry-stone walls around or within a garden make ideal planting places for crevice-loving plants.

Fig. 8.2 Retaining walls are not too difficult to construct and will act as a perfect home to a wide range of alpines.

Young plants are the easiest to get going but rooted cuttings make a better bet. All should be regularly watered until they are established.

The best way to get plants established in a wall, however, is from seed. Place a few seeds on the palm of one hand and then, with the aid of a drinking straw, blow them into a crack in which there is a little compost (Fig. 8.3). Once established in this way, many plants will continue to self-sow into the wall. In some plants, *Cymbalaria muralis* for example, the stems carrying the seed pods turn naturally away from the light into crevices and deposit the seed inside ready for germination.

A free-standing wall will have two sides, one of which is bound to catch more sun than the other, unless it is on an exact north/south axis. This variation in the amount of received sunlight can be exploited by planting sun-lovers, such as *Erinus alpinus* and several *Campanula*, on the sunny side while those that prefer the cooler, shady side, such as *Ramonda* can be planted on the other. If a retaining wall has its face away from the sun then it tends to make a cooler and moister habitat than a free-standing wall. This kind of situation is much appreciated by ferns and an interesting fernery can be developed.

Maintenance is quite simple. New plants should be kept watered until they are established, but otherwise natural rainfall should be sufficient except in times of severe drought. Many spreading plants, *Aubrieta* and *Helianthemum* should be sheared over once

they have finished flowering to keep them compact. The only other task is the ever-present one of keeping an eye out for weeds and removing them. Walls can become the natural home for ivy and this must be kept at bay if there is to be any hope of growing other plants on it.

Paving

Most gardens have a paved area somewhere within it, often at the back of the house as an area for sitting and relaxing. The covering is either stone or concrete flags, or brick pavers. In much modern housing the whole garden is so small that it is covered in this way, with no room for conventional borders or lawns.

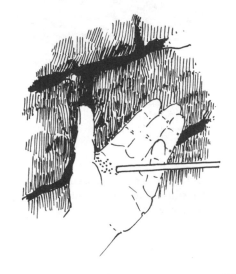

Fig. 8.3 Seed can be easily sown into vertical crevices by blowing it with a drinking straw from the palm of a hand.

This paved area can be utilized to grow a large number of alpines. One way is to grow them in sinks or troughs, as already described on p. 36. The slabs or brick make an ideal base for such containers and in their turn the containers make a very decorative feature on the terrace or patio. If a wall is built round the edge of the terrace it is possible to build it as a double wall so that it becomes a raised bed (see p. 29). This form of raised bed can provide a wide range of habitats, both in the sun and shade and the number of delightful plants that can be grown will make a marked contrast to the usual brash bedding plants that are so often grown in such positions.

However, it is the paving itself that can provide a unique habitat for many alpine plants. These can be planted in the cracks between the stones or the occasional slab or brick can be removed and this area planted up as a miniature garden.

The gaps between paving stones can be left when they are laid or they can be scraped out at a later stage. If the slabs have been laid on a concrete base it may be necessary to drill a small hole through this so that roots can get down into soil, but many plants will find enough nourishment from the dust and detritus that accumulates between and under the slabs.

Fig. 8.4 Removing a slab, replacing the soil beneath it with a gritty compost and then planting alpines creates a decorative feature for a patio.

The plants that are used in these positions should be tough as they are liable to be walked on when the terrace is in use, or even knocked severely when the terrace is swept. The kind of plants that do well here are dwarf shrubby ones such as the thymes (*Thymus*) or *Mentha requenii*, which have the advantage that their leaves give off a fragrant smell when crushed or walked on. Another good, tough plant is *Acaena* but these have burrs that could be painful if used in areas where people are liable to walk with bare feet. There are always areas where people do not walk and these can be used for more delicate plants.

Lifting slabs or bricks can give the gardener more scope as he is, in effect, making a raised bed level with the ground (Fig. 8.4). The soil beneath the slab is removed and a mixture suitable for alpines (see p. 16) is put in its stead. If there is any possibility that the water from the terrace will drain into this hole, so that it acts like a sump, then some action must be taken to incorporate a drain. Any plants can be used here but it is often a good idea to use some spreading plants to soften the edge of the paving round the hole. Taller plants such as *Juniperus communis* 'Compressa', or small pieces of rock or tufa can be used to add height and structure. A good arrangement can be made by placing troughs next to areas that have had the slabs removed so that plants can sprawl around their bases. Another idea is to partly bury a large lump of tufa in the hole and plant it up as shown on p. 43. Top-dress these small gardens with stone chippings or grit in the same way as a raised bed (see p. 33).

Maintenance of these small gardens is not difficult and mainly consists of making certain that any weeds that germinate are removed. Watering, of course, is important, but it is not so critical as in some other parts of the garden. The reason for this is that the terrace or patio traps water below its surface, so that it cannot evaporate, thus providing a reservoir of moisture for the roots of the plants.

The big benefit of using paved areas as alpine gardens is that they are readily accessible to the elderly and disabled. In areas designed specifically for these groups then the troughs and raised beds should be built up to a convenient height, but it is imperative that they are stable. Planting between cracks should be restricted to the margins of the terrace where they are unlikely to be tripped over.

Alpine lawns

Many visitors to the mountains come away with the image of the floriferous meadows firmly fixed in their minds, with every intention of trying to recreate them when they get home. Unfortunately it is likely to remain a dream, because the reality is that it is impossible to recreate the conditions in which these meadows could grow in our gardens.

The nearest one can get to it is to create a wildflower meadow, using native plants, but even this is extremely difficult to achieve satisfactorily. Indeed a wildflower garden is a hundred times more difficult and time-consuming to create than a conventional garden; it is certainly not just a question of letting the garden get on with it.

The first thing to create is the meadow itself. This can be achieved either by cleaning a piece of ground to remove all perennial and annual weeds and then sowing it with a mixture of fine grasses. Alternatively a piece of existing meadow or a lawn can be used. In the case of the former it will need to be mown regularly, like a lawn, for several years until all the coarse grasses have died out. Once a fine sward has been achieved then meadow flowers can be planted into it. In the first instance it is better to plant rather than sow, at least during the initial stages, as this reduces the competition for the new plants. The plants should be spring-flowering and can include some bulbs such as the small daffodils.

Once the flowers have seeded (about mid summer) the lawn should be cut and then mown monthly until mid autumn. If autumn-flowering plants, such as colchicums, have been introduced then the mowing will have to stop earlier. This pattern follows the natural cycle in the alpine meadows where the meadows are left to grow for hay until summer and then, once cut, they are grazed by cattle until the autumn. It is essential not to allow the lawn to grow rank and any coarse weeds that find their way into it should be removed at once, and should certainly never be allowed to seed. To be successful a lot of attention is needed.

However, there is a form of gardening where the plants are left to 'get on with it' which can prove quite satisfactory in alpine terms. There are a number of plants that are really too rampant and too bullish to include in a conventional rock garden or raised bed. For example, many *Sedum, Acaena, Cotula* or *Pratia* have a tendency to travel far and wide smothering other plants on their travels. It is an interesting exercise to confine them all to one bed and let them fight it out. All weeds, particularly perennial ones should first be removed from the site.

A good example of this kind of garden can be seen at Sissinghurst Castle in Kent, UK, where there are two beds entirely devoted to different types of thymes. These form a lawn of merging hummocks of different colours from pink to red; a delightful sight in high summer. However, pretty as it looks, it does need a lot of maintenance as it has to be torn apart every few years and replanted, otherwise the centres of the plants die out and brown gaps – and ultimately weeds as well – appear.

Perhaps a more modest form of alpine garden can be created by adding bulbs to an existing lawn. Miniature daffodils (*Narcissus*), snowdrops (*Galanthus*) and crocuses can be introduced to certain areas which should not be mown when the plants are in leaf. The secret of this type of garden is to prevent any coarse grasses getting into the lawn. One or two other flowers can be introduced but they must flower at the same time as the bulbs so that it can all be cut down and restored to a conventional lawn before the season is too far advanced, otherwise it will all become rank and a severe problem with which to cope.

Odd corners

It is amazing the number of odd spots around a garden that can be used for growing plants. For the visitor this makes an absolute delight as one is always discovering more plants tucked away. For example, it is perfectly possible to utilize a damp shady area behind a shed by beefing up the soil a bit with organic material and planting rhododendrons or many of the other shrubs or woodland plants that will enjoy these conditions.

Sinks and other containers can be placed in all manner of places; alpines can even be grown in window boxes for example (but be certain that they are secure and not likely to rot). Raised beds can be built in odd places that are of no use for anything else.

The idea that paved terraces can be used has already been dealt with (see p. 60) but there is also the possibility of using paths and drives in the same way. If covered with loose gravel or shingle they are forming what is in effect a scree bed and quite a number of plants can be introduced to form small colonies. Thymes are good for this as are *Erinus alpinus* and many others. If a drive consists of two parallel concrete paths on which the wheels run and a central earth or gravel reservation then this can certainly be planted to advantage. This would make an ideal site for an alpine lawn in which the more vigorous plants can be safely left to fight it out.

Walls have already been mentioned but low roofs can also utilize certain plants, in particular sedum and houseleeks (*Sempervivum*). I have a very vigorous colony of these two growing on my north-facing porch mixed with lichen and moss. They were started by the very un-alpine method of putting a cowpat on the roof and planting it up with a piece of the sedum and a rosette of the houseleek. No further attention has been required for twelve years, during which time they have colonized the whole roof. This is the only true example of maintenance-free gardening I have ever come across.

Small bulbs are possibly the most adaptable of alpines as these can be grown in a wide number of habitats including under hedges and under shrubs of all sizes, in particular deciduous ones. Whereas most alpines would look incongruous in such places (even, indeed, if they would grow there in the first place) quite a number of small bulbs, such as snowdrops (*Galanthus*) and cyclamen, would look perfectly happy and, if well suited, would soon spread.

So with ingenuity a large number of habitats can be provided for alpine plants, even within a small garden, but do remember the dignity of the plants and do put them in surroundings which are sympathetic to their beauty and character.

PART II

ALPINES UNDER COVER

CHAPTER 9

Introduction

The secret of growing alpine plants is to provide them with conditions in which they will thrive. This normally means that they should be grown in circumstances that are as near as possible to those that they enjoy in the wild. However, although botanical gardens can enjoy the luxury of having specially chilled houses, the majority of gardeners find it impossible to emulate the conditions in the mountains.

Within certain limitations it is possible to get the soil, watering and feeding right, but it is the climate which is extremely difficult to copy. The light for example is very intense in the thin, unpolluted air. It contains far more ultraviolet rays than lower down where most people garden. The difference in this light means that whereas a plant in the mountains will be short and compact, in the garden it will become lax and bushier.

It would seem natural to suppose that any plant that comes from the high mountains would be totally hardy as it is exposed to below-freezing conditions for long periods as well as strong winds, but it is easy to forget that many plants are covered with snow, often metres thick. The temperature at ground level, under this snow, is usually around about the freezing mark, usually slightly above, so that the plants are not frozen solid and still have a certain amount of water for their roots.

Another important factor is that once winter has started in the mountains it usually continues until the spring. In Britain and most of the other countries where alpines are grown, the pattern of winter is more of a stop/start nature. A cold spell will be followed by a couple of weeks of warm, muggy weather followed in turn by another cold snap, perhaps severe, and so on. This sequence means that after the initial cold spell the plant thinks that the warm weather is the coming spring and starts to put on growth, only to be checked by the next sudden drop in temperature. This check can be severe enough to kill the plant. In other words, although the plant may be completely hardy in the wild, the fluctuating temperature makes it susceptible to the milder weather found in many lowland gardens.

Many plants, bulbs in particular, put on most of their growth in the winter and early spring. After flowering and seeding they die down and rest until the autumn rains once again start them into growth. During the summer they are used to a certain degree of baking by the sun. In an average British summer plants grown in the open will not usually be subjected to a drought or be baked.

Quite a number of plants will flower early in the year. Many of these, *Ranunculus calandrinioides* from the Atlas Mountains in Morocco being a good example, have delicate petals that can easily be damaged by the wet weather experienced in an average maritime climate. The only way to see these plants at their best is to prevent the rain getting at them while they are in flower.

It is possible to a limited degree to control the weather by the judicious use of sheets of glass but it is not a very satisfactory method to use on a large scale and most growers prefer to grow some of their alpines under a more permanent cover of some kind. This is most usually an alpine house, in which conditions, to a certain extent, can be controlled. These conditions, of course, not only affect the plants; most gardeners like to be tucked up away from the winter weather while they tend their plants during the most inhospitable months of the year.

CHAPTER 10

Growing in Pots

If plants are to be grown under cover the most convenient way of doing this is by using pots of some sort. The big advantage of growing plants in this way is that they are portable, i.e. they can be kept inside during the winter and moved out during the summer, or they can be grown outside and just brought into the alpine house while they are in flower. They can also be taken to shows or along to local alpine meetings. A plant in a pot can be given away more easily than one in a bed. If a plant gets too big for its allotted space it can be moved, or those around it can be moved to give it more space.

Being grown in a pot also means that plants can be placed on benches so that the grower can see them more closely, both to admire them and to give them better cultural attention. The best growers of alpines are those who spend a lot of time observing their plants and thinking about what they see. Water, for example, can be administered individually to the plants, according to their perceived needs. Indeed, the very compost in which they grow can easily be varied from pot to pot. This individual, close attention is not only beneficial to the plants but also rewarding in what the grower learns about plants and their cultivation.

One final advantage of growing plants in pots is that a large number of plants can be grown in a small amount of space. This is useful both for the number of different plants one can grow and also for the number of similar plants that can be grown for exchange, sale or simply giving away. It is also advantageous when there is a necessity to grow on a large number of seedlings to find out which have the best flowers or the best form.

Types of pots

You will not have to be interested long in alpines to discover that there are two types of pots, clay and plastic, both having their devotees. A few years ago the advocates for the use of clays would have fought to the death in defence of their chosen medium but today good sense prevails and it is generally acknowledged that both types of pots have advantages and disadvantages and that one or the other is better in different situations.

Until the second half of the twentieth century nearly all pots were made of terracotta (there was the occasional one made of another material such as cement by way of experiment). They came in a variety of sizes, usually determined by the whim of the potter. The sizes were not given by diameter or capacity as is the custom today but by the rather odd custom of quoting the number of pots that could be made from one wheelful of clay. Thus the higher the number the smaller the pot. Thus a 60 is the equivalent of a 7.5 cm (3 in) pot while a small 60 and a large 60 were 6.3 cm ($2\frac{1}{2}$ in) and 9 cm ($3\frac{1}{2}$ in) pots respectively; 44s were 11.5 cm ($4\frac{1}{2}$ in) and so on up to 8s which were 30 cm (12in) in diameter. Those pots that were taller or deeper than normal were called (and still are for that matter) long toms and the shorter-than-normal pots were named pans. Long toms are used for plants with deep root systems, particularly those with tap roots. Pans are used for wide-spreading plants with shallow root systems or for growing several of the same plant in order to put on a good display. Pans are not only round but also square and rectangular.

Before recent standardization in terracotta pots, this variation in size was a great disadvantage to the gardener, particularly when it came to potting on or repotting. It was often difficult or impossible to find the right-sized pot in which to put the plant; they were usually too narrow or too wide, too deep or too shallow, or tapered too quickly. For twenty or so years it was very difficult to buy clay pots and many growers found their dwindling stocks very frustrating to use and many went over to plastic to avoid the problem. In the late 1980s clay pots again became generally available, although at a much greater price. Now the pots are manufactured to standard sizes and this has made life considerably easier. If the beginner (or anyone else) buys a job lot of old clay pots this will help explain why he is unlikely to find no two pots are the same.

Variation in size is only one of the disadvantages of clay. Another is that they break if dropped or knocked and are prone to fracture by the frost. They are heavy, particularly when filled with compost. They and their contents dry out quickly (this is also an advantage; see below). To many people the greatest disadvantage other than cost is the fact that they are the very devil to clean.

Their advantage is that alpines generally seem to be happier growing in them. One reason for this is that it is virtually impossible to overwater a clay pot as water evaporates from its side as well as running out of the drainage hole at the bottom. This is a nuisance in summer as the pots will need constant watering, but in winter when the plants are taking up less water it prevents them from becoming waterlogged. The porosity of the pot works both ways and if it is plunged in damp sand the compost within will take up moisture through the walls. This is particularly useful in winter. Another factor concerning winter is that clay pots are warmer than plastic ones during cold spells, and yet during the summer, because of the evaporation from their sides, they are cooler.

A minor, but nonetheless a very important advantage to many people is that clay pots look infinitely more attractive than their plastic counterparts, and the plants look more at home in them. The clay pots are rigid and do not collapse as plastic ones sometimes do when they are being carried.

Plastic pots overcome some of the difficulties presented by clay pots but in turn have some of their own disadvantages. The biggest one is that moisture cannot escape through the sides of the pots and even with well-drained compost plants can be overwatered and become waterlogged. This is particularly a problem during the winter when it is difficult to tell how much water a plant is taking up. There are times, however, when a moisture-retentive compost is required and then water retention is in the plastic pot's favour. As already mentioned they are colder in winter and hotter in summer as the plastic cannot breathe. Plants never look as happy in plastic pots as they do in clay ones; plants on the show benches, for example, always look more attractive when set out in clays.

The two main advantages of plastic pots are that they are cheap (or at least cheaper than clays) and that they are easier to clean. Another advantage, particularly for the elderly, is that they are much lighter to carry.

Today most growers have preference for one type of pot or the other, but few exclusively stick to this choice as they appreciate that the other also has advantages in certain situations. The only advice that one can give (as in so many matters concerning gardening) is to try both and to see with which you and your plants are happiest.

There are many other types of containers in which alpines can be grown, empty yoghurt cartons and used plastic coffee cups being the most frequently met. In many alpine circles use of this kind of container is usually frowned upon. They should not, for example, be used for plants that are brought along to many of the alpine sales that regularly take place at society meetings. The main reason for this is that the plants do look out of character in such containers, especially if they have writing and illustrations on the sides. Another reason is that these pots come basically in one size and plants that are grown in them soon become cramped and starved. Plants are often left too long in such containers and this does little to help their appearance.

The beginner, confronted with the other expenses of setting up an alpine garden, can ill afford to spend much money on a large collection of pots and can make good use of such free cartons. He or she should do so bearing a couple of points in mind. The first is that drainage holes should be cut or burnt in the bottom of all cartons. The second is that he should convert to pots as soon as he can afford to do so.

Whatever pots are used they must always be clean. They should be scrubbed inside and out with warm water, removing all soil. The white salt deposits should also be removed from the outside of clay pots, particularly if they are intended for show plants. Special round brushes that fitted inside different sized pots used to be available and these can occasionally still be found.

As well as cleaning pots some growers like to sterilize them as well, particularly clay pots which may harbour disease in their pores, by boiling them in water for a short while. With suitable precautions household bleach containing sodium hypochlorite can be used; pots should be soaked for 30 minutes in a solution of 1 part bleach to 4 parts water. A much safer but more smelly method is to use a solution made up from water and Jeyes Fluid to the manufacturer's specification.

Compost ingredients

There are three basic composts that are used in pots; potting, seed and cutting composts. The last two will be dealt with under propagation (see pp. 112 & 116) but the first will be dealt with here as it it one of the most important aspects of alpine gardening.

There is no hard and fast rule as to what is the best compost. Even if there were it would be difficult to make as the ingredients vary so much. For example the loam, which forms the basis of any compost, can vary in composition from one part of the garden to another, let alone from one garden to another or different parts of the country. It will vary in its mineral content, and its amount and type of humus, sand and stones. Its pH can also vary considerably. If peat is used as the organic content than again there is a large range of pH values from neutral to extreme acidity. Grits will produce sharper drainage if they are more angular than if they are rounded. Anyone who has bought a John Innes potting compost will know of the great variation that they have obtained from different manufacturers, or even from the same manufacturer over a time; in spite of a supposed rigid formula and a seal of approval they could all come from different planets.

Any formula will therefore only act as a guide and it is up to the gardener to experiment further. Many of the best growers vary their standard composts from plant to plant by adding a bit more grit or a bit more leafmould, or perhaps just a dash of tufa dust. This kind of treatment can only come with experience and observation — two key aspects in growing alpines well.

The three basic materials are garden loam, humus in the form of leafmould or peat (or some modern alternative) and a drainage material such as grit. The *loam* provides the body of the compost, containing the nutritional elements and the mass for the roots to get a grip and give the plant stability (most indoor gardeners have experienced at some time the impossibility of keeping a house plant upright in dried out soilless compost). The texture of garden soils can vary from stiff clay to almost pure sand. The kind of loam that the alpine gardener requires lies somewhere between the two. It is preferably a soil that has been worked for many years and now incorporates organic material and free drainage.

The classic way of acquiring good loam is to make a stack of inverted turfs and leaving it until it is well rotted. If you are taking up a lawn, or know of anybody that is, then it is well worth putting the turfs on one side. Not everyone has access to either good loam or to turfs and they must rely on buying loam. Increasingly there are places where this can be bought either by the lorry load or bagful. In many cases this is sterilized before delivery which is a great bonus. The alternative is to buy in a John Innes potting compost and modify it, as will be described later (p. 69).

The main role of the *humus* in the compost is to act as a water reservoir. It prevents the compost from drying out too quickly and holds the water in a form that is readily assimilated by the roots. If leafmould is used then it will also contain valuable nutrients and minerals. As we have seen, the acidity of peat can vary from area to area and some leafmould can likewise be more acidic than others. For environmental reasons the use of peat is now frowned upon and it is likely to become difficult and expensive to buy. There are many alternatives being offered including compounds based on coconut fibre. I know of nobody who has yet experimented with these regarding their effect on alpines.

Leafmould is generally available to many growers who are prepared to gather their own leaves and to stack them for a year or so to rot.

One or two old-fashioned nurseries used to offer leaf-soil (a combination of rotted leaves and woodland soil) but I am not certain whether any still do; it might be worth asking. Any temptation to pop down to the nearest wood and strip it of its leafmould should be resisted as leaves form a vital part of a tree's life-cycle and removal could soon impoverish the soil to their detriment. There are generally plenty of leaves available that would normally go to waste; many local authorities and public parks, for example, either dump or burn many tons each year and could provide a ready source to the keen gardener. Some leaves are more reluctant to rot than others (sweet chestnut, for example) while others can be decidedly acid (pine needles). While acidic leaves should be avoided for most composts they can be useful in special ones made for acid-loving plants.

One advantage that peat has over leafmould is that it is generally sterile. Leafmould can contain all manner of things from insects and worms to fungi and diseases. It is sensible, therefore, to sterilize it. Although this can be carried out with chemicals it is best undertaken with heat by the amateur. The leafmould should be passed through a 6 mm ($\frac{1}{4}$ in) sieve to make certain that there are no large pieces of leaf present. It should then be sterilized as described on p. 69. As long as no chemical fertilizers have been added then the compost can be sterilized as a whole after it has been mixed.

The importance of *grit* to a compost is that it keeps the mixture open and free-draining. The more grit the sharper the drainage. The maximum size of this grit should be 4 mm ($\frac{1}{8}$ in) and it should be crushed so that it has angular faces as this helps with the drainage. Washed grit is the best to buy, but it is likely to need washing again to make certain that it is not importing any impurities. If it comes from the sea it could contain salt; if it comes from old river beds then it could well contain mud and all manner of things. Flint is the best buy as this is usually chemically inert and should not affect the pH of the compost. It can be purchased from some garden centres but it is cheaper to buy in large sacks from agricultural merchants as chicken grit (there is a small size called chick grit and a larger called turkey grit).

Some flint grits include small pieces of limestone and an eye should be kept out for this. Alternatives that might be available include grits manufactured from granite and quartzite. Purchasing in sacks does not guarantee that there are no impurities and it is advisable to wash them before use.

Some growers prefer to use *sharp sand* instead of grit. This is not the soft builder's sand that is used for most cements, but a coarse variety with small pieces of sharp grit. One of its main uses is in the cement that is used for levelling internal floors and hence its other name: screeding sand.

Many of the old books recommended crushed bricks as the drainage agent. Modern bricks are harder and less easy to crush to grit size. Use old bricks by all means, but be careful that they do not have a covering of old mortar on one or more sides as this contains lime and could drastically alter the alkalinity of the compost.

Moving from the traditional methods to the modern we come to the use of *mineral aggregates* with which many gardeners have been experimenting. These, such as perlite and vermiculite, perform the function of both the grit and the peat by holding a certain amount of water and yet ensuring free-drainage to the compost. They are almost weightless and thus reduce both the weight that has to be carried in pots and the weight that is brought to bear on the staging in the alpine house. Controversy rages over their use: some growers swear by them while others reject them equally vehemently. As with clay versus plastic pots, a practice will eventually emerge that is agreeable to most alpine gardeners. In the meantime it is up to the individual to experiment and if he or she finds that the plants are happy then that is the purpose of the exercise. For the beginner it is probably best to get to know conventional loam-based composts, noting how the plants' reactions vary according to the composition.

The final ingredient of compost is *fertilizer* and here again controversy raises its head. Some growers are happy for the loam to provide all the nutrition that the plant needs. Since it is repotted annually (in theory at least) its source of food is replenished each year. If plants begin to look starved then a liquid feed is applied during the growing season. Others prefer to add a slow-release fertilizer to the compost at the outset. The idea is not to grow cabbages so it is generally agreed that any added fertilizer should be a low nitrogen one. If John Innes potting composts are used then they will already contain a balanced fertilizer and the dilution by adding other ingredients will make them adequate for alpine use. For the beginner the recommended course of action is to add some slow-release fertilizer at a third or half of the manufacturers' recommended level. It is essential that in the balance of the chemicals in the fertilizer (the NPK ratio), the nitrogen should be the lowest.

Any fertilizers that are added to a compost should be added after the compost or its individual components have been sterilized. They can become very soluble in water when heated, causing phytotoxic levels in the compost which is dangerous to the plants.

The other chemical that can be added to composts is *ground chalk*. The rule here is not to add it unless it is deemed necessary. Unfortunately it is automatically put into manufactured John Innes potting composts which can cause problems for some lime-haters, ericaceous plants for example. However, as it is only used as the loam constituent and other materials are added, the lime content becomes negligible for most plants.

Compost preparation

The first thing is to sterilize the components. Not all alpine growers agree with this process as they feel it takes something from the soil, in particular beneficial micro-organisms. Others not only sterilize the compost but also all pots and tools as well.

Peat and washed grit should generally be clean and it is the loam that needs the attention as it is likely to contain small insects and worms as well as weed and possibly various diseases and rots. Either the loam can be sterilized separately or, if it is more convenient or there is doubt about the sterility of the other components, in combination. Do not heat sterilized composts that already contain fertilizers.

The loam or compost should be damp as it is the steam that is given off that does the actual sterilization. Moisture will also start any seed or spore into active growth, greatly improving the chances of their demise. Put it in a covered container (or on a tray, covering the compost with aluminium foil) and place it in an oven at 82–100°C (180–212°F) for 30 minutes. A meat thermometer can be inserted to indicate when temperature has been reached and the 30 minutes begin.

The most widely available loam-based potting composts are those named after the John Innes Institute. These contain:

7 parts (by volume) of sterilized loam
3 parts of peat
2 parts grit or sharp sand

Added to each 36 l (8 gallons or 1 bushel) is:

21 g ($\frac{3}{4}$ oz) ground chalk
110 g (4 oz) John Innes base fertilizer (2 parts (by weight) of hoof and horn meal, 2 parts of superphosphate of lime and 1 part of sulphate of potash).

This makes up what is known as John Innes Potting Compost No.1. No. 2 and No. 3 have amounts of fertilizer doubled and trebled, while the ground chalk remains the same.

For most general gardening purposes this is the compost that is commonly used, either purchased or made up at home. From the alpine gardening point of view it is generally considered a starting point only. The mixture depends on its use but many growers will add 1 part (by volume) of JI No.1 to 1 part of grit. If sharper drainage is required then the ratio should be 1 of compost to 2 or even 3 parts grit. For a compost for woodland plants then 1 part of JI No.1 should be added to 1 part of leafmould (or peat) and 1 part of grit. JI No.1 is usually strong enough for most alpine plants but for larger and more vigorous plants it might be felt that the stronger No.2 or 3 should be used.

Starting from scratch the basic formula can be 1 part (by volume) of loam, 1 part leafmould (or peat) and 2 parts of grit, to which can be added a low nitrogen base fertilizer at a third of the manufacturer's recommended level.

As well as loam-based composts there are of course the soilless composts. Most alpine gardeners reject these out of hand as being unworkable, but many well-known growers use them very successfully. The problem here is that they are peat-based and with the recent campaign against the use of peat, they could become increasingly difficult to find and more expensive as manufacturers change over to all manner of alternatives. None of these alternatives, as far as I know, has yet been tried with alpines.

Soilless composts are easy to make if peat can still be acquired (and if the grower does not object to using it). Sphagnum moss peats are best and to these drainage material in the form of sharp sand or grit is added until the compost is open and free-draining. Peat contains little or no nutritional value of its own so a low nitrogen, slow-release fertilizer should be added to the compost.

The biggest problem with soilless composts is watering. It can be very easy to overwater this kind of compost unless it is well supplied with sharp sand or grit. Ready-made peat-based composts may need additional drainage material added to them as they are often too retentive for use with alpines. On the other hand, if the compost dries out it is the very devil to rewet, any water applied to the pot usually pouring straight down the sides and out through the drainage hole without stopping to look at the contents of the pot. Make certain that the compost is always at least just moist.

Planting

As is constantly emphasized throughout this book, drainage is the keynote to growing alpines. Any pots, whether plastic or clay, should have adequate drainage holes in the bottom through which water can drain. Unfortunately not only can water pass out, but so can compost, and worms can make the reverse journey. The traditional way of preventing compost from trickling out is to 'crock' the bottom with a piece of broken pot. This covers the hole sufficiently to prevent the compost escaping, while leaving enough space for the water to pass through. If worms are likely to be a problem (more likely in a cold frame than in an alpine house), then a circle of zinc mesh used to be placed in the bottom of the pot. Nowadays a piece of plastic netting is a good alternative.

Traditionally, and still practised by many growers, the next step was to put a layer of grit in the bottom of the pot before filling it with compost. However, modern theories that are based on experiments, advocate that this layer of grit be abolished, the argument being that if the compost in the pot is in contact with the plunge or the material on which it is standing (both likely to be sand (see p. 84)), then better drainage will be afforded because of the capillary attraction that takes place.

On this basis, many growers have given up using the grit layer. They have also given up crocking the bottom as this also breaks the contact with the plunge material. Netting on the other hand still allows the compost to meet the sand, allowing moisture to flow out of the pot when it is in excess and to draw it in when it is deficient. Unfortunately, netting has the disadvantage that roots penetrate it and it is difficult to remove without damaging them when the plant is repotted. Plastic pots generally have more, but smaller, holes than clay pots and the netting can be dispensed with as the compost is less likely to fall out (on the other hand it may still be needed if worms are deemed to be a nuisance).

So ignoring all that has been said so far, most alpine growers now usually put their composts directly into the pots, relying on its ingredients to provide all the drainage they need.

The size of pot should not be too big for the plant that is going into it. It must be remembered when talking about drainage, that the plant itself removes a great deal of moisture from the soil. Any compost that is beyond the reach of the roots is likely to contain stagnant water which will turn the soil sour and possibly rot the plant. Plants with tap roots will need deeper pots than those with normal roots.

Part-fill the pot with compost and then holding the plant between index finger and thumb (resting the little finger on the rim of the pot for support) in the centre of the pot, trickle compost in around the roots (Fig. 10.1). Tap the pot on the bench a few times to settle the compost and *lightly* press it down. Fill it up to the lower edge of the top band of the pot.

On top of this place a layer of grit to a depth of about 1.25 cm ($\frac{1}{2}$ in). This grit will help in several ways. It prevents the soil panning down when watered so that the compost is more evenly watered; it prevents moisture hanging about round the neck of the plant which is one of the most likely places for rot to set in; it keeps the foliage off the damp compost; it helps prevent moss and liverwort growing on the pot, and if they do it makes them easier to remove; it acts as a mulch and reduces loss of water through evaporation; and finally it presents an attractive background against which to view the plant. Plants can also be top-dressed by having small pieces of rock placed under the foliage. This has the same effect as the use of grit and generally sets off the plant well.

Although any compost used for potting up plants should be moist, it will still require watering once the plant has been installed.

Watering

Watering is vital to all plants and achieving the right balance between too much and too little is one of the major arts in all types of gardening and is particularly so when growing alpines. Most plants do not like to be dried out completely. Until recently it was thought that bulbs should be thoroughly dried out each summer and given as strong a baking in the sun as possible. Now it is felt that many of these bulbs seem to benefit from just a modicum of moisture that their questing roots are likely to discover in the wild.

In the main it is when plants are in active growth that they require the most water, thus it is most convenient in an alpine house or frame to arrange plants in groups according to when they are in growth. This makes watering much easier. When the plants are not in growth the compost should be kept just moist, for most plants this is during the winter time. If an excess of water is given at this time of year it will simply hang around in the peat, not being utilized by the plant, and is likely to cause rotting.

Plants in plastic and clay pots will dry out at different rates and will therefore require different watering regimes. Clay is porous and water escapes from its sides, drying the compost much more quickly than that in plastic where evaporation can only take place from the surface of the compost itself. To facilitate watering, it is preferable to keep the two types of pots apart in the alpine house or cold frames.

Fig. 10.1 The plant should be held between finger and thumb in the centre of a pot resting the little finger on the edge of the pot to support it.

Fig. 10.2 If a wet ring shows beneath a pot when it is lifted from a bench, the compost is moist enough.

When to water is very difficult to explain satisfactorily; it is something learnt by practice and experience. Many plants will tell you when they are short of water as they will visually start to flag or the leaves will become limp to the touch. The pots can be lifted and those short of water will be noticeably lighter than those that have an adequate supply. If the pots are standing on a bench there can be seen a circular patch of moisture under each one that is moist enough when it is lifted (Fig. 10.2). Those that are dry underneath require watering. If clay pots are used they can be tapped and if they are too dry they will give off a ringing note.

All these are indicators which will help the grower, but eventually he or she will be able to tell intuitively when watering is required. The most difficult time is during the winter when so many plants are dormant. As already stated they only require a small amount of moisture at this time; this is not too difficult to maintain, particularly if the pots are in a sand plunge (see p. 84), but a couple of days of moderate sunshine, even at this time of year, can dry out pots under glass without the grower being aware that it has happened, so keep an eye on them even if it is a time when you would not normally be watering.

Actual watering systems will be dealt with when the alpine house is considered (see p. 84) but there are several general principles to be considered here. Many growers prefer to water their plants from below. In other words they stand the pots in water and allow it to percolate up from beneath. Once the surface of the compost or the grit top-dressing changes colour they are removed from the water and allowed to drain. This, they claim, does not compact the compost, precluding air reaching the roots. It also ensures that the whole of the compost is evenly moistened. Normally the pot would be stood in a tray of water that comes partly up the side of the pot. With the odd pot that is in urgent need of water it is also possible to hold it in a water butt or bucket with the water level just above the top-dressing, holding it there until air bubbles stop rising. Another advantage of watering from beneath is that many plants do not like their foliage or rosettes to get wet; the drastic method just mentioned should not of course be used for this type of plant.

Watering from above is simpler and saves having to move plants around. A fine-rosed watering can is the usual method employed for those plants that can be watered *en masse*, for example seedlings in a cold frame, but those in an alpine house, particularly those that require that their foliage be kept dry, usually need individual attention. Water again should be applied by can, either one with a modified spout which only allows a trickle to come out or by placing a finger partially over the spout's opening. This control of the water allows precise watering so that the correct amount of water is directed to the right place.

Some plants are very susceptible to excess water and these can be double-potted. The plant is potted up as normal in a very free-draining compost in a clay pot. This is then placed inside another pot which is filled with sand (Fig. 10.3). Any water that is given to the plant is poured into the sand between the two pots. Enough water is then absorbed through the clay and drainage hole to maintain the plant without giving it cause to rot off.

Overhead watering should only be undertaken in the early morning or evening. During the day a droplet of water on the plant can act as a lens intensifying the sun's rays to the extent that the leaves can become scorched. During hot weather if the base of an alpine house is kept wet and the plunge moist, then the air will remain buoyant and prevent the plants transpiring too heavily, thus using up their moisture.

Additives can be mixed in with water before it is applied. Some growers, for example, use liquid or foliar feeds on a regular basis (see p. 73). Another practice, quite common amongst some leading growers, is to add a systemic pesticide at half-strength at least once a week (see p. 121). Not all additives are welcome as many people find that the water from taps either has too much chalk in it or other additives put there by their water authorities (or even farmers). If this worries you then the answer is to collect rainwater in barrels (hoping that even this does not contain too many pollutants!). The pure water from the snow melt in the high mountains is very difficult to emulate. Doubtless garden centres will one day be offering bulk-packed pure mountain water to customers.

Most plants require at sometime during their year's cycle that their water supply is reduced or even stopped, normally when they

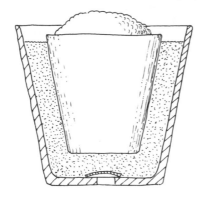

Fig. 10.3 Double potting using sand in the outer pot prevents a plant from getting excessively wet.

are dormant. It is useful to prepare some coloured labels that can be left in pots to indicate those that should not be watered or those that should only have a limited amount. This is a particularly useful device if the grower goes on holiday leaving the plants in somebody else's care. Similarly coloured labels might be used, if an inexperienced plant-minder is in charge, to indicate those plants that under no circumstances should have water splashed on their foliage.

Feeding

Plants that come from the higher mountain areas receive relatively little in the way of nutrients; their diet is quite sparse. Further down the mountain, in the meadow regions, the plants are likely to get a much richer diet. Here rotting detritus is washed down from the mountain; the dying grasses, leaves and other vegetation are recycled into the soil and there are often grazing animals that contribute to the amount of food there is in the soil.

There is a divergence of opinion amongst alpine growers as to the extent that feeding should take place. Many feel that if the plants are repotted each year with fresh compost then this will provide sufficient nutrients. Others prefer to give the plants a low nitrogen, liquid feed at fortnightly or even, in some cases, weekly intervals during the growing season. Fertilizers rich in potash, such as those used in tomato feeds, are the most popular type.

The beginner must learn to strike a balance based on the natural conditions of the plant and its requirements. High mountain cushion plants, such as the *Androsace*, should be given a sparse diet whereas the bigger plants from lower down, such as the *Pulsatilla*, should be given a regular feed. This latter type of plant is herbaceous and must put on a great deal of growth each year in order to survive and therefore is in need of more sustenance than the small perennials higher up. There is no doubt that the use of high potash fertilizers improves the flowering qualities of a plant in the ensuing season. Bulbs in particular enjoy this kind of treatment.

Maintenance

Keeping plants in a restricted space in a limited amount of growing medium means that they require quite a bit of maintenance. In the first instance they will require constant attention as to their water and nutritional requirements as we have already seen. Alpine gardeners cannot afford to go on holiday unless they have somebody they can trust to do the watering or have a foolproof automatic system of some kind (see p. 84).

Keeping plants in pots under cover is also likely to increase the chances of disease and attacks by pests. Part of any alpine grower's routine should be a regular check of all pots to look for any signs of disease or attack (see p. 120). At the same time any dying leaves or petals can be removed.

Green liverwort or mosses can form on pots kept in damp conditions. The use of a grit top-dressing helps prevent this and, should it occur, makes it easier to remove, the whole top-dressing being taken off and a new one put in its place. It is possible to water plants with a proprietary algicide, which will kill off both the moss and liverwort, but the blackened remains still have to be removed which is almost as difficult as removing the problem in the first place. Although it is claimed that most of these herbicides only affect the plants for which they were designed there is no doubt that many alpines are far from happy if they come into contact with them. So use any algicide with caution and preferably remove any moss and liverwort by hand.

As has already been mentioned, any dead leaves, stems, petals, or seed cases should be removed. Any of these are likely to decay and introduce rots into the plant. A regular patrol of the pots using a pair of finely pointed scissors and a pair of tweezers will keep them under control. This kind of attention is far from boring as it means that each plant is carefully examined, giving a chance for the grower to see it at all stages of its growth. With the kind of intimate knowledge that this provides you are then much more likely to spot when things start to go wrong, as well as experiencing the full beauties of the plants.

The biggest maintenance job each year is potting on and repotting. The difference between these two terms is that in the former a plant is taken from its pot and then potted on, with new soil, into a larger pot, and in the latter it is repotted into a same-sized pot.

Once a plant has become pot-bound, i.e. its roots have filled the pot and are beginning to circle round it, it is time to move it into a bigger pot. Roots emerging from the drainage holes at the bottom of the pot are an indication of this. There are some plants, *Cyclamen* being a good example, that seem to thrive on being pot-bound and always flower better under this condition. These should be left until the roots really fill the pot before moving them on.

Never pot on too far, the next size of pot up should be sufficient. Over-potting can result in sour soil as the plant is incapable of utilizing all the moisture present.

Repotting and potting should generally be carried out when the plants are in active growth. This allows them to re-establish themselves quickly. Plants, such as bulbs, which have a positive dormant period should be repotted towards the end of this period, just before they restart growth.

The soil around the plant to be repotted should be just moist but not wringing wet; nor should it be powder dry. Water the day before or earlier in the day to get the consistency right (experience will soon show you when the soil is in the right condition for potting). Take the plant to be repotted and tip it, so that all the top-dressing falls off or can be worked off with the fingers. Next invert the pot, holding it with one hand which supports the compost and the plant which emerges from between two fingers. Give the rim of the pot a sharp downward tap on the edge of a table or bench and the plant and compost will come out safely onto the palm of the hand (Fig. 10.4). Cushion plants are particularly difficult to remove without damaging their shape. Here a piece of

nylon stocking or tights can be stretched over the plant and gently tied round the stem to give it support during the operation.

Gently untangle any roots that have become matted around the edge (some authorities tell you not to touch the roots under any circumstances, but they are useless if they have become matted in a tight cylinder and they must be teased out if the plant is to thrive) and break away some of the loose compost. Opinion differs as to how much compost should be removed. Some, pointing out that it is stale and therefore of little value, advocate that it should all be removed. Others wishing to avoid disturbing all the roots only remove up to a third, taking it from around the edges. Yet others, frightened to touch the plant, remove none. Experience will show you which of the first two methods you are most at home with and which suits the plant best.

Take a clean pot one size up and, with fresh compost, repot the plant. Tapping the pot on the bench will help to settle the compost and help to prevent any air pockets forming. Top-dress with grit or stone and then water the plant preferably from below so that all the compost is evenly soaked. Put the plant in a cool spot, out of the sun and any draught for several days before restoring it to its normal position.

Repotting follows the same procedure except that a clean pot of the same size is used. Not all plants need potting on, some are slow growing and do not need the extra space for a number of years. Others have reached their ultimate size and thus need the same amount of space. Yet others, while still in active growth, have reached the largest practical size of pot. Because there is no additional compost being added it is more essential to remove soil from the plant and replace it with fresh compost.

While repotting, examine the plant to see that it is not suffering from some unseen pests and diseases. Root aphids or vine weevils (see p. 122) may be at work unseen below the surface. It is also the time to consider splitting a plant. Bulbs present an obvious example of this but many of the more herbaceous type of alpines can be divided at this time to make extra plants. Some, especially stoloniferous plants, will require it otherwise they will become too congested and die out.

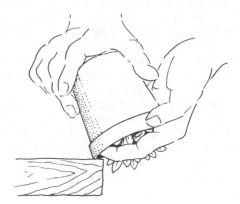

Fig. 10.4 To remove a plant from a pot support it between your fingers and tap the inverted pot smartly on the edge of the bench.

CHAPTER 11

The Alpine House

An alpine house is a specialized form of greenhouse or glasshouse, the main function of which is to protect the plants from inclement weather, usually excessive rain and occasionally excessive cold. Sooner or later most alpine gardeners yearn to own one so that they can extend the range of plants that they can grow. In any list of alpines there are always some which are marked 'for the alpine house' or 'needs alpine-house protection', but in fact it is not essential to have such a building. Many successful growers have managed all their lives with cold frames, which are in fact miniature glasshouses.

The big advantage of an alpine house over cold frames is that plants are normally grown on staging which puts them close to the grower's eye, where he can easily examine and enjoy them. The colourful sight of an alpine house in spring is one of the glories of gardening. The fact that the grower can similarly benefit from the house's protection is also important, as an alpine gardener is bound to spend a lot of time tending his plants during the winter and early spring when the weather is likely to be at its most uncomfortable.

A specially designed alpine house is a sight to behold, a veritable Rolls Royce amongst glasshouses. They can be purchased from specialist firms and if looked after can still hold their own on the second-hand market. Most growers, however, find that the expense of such a house is way above their pockets, desirable as it may be, and they have to settle for a modified greenhouse. The main modification, as we will see later, is to the ventilation, something that modern greenhouse manufacturers seem to neglect woefully.

Siting

The traditional orientation for a glasshouse is on an east–west axis, so that the interior receives maximum light from the winter sun. This is not strictly adhered to today; other factors such as the design of the garden, position of paths and so on taking precedence.

Most gardeners try to ensure that the alpine house is in the open, away from any shade. Not all agree with this and a few position their houses under open trees that produce a light dappled shade (an apple tree for example, but beware of falling apples!). The argument for this is that during the winter when maximum light is required there are no leaves and hence optimum light, but as the sun gets stronger so the leaves emerge and produce automatic shading. This is fine as long as the leaves are not too dense, but does not take into account dull overcast periods when shading ought to be removed from the house. Although positioned in the open for maximum light, an alpine house should be protected at a distance to prevent it being buffeted and chilled by winds.

Aesthetics can play an important part in the glasshouse's position and in a decorative garden it might well be tucked away at the bottom of the garden behind a screen of some sort, but there are practical considerations to remember. Any good alpine gardener will visit the alpine house regularly during the winter in all weathers, so that it should be easily accessible, with good paths and possibly sited close to the main house so that one is not put off from making the journey.

Materials

The choice of materials is between wood or aluminium for the structure and glass or plastic for the cover.

Traditionally alpine houses were only glazed from the staging upwards. The walls were built of brick or concrete blocks on which the wooden framework was built. Nowadays the glazing usually goes right down to the floor and the framework is made of either wood or aluminium (Fig.11.1). Needless to say both have their devotees.

Fig. 11.1 Alpine houses can be in the traditional style, with solid walls to bench height, or glazed to the ground.

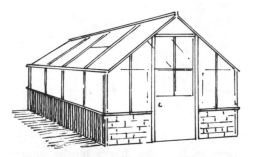
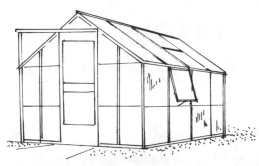

The main advantage of wood is its appearance: it looks a much nicer building than an aluminium one and it fits into the landscape, as far as a greenhouse can, much better than the metal one. In cold weather it is marginally warmer than the aluminium house and, surprisingly perhaps, it is stronger. The gales of recent years damaged many aluminium houses, particularly the cheaper varieties, and left the wooden ones untouched. One reason for this appears to be that the aluminium glazing bars flex in strong winds, allowing the glass to pop out.

The big disadvantage always levelled at the wooden house is that it requires a great deal of maintenance. The few hours a year required to treat the woodwork may well be considered worthwhile for a more attractive house.

Most wooden houses these days are made from cedar, which is relatively long-lasting, especially if cared for. Structures made from cheaper woods are sometimes offered but these are usually a false economy as their lifespan is much more limited (another point to remember is that firms offering these cheaper options rarely provide a back-up range of accessories, such as extra ventilation, which may be required).

The big attraction of aluminium houses is that they are cheap and much easier to maintain. The glazing bars are usually thinner and therefore let in more light.

Glass was, and remains, the main material for glazing alpine houses. Recent years have seen the rise in popularity of the poly tunnel and the conservatory. The former has introduced gardeners to structures with polythene stretched over them, which were originally used in the horticultural trade. They are useful in the garden but not normally for the alpine grower and it certainly is not a substitute for the alpine house. With conservatories has come the increased use of clear plastics as a substitute for glass. They are used mainly where safety is important or where curved sheets are required. There are some greenhouses on the market with this type of glazing, but until proved to the contrary, I doubt their suitability for alpines. It is questionable as to whether the plastic has as long a life as glass and it is certainly softer, making it easy to scratch (when cleaning it or removing a painted-on shading for example) and thus reduces the transmission of light.

Structure

Talk to any alpine house or glasshouse owner and you will usually be told that their house is too small or that they need another one. When selecting a house the most quoted rule is to work out what size you want and then double it. There certainly seems a lot of truth in this as what, at first sight, seems to be a large structure when it is empty, soon becomes filled to bursting with plants. There is no doubt that you should buy the biggest alpine house that you can afford and the site will allow. Having said that many growers do manage quite happily with a small house supplemented by a number of cold frames. The plants are grown in the frames and brought into the house when they are in flower or need attention.

Most of the traditional alpine houses were built with solid walls up to bench level and then glazed above. These walls were made of brick or stone and were wide enough to support one edge of the staging, brick piers being built for the other side. Many of the old houses were actually built into the ground with a central gangway excavated into the soil and the glazing rising straight off low foundations just above ground level (Fig. 11.2). One of the big advantages of this type of structure is that the ground acts as a storage heater and the house is warmer at night, especially if the staging is built directly on the earth, on either side of the path. Since the structure is lower it is not so prone to being chilled by the wind as a conventional house. The obvious problem is that drainage precautions must be taken to ensure that the gangway does not flood.

Nowadays most greenhouses are glazed right to the ground. Some have wooden panels up to bench level and others have aluminium panels that can be purchased as optional extras which can be attached over the glass, again up to bench level. Unless you require the area below the benches to be dark there is little benefit in this.

Some glasshouses are now manufactured with slightly sloping sides, the intention being that the sun will meet it at right angles in the winter, thus allowing in more light. There seems to be no advantage or disadvantage in this to alpine growers.

Where space is restricted or money limited a lean-to alpine house might be considered (Fig. 11.3). This can be attached to any type of building including garages and sheds, but if it is close to a house it may need planning permission. The big disadvantage of such a structure is that it does not get light from all directions and plants can become drawn. One way of limiting this is to paint any solid wall white. However, a solid wall, especially if it is a house wall, does have the advantage that it can provide some warmth to the glasshouse.

It seems sensible to have firm foundations for the house. Most manufacturers offer concrete blocks or bulks of timber for this purpose. These are easy and convenient and enable the gardener to move the structure elsewhere in the garden if he so wishes with the minimum of trouble. It is worth remembering that in England if the gardener is not the owner of the property, then any structure fixed to permanent foundations becomes the property of the owner. Proper concrete foundations do, however, allow for a feeling of security, as many of the concrete block foundations can move causing distortions. Certainly concrete blocks are to be preferred to wooden foundations in windy areas.

Floors
The main criterion for any floor is that it

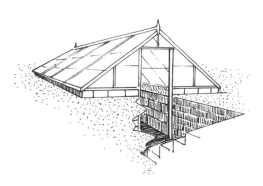

Fig. 11.2 By using a sunken pathway the alpine house can be considerably reduced in height, making it a much warmer structure.

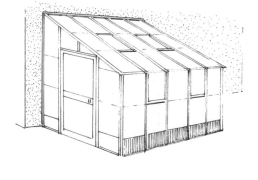

Fig. 11.3 Lean-to alpine houses can be attached to other buildings. They are often warmer but light is reduced.

should be firm and easy to clean. In really hot weather it is useful to be able to flood it with water so that the ensuing evaporation considerably cools down the alpine house. Undoubtedly the simplest floor is a beaten earth one, but it is not particularly hygienic; it is difficult to keep clean and can get very muddy, but it is cheap.

The simplest constructed floor is a raft of concrete covering the whole area so that it also doubles as foundations for the walls and for the piers that support the staging. This can be laid before the alpine house is erected, making all subsequent work easier. The big disadvantage of laying a raft is its inflexibility. For example, some growers have propagating frames built below their staging and these can either be built on the floor, or, in order to obtain more

Fig. 11.4 Make certain there is adequate ventilation both along the ridge and along the sides.

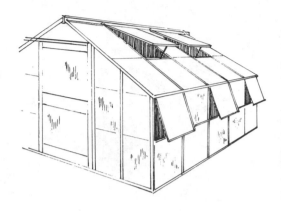

Fig. 11.5 Louvres provide effective ventilation, and their narrow profile is ideal if there is a path beside the alpine house.

When laying the base of the alpine house it is worth laying a path from the house if none already exists. It will be well used in winter and during inclement weather, perhaps in the dark, and a proper path will be much appreciated.

Ventilation

One of the most important aspects to get right in the construction of an alpine house is the ventilation. Short of a gale, the more air that passes through the house the better. This will help prevent damp, stagnant air hanging around the plants which is one of the major causes for the development of rots. Freely circulating air also helps to keep the plants cool in warm weather.

If the house is big enough it is a good idea to have doors at each end to ensure a through-flow of air. If this is not possible then an opening window or louvre should be placed in the end opposite the door. Most glasshouses are short of ventilation, even in the bigger houses. For preference the alpine gardener will require opening lights along both sides of the ridge and along each side level with the staging (Fig. 11.4).

Most glasshouses are manufactured on a unit system so that it is possible to buy extra vents that can be inserted in place of straightforward glass. It will undoubtedly be expensive to have these vents inserted right along the ridge and all along the benches, but a satisfactory compromise is to replace every other pane of glass with vents. These vents can be the conventional ones that are hinged at the top and held open by a bar at the bottom, or on the sides they can be the modern louvre windows (Fig. 11.5). The latter have the advantage that they do not stick out so far when they are open and rain is not so likely to be blown in. However, they do tend to suffer from damage in high winds.

A cheaper alternative is to simply remove some panes of glass during the summer. These must be on a sheltered side so that rain does not blow in and they should be covered with wire or plastic netting to prevent birds and other animals entering. This is only really feasible with aluminium houses in which the glass is easily clipped in or out.

Any vents, not only the ones just mentioned,

light from the side walls, sunk into the ground with the lid level with the floor. Unless provision is made at the time of laying the concrete it is difficult to make such modifications. As an alternative, it is possible to concrete just the central gangway, perhaps making it wide enough to take the central piers of the staging. The rest of the floor can then be covered with gravel on a polythene base.

An alternative to laying concrete is to use it in the form of paving slabs. These have the advantage in that they can be taken up and moved if necessary. A brick floor is another possibility along the same lines.

are likely entry points for animals and netting of some sort should be pinned or permanently fixed over them. The doors are the greatest problem and here it is best to make up a frame the same size as the door and cover this with wire netting. When the main door is open, and in most alpine houses this is for most of the year, the wire-covered one can be inserted in its place. With a bit of ingenuity this can be arranged so that it is hinged on the opposite side of the door frame to the main door so that either one or the other is always closed except when someone is walking through (Fig. 11.6).

There are certain times of the year when the vents may all have to be closed, when it is snowing or in a thick fog, for example. It is still essential that the air should be circulating so an electric fan, permanently installed, can be of great benefit. It is also a great help during still, hot summer days in keeping the air moving, cooling the plants and preventing rots developing which are one of the main curses of stagnant air.

Shading

Next to ventilation, shading is the most important consideration. The hot sun from late spring onwards will be too strong for most of the plants in the alpine house and the temperature within the house will rise, even with a good ventilation system.

There is no doubt that whatever shading system is used it should be on the *outside* of the house. If netting, for example, is put up on the inside of the house it might protect the plants from direct sunlight, but by the time the sun reaches the netting it has already penetrated the house and so the temperature will rise appreciably.

There are basically three types of shading: paint, netting and wooden frames. The paint is a white powder that once mixed with water can be sprayed or brushed onto the glass. It forms an opaque cover through which light passes but the sun is reflected back. The main difficulty is that on cloudy days it has to be wiped off and then the glass resprayed when the sun reappears. There is one particular brand that becomes transparent when it rains, thus allowing in more light, but it maintains its normal opaqueness when the sky is merely overcast. In practice what happens is that most

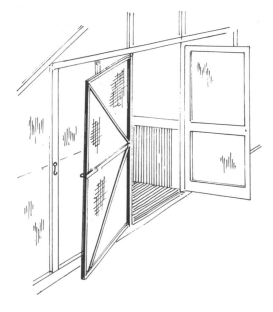

Fig. 11.6 A second door of wire netting will prevent animals getting in while allowing air free access to the house.

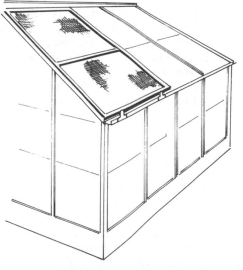

Fig. 11.7 Shading is best provided on the outside of the house. The easiest is frames that can be clipped on.

gardeners put it on at the beginning of the season and leave it there until the autumn unless a prolonged dull spell occurs, when they might temporarily remove it. It is cheap and not too time-consuming to apply and remove.

Netting is not too expensive and is reasonably effective. It can be pinned to the top of the house and rolled down over the glass. During dull spells it can be easily removed. It can also be fastened to rectangular frames that can be clipped to the house (Fig. 11.7). In some ways this is more satisfactory, as, although it

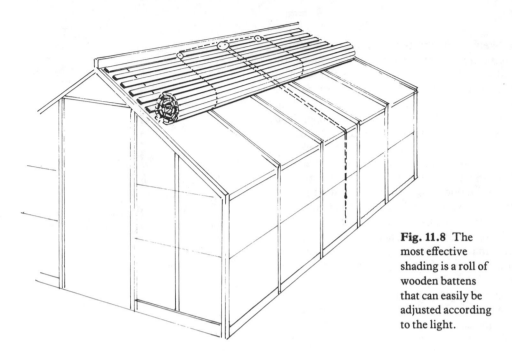

Fig. 11.8 The most effective shading is a roll of wooden battens that can easily be adjusted according to the light.

obviously becomes heavier, it is easier to handle; it is easier to keep the frames on during high winds, for example. When using frames it is also easier to make provision for any opening lights on the glass house.

The use of parallel wooden laths is an old-fashioned method, but still considered the best by many people, giving a wonderful dappled light. In expensive systems the laths are not attached to frames but are kept parallel by a system of webbing or strings which allow the whole shading to be rolled up. The roll is permanently installed on the ridge of the house and unreeled by a system of pulleys when it is needed (Fig. 11.8). A simpler and less expensive method is to fasten the laths to a rectangular frame and attach it to the roof of the glasshouse with clips. Again provision must be made for opening vents. The use of the laths is the most expensive system but in many respects the most satisfactory if the gardener can afford it.

Opening vents should have their own shading. Those that are inconvenient to reach, such as at the ridge, can have a permanent shade fitted to them as long as this does not represent too much of the total glazed area. A piece of netting, for example, can be stretched across the inside of the opening to act as both shading and protection against birds and cats.

Heating

The question of heating in an alpine house is a very delicate one and promotes more argument amongst alpine gardeners than probably any other subject. The main function, most gardeners feel, of an alpine house is to keep the moisture out and should act more like a bus shelter than a conservatory. Indeed most growers never shut up their houses completely, leaving doors and windows open as long as neither rain or snow is blowing in. The plants are considered hardy and can be left to their own devices; if they succumb to cold then they are not alpines anyway and can be dispensed with.

In an average temperate climate winter, losses in an alpine house – even an open alpine house – are few and there is no reason to worry about the cold; however, every so often there is a winter or run of winters when the temperatures are particularly low and remain so for days on end. In an unheated house the pots freeze and the plants' roots are unable to obtain the little moisture they require, with dire consequences. In these rare circumstances, it seems very prudent to put in an electric heater that will maintain the temperature at round about freezing point. There is no need to go higher as there is no intention to promote growth, only to keep the plants frost-free.

A practice that most growers deprecate and that is probably at the root of their antagonism to heat, is the use of heat to push on plants for shows. Plants in a backward season can be brought forward, or plants just coming into flower can be given a boost. Experienced judges can usually spot such practice as the plants are not in character and have a more lush growth.

Because heat it not regularly required in the alpine house it is most conveniently supplied by an electric heater, preferably equipped with a thermostat. Avoid using a paraffin (kerosene) heater as this gives off moisture which can cause problems in a still atmosphere. Some alpine houses contain heated propagating frames and these can be used at times of frosts for one or two pots of the more tender plants.

As an alternative to using heat, plants can be insulated. A popular, and cheap, method of doing this is to drop sheets of newspaper on top of the pots (Fig. 11.9). The sheets are dropped on one another so that air is trapped between them. These should be removed first thing in the morning unless the temperature in the house does not rise above freezing. This is particularly effective in the old-fashioned houses with a sunken pathway and staging that is built directly on the earth. This earth acts as a storage heater and prevents the cold approaching the pots from underneath. Another idea is to make a framework covered with polythene (preferably the type with air bubbles in it) that can be dropped over part or all of the bench. It is essential only to have it in position when serious frosts threaten, otherwise the close atmosphere will be detrimental to the plants. Pots plunged in sand are much less likely to freeze than those standing on an open bench. In a cold area the staging containing the plunge material (see p. 84) can be lined with sheets of polystyrene which will help prevent the pots from freezing solid.

Another possibility is to insulate the house itself, either by the expensive method of double-glazing or by lining the inside of the house with sheets of bubble polythene that can be bought for the purpose at most garden centres. The benefit of insulation is only felt on the few occasions when all vents and doors are closed; any draught that enters will drastically reduce its efficiency. If the alpine house has been hermetically sealed during a cold period to prevent the ingress of cold air then it is vital that the air be kept circulating and a fan must be installed.

Precautions, then, can obviate the need for heat, but if temperatures do dip sharply and there is the likelihood of pots freezing solid then a modicum of heat to keep the plants alive will do no harm. The use of excessive heat will produce plants out of character and probably more susceptible to disease and the cold.

Staging

It is, of course, perfectly possible to grow alpines on the floor of the house (see p. 86) but most people prefer to install some form of benching which not only brings the plants up

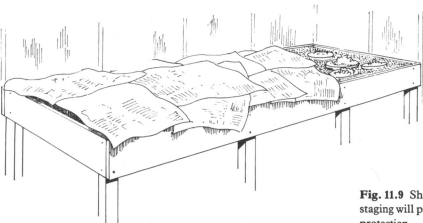

Fig. 11.9 Sheets of newspaper dropped over the staging will provide surprisingly effective frost protection.

Fig. 11.10 Staging filled with wet sand is extremely heavy and the supports should be strong to take account of this.

to a convenient height but also gives space beneath for storing dormant plants. Another advantage of staging is that it can be used to support a sand plunge which helps keep the plants warm and watered.

The most important criteria of any staging is that it should be very strong. The amount that it will have to support, especially if a plunge material is used, is considerable. Ideally the legs that take this weight should be either brick or concrete block piers (Fig. 11.10). These are immensely strong and will give the grower peace of mind in that he should not enter the alpine house one day and find a jumbled heap of pots, plants, and plunge amongst the collapsed staging.

If the whole of the staging is constructed from wood then the legs should be of reasonable dimensions, say 5×7.5 cm (2×3 in), and should be tannalized to prevent them from rotting. Do not rest them directly on the soil otherwise they will sink under the weight; build foundations or place them on paving stones that will spread the load. Normal glasshouse benching does not have to take quite the strain as that in the alpine house and so look carefully at any off-the-peg aluminium staging and make certain that the legs are strong enough. They should preferably be made of angled metal to give them rigidity and should be braced. Again foundations or blocks

of some kind should be provided to prevent them sinking.

The height of the staging is not critical, the most convenient working height being about waist high, i.e. about 76 cm (30 in). The depth should not exceed the distance that you can reach, bearing in mind that you may have to lift a heavy pot from the back. In a large alpine house as well as having staging round the sides it is also likely to have a free-standing section down the middle.

In the more traditional greenhouses the benching consists of wooden slats nailed to a wooden framework (Fig. 11.11). The gaps between the slats allow plenty of air to circulate between the pots, but also allow the pots to dry out rapidly, especially clay ones. In more modern glasshouses the staging usually consists of a framework containing sheets of aluminium that, in effect, makes a table or a shallow tray along one or more sides of the house (Fig. 11.12). This allows pots to be stood on a capillary matting, gravel or sand which is useful in allowing the pots to drain, or, if they become dry, automatically to introduce moisture through the drainage holes. Many growers have at least a small area of this type in their alpine house where they can place short-time occupants, particularly those in plastic pots, which will not gain the benefit of a full-depth plunge.

However, most growers prefer to use benches that have sides to them so that a plunge material, usually sand, can be used (Fig. 11.13). Such staging can be purchased ready made or made by the grower from either aluminium or wood. If wood is used then it should be treated with preservative (*not* creosote) and lined with polythene or aluminium sheets (I have found that old aluminium printer's plates are ideal). Sheets of corrugated iron or plastic can be used to give rigidity to the base of the bed. In the past many growers used sheets of corrugated asbestos but this is now not advised on health grounds. Corrugated iron will eventually rust through, especially if second-hand material has been used, so it should be carefully monitored and replaced at the first sign that it might be unsafe.

Drainage holes should be made at the lowest points. Some growers prefer to have totally waterproof linings to their plunge beds as they like to fill them partially with water to give all the plants a good soak and then remove the bungs in the holes and drain off all the excess.

The sides of the staging should be about 15–20 cm (6–8 in) deep and well supported as they will not only have to carry the weight of the plunge pushing outwards but also, in all probability, the weight of the gardener as he either leans across to attend plants or leans against it while in deep discussion.

There are all kinds of modifications that many inventive growers have made to their staging. One that is relatively commonplace and worth considering is to have a work surface of some kind. This is difficult to build into a cramped alpine house and it is a waste of bench space if part of this is given over to it. However, it is quite possible to build one or more sliding boards that pull out into the gangway from beneath the staging. Alternatively, a hinged table can be made that folds down against the side of the staging or, the simplest of all, a moveable board that can be clipped on to the top of the staging on either side of the gangway at any point along its length (Fig. 11.14).

One of the advantages of staging is that it provides space below that can be used for a variety of purposes. A further layer of staging can be built below it, giving in effect a wide shelf; or the ground itself can be utilized. This

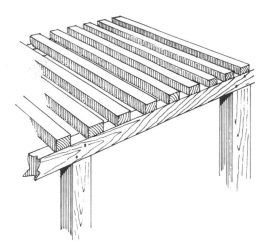

Fig. 11.11 Wooden slats allow air to circulate between the plants but are very cold in winter. Pots can fall over on them.

Fig. 11.12 A low-sided bench allows pots to be stood on sand or capillary matting. The pots are also more stable.

Fig. 11.13 A deeper-sided bench allows the use of sand in which the pots can be plunged to the rim.

Fig. 11.14 A work surface in the form of a drawer, flap or span is very useful when tending to the pots.

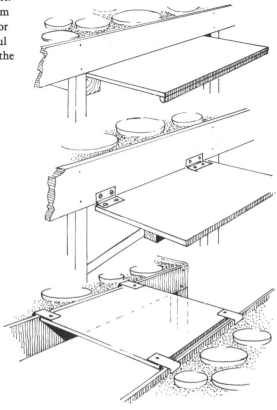

The conventional material for a plunge is sharp sand. Many growers add from one third to a third of peat to this, partly to help preserve moisture and partly to ensure that when a pot is removed for attention, its hole does not cave in, making it difficult to replace. Peat, however, tends to help promote moss and liverworts and as long as the sand is not allowed to dry out, replacing pots in their original holes should not be too much of a problem. Another material that is sometimes used is fire ash.

The pots are plunged into the sand up to the bottom of their neck band. Some of the bigger pots can be plunged in a deeper bed or left with part of the pot exposed.

Watering systems

Alpine-house management depends very much upon the temperament of the gardener and the time available. This is especially apparent in the techniques of watering plants. No two growers water alike and one of the most difficult of alpine tasks is to take over mature plants from another grower and try to keep them alive.

Watering itself has already been covered (see p. 71), most growers using a watering can and giving each plant individual attention. Keeping the plunge around the pots wet helps to prevent pots drying out, and in winter (and also for plants that must be kept on the dry side all year) it provides just enough water to keep the plants 'ticking over'. Hand watering has much to recommend it but there are many gardeners who are unable to give this kind of continuous attention and need some form of automatic watering system.

One method, which is not so much automatic watering as bulk watering, has already been mentioned when describing the staging (see p. 73). More automatic systems rely on water being fed from a container onto capillary matting. Matting is laid on a bench with the edge hanging over into a piece of guttering (Fig. 11.15). The gutter is kept topped up with water either by a drip feed from a container suspended above it or by a tank whose outlet is level with the water in the gutter and whose inlet is controlled by a ball cock. The capillary matting takes up the moisture onto the bench where, in turn, it is

is mainly used for storing plants that are out of growth (see p. 88) but it is also possible to build frames for cuttings that make good use of this space (see p. 109). To give extra depth, the area on either side of the path can be excavated and filled with plunge, but if there is the possibility that this will fill with water from the surrounding area, either it must not be attempted or a drain installed. The advantage of lowering the level on either side of the path is that if plants or cuttings are placed under the benches, then they will be getting more light from the windows and from the central aisle itself.

Plunge

The purpose of the plunge is twofold. It prevents pots drying out too quickly and helps prevent them freezing in winter. It is mainly of benefit to clay pots, which have porous sides, but even plants in plastic pots will appreciate the extra winter protection it affords.

absorbed through the clay and through the drainage hole of the pot. Only short pots can be dealt with in this way as no significant amount of water will travel far up into the compost. At best this is only a holding system, rather than a system that can be regularly employed.

A drip system can be employed to keep the plunge moist, which reduces the necessity to water. A container of water can be strapped to the framework of the house, either inside or out, above the plunge level. It is fitted with a series of tubes letting out regular drips of water at intervals along the surface of the sand (Fig. 11.16). As with the previous system this is a holding operation rather than one that provides enough water for active growth; small pots might receive enough water but the bigger plants in larger pots, especially those that stick out of the plunge, will certainly not.

A sprinkler system can be installed which is worked by a time switch but again there are disadvantages. In the first place only plants that can be watered overhead can utilize it; secondly, all plants receive the same amount of water, and thirdly the plants are watered at a precise time whether they require water or not. This last problem can be overcome by installing moisture sensors, which indicate the need for water, instead of a time switch. The system can be adapted to flood the plunge rather than water from overhead.

Fig. 11.15 Capillary matting, drawing water from a piece of gutter, provides one form of automatic watering.

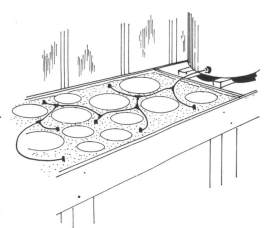

Fig. 11.16 A drip feed can be installed to keep the sand plunge constantly moist.

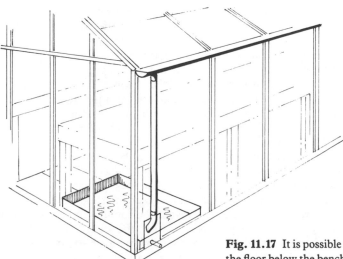

Fig. 11.17 It is possible to build a water tank into the floor below the bench so that water is always at hand.

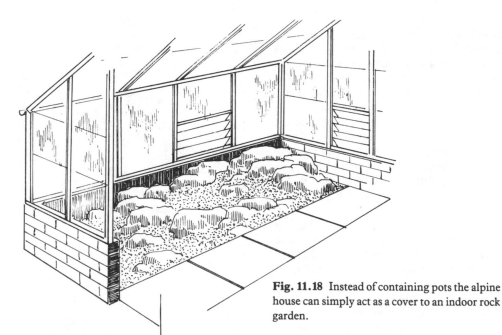

Fig. 11.18 Instead of containing pots the alpine house can simply act as a cover to an indoor rock garden.

The only (usually) reliable system if you are unable to water yourself is to find somebody else who is able to undertake it in your absence. One of the values of joining a local alpine group is that you meet many like-minded gardeners who are often more than willing to help out, especially if the only time that you require automatic watering is when you are on holiday. As suggested earlier, a system of coloured labels or notes should ensure that plants receive the correct amount of water. Whatever system is used, great care must be taken during winter months (see p. 71).

Many gardeners always like to use rainwater on their plants as they are worried about the chemicals added to the mains water supplies. Chlorine especially can be a problem, as can the calcium found in the supplies in hard water areas. Gutters can be attached to the alpine house and other buildings such as garages and sheds to catch as much water as possible which can be stored in barrels. Those with larger alpine houses sometimes bury a water tank below the staging inside the house, leading the gutters into it (Fig. 11.17). This means that good quality water is always readily at hand, which saves a lot of time and, as it is only necessary to dip a watering can into the tank at one's feet, it lessens the chances of putting off the chore of watering.

Raised beds

So far we have been considering alpine houses that are designed for the growing of plants in pots, but not all houses are used in this way. Some growers prefer to grow the plants in the equivalent of raised beds so that they can be free-draining and spread their roots. There are two basic ways of achieving this: firstly to create a small rock garden on the floor of the house and secondly to use the staging as an extended trough.

A rock garden is easy to create and should be constructed along the lines suggested for a full-sized garden in the open. Rocks can be used to set the plants off as well as giving them cool root runs. Tufa is a popular rock as it provides a convivial habitat for many species that appreciate the extra protection that the alpine house affords. The compost can be the same mixture as advocated for the rock garden (see p. 16).

The bed can be a flat one but it has a more attractive appearance if it is built up in the fashion of a rock garden (Fig. 11.18). This means that there must be some form of backing to prevent the compost and rocks coming into contact with the glass. If the bed is wide enough then it is possible to build up rocks into a sloping wall at the back. The depth of compost should be at least 25 cm (10 in) and if a

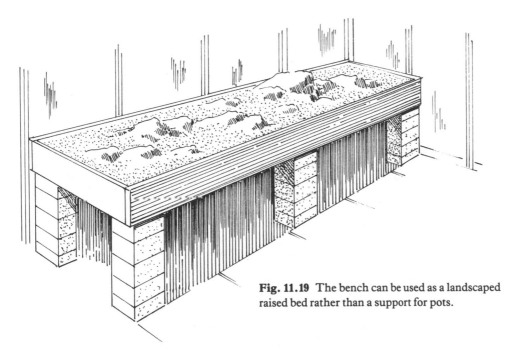

Fig. 11.19 The bench can be used as a landscaped raised bed rather than a support for pots.

drain can be incorporated, part or all of this can be below the level of the floor. This has the advantage of keeping the compost cool in summer and warm in winter. If possible louvres or opening windows should be available at the height of the bed so that fresh air is constantly passing over it. If the bed is too wide to reach all parts from the central gangway, make certain that there are firm stepping stones available; if the gardener loses his balance on such a bed then he may well fall through the glass.

Plants are planted directly into the compost or they can be introduced in pots. The advantage of the latter is that it is possible to bring in plants from the cold frames that are in flower and plunge them in the compost so that the pot is hidden. By doing this there is always something in bloom and of interest in the house. However, do not leave them in position too long otherwise the roots will grow through the bottom of the pot into the compost. If you want them to be on permanent display take them out of the pot and plant as normal.

The second type of bed is on the staging (Fig. 11.19). Here the plunge is replaced with compost and, again, the plants planted directly into it. The sides of the bed should be a minimum of 20 cm (8 in) but some areas can be locally deeper by building it up with rocks and filling the spaces between them with compost. A bed that has been landscaped, even with small pieces of rock, looks much more interesting than those that are flat and just top-dressed with grits.

This type of bed is immensely heavy and should be well supported on solid piers. There should be drainage holes to allow any excess water to drain away.

In essence the attention required to look after such a bed is the same as that in the open garden with just two provisos. The first is that since there is no natural rain, all watering must be done by hand and under no circumstances should it be neglected as these beds, being under glass, will dry out faster than in the open. The other thing is that not only will the plants appreciate the protection of the house, but so also will the pests. A close eye should be kept out for them, aphids and red spider mite in particular.

Running an alpine house

An alpine house needs a great deal of attention; there are very few short cuts. Many growers like to check it at least once a day. This is often in the evening after work so it might be useful to lay electricity on so that lighting can be provided for the winter (as well as the ability to use electric heaters or fans if required).

Routines are basically the same as any other aspect of alpine gardening, namely checking that the plants have adequate water, removing dead leaves, petals, stems and seed cases and looking out for pests and diseases. These are likely to be more rampant in the congenial conditions of the alpine house than in the open garden and must be suppressed at the first sign. An eye must also be kept out for plants that are becoming root bound and in urgent need of potting on or repotting.

Plants have a tendency, as all gardeners know, to grow towards the light. Nearby objects such as houses and trees may reduce the light reaching certain parts of the alpine house and in shaded houses there is often slightly more light coming in from the side than the top. Lean-to glasshouses, having at least one solid side, present a particular problem with unidirectional light. Plants need all round light and can become deformed by growing in one direction. For the majority of plants, particularly if the grower is not taking them to shows, this does not matter but it can cause problems if the intention is to grow perfectly rounded cushions. The problem can be overcome by rotating each pot through 90° every two or three days so that the pots make a complete cycle every ten days or so.

Plants need not stay in the alpine house all the time. Many can be quite happily grown in cold frames and just brought inside when they are in flower so that they can be fully admired. Once the blooms begin to fade, they can again be moved back outside. Not all need to be moved outside. Those that become dormant, and need little in the way of light or moisture during this period (bulbs are a very good example) can be placed below the staging. Here an eye can be kept on them without their taking up valuable bench space. Many plants that do not like the summer heat, on the other hand, will be better off in the open plunge beds, covered with shade netting (many of the primulas fall into this category).

The alpine house must be kept clean at all times. It is very easy to remove some dead leaves or old petals while standing talking to somebody and simply drop them on the floor. These odd fragments of vegetation will rot and act as ideal homes to pests. Removing all rubbish is one of the first requisites in disease prevention. Light is essential to good growth, and except when shading is in position to reduce the effects of the sun, all glass should be kept clean.

If there is not time to undertake all the necessary jobs a list of things to do must be kept. A notepad should be kept permanently in the house. The use of coloured labels can be a great help in marking those plants that need attention of various kind, such as potting on, or giving instructions about various plants, such as not to feed or water, for example.

CHAPTER 12

Cold Frames

Cold frames are a great boon to any alpine gardener. Although they cannot house the gardener himself, they are able to undertake most of the functions of an alpine house. They have the advantage that they are cheaper; they can have the lights removed in summer giving them complete ventilation; they can be completely covered in winter making it easier to keep the plants warm in cold spells; and they are lower structures and therefore do not intrude so much on the landscape.

Their basic function is the same as an alpine house, namely to give protection from inclement weather to plants in pots. They also have a secondary function in that they serve as a storehouse for plants that are out of flower, or resting, that would otherwise be housed in the alpine house. They are also used for housing young plants that are being brought on or plants that have just been propagated (see p. 114).

Structure

There are two basic types of cold frame: those with solid sides and those with glass sides (Fig. 12.1). The former have the advantage that they are much warmer and often much stronger (often able, for example, to take the gardener's weight as he sits on the edge). The latter have the advantage that the glass sides let in light, thus drawing the plants less.

Most of the ones that can be purchased have a framework of aluminium and if the sides are not glass then these are made up from aluminium sheets. You pay for what you get, the cheaper structures usually being more flimsy. The opening glass may not be encased in proper lights but simply slid in and out of the main frame.

Home-made frames are simple to make, can be of any size and can be decidedly more robust. The walls can be made from brick, or thermal or concrete blocks (or, as they are not

Fig. 12.1 Cold frames can have solid, warm walls, or lighter, colder glass ones.

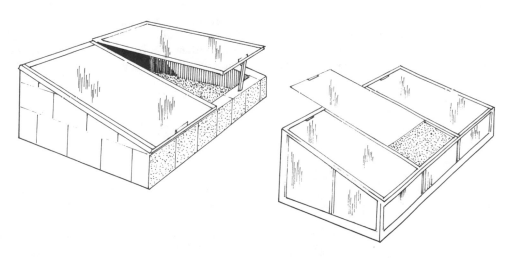

very high, actually cast in concrete). Alternatively they can be made from wooden planks on a wooden frame. Many regard the best of such materials to be railway sleepers as these are easily stood one on another, are extremely strong (you can certainly sit on the edge of these) and very warm in winter. The big disadvantage with sleepers is that they can ooze tar which inevitably gets on the hands and clothes.

Frames can be put anywhere. They should preferably be in sun but some growers have at least some under trees that have had their lower branches cut off so there is ample, dappled light. These frames are particularly useful for plants that require cool or this kind of woodland conditions. Those in the sun should have their lights sloping towards the sun (i.e. south in the northern hemisphere). Wherever they are placed there must be ample space around them. Remember that if the frame has sliding lights then there must be room behind the frame to accommodate these while the contents are being attended to. Another factor often overlooked is that if the lights are to be totally removed during the summer then there must be room to stack them safely.

The site needs to be a level free-draining one. If it is intended to use a plunge material then the base can be excavated to a depth of 15–20 cm (6–8 in) and lined with polythene. This not only provides a rot-free container for the plunge material but it will help keep the plants warm and you will be able to put taller plants into the frame as the pots will be sunk into the plunge.

An earth base, however well levelled to start with, eventually seems to turn into a switch back, with the activity of worms, mice and the roots of nearby trees. A trouble-free base can be achieved by covering the whole site with concrete. This will not only give a firm, even base but exclude worms and the questing roots of trees which seem to be always teasing away at the polythene trying to get at the moisture. It is essential that there is a slight slope on the concrete to allow water to drain away and a hole must be left either in the concrete or in the wall itself to let the water escape. While making a concrete base for the frame it is sensible to extend it a few feet around the actual frame so there is a permanent path from which to work.

A concrete floor will also provide a firm base for the walls but if otherwise, shallow foundations can be built to advantage, although it is not necessary with the lighter structures as long as it is possible to anchor them to the ground so that they will not blow away. The basic shape in profile is a trapezoid one, with the back wall higher than the front and sloping walls between (Fig. 12.2). It should slope so that the lights will shed any rain, and any condensation from the inside of the lights will trickle to the front before dropping off, i.e. it will not drip onto the plants. Another reason is that the lights will be at an angle to the winter sun, allowing maximum light penetration.

The frames should not be too deep but should allow for the height of a pot and the height of the plant, bearing in mind that shorter plants can go in the front and taller ones at the back. Suggested heights are 25 cm (10 in) at the front and 45 cm (18 in) at the back. The distance from front to back should be determined by how far the gardener can reach. All pots should be able to be removed safely from either the back or front of the frame without having to climb into the frame (this is

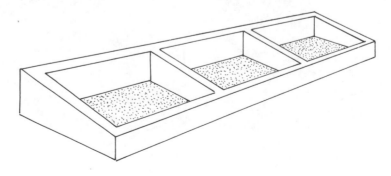

Fig. 12.2 The basic shape should provide for sloping lights so that water and condensation are easily shed.

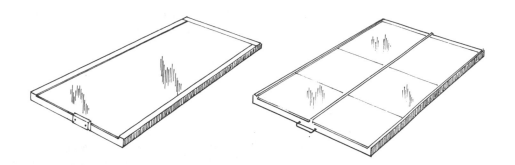

Fig. 12.3 Lights can be made of one large sheet of glass or several smaller ones.

not strictly true as most horticultural frames need to have a stepping stone placed somewhere in them to give the grower access). The maximum width should be about 120 cm (4 ft). The length of the frame is mainly dependent on the amount of space available and the size of the grower's pocket. It should, however, be a multiple of the size of light you propose to use.

The lights are aluminium or wooden frames that support either one large sheet or several small sheets of glass (Fig. 12.3). A single-sheet light has the advantage of letting in more light. A multiple-sheet light usually has a glazing bar down the middle and two or three sheets of glass on either side. The glazing bar does absorb some light but it is more rigid and has the advantage that if there is an accident only one small sheet (if you are lucky) needs replacing instead of an expensive large one. If there is more than one light on each frame then there must be supports between each light. This can be either a piece of wood running from the top to the bottom of the frame or, particularly in larger frames, it can be an intermediate wall.

The lights should either be able to slide backwards and forwards to gain access to the frame or they should be hinged at the back so that they can be tilted on their rear edge and locked in an upright position. The latter is preferable where there is a wall or other rigid support, otherwise strong winds may cause havoc. Winds can also play havoc with lights that are on the frames and it is a very sensible precaution to provide some form of catch that will prevent them being blown off (Fig. 12.4).

If a wooden frame or lights are used then they must be painted or treated with wood preservative (*not* creosote). With all types of

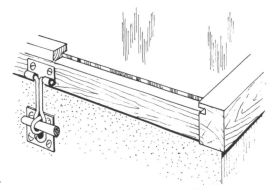

Fig. 12.4 It is essential to provide each light with a catch to prevent the wind blowing it off the frame.

solid-walled frames the insides can be painted white to reflect some of the light in compensation for their opaqueness.

The floor of the frame can be concrete as described earlier or beaten earth covered in black polythene. Either can have one of several coverings. There can be a plunge material, sand for example, to the depth of 15–20 cm (6–8 in) which performs the same function as in the alpine house. Another possibility is to have a shallow layer of sand or gravel on which the pots can stand, allowing them free drainage.

Cold frames in use

The frames should be used in the same manner as an alpine house. They should be regularly checked to make certain that all the plants are receiving enough water and all dead and dying material should be removed.

Fig. 12.5 In summer the frames can be covered with a shading material to protect the young or newly potted plants.

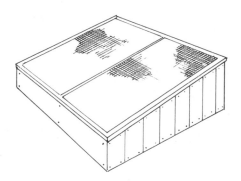

Ventilation is important as shut frames have a very closed atmosphere, which may be useful for short periods (immediately after potting up seedlings, for example), but is generally a bad thing for plants. Except in the most inclement weather the lights should be propped open at least 5 cm (2 in) with blocks of wood. This will allow the air to circulate but prevent rain and snow getting in. During the summer months the lights can be totally removed except when there is a threat of continuous heavy rain. Plants that do not like any moisture on their leaves are likely to be kept in an alpine house but should they be kept in a frame then the lights should be left on to guard against rain (but again they should be propped open about 5 cm (2 in) all round to allow air to circulate freely).

As most frames will be open in the summer, shading is not so critical as it is for the alpine house as there will not be the build-up of heat. However, some plants, especially woodlanders, like a bit of shade and this can easily be provided by making a frame the same size as a light and covering it with shade netting (Fig. 12.5). These can then be placed directly over the open frames. Should there be any need to have the lights on in the summer then the shade frames can be put on top of the lights to protect the plants within.

These shade frames will also help to insulate the frames in winter. On cold nights they can be put on top of the lights as extra protection. Being netting they will not give a great deal of extra insulation, but enough to help keep the average frost out. For better insulation the whole of the frame can be draped in sacking or an old carpet. In very cold areas bales of straw can be stacked beside and on top of the frames to give complete insulation but this is really needed only in extreme conditions.

CHAPTER 13

Plunge Frames

Most alpine growers propagate and acquire far more material than they can use. Most, following the happy tendency that most gardeners are very generous, give plants away to visitors or donate them to local alpine group plant sales. Whatever they ultimately do with them, there always seem to be a lot of pots and little space to put them — either in the alpine house or frames. Another problem that many growers come up against is the number of seed pots awaiting germination. These all need somewhere to be stored, many being around for two or three years before their contents can definitely be discarded as being non-viable. One way of dealing with the inevitable excess of pots is to make some plunge beds out of odd bits of material.

The basic idea is to make a rectangular frame which will contain a standing area for pots. The base of the frames can be concrete if you can afford it, or simply packed earth covered with polythene. In either case to give the plants the warmth of the earth during the winter and to bring them down out of the wind, the inside of the frame can be excavated to a depth of about 15 cm (6 in). The sides can be made from bricks or blocks (old kerb stones make an excellent surround) or from wood, the best of which is railway sleepers. If you have the materials then they can be built as ordinary cold frames with sloping ends, but this is not necessary. If possible it is best to be able to make the walls taller than the tops of the plants that the frame will contain as it then allows temporary lights to be used in winter.

The base of the frame can be left either as concrete or polythene and the plants can be stored directly on this. However, it is better if they are plunged in sharp sand or even ashes. This makes the plants easier to water if they are in clay pots and warmer in winter no matter what pot they are in. Alternatively there can be 2.5 cm (1 in) of sand or gravel on which the plants can stand. This will help with drainage and also maintain a certain amount of moisture around the bottom of the pots in dry weather.

There is no reason why these stock beds should not be housed in ordinary cold frames, there is nothing special about them, but costs usually preclude full-scale frames, hence the less detailed structure. Lights are not usually needed. Any plants that are either on the tender side or prone to the damp are kept in the cold frames, but they can also be provided cheaply with wooden frames covered with clear polythene. These can be put on in times of snow or excess rain. There should be some way of securing them against winds. Two ropes or wires tied over the length of the frame will often suffice.

The frames are treated in the same way as proper cold frames with plants being regularly examined. Because the frames are normally open to the weather it can become all too easy to assume that the plants are receiving sufficient moisture from the natural rainfall. Both the wind and sun can dry them out very quickly so check them for water as frequently as other pots in the alpine house and cold frames. Plants that are to be given away can often be neglected and can quickly become pot-bound. Treat them with the same consideration as you would show plants.

Some plants, such as primula, appreciate a shady cool position. These can be catered for by building the plunge beds in dappled shade. They can also benefit by making the plunge a mixture of sand and peat or just peat itself. If this is kept moist it will surround the plants with an atmosphere they like.

CHAPTER 14

Bulb Frames

Bulbs are the one category of alpines that are given their own special treatment. Many gardeners happily grow them in their alpine houses or cold frames but many others find that they can give them better growing conditions if they construct a bulb frame.

The majority of bulbs, but certainly not all, come into growth during the winter, flower in spring and then die back. During the period of dormancy which lasts from summer into the autumn, the bulbs need to be kept dry and to be baked by the sun. Until recently it was assumed that the drier the better, but now there is a tendency amongst some growers to allow a modicum of moisture as they have found that many bulbs seem to prefer it. Indeed in the wild, although they receive no rain during their dormant period, the depth of bulb and the questing roots means that they are able to find a certain amount of moisture below the parched crust. Many bulbs can be over-baked during hot summers in temperate climes. The reason for this is that although their natural climate is hotter they are usually much deeper in the soil and therefore do not feel its full effects.

Construction

There are several ways of constructing a bulb frame but to all intents and purposes it is a miniature greenhouse, designed to keep the summer rains out and to let in as much sun as possible. In contrast to the greenhouse, however, it is usually opened up for at least part of the winter to allow the rain in.

Bulb frames should be sited in as open a situation as possible with maximum sunlight and no shade. Protection from cold winds would be appreciated as long as the trees or shrubs that provide the protection are not too close.

Essentially a bulb frame is a raised bed (or even a sunken bed) with a frame over the top (Fig. 14.1). Some growers like to have the plants at reasonable working heights (waist high, for example) and therefore build a raised bed (see p. 31) with bricks or concrete blocks, filling the upper 25 cm (10 in) or so with compost. It is also possible to have the bed at ground level, either by building a low wall or excavating a bed out of the ground. In either case the drainage must be extremely good as any stagnant water will be fatal to the bulbs. Do not attempt to create a sunken bed if there is any chance that water may drain into it rather than out of it. If the frame is to rest on the ground, i.e. if it is a sunken bed, then it is not necessary to have foundations but it is to be preferred as this ensures that the frame has a level base. It will also help contain the compost and help prevent the encroachment of weeds and attacks by rodents.

The most commonly seen frames are those that have been bought from commercial firms. These are aluminium frames with glass sides and sloping tops. The glass is removable, either as individual sheets or as lights (i.e. sheets of glass within a frame). These are quite lightweight and should be well anchored to the walls of the raised bed or to the ground.

There is no reason why frames should not be home-made. They can be made in the same

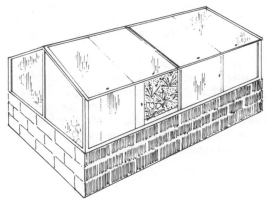

Fig. 14.1 A simple bulb frame is a raised bed with a miniature greenhouse on the top.

fashion as the ones just described, either from aluminium or from wood. If wood is used it should be treated with a preservative (*not* creosote) or painted. It is also possible to make a solid frame more in the manner of a cold frame or plunge bed and cover it with a light. Railway sleepers make excellent solid walls that do not rot when filled with compost. Make certain that the light can be propped open (ventilation is important) without any rain being able to get in. One way to ensure this is to make the lights so that they overhang at both ends.

Any frame that is on the ground or on a low wall should have the base covered with a fine-mesh wire netting to keep out mice and moles (Fig. 14.2). On top of this should be 7.5–10 cm (3–4 in) of drainage material. The next 20–25 cm (8–10 in) should be a mixture of 1 part (by volume) of loam (or John Innes potting compost No.3), 1 part leafmould or peat and 2 parts grit. The whole can be top-dressed with grit or stone chippings after the bulbs are in place.

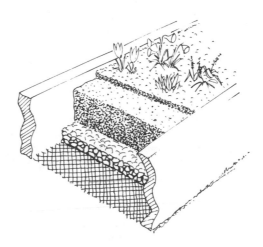

Fig. 14.2 A cross section through a bulb frame showing the fine-mesh wire netting in the base.

Using bulb frames

Although the bulbs can be grown in pots and plunged in sand in the bulb frame (instead of the compost already described), most growers prefer to plant the bulbs directly into the frames. Bulbs, unfortunately, have a tendency to wander and even if they are planted in distinct, well-labelled groups they will inevitably get mixed up with their neighbours, so out of flower, it will be impossible to tell what bulb is what.

There are two ways that can avoid this. The first way is to divide up the whole of the bulb frame into little cells. This can be done with lengths of wood or aluminium laid both across the width and along the length of the frame, separating it up into what really amounts to a series of square or rectangular boxes. The bulbs are planted in these, restricting each box to one species. The bed can also be divided by tiles or slates inserted on the edge into the compost.

An alternative which has gained much popularity in recent years is to use the lattice pots that are normally used for plants in ponds (Fig. 14.3). These pots have holes in the side and bottom so that the roots of the plants can

Fig. 14.3 Bulbs can be planted into lattice pots before plunging into the bulb frame.

wander out into the water and mud of the pond. In the bulb frame they keep all the bulbs together, as they are too big to wander off through the holes, but at the same time give the roots the freedom of the whole bed. Another advantage that many have found is that the pot can be lifted when the bulbs are in flower, slipped inside a conventional pot and displayed in the house or at a show and then replaced in the bulb frame without any apparent discomfort to the bulbs. A minor, but none the less convenient, advantage is that labels can be tied direct to the side of the lattice pot thus making sure that the bulbs do not lose their label, a nightmare that all growers dread, but one that can so easily happen if the labels are simply pushed into the soil.

Most bulbs are planted during their dormant period, which is usually in the summer or early autumn. A hole is excavated in the compost and a pot is inserted so that its rim is just below the surface. An aluminium label bearing the details of the bulbs is wound round one of the bars of the lattice work. If plastic labels are used they should be attached with a piece of thin garden wire. The pot is part filled with the soil mixture, the bulbs placed in position and the compost made up to the surrounding level. The label that was tied to the pot may well be below the surface so it might be necessary to have a conventional one stuck in the ground as well. Once all pots are in place top-dress the bed with either grit or stone chippings. If the bed has been divided up into sections then the same procedure should be followed except, of course, there will be no pots. The lights or glass are kept on the frames until the autumn, when they are opened to allow the rain to get in. If there are no rains then watering will have to be started with a watering can. During the winter they can be left open unless there is excessive rain or unless the temperature drops too low, but this will depend very much on which bulbs you are growing. Many bulbs will tolerate a certain amount of cold, some more than others. Experience (and information from books) will soon tell you what is best both for your area and the bulbs you are growing. Once the bulbs begin to flower they are likely to need protection in order that the petals are not ruined. If the frames are kept closed it is essential that they are not allowed to accidentally dry out. Nor should they be completely closed except at night against the cold. Air should be allowed to circulate freely.

When the bulbs have finished flowering and have set seed, the foliage and stems will die off. Watering should now cease and the frames covered to allow the soil to dry out.

Towards the end of the summer or early autumn the pots can be removed and the bulbs tipped out. If they have increased in numbers they may require dividing, putting some into another pot. The pots are reinserted and filled with fresh compost. Even if the bulbs do not require dividing, it is a good idea to tip them out of their pot to examine them for possible rot or some other disease which may be setting in; there might be time to arrest it. Familiarity with the bulbs themselves, as well as the blooms they produce, will help you to grow them well.

The bulbs are put into fresh compost each year which gives them a certain amount of nourishment, but most growers like to feed at least once a fortnight during the growing season. The preferred feed is a liquid high-potash one, such as a tomato food.

Some alpine gardeners, who grow a lot of bulbs, use small glasshouses as bulb frames, planting the bulbs (in lattice pots) directly into raised beds constructed on the staging. Here the bulbs are enclosed all year and therefore need regular watering while they are in growth; otherwise their culture is the same as those grown in bulb frames. Others grow them in ordinary pots plunged in sand. Not all can afford to devote the whole house to bulbs and other alpines are to be found on the same staging. If they are mixed then care must be taken not to water them accidentally during their dormant period, which does not necessarily coincide with that of the other plants. Feeding and culture should be the same as for bulbs raised in a bulb frame.

Boykinia jamesii
(*Telesonix jamesii*) is
a curious plant
from Colorado that
needs a cool root
run in a crevice, as
here, or in an alpine
house.

Right: There are
many campanulas
for the rock garden.
This is *Campanula
barbata*, which has
delightful, hairy
bells. It is best
grown from seed
every year as it is
usually a biennial.

Far right: Many
campanulas creep
underground
forming clumps or
mats. This is
*Campanula
cochleariifolia*, seen
here in the wild.
There are several
cultivated forms.

Left: *Crocus* is à genus widely grown by alpine gardeners, both in the open and under glass. This is a handsome pot of *Crocus dalmaticus*.

Below: Every rock garden should include at least one daphne. This is *Daphne cneorum* photographed in the wild in the central Pyrenees.

Right: *Dianthus pavonius* is an easy and delightful pink to grow in the open. It is seen here growing in a natural rock garden in the Italian Alps.

Below: The shooting star, *Dodecatheon pulchellum*, is a fascinating plant related to *Cyclamen*. Here it is seen in the Medicine Bow Mountains in Wyoming, USA.

Left: The shrubby *Dryas* is a popular rock garden plant. The more unusual *D. drummondii* is seen here growing in its native habitat in Alberta, Canada.

Eritrichium nanum (right) is one of the most desirable but most difficult alpines to grow. *Douglasia montana* (left) is also a demanding plant, although both do well in the wild.

CHAPTER 15

Shade Houses

Many alpine gardeners love to grow woodland and other shade-loving plants. In the open garden they can easily be grown in shady spots as long as the soil is right (see p. 47), but growing them in pots in frames or alpine houses can be too hot for them. An alternative is to build a shade house especially for this type of plant.

Shade houses can take many forms, but they will all have to be built or specially commissioned by the gardener as they cannot be purchased in the same way as alpine houses or greenhouses.

The basic principal is to provide dappled shade over either plunge beds for pots or raised beds in which the plants can be directly planted. For the most part it is only desirable to keep out the sun, letting in both the rain and frost.

The easiest way of making a shade frame is to find an old greenhouse that has lost its glass (these are not too difficult to find and can often be had for the price of moving them). The frame can be covered in plastic shade netting, reinforcing or padding the places where it passes over sharp corners to prevent chaffing. Only the top and those sides that face the sun need be covered. The rest can be left open to help promote maximum air circulation. Woodland plants are usually protected to a certain extent from strong winds by trees and shrubs, so if the unnetted side faces the prevailing wind it might be necessary to cover it with a wind-break netting.

In colder areas or where there is particularly heavy rainfall an alternative would be to glaze the roof of the house, leaving the sides open, and before covering the whole with netting as before. If the top is glazed and the sides left open it is essential to have guttering installed, otherwise all the water from the roof could blow inside, negating the purpose of the roof.

There is no need to use a conventional pitched greenhouse shape. If it is being built from scratch then a simple flat-topped, wooden framework will do. Shade netting will catch the wind in the manner of a sail, so any structure should be well built and firmly anchored. If it is intended to leave the netting on permanently, i.e. it will not be removed for the winter, then make certain that there are enough cross-members to take the weight of the netting when it is full of snow. These need not be part of the structure itself but galvanized wires stretched tautly across it. The beds for these simple frame houses can best be made with railway sleepers. These make good solid walls which will last for years, not only providing a warm, strong support for the soil but also an edging on which it is possible to walk or sit. Although it is desirable to make the beds so that the centre can be reached from the sides, it is possible to make them bigger and to include stepping stones.

Access can be via a central aisle, as in a conventional alpine house, or from the sides. If the latter is required then a round pole (a broom handle perhaps) can be tacked along the bottom of the netting so that it can be rolled up in the manner of a blind. Alternatively it can be simply looped up.

The raised beds in a shade house can be either low, up to 30 cm (12 in) from the ground or built up to the height of normal staging. If the plants are to be planted directly into the beds then the soil mixture should be the same as that for peat beds.

Attention should also be the same as for peat beds. The bed can be top-dressed with bark if it is felt necessary or desirable. The use of shade netting may cause an uneven spread of the rain pattern on the bed so an eye must be kept out for any area that is too dry; do not assume that because it has rained that all the plants have had sufficient water. To prevent the soil becoming depleted of nutrients it will need an annual treatment with a balanced fertilizer.

CHAPTER 16

Lean-to Protection

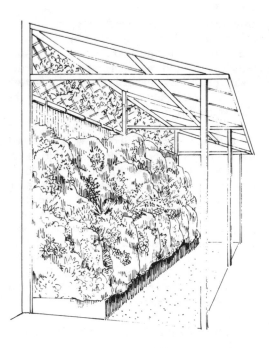

Fig. 16.1 A bus-stop type roof makes ideal protection from the rain while allowing maximum air movement.

In a maritime climate, most of the protection afforded to alpine plants is against rain. This being so, there is no reason why a conventional alpine house cannot be dispensed with and a simple cover in the manner of a car-port or cantilevered bus shelter should not be used instead. Many successful growers have used such protection either instead of or supplementing the conventional forms of alpine house or cold frames. They can be used for growing plants in pots or building beds of one sort or another. One of the most successful known to the authors was over a large tufa cliff (described on p. 45) in which many plants grew in a natural way that would have been impossible to cultivate in the open (Fig. 16.1).

It is possible to build the shelter in the open but it performs best if it is attached to another building, particularly if the latter is on the windward side. Buildings also seem to provide an extra bit of protection from the frosts in winter. The best position is on the sunny side of a building otherwise the plants will all become very drawn. Care should be taken to see that it is not placed alongside a building that will produce the effect of a wind tunnel. This effect is particularly prevalent at the sides of buildings where another house or a garage is nearby, forming a passage.

The design and construction is not too difficult. Basically it is a wooden frame holding either panes of glass or sheets of clear, corrugated plastic that form the sloping roof. The supporting posts can be of wood or metal. There should be a gutter to prevent large amounts of water blowing back under the roof. To help break any wind that may be funnelled through it, one or more sides may be covered with a wooden trellising, but it should be as open as possible to prevent the build up of heat and to provide adequate ventilation.

The use of a lean-to can take any form the gardener requires. Conventional staging can be erected for pots or a raised bed can be built for those plants that disapprove of too much moisture or require that little bit of extra winter protection. It can also provide temporary shelter for plants in pots that are in transit from potting shed to plunge frames, for example, or for assembling pots for a show or sale.

PART III

TECHNIQUES

CHAPTER 17

Potting Sheds

While the alpine house is an ideal place for growing alpines it is not a very good place for carrying out the various operations such as potting and propagation that the grower has to attend to throughout the year. Nor is it a very good place to store all the bits and pieces that go along with this. From the gardener's point of view it can be uncomfortably cold in winter and too hot for the rest of the year to work in. Heat and sunshine are not really the best of conditions for preparing cuttings, nor for exposing plants' roots when potting.

A potting shed is the ideal solution if there is space and money enough to provide one. A counsel of perfection would advocate a brick-built one that remains cool in summer and warm in winter but an ordinary wooden garden shed will suffice. As with the alpine house, potting sheds never seem big enough and the gardener should buy the largest he can afford. Having said that, many make do with small ones in which there is just room to stand.

Since the gardener will spend many hours standing in the potting shed it is sensible to have a proper floor. Another advantage of this is that it is easier to keep clean. It can either be concrete or wooden, the former being stronger and latter being warmer. If it is a large shed then compost can be mixed on the floor, for which concrete may be the better surface. A concrete floor also means that the shed can be well fixed to it as a base. If it is of wood then bearers will be required to keep both the floor and the walls from touching the earth. In either case the shed should be level, stable and able to survive any winds that may attempt to blow it into the neighbour's garden.

The arrangement inside is up to individual taste and working methods. A bench along one side, preferably under a window is one of the main requirements. This should be at about waist height and fixed firmly on stout legs. A thick marine ply as used in some kitchen work-surfaces is an ideal material. This is waterproof and can be used as it is but other materials might need the protection of a layer of formica or lino to prevent the moisture from composts and watered plants from breaking it up. Beneath the bench can be space for bins of various sorts to take the larger quantities of materials, grit, vegetative waste, other waste (packaging material, for example), spent compost and so on. The walls of the shed can be fitted out with shelves to take pots, fertilizers and all manner of other things. Unless there is a separate tool shed space can also be allocated for hanging tools on the walls. In my shed I have an old kitchen unit on the opposite side to the main bench. This provides a stainless-steel sink in which pots can be stood to draw up water and a draining board on which they can be placed to drain, all within convenient reach of the potting bench.

It is entirely up to the individual as to whether the potting shed contains a tall stool, but a long session in front of the bench can be tiring. If there is a lot of standing it can be advantageous to have an old piece of carpet or matting on the floor. This is not only softer to the feet but also warmer. It should, however, not be fixed as the shed will require regular sweeping to remove all the compost and other materials that inevitably fall on the floor.

Electricity is a boon if it can be laid on, as it means there can be light and heating to enable work to be undertaken in the evenings. Water is likewise convenient, although the tap can be installed outside. Water should also be collected from the roof and stored in one or more barrels in a convenient position.

If space is short and work has to be carried out in the alpine house then a section of the staging should be converted to a work bench with a couple of shelves above it and space beneath it to take containers of compost, grit etc. As there are growing plants nearby, it is particularly important to keep the area clean and to remove all odd pieces of rejected propagating material, such as leaves, as soon as possible.

It is of course quite possible to work outside and many alpine gardeners do but any table or bench should be placed well out of the drying sun and wind, otherwise these will take their toll of the plants and cuttings with which the gardener is dealing.

If there is space outside the shed it is useful to have a concreted area as a temporary resting place for pots and on which to have a large metal tray that can be filled with water for part-immersing pots after they have been dealt with. If a lot of potting is undertaken it is often convenient to build a series of brick bins near at hand. These can be used to store bulk materials like peat, prepared leafmould, grit, used compost and so on. They can be constructed like coal bunkers with a lid to keep off the rain and impurities that might blow in.

Potting sheds and the area around them can become very dirty and untidy and a special effort should be made to keep everything neat and tidy. Old compost and top dressing, in particular, seem to get everywhere and it is not unusual to find oneself walking on several inches of the stuff. Dead pieces of vegetation and old leaves seem to drift into corners both inside and out.

It is essential that these should be cleaned up as they can harbour all manner of pests and diseases; good housekeeping and hygiene is the first line of defence against such problems. A solid floor inside and concrete paths and yards outside makes this much easier.

A potting shed and the space around it may be a luxury but one well worth indulging in if you possibly can.

CHAPTER 18

Tools

Tools to most gardeners are very personal items. We all have our favourites and will often scorn those used by others. To the alpine gardener the most important tool is undoubtedly the *trowel*. Those with a solid welded shaft are much stronger than those made from pressed or folded steel. These are not so easy to find nowadays and usually only come in stainless steel. Avoid those made from aluminium as these blunt very quicky, especially with constant use in gritty composts. A narrow trowel, a fern trowel for example, is useful for digging down deep to get out obstinate, tap-rooted weeds such as dandelions. Some gardeners prefer to weed with a small handfork for which all the above constructional comments also hold true.

A good pair of *secateurs* is very useful, especially if there are shrubs in the rock garden. It pays to buy a good pair as these will last a lifetime. In the open garden most jobs undertaken by an alpine gardener can be done with trowel and secateurs (once, that is, the basic digging and construction are over for which ordinary gardening tools are used), but many gardeners have their own personal tools that they have either devised or adapted from existing tools. I, for example, find that a

triangular-tipped tool that I originally had for turning while making ceramic pots is marvellous for weeding as I can easily get amongst the roots under the crown and pull them out. The point is also useful for teasing open the soil and the bevelled edge for scraping off seedlings.

In the alpine house standard equipment usually includes a pair of long-nosed *scissors* and a pair of *tweezers*. Both should perferably be of stainless steel. These are mainly used in trimming plants and removing dead material, although the tweezers are also good for collecting small seed. A *scalpel* is also sometimes used, especially when preparing cuttings but this will be mentioned, along with some other specialized tools, under propagation (see p. 115).

One piece of home-made equipment that is indispensable is a *carrying tray*. These are useful for carrying pots to and from the potting shed to the alpine house, cold frames, plunge frames or even to the garden for planting. One can be permanently reserved for carrying tools, labels, pencils, string, gloves and so on, about the garden. The simplest way to construct them is to take a stout wooden tomato tray and nail two upright pieces of wood to the centre of the end-sides and then another piece between these to form a handle (Fig. 18.1). These are simple to make from throw-away trays and scraps of wood and it is therefore possible to make a half-a-dozen or more at very little cost (although you only have two hands, it seems that you can never have enough carrying trays). A stronger tray can be made by making the box part out of heavier materials, preferably wood that has been treated with preservative. The dimensions are not critical though for convenience the width and length can be based on a multiple of 9 cm ($3\frac{1}{2}$ in) or 7.6 cm (3 in) pots so that they pack in tight when full. They are easiest to carry if the handle runs down the length of the tray, not across it.

Fig. 18.1 An easily-made carrying tray that will prove indispensable.

CHAPTER 19

Acquisition of Plants

There are various methods of acquiring plants including buying them, being given them, growing them from seed or cuttings and stealing them. The last mentioned is not given as a joke but as a warning that in recent times many alpine gardeners have lost plants, sometimes rare or valuable, that have obviously been taken from the garden or alpine house. One need not dwell on the indefensibility of this practice, particularly as gardeners by their nature are some of the most generous people around; however, it should be stressed that even stealing the odd cutting or seed is equally reprehensible. If you want something badly ask for it and the chances are you will be given a piece or put on a list for some at a later time. (Another prevalent practice that is to be abhorred is stealing labels to save having to write out plant names — these often contain all the details of the plant and are the only record the grower has.)

Choosing plants

Whenever you acquire a plant try and get the best available. The first criteria is to choose one that looks healthy. Avoid any plant that has stunted growth or obvious signs of pests such as aphids. On the other hand do not go for the largest plants as these can be the most difficult to establish; a good, medium-sized plant, or even a small plant as long as it is not weedy, is what is required.

If roots are emerging from the bottom of the pot check that the plant is not too root-bound. Many that have a solid cylinder of roots will be very difficult to establish (Fig. 19.1). Occasionally, particularly with some of the stoloniferous woodland plants, being pot-bound can be to your advantage. I recently bought a pot of a *Tricyrtis* that was so pot-bound that the plastic container was completely distorted. When I knocked it out (or as it was so distorted, when I cut the pot off) I was able to divide the knotted clump up into 40 individual plants each of which grew away

Fig. 19.1 Make certain that you do not buy plants whose roots are pot bound.

when potted up. Experience will tell you what can be purchased in this state, but as a rule of thumb avoid anything that is too root-bound, especially in the field of trees and shrubs.

There are some plants that are best seen in flower before purchased. These are plants that have different colour forms or different flower-shapes, some much better than others. For example, there are quite a number of different *Ranunculus* species that have a range of petal shapes from thin and sparse to wide and generous. Obviously it is the latter you want as these make much more attractive flowers. Plants raised from seed are especially prone to variability so these should be treated with suspicion until you have seen them in flower. There are some nurseries from which you can rely on getting good forms but there are others where it is absolutely essential to see the plants. To start with the beginner will make mistakes but this is all part of learning, and he or she will soon get to know which plants are variable, and which nurseries can be trusted and which to treat with caution.

Some plants have to be taken on trust if purchased during their dormant season. For example, there may or may not be bulbs in a pot which appears to be nothing other than compost once they have died back. Again purchasing in season will obviously prove whether there is anything in the pot, and if in flower, it will prove the quality of the flower and also the accuracy of the naming of the plant.

In alpine group sales, treat with suspicion any plants that have obvious signs of having just been dug up and hurriedly rammed into the pot. Some of these will undoubtedly make good plants, but may have no roots or broken stems and will never recover from their traumatic experience. Some bulbs, *Galanthus* being a good example, are best moved 'in the green', i.e. while they are still in leaf, and it is quite acceptable for these to have been recently dug up, indeed, the more recent the better.

If you are a beginner do not attempt to grow the more difficult or rarer plants; they will more than likely die on you which is a waste of plants and money. Many of the easier-to-grow plants are also some of the most beautiful; rarity does not necessarily equate with beauty. Start with the commoner plants as these will give you plenty of valuable experience in growing and propagating and from which you can progress to the more challenging alpines.

Buying plants

The best source for buying plants is the specialized nursery. They can be purchased from garden centres but the range and the treatment and the quality of the plants usually leave much to be desired.

Plants from most nurseries can be bought either direct or by post. Obviously a personal visit to the nursery enables the gardener to see the plants he or she is about to purchase but, more than this, it allows him to talk to the nurseryman. Nurserymen are very busy people and not too much of their time should be taken up, yet generally they do enjoy talking about plants. They are very experienced growers and a lot can be learnt from a few minutes' chat. They will help the beginner avoid the more difficult plants and provide valuable advice on the more challenging types. Talking about plants is one of the great joys of alpine gardening and many gardeners owe their enthusiasm to formative talks with nurserymen.

Most of the best nurseries also provide a catalogue of their stock. These are always worth acquiring as they not only tell you what is available, but also often give descriptive and cultural details of the plants. Regretfully nurserymen now have to charge for their catalogues but they are still worth the small sum they cost.

With these catalogues to hand it is possible to order plants by post. You obviously do not see the plants before they arrive but most reputable nurseries can be trusted to send out good plants. Another disadvantage (and an increasing one it seems) is that the cost of postage and packaging has to be added to the bill. That aside, post is a good way of acquiring plants from distant nurseries, especially those that specialize or have a reputation for certain plants.

When ordering plants by post it must be assumed that the nursery will not have all that you require, some items are bound to be sold out. It is impossible, therefore, to know how much to make your cheque out for. The method that most nurserymen prefer is for the cheque to be made out for a limited amount, i.e. leave the total blank but write on it 'limited to a total of . . .' giving the limit as the maximum to which the bill will come. The nurseryman will then fill in the exact total. An alternative is to make out a cheque to the maximum amount and give a list of substitute plants that you will be willing to accept in the event of some of your first choice not being available.

Plants are normally only sent out by post during the spring and autumn. These are the busiest periods for the nurserymen when they have to send out all the orders accumulated during the previous months. This means that there may be a delay in dealing with your order. Nurserymen do not normally acknowledge the receipt of an order but if you want them to do so send a stamped addresssed envelope. If you are going away on holiday even for only a few days, when it is possible that the plants may arrive, either inform the nurserymen so that he can delay posting them or arrange for a neighbour to open the parcel. Plants sitting in a package for a fortnight are a sorry sight.

When the plants arrive, unpack them immediately, water them if necessary and stand them in a cool shady place for a few days to acclimatize. Some nurseries still grow their plants in clay pots and knock them out before posting. These plants will require putting straight into a pot even if they are destined eventually for the open garden. Once the plants have recovered they can be transferred to their final position either in the alpine house, frame or open garden. However, do not be in too much of a rush to plant outside; make certain that the plant is big and strong enough. Some growers are deeply suspicious of all other growers, irrespective of whether they are professionals or amateurs, and prefer to wash off all the compost, to remove any pests or diseases, and repot in their own mixture. Certainly once the plants have settled down it is sensible to get them into your own compost so that you are better able to control the amount of watering required.

Some growers feel that they have been cheated if they have to buy a plant from a nursery; they begrudge spending money on plants when they can grow them for free from seed or cuttings. This is a somewhat short-sighted view, however. Buying plants is often the only way to acquire certain species or cultivars and, as already has been stated, the contact between the customer and the nurseryman is an invaluable one. Few nurserymen are in the business to make a fortune, for most it is the love of plants that has drawn them into the trade and they pass on a bit of this with every plant they sell.

If you possibly can, get into the habit of regularly visiting any local nurseries even if you only buy the occasional plant. In that way you will get known and if there are any specialities tucked to one side you will probably be informed. Another aspect of knowing your local nurseryman is that once he trusts your skill and judgement he will often swap or even buy plants from you — a real compliment.

CHAPTER 20

Recording Plants

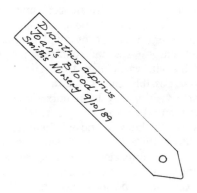

Fig. 20.1 Write information on labels from top to bottom to make it easier to read when in the ground.

Much experience in gardening is dependent on observation but, unless you have a phenomenal memory, observation will need backing up by records. These records are basically of two forms: a label which is kept with the plant and a more detailed record kept in a book, on cards, or on computer.

Labels are vital. The worst nightmare that most alpine gardeners can imagine is to have all their labels removed. These not only include details as to the name of the plant but also its provenance, when acquired and possibly other information. The name of the plant should be given in full including cultivar name if it has one on the front of the label, preferably written from top to bottom (Fig. 20.1). If they are written the other way round only the ends of the words, which tend to be meaningless, may be seen when the label is stuck in the soil, necessitating its removal every time the name of the plant is sought. As soon as a plant is put in a pot, label it, as it is remarkable how quickly it can be forgotten. It is even more important with pans of seeds as there is no way of identifying them until they have germinated and have fully grown, and not even then with some plants. Every gardener must have had the experience at some time of leaving the labelling until later only to find he has forgotten which is which.

If seed has been collected in the wild then it is likely to bear a collector's number. This is usually in the form of the collector's or collectors' initials plus a running number, for example P & W 6386 refers to seed from a particular form of *Lupinus microcarpus* collected by Pearn and Watson in Chile; and plants deriving from this seed would normally be recorded on the label as *Lupinus microcarpus* P & W 6386. It is particularly important to include the collector's number when the species has not been identified as, for example, in *Hypericum* sp. ACW 2760.

Other information that can be carried on the label are various dates such as date of sowing, pricking out, planting out or potting on. Each can be prefixed by a letter to show to which operation they refer. If the plant was not grown from seed by its owner, it is common practice to include on the label the name of the person or nursery from which it was obtained. If the plant requires periods of no water or has special dietary requirements then these can also be recorded on the label.

The best form of label is that made from aluminium. Unfortunately the firm that produced labels for generations of alpine gardeners is no more and the only ones that are now available are very expensive. Printer's aluminium plates, cut into strips, make a good alternative, but for most people the only real alternative is a plastic label. These are brittle and have to be replaced every two years or so. Labels in the open ground are very easily disturbed, both accidentally by the gardener and also more deliberately by birds and other animals. To prevent this they should be tied to a length of galvanized wire which is securely pushed into the ground.

Special pens with waterproof ink can be used for writing on labels, but the lettering is relatively short-lived and an ordinary lead pencil lasts much longer. If you want to go to the trouble, labels can be varnished after inscription and this will make the writing last for quite a number of years. Some growers print the plant's name on embossed tape and stick this to the label. Unfortunately, it does not last very long, soon fading and looking rather tatty. Another disadvantage is that the letters are large and spaced well apart, limiting the amount of information that can be accommodated on the label. A pencil is the answer. It is always easily available to add extra information and it lasts as long as any other method.

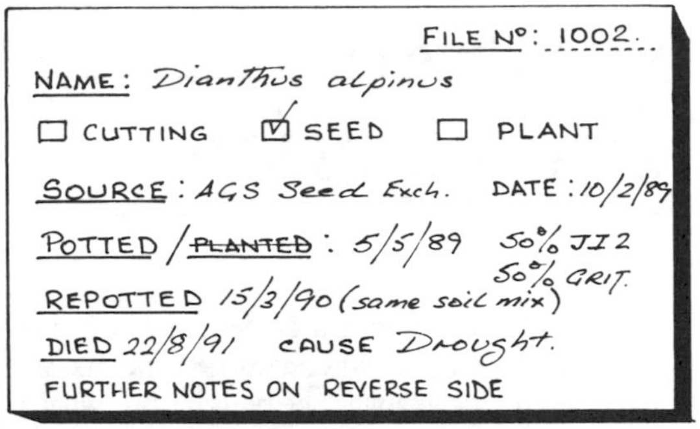

Labels are the only records that many gardeners keep, they find that they will carry all the information they require. Other growers, however, keep much more detailed records of their plants. The two basic records are a *seed record* and a *plant record*. In the first a record is kept of all seed sown: when sown, source of seed, what type of compost, temperature, date of germination, and germination percentage. All these facts come in useful when assessing how well the germination went and whether any factors need to be altered next time that particular seed is sown.

Similar types of information can be kept for particular plants and this would be regularly updated throughout their lives. For example, details might include date of planting, provenance, watering and feeding regimes, date of emergence (if herbaceous), date of flowering, date of dying down, amount of flower, amount of seed set and so on. The last few entries would be added on an annual basis. A lot of effort is required to keep this type of record but the fund of information that it makes available to the grower is enormous. Similar records can be kept for other methods of propagation, such as cuttings.

There are various ways of keeping this type of record. The easiest is on *index cards* (Fig. 20.2). The advantage of these is that they can be kept in alphabetical order of the plants' names. They are also easily transportable and can be carried round the garden while notes are taken. They can just as well be kept in a note book as this is even more portable (Fig. 20.3), but the problem here is that it is generally not possible to keep the records in alphabetical

Fig. 20.2 Index cards are a very versatile way of keeping records and can be taken to the plant.

Fig. 20.3 Note books are one of the easiest methods of recording but, having fixed pages, they are not very flexible.

order although in a book with a thumb index it is at least possible to keep all plants beginning with 'A' together and so on. A compromise is to use a loose-leaf binder with one sheet per plant.

The use of *computers* has become very widespread and many gardeners now keep their records on them. However, unless you have a portable machine all the information has to be written in a notebook and then taken inside and transcribed into the computer. Another disadvantage is that the gardener often pops indoors to look up something quickly while working. With a book or a card it can be quickly looked up, but a computer needs to be switched on and the programme and files loaded before the search can be begun and all this with muddy fingers. In spite of the computer's apparent speed, books and files are much quicker especially if kept in the potting shed.

CHAPTER 21

Propagation

There is no reason why a gardener should ever learn to propagate; whenever new plants are required they can always be bought, but what a lot the grower would miss. Much of the pleasure of gardening is in producing healthy attractive plants from seeds that are no more than specks of dust, or from cuttings that are but mere slips.

There are many practical reasons why a gardener should want to propagate plants. It allows him to acquire plants much more cheaply than buying them and also to have several of a particular plant of which he would only buy one. Propagation is a form of insurance against losing rare plants. As soon as is practicable a rare plant should be increased so that if it should perish there will be others to succeed it. One of the most important methods of plant conservation is to propagate as many as possible and spread them round to friends and other alpine gardeners, the more there are in cultivation the greater the chance that the plant will survive.

Growing plants from seed allows the grower to move to the frontiers of gardening. There are many seed collecting expeditions to different parts of the world that bring back seed of plants that are not in cultivation. By taking shares in such trips the grower has the opportunity of growing plants that he would otherwise not be able to obtain. Another aspect of growing from seed is that there is always the possibility, either accidental or by deliberate breeding, of producing superior or different forms from those already in cultivaiton.

Most gardeners grow far more plants than they require. This is partly a hedge against the possibilty that some might die and partly a desire to build up stocks to give away.

All these, and several more, are reasons why a gardener should learn to propagate. There are those to whom gardening *is* propagation, but to most of us it is just one of the many fascinating facets.

Propagators

It is perfectly possible to increase stock successfully without any propagators but having one or two does make life considerably easier. They are certainly not essential for growing plants from seed, but if cuttings are attempted than they do become a bit more than a luxury.

Essentially a propagator is a miniature greenhouse, with a base that is filled with compost or contains pots or trays of compost. Over this is a transparent glass or plastic cover which helps maintain an even, warm temperature and a moist atmosphere. Temperature can be further enhanced by having electrical heating in the base. They can be bought or home-made.

The ones that can be purchased from garden centres or from advertising in the gardening press vary from a simple plastic base tray with a moulded plastic cover to much larger, elaborate affairs with a metal frame and glass or plastic panes.

The simplest home-made propagator is a plastic bag tied over the top of a pot, but I find these rather messy and unsatisfactory. A more satisfactory, but no more complicated method is to use a plastic sweet jar that has had the top cut off. This can be easily inverted over a 9 cm ($3\frac{1}{2}$ in) pot forming a close atmosphere, particularly if it is standing on a bed of sand so that the cut rim of the jar sinks in forming a perfect seal. It is very easy to lift to examine the cuttings and excess condensation can be removed from the inside of the jar with a flick of the wrist. Being rigid it does not collapse over the cuttings. These types of jars can be had for free from most sweet shops as they generally throw them away after use. The method is akin to the old-fashioned use of glass bell jars. This is sufficient to cover one pot of cuttings but a bigger frame can be made with not much more effort.

The four sides of a box can be made from some lengths of 15×2 cm ($6 \times \frac{3}{4}$ in) wood. This can again be bedded on sand and a lid made from a pane of glass (Fig. 21.1). The dimensions are variable and can be either made to fit the space available or the size of any odd piece of glass that you happen to have. The frame can be made a bit more sophisticated by sloping the sides and enclosing the pane of glass in a frame and hinging it at the back (Fig. 21.2). Bought frames usually have glass or plastic sides; with a bit of ingenuity these can also be produced at home but the evenness of the light in the solid-walled versions can be improved by painting the inside of the frame white.

A further sophistication can be introduced by installing soil-heating cables in the base of the propagator. This speeds up the production of roots by a cutting as well as decreasing the germination time of many seeds. The cables are usually laid on a bed of sand and then covered with a further layer to protect them and to hold the heat (Fig. 21.3.). If desired another set of cables can be installed round the sides of the frame to heat up the air but most growers find it sufficient just to heat the soil which in turn increases the air temperature. To use the heating system efficiently it is advisable to install a thermostat. Heating cables and thermostats are commonly available and usually come with full installation information.

As well as heating, another professional technique that is now being made available to the amateur is the use of *mist units* (Fig. 21.4). These are connected to the water supply and, either at a predetermined time or when an electronic 'leaf' indicates that the atmosphere is drying out, emit a fine spray or mist. This does away with the need to have a top to the propagator, but if used in an alpine house near plants it should have a screen round it to prevent the drift of water droplets. Most growers find that cuttings root better under such a system but, of course, they are of no use for germination of seeds.

Propagators should be placed in a light but not sunny position. If it is not too dark an ideal position is under the bench in an alpine house (Fig. 21.5). If the frame is built into the ground then more light is available from the glass walls of the house (but make certain if the frame is built into a hole that it will not fill with water).

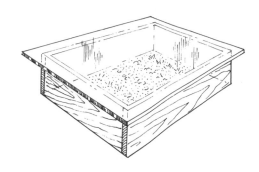

Fig. 21.1 The simplest propagation frame is simply a rectangle of planks covered with a sheet of glass.

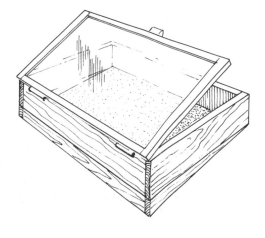

Fig. 21.2 A more effective frame has sloping sides and a hinged lid.

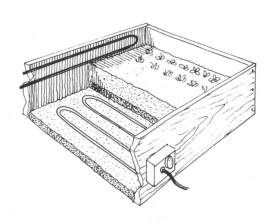

Fig. 21.3 The most efficient frames have heating coils built into the base and sides.

Fig. 21.4 Increasingly mist units are becoming available to amateur growers.

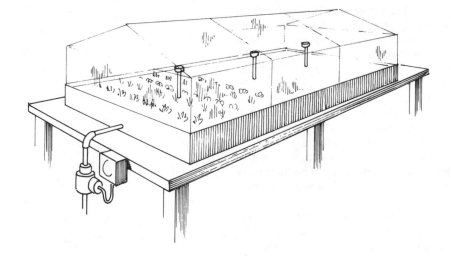

Fig. 21.5 To save space propagating frames can be built under the bench if there is enough light.

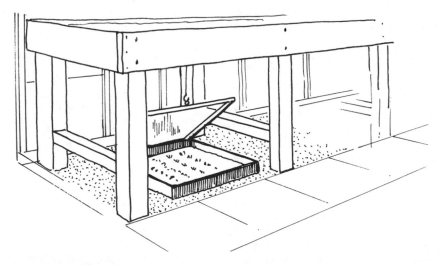

The ground in such a frame will help to hold the heat but, of course, it is much further for the grower to bend. The lid can be hinged from the back and kept open by a catch attached to the staging. It is preferable to have two or more frames so that one can be kept closed while another is partially open to initiate the hardening off process. Mist units have to be placed on a bench and should be sited away from any plants that might suffer from a constant drenching with fine mist.

The frames can have a bed of a mixture of 50% sand and 50% peat into which cuttings can be directly struck or on which pots or trays can stand. Further details are given when cuttings are considered (see p. 115).

Seed

Growing plants from seed is one of the first methods that most gardeners try and it is also one of the most fundamental ways of reproduction in nature. For the majority of plants it is a simple system that always provides at least a few seedlings, but there are some that need all the experience and ingenuity that a grower can muster.

Variability

There are several points that should be borne in mind about the plants that are grown from seed, the main one being that there is no guarantee that the offspring will be identical to the parent. If the seed comes from a species that has very little variation then there is the strong possibility that the new plants will conform but many species produce all kinds of variations, particularly in colour and if you sow seed, for example, of a white cyclamen, the chances are that you will get a mixture of pink and white seedlings as a result. Indeed it is quite possible that there may be no white seedlings at all.

As well as variation caused by the unseen genetic make-up of the plant there can be substantial differences caused by cross-pollination, either with different forms of the same species or even with different species. Most plants are either wind or insect pollinated and in an open garden it is difficult to control how these wander from plant to plant, carrying pollen with them. This form of cross-pollination can produce some interesting results, in some cases new forms or hybrids that are worth keeping and propagating by vegetative means to ensure that the new characteristics continue.

Of course, this variability of plants grown from seed can be turned to the gardener's advantage. By deliberately introducing pollen from one plant to another he can create new forms. If carried out in a controlled way he can transfer certain characteristics, such as a colour, flower size or hardiness and improve on the plants in cultivation. 'Improve', however, is very subjective and while other areas of gardening tend to produce larger and brasher flowers each year, most alpine growers, on the whole, prefer to grow plants as they appear in the wild; seeking out the best of these 'natural' forms.

Sources

Seed can be obtained from a variety of sources. Most commercial seed merchants include a few alpines on their list but they are usually the commoner ones and have often been 'improved' by selection. Many of the alpine nurseries sell seed as well as plants and it is worth asking whether they produce a separate list. Several individuals collect seed from their garden or from the wild and sell it. It is not always easy to find out who they are, as their reputation is usually spread by word of mouth.

The richest source of seed is through seed exchanges that most of the alpine societies run.

Here members collect seed and send it into the exchange. All members than have the opportunity of selecting a set number of packets at a nominal charge to cover the cost of the scheme. The Alpine Garden Society, which runs one of the biggest schemes, currently has about 5500 different varieties on offer.

One very interesting source of seed is obtained by taking shares in seed collecting expeditions to various parts of the world. The going rate is about £50 per share in the U.K. (and approximately $100 per share in the U.S.), and for this you obtain between 30 and 100 packets. Compared with commercial seed this is good value for money particularly when you consider that you are getting seed that is as pure as you are likely to get; in other words, its make-up has not been adulterated by other garden plants, and you may well be getting seed of plants that are not in cultivation. Some of these seed collectors now issue lists and you pay by the packet rather than taking out shares. This is gardening at its frontiers and can be very exciting indeed. These expeditions are usually advertised in the alpine garden journals.

The last source of seed is from your own garden. It is a good idea to propagate many of the plants in the garden so that you have spares to replace an aged or dying plant and also so that you have stock to give away when visitors admire the parent plant. Seed should be collected as soon as it is ripe and stored at first in open containers until it has dried and then in sealed paper bags or envelopes. Do not leave it at any stage in a hot atmosphere or sunlight; a cool position in a potting shed, away from mice is ideal. If they are going to be stored for any length of time the packets should be put in a sealed polythene box in a refrigerator. The seed need only be kept at the normal domestic refrigerator temperature, which is just above freezing; there is no need to freeze it.

When to sow

When to sow can be a difficult decision to make for the beginner, or, indeed for more advanced growers. If you buy your seed from seed merchants or get it from seed exchanges you are limited to a spring sowing as this is when the seed becomes available, which solves the problem for you. On the other hand, if you collect your own seed or have access to it while it is still fresh, there are many species that prefer to be sown as soon as possible after collection. Members of the Ranunculaceae, such as *Ranunculus* itself, *Anemone*, *Pulsatilla*, or *Helleborus*, all germinate very freely and quickly if sown fresh but have a poor and slow germination rate, often spread over two or more years, if sowing is delayed until spring. Another family that includes members that like an early sowing is the Primulaceae of which many *Primula* and *Cyclamen* do well if sown fresh.

Experience and knowledge gained from other growers and books will tell you which need sowing fresh and which can wait until late winter or early spring. Many gardeners when confronted with seed that they have not grown before divide the contents of the packet in two and sow one batch in autumn and the other in spring.

Breaking dormancy

Much of the seed that the general gardener comes across is of annual plants from Mediterranean regions which need little other than warmth and moisture for germination. Seed from alpine plants can be a little more complicated. Much seed needs a chilling to break dormancy. Under normal circumstances much seed would germinate soon after it reaches the ground and the resulting seedlings would then have to survive the harsh winter that immediately follows. To obviate this nature has provided a lot of seed with a built-in inhibitor which prevents it germinating until the spring when chances of survival are greatly increased.

For many alpines this inhibitor needs a period of cold to break it down, the idea being that if the seed has been subjected to the cold for a couple of months and then the temperature rises, this rise must indicate the beginning of spring when it is safe to germinate. If seed is sown in autumn or winter and left in the open then, in an average year, it will be subjected to frosts and sufficient cold periods to break the dormancy. (The problem with temperate climate winters is that they can blow hot and cold and after a cold spell, it can turn mild followed by another cold snap. Any seed that is fooled into germinating during the

mild spell may well need to be brought into the protection of an alpine house or cold frame during any subsequent cold spells.) In a mild winter, or if seed is received too late to have sufficient chilling, it is possible to break dormancy by putting it in a refrigerator for six to eight weeks before putting it out in the open.

There are other forms of inhibitors such as hard coats that delay the seed germination until the seed coat has broken down. The commonest example of this is in the pea family, particularly amongst the *Lathyrus*. Here the traditional way is to soak the seed in warm water for a few hours and any seed that does not swell up should have its hard coat pierced in some way. Putting the seed in a jar with a small quantity of sharp sand and giving it a good shake is a good and safe method. Chipping with a knife or file is only for those with sure fingers and the traditional method of using acid should be avoided unless you really know what you are doing. If *Cyclamen* dry out or you obtain old seed they will benefit from being soaked in water. A drop of washing-up liquid breaks the surface tension around the seed and allows it to imbibe the water more easily.

The many other forms of inhibitors need not detain us here as not many apply to alpines but those interested should consult specialist books on propagation.

Not all seeds need this treatment and, again, experience will soon show which do. There is no need to worry unduly at all this as it belongs to the more sophisticated side of seed growing. Many gardeners have germinated seed quite happily by putting it in pans and leaving it outside until it germinates, even if this does mean a two- or three-year wait.

Composts

As with all forms of composts, most growers have their own preferences for seed compost. One eminent grower uses any old compost that is left over from potting, on the basis that all the seed requires is something to hold a little moisture and something to support its roots and shoot. Other growers prefer to use unsterilized compost, while still others prefer to use compost as freshly sterilized as possible. All the different preferences have theories behind them; many sound very plausible, and most have a success that proves their theories.

The actual make-up, then, of seed compost is not something over which the beginner should lose much sleep. A good mix would be equal parts by volume of loam, peat (or sieved leafmould) and grit. There should be no need for any fertilizers as the loam should contain sufficient nutrients to keep the seeds going for the short time between germination and when they are pricked out. Some of the primulas and ericaceous plants such as rhododendrons seem to prefer a compost that has more peat in it. Special peat-based ericaceous compost can be bought or mixtures made up that either contain double the normal amount of peat and one part sharp sand. Although this compost will remain moister than the usual mix it should still be free-draining.

Sowing

There is no need to sow vast quantities of seed. The general gardener is used to sowing whole trays of seed for bedding plants but when growing alpines such quantities can become an embarrassment, not to say a nuisance. The grower generally only wants one or two plants for himself and perhaps up to half a dozen to give away. For most plants a pinch of seed, thinly sown in a 7.5 cm (3 in) pot will produce more than enough plants. Larger seed can be space sown in a bigger pot, 9 cm (3½ in) for example.

The pot is filled with compost almost to the brim and then tapped smartly on the bench to settle it so that it is about level with the lower edge of the rim. If after tapping the compost still looks a bit loose and fluffy it can be pressed down *lightly* with the fingers or a circular piece of wood. The surface of the compost should be flat and even. Spread the seed evenly on the surface either by placing it on the palm of one hand and gently tapping it with the other, allowing the seed to fall over the edge of the hand, or by sprinkling it from between finger and thumb. It can also be spread by allowing it to trickle gently out of the packet, tapping it lightly to encourage an even rate of fall.

Large seed, such as that of the lily family, can be space sown. Each seed is placed individually on the compost leaving an even space all round it. Small seed can be mixed with a little silver sand to help produce an even spread. A pinch of sand is put into the packet along with the seed and shaken up. The mixture is then sown as with ordinary seed, the sand can be seen and indicates where it and the seed have fallen, allowing a consistent spacing over the whole pot to be achieved.

Once the seed has been sown it can be covered with a fine chick grit, obtainable from agricultural merchants or pet stores. A layer of between 0.6 and 1.25 cm (¼ and ½ in) is sufficient depending on the size of the seed. Very fine seed, such as primula, can be sown after the grit has been applied, scattering it over the surface so that it falls between the small particles of stone. Even seed that needs light for germination can be treated in this way as sufficient light filters down between the individual pieces of grit.

The pots can now be watered. They can be placed in a water bath, the level of which should come about half-way up the pot, until the surface changes colour, indicating that it is now damp throughout. Alternatively it can be watered from above with a fine-rose watering can. For small seed sown by scattering them over the grit, the latter is the best method as it washes it down to the compost.

Label the pots as soon as the seed is sown. If it is delayed it is amazingly easy to forget what is in what pot. If only a few seed have been sown in a pot it is worth putting down the total on the label along with all the other details. The reason for this is that if there are, say, only five seed to a pot, then once five seedlings appear you know you have the lot and will not delay pricking out or putting the pot back expecting more to germinate. As well as labelling pots some growers keep a seed register (see p. 107).

Germination

Pots can now be placed outside in a sheltered, shady spot. It is preferable to cover them with a net to prevent animals and birds supplementing their diet or even just simply knocking the pots over. They should be left open to the frosts but should be covered in times of excess rain. Do not allow them to dry out. If germination takes place in a mild spell during the winter and more cold weather is due, place the pot of seedlings in the alpine house or in a cold frame.

If seed does not germinate in its first spring leave it where it is until the following spring or beyond. Some seed may take up to three or more years to germinate, so do not be in a hurry to discard it. Keep the pots just moist throughout the summer although there will be no germination until the following spring. Some plants, such as lilies, have delayed hypogeal germination which means that they put down normal roots but produce the seed leaves which stay below ground for at least the first year, giving no sign of their presence above the ground. These will, again, require moisture throughout the year.

Most growers find there is no need for extra heat for germinating alpine seed but some find that it helps with some plants. These they place in a propagator with bottom heat. For the most part there is no need to go to this expense but should the beginner want to experiment, he can split his seed between pots outside and pots in a propagator to determine which appreciate the extra warmth.

Pricking out

The first leaves that appear above the surface are the seed leaves. The next pair are the first true leaves and it is with their appearance that the seedlings should be pricked out into individual pots. Do not put them into too large a pot. Most alpines are more than happy with one of 7.5 cm (3 in) diameter; some of the smaller, slow-growing plants will even take a smaller pot.

Gently tip the seed pot, releasing the grit on the top; next invert the pot and tap out its contents, supporting the ball of compost and seedlings with one hand. The compost can now be gently separated removing the seedlings one at a time. If only one or two seedlings have germinated then these can be removed individually from the pot without tipping out the contents. Fill the ensuing holes with fresh compost and replace outside in case more germinate.

Pot up the seedlings into a potting compost to the same depth that they were in the seed pot, allowing enough room to top-dress with grit. Once potted up make certain that they are labelled immediately and then place in a water bath that comes about half way up the pot until the change in surface colour shows that the compost is thoroughly wet. Drain and place in a covered cold frame screened from the sun.

With some bulbs, the pot should be left undisturbed until the second year as the individual seedlings will be too small to prick out. There are some, such as *Erythronium*, which seem to do better if sown thinly in the pot and once germinated left until their second or third year without being disturbed; then the whole potful (or some growers split it in half) is planted out in its final position in the garden. Plants treated in this manner will require a stronger seed compost (the normal potting compost will do) and regular feeding while they are in active growth.

Vegetative propagation

Vegetative methods of propagation consist of removing a part of the plant and creating a new plant from it. The methods include taking cuttings, making divisions, layering and grafting. They are very important as they allow the grower to produce plants that are identical in every way to their parent.

Although all the plants in a species have certain characteristics in common there are often further attributes in which they differ, colour being a frequent one. The species itself may be perpetuated by any means of reproduction, including seed, but the resulting plants although of the same species, will not necessarily have all the characteristics of its parent. With vegetative reproduction the grower is taking a part of the plant and enlarging it into another plant. In doing so he is creating a plant or plants that exhibit exactly the same characteristics as the parent. These identical offspring are known as clones.

Sometimes one plant is particularly distinct within a species (it may, for example, have larger or brighter flowers than the rest) to warrant being given a cultivar name (distinguished by being put in quotes, e.g. *Primula allionii* 'Crowsley'). In order to keep intact all the characteristics that make up this cultivar, it must be increased vegetatively.

Another reason for using vegetative methods of propagation is that not all the plants produce seed in cultivation. There is a wide variety of reasons for this. For example, there may not be any pollinators around, the temperature may be wrong, a plant might be dioecious (i.e. male and female flowers are borne on different plants) and a partner might not be available, or all plants belong to the same clone whereas a different one is required for successful pollination. Whatever the reason there is quite a number of plants that can only be raised by vegetative propagation.

Most vegetative methods of reproduction are quite straightforward, although some plants respond more easily to one method than another.

Cuttings

Taking cuttings consists of removing a shoot or a stem and placing it in a growing medium until it has acquired roots, from which time it can be treated as an ordinary plant.

Cuttings are normally taken when the plant is in active growth. This can vary from spring until late summer; however, the earlier the cuttings are taken the stronger the plant will be by the onset of winter. The majority of cuttings are taken in the summer when the new growth is beginning to harden slightly but, like so many aspects of alpine gardening, each grower has his or her own favourite time for taking cuttings from individual plants and the beginner will soon learn from experience which is the best time. If a plant shows signs that it is about to die then cuttings should be taken immediately, whatever time of year.

The condition of the cutting material to a certain extent determines the time of year that propagation should take place. Some plants root more easily from soft cuttings (i.e. new growth that is still very pliable to the touch), others prefer to be semi-ripe or ripe. Ripe cuttings are where the shoot has hardened and become stiff. It is normal to take cuttings from trees and shrubs in this ripened or hardwood stage in the autumn.

Cuttings should always be taken from non-flowering material; in other words, there should be no flowers or buds on the shoot selected for a cutting. This can be extremely difficult with some floriferous species and it may be necessary to wait until flowering is over. With some mat-forming species, for example *Aubrieta* and some of the *Viola*, the plants can be sheered over after flowering and the new growth that appears provides excellent cutting material.

Fig. 21.6 Trim a cutting just beneath a node with a sharp knife, scalpel or razor blade.

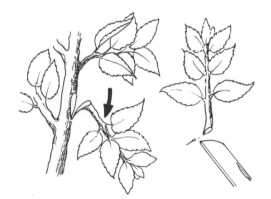

Fig. 21.7 A heeled cutting should be gently stripped from the shoot, taking a piece of the old wood with it, and then neatly trimmed.

Most cuttings will be about 2.5–4 cm (1–1½ in) long but others, particularly of cushion plants, will be much shorter. They should be removed from the plant and used straight away. If there is likely to be any delay or if they need transporting any distance (even from an alpine house to potting shed on a hot day) they should be put into a sealed polythene bag to prevent them flagging. The majority should be trimmed off with a sharp knife or scalpel just below a node (the swelling where a leaf stalk joins the stem) (Fig. 21.6). Those which are taken from a woodier stem should be taken with a 'heel'. That is the shoot should be pulled downwards tearing away a little of the stem with it. This is then neatly trimmed back, leaving a short spur (Fig. 21.7).

115

Fig. 21.8 Remove all the lower leaves with a scalpel leaving no jagged edges.

All leaves that will be below the soil level when the cutting is inserted in the compost should be removed (Fig 21.8), again with a sharp knife, as these will rot, spreading disease to the rest of the cutting. Since the cutting will not have any roots it will not be able to pick up water efficiently and the transpiration of too many leaves above the soil level will cause the cutting great stress, so these should be reduced to just two or three depending on their size.

When cuttings are ready they should be placed in the growing medium straight away or returned to a polythene bag. The tip of the cutting is dipped in a rooting compound and inserted for part of its length into the growing medium. It is then enclosed in a cutting frame or propagator and left until the roots have been formed.

Most growers use a special cutting compost as their growing medium. For the most part a 50–50 mixture (by volume) of sharp or silver sand and peat is used. Some growers use just sand. Traditionally no fertilizer is added to a cutting mix but recent research has shown that the addition of a base fertilizer can be of benefit. The propagator should be regularly checked as the compost should never be allowed to dry out. Those composts with the addition of peat remain moister than those without it. Some growers have successfully been using perlite or vermiculite as alternatives to sand as these have good moisture-retentive qualities.

The majority of cuttings can be housed in propagators as described on p. 108. In the larger propagators they can either be placed directly in the sand in the base or can be placed in pots or trays which are in turn stood on the sand. Small quantities of cuttings can be placed in pots and covered with either a plastic sweet jar or polythene bag. The enclosed atmosphere of the propagator helps reduce the transpiration from the leaves. A gentle bottom heat of around 20°C (68°F) will help to speed up the formation of roots.

However, not all alpine plants like a close atmosphere; silver-leaved plants in particular resent it. These can be placed in a propagator that is covered with a shade net or even pushed directly into the plunge on the staging in the alpine house. In the case of the latter, they should be shielded from direct sunlight by partially covering with a small piece of netting. It is not particularly recommended as regular practice but it is surprising how many plants, silver or not, will root if a piece (perhaps that accidentally breaks off) is pushed into the plunge next to the parent plant.

As an alternative to the closeness of a propagator a moisture-charged atmosphere can be created by the use of mist propagators which are becoming more generally available (see p. 109).

The cuttings are left in the frame until signs of growth are seen. This can usually be seen by the appearance of new leaves or the formation of new shoots. For confirmation it is possible to gently dig up one to see if it has roots; if there are enough cuttings to spare one if it is damaged, gently pull on one to see is there is resistance from the roots. Any cuttings taken in autumn should be left until spring before potting up even if they establish roots. Hardwood cuttings which are usually taken at this time of year are unlikely, anyway, to root until the spring.

Once roots have been established the cuttings must be potted up. First the propagator, if one has been used, must be left open progressively each day so that the cuttings harden off. They can then be removed and potted into individual pots using a potting compost. Do not use over-large pots. These cuttings should be kept in a covered frame until established and again hardened off.

Leaf cuttings

Propagation through leaf cuttings is not widely used in alpine gardening although there are a few plants, such as *Ramonda* and *Sedum*, that can be increased in this way.

An outside leaf is removed in spring from the plant by cutting it as close to the main stem as possible with a sharp knife, and pushed into a compost consisting of equal parts by volume of sharp sand and sieved peat. The leaf is pushed in base first to a depth of about 1.25 cm ($\frac{1}{2}$ in). The pot is placed in a propagator and the compost kept moist. Once growth is seen it can be potted up in the normal way.

Root cuttings

So far the cuttings we have looked at are from parts of the plant that are above ground. It is also possible to take cuttings from the roots of some plants. Although not all gardeners practise this technique anyone who has accidentally left a piece of a dandelion or bindweed in the ground will be aware of it.

There are not a great deal of alpines that can be increased in this way but there are a few such as *Anchusa caespitosa* and *Morisia monanthos* that are suitable for this treatment. They are normally plants that have thick fleshy roots, often tap roots. The plant is dug up and one or more roots removed and cut into sections about 2.5 cm (1 in) in length. Traditionally the top cut is directly across the root and the lower cut is at a 45° angle. This is so that the grower can distinguish at a glance which is the top so that it can be planted the right way up (Fig. 21.9).

Cuttings are normally taken during the period when the plant is not in active growth, which generally means from early to late winter. They are placed vertically, just beneath the surface, in a pot or pan of cutting compost which consists of either sharp sand by itself or an equal mixture by volume of sharp sand and peat. The cut surfaces can be dusted with a fungicide as a precaution against disease. By the end of winter shoots will be seen rising from the root and at this point they can be potted up individually in a potting compost.

Division

Some plants, particularly those that are stoloniferous, lend themselves to division. This is a relatively simple technique that involves digging up the plant, or removing it

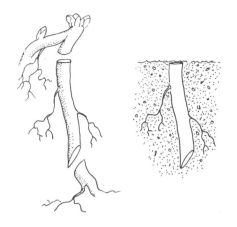

Fig. 21.9 Root cuttings should have a horizontal cut at the top and a sloping one at the bottom to identify their orientation.

from its pot, and dividing it into several portions, each of which has roots.

Division can be undertaken in spring as the plants come back into growth or in the autumn as they die down. Theoretically it is also possible to do it in the summer but the plant is liable to transpire moisture faster than the disturbed roots can pick it up. If divisions are potted up and kept in a close atmosphere then it is possible to do this in summer, but it should be avoided in the open garden unless there is the likelihood of a prolonged dull showery period.

Plants that can be divided fall into several different categories. Some naturally increase themselves and form one large congested clump made up of several individuals. An obvious example of this is bulbs. Once the clump is lifted the individuals can be easily separated, indeed they often fall apart, and potted up. Some plants of a more herbaceous character appear to be an intertwined mass of roots. If these cannot easily be separated, remove all the soil by dipping the plant into a bucket of water, then by jiggling and teasing at the roots with the fingers; the individual plants should separate. *Gentiana sino-ornata* falls apart very easily this way, while *Hepatica* take a bit more effort to separate the crowns.

Some plants appear to have individual crowns but are still firmly attached to each other. Here the connecting portions will have to be severed with a sharp knife or scalpel. Some of the *Iris* and *Primula* would be examples of this type.

The third type of plant is that which has a creeping or stoloniferous rootstock. Here either the whole plant can be lifted and divided or a small portion can be dug up with a trowel without disturbing the main plant. *Campanula cochleariifolia* is a good rock garden example of this, and there are numerous woodland plants which enjoy creeping through the leafy soil.

Sometimes it is possible to break a single shoot from the side of the plant, in the manner of a basal cutting, except in this case it already bears some roots. This is known as an Irishman's cutting and should be potted up until it has established itself.

Fig. 21.10 A branch or shoot can be layered directly into a pot of compost using a stone to hold it in place.

Although division is usually considered as a method of propagation it is also important to remember that many plants will die out, from the centre, through congestion if they are not periodically dug up and divided.

The division can be either replanted directly into the soil or potted up. An eye should be kept on those that are replanted in the open garden as they should not be allowed to dry out. The central portion of the plant, which generally consists of the older, woodier part, should be discarded and only the younger material from the extremities used.

Layering

Although used quite widely in other areas of gardening, layering is not used to any great extent in alpine gardening except for a few shrubby plants. Basically it is a method that is useful for rooting stems of plant that are difficult subjects to root as cuttings. Unlike a cutting the layer is placed in compost while remaining attached to the plant.

A stem of the plant is bent over and secured against the ground or in a pot of compost by a heavy weight, such as a stone, or by a pin of some sort (Fig. 21.10). A stone has the advantage that it conserves moisture around the layer and also keeps it cool. A hole can be scooped out of the ground and this can be filled with a potting or cutting compost. Alternatively a deeper hole can be dug and a pot of compost positioned beneath the layer so that the roots descend into it.

Better rooting is achieved if the layer is partially cut through at the point where it comes into contact with the soil or compost (Fig. 21.11). The soil should be kept moist.

It can take a long time for a layer to send down roots, sometimes years, but eventually they appear either in the ground or in the pot. When they have developed enough for the plant to be self-sufficient, the layer can be separated from the parent plant.

Many growers do not have a regular programme of layering but do it whenever they see a suitable branch or shoot, irrespective of whether they need a new plant of that type or not. This kind of foresight can be very advantageous for plants that take a long time to propagate as it provides a spare plant or two against an unexpected disaster.

Fig. 21.11 Many layers root more easily if they are split first. Here pegs are used to hold it in place.

Grafting

Grafting is another technique that, while common in general gardening, is not frequently used in alpine gardening. It is used on woody subjects that are very difficult to propagate in any other way. The most frequent use in the alpine field is for some of the *Daphne*, in particular *D. petraea* 'Grandiflora'. Basically the technique consists of taking a shoot (the scion) from the plant you want to grow and 'welding' it onto the rootstock of a more common plant that is easier to grow.

There are several types of graft and the grower who wishes to explore this area thoroughly should search out a good book on the subject but one graft, namely the saddle graft or its reverse, the wedge graft, is sufficient for most alpine uses.

A young plant, usually a seedling, of the rootstock is selected — in the case of *Daphne*, *D. mezereum* is usually chosen — and the stem cut through just above ground level, below the lowest leaves. The cut is in the shape of an inverted 'V'. The stem that is to be united with it (the scion) has its base fashioned into a matching inverted 'V' so that when the two are brought together the scion fits snugly into the rootstock. The union is then bound together with either a strip of polythene or a special grafting tape (Fig. 21.12). The wedge graft is similar except that the cut in the stock is a deep 'V' with the scion cut to a similar shape.

The important thing about any graft is that the cambium layer (the layer just beneath the bark) of both the scion and the rootstock should be in contact. This is facilitated by both being the same size, but should the scion be of a smaller diameter then it should be moved to one side so that the two layers come into as much contact as possible.

The grafted plant is put into a closed propagator until the two are firmly united and the plant grows away. At this stage the polythene strip can be removed and the plant hardened off.

Micropropagation

Micropropagation is one of the most recent methods of propagating plants. As yet the technique, which requires laboratory-like conditions, is still mainly undertaken on a commercial scale although one or two amateurs are

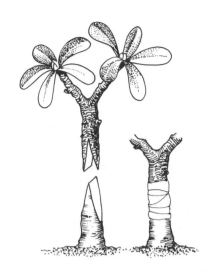

Fig. 21.12 Grafting a daphne using a saddle graft and binding it with a strip of polythene.

beginning to explore the field. A full description is beyond the scope of this book but a brief outline is given so that at least the gardener will have some idea as to what the technique involves.

The basic idea is that a small part of the plant, often as small as a few cells, is taken from the tip of a shoot or a piece of stem and is grown in sterile conditions on a nutrient agar in a test tube until it begins to resemble a recognizable plant or cluster of plants. At this stage the plant is weaned onto a conventional growing medium and, once hardened off, continues life as a normal plant.

The great advantage of this system is that it is possible to propagate plants that are difficult to increase with the usual techniques. Using small quantities of material a lot of plants can be produced from one parent plant, far more than with conventional methods. Another advantage is that it is possible to 'clean up' the plants and remove various virus infections that are transmitted from parent to offspring if normal vegetative methods are used.

The main difficulties of the system are to ensure complete sterility and to balance the nutrient mixture on which the culture grows. These are difficult for the amateur to overcome but already some have ventured into the field and are meeting with success.

CHAPTER 22

Pests and Diseases

Unfortunately the gardener very rarely has it all his own way. Nature seems bent on throwing the occasional obstacle in his path just to let him know that he has not yet reached, and probably never will reach, the point where he is in control. This mainly manifests itself in the form of pests and diseases.

Alpine gardening is certainly no more, and possibly much less, prone than many other areas of gardening. The open rock garden is generally quite free from any serious problems, except possibly from an aphid attack and if the gardener is happy to put up with the odd hole in the leaf, then pests and diseases should not unduly worry him. The alpine house can be another matter. Because the habitat is tailor-made for plants, it is also tailor-made for their predators which can feed, multiply and over-winter in relative luxury. Even here with a bit of care and foresight things can be kept under control.

Some problems such as a mild outbreak of aphids can be ignored as they are unlikely to cause too much damage. However, besides the possibility of the mild outbreak suddenly turning into a full scale epidemic there is the problem that such insects do not just cause damage in their own right but can introduce viral diseases, which are much more serious.

Prevention

Hygiene, especially about the alpine house, is vital in the fight against pests and disease. Dead vegetable matter can provide shelter and food for all manner of pests as well as acting as hosts to diseases. It should be scrupulously removed from the house. Do not pick off dead flowers and simply drop them on the floor. Do not allow leaves that have blown in through the vents or door to accumulate anywhere in the house.

Check all plants that are being introduced to the house, either through purchase or donation, to make certain that they are not carrying pests or diseases. If necessary knock out the plant from its pot and repot it in fresh compost if there is any reason to think that there may be problems below the surface; some growers do this automatically with all new plants, however impeccable their source.

As soon as any signs of trouble appear take preventive action straightaway, do not wait until the situation has got out of hand. This is particularly important if you loathe to use insecticides as, for example, the odd aphid can be removed with the fingers but once they have multiplied it becomes more of a problem.

Pests

Most pests are insects but they can include other animals such as slugs, birds and mice. Most animals are relatively easy to deal with by mechanical methods (such as putting wire over alpine house vents or removing slugs by hand) but insects pose a different problem. The quantities in which they appear, the fact that they are often so small that they can be barely seen, and that they hide in crevices and avoid detection, make them difficult to eradicate except by chemical means.

Not all gardeners are keen on using chemicals but most are happy to do so as long as they are safe and not used too frequently. If chemicals are used it is essential to follow the manufacturer's instructions. An extra quantity of pesticide will not be any more efficacious in eradicating a severe attack than the recommended dosage; indeed, it may harm the plants. It is particularly important to follow the suggested safety precautions. Not all chemicals are safe to be used with alpines and caution must be exercised if there is any uncertainty.

Chemicals can be applied as a spray, as a liquid to be added to the contents of a watering can when watering or as a vapour in the form of a smoke cone. For plants that do not like water in contact with their foliage, use a systemic insecticide that is watered into the pot so that the plant takes it up, and then poisons the insect when it is chewed. The smoke cones need to have the whole house shut tight and any holes sealed. The plants should be dry as the vapour can cause problems for the plants if it comes into contact with moisture on their leaves or stems.

As a preventive measure some growers include a weak solution (half the manufacturer's recommended dosage) of systemic insecticide with one of their waterings each week. To prevent insects becoming immune to the insecticide, they use a different one in rotation. They claim that this keeps their plants insect-free and that the weak solution appears to do no harm to the plants. Others are horrified at the prospect of regularly using insecticides, particularly if there are no signs of pests requiring this treatment. They prefer to keep a keen eye on the situation and deal with the insects as they appear. Apart from straightforward observation there are two methods that can help to indicate what insects are around. The first is achieved by sinking a yellow dish in the plunge so that its rim is level with the surface and filling it with water. Insects will be attracted to it by the colour and once in the water drown. This gives a clear indication of what pests are around as well as killing off a few. The other indicator is in fact sold as a method of control although the small quantities killed make it more valuable as an indicator. It consists of a rectangle of yellow plastic covered with a sticky substance. The action is the same as the old-fashioned flypapers in that once an insect comes into contact with it, it sticks and cannot get away. Being yellow it is slightly more effective than its predecessors. One or two of these positioned around the alpine house will give a fair indication of what is around. If the whole place is festooned with them they will help to keep the pests down but will undoubtedly also ensnare the grower's hair at some point.

If the grower wishes to avoid the use of all chemicals, he or she is reduced to using one of two methods: either mechanical or biological. Mechanical methods basically involve using the fingers or tweezers to physically remove the pests. Alternatively a spray charged with the traditional solution of water and soft soap can be used. This is unlikely to poison the insects but more likely to simply wash them off the plant. Another method involves the sticky papers, as already mentioned.

Biological control has now become quite well developed and has left the realms of science fiction, so much so that this form of control is now available to the home gardener as well as the commercial grower. The basis of this technique is to acquire and release an insect that predates on the one that is causing the trouble. Advertisements appear in various gardening journals offering a range of predators. Once the outbreak is under control the introduced insects die out and another lot have to be purchased if the outbreak reoccurs. It is a relatively cheap method and claims to be effective, especially in confined conditions such as an alpine house.

The commonest of the pests are *greenfly* and *blackfly* or *aphids* (Fig. 22.1). As their names imply they are small fly-like creatures that in fact can be a variety of colours depending on the species involved. These, often in large colonies, chew the young shoots or leaves, reducing them to a sorry sight of contorted and stunted growths. As well as lowering the strength of the plant and possibly even killing

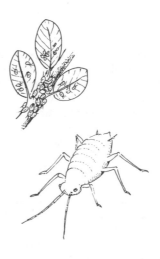

Fig. 22.1 Aphids or greenfly, the commonest of pests.

121

Fig. 22.2(*a*) Capsid bugs,
(*b*) leaf-hoppers,
(*c*) mealy bugs, and
(*d*) whitefly.

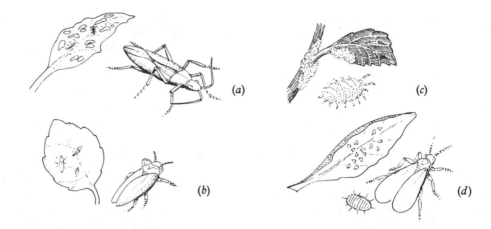

Fig. 22.3 Both the adult and grub weevil are a pest of the first order.

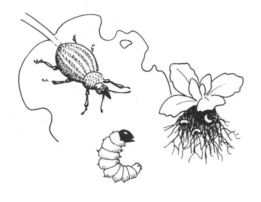

contorted and stunted stems and leaves on plants. These insects include *capsid bugs, leaf-hoppers, mealy bugs* and *whitefly* (Fig. 22.2). The controls are the same as for aphids.

One of the most troublesome of insects in the alpine house, particularly in hot dry summers, is the *red spider mite*. It is a microscopic pest whose handiwork is more readily seen than the insect itself. The first indication of its presence is a dulling of the leaf followed by a fine brown mottling and finally a withering of the leaf. It is not the easiest of pests to get rid of without fumigating the whole of the alpine house; and outside, where they seemed to have increased in recent years, they are almost impossible to deal with. Biological control is now offering some hope as predators have been bred on a commercial scale.

Another scourge which has been increasing in recent times is the *vine weevil* (Fig. 22.3). This is a menace at two stages of its life. As an adult it chews leaves, making an unsightly mess and, as a grub it chews through the roots of the plant. It is particularly partial to plants with a fine root system such as *Primula, Cyclamen* and *Geranium*. Often the first sign of the grub's presence is the plant's total collapse, it just comes away from the soil, and if the infected plants are in the open garden they can simply blow away. Vine weevils are both a nuisance in the pots in an alpine house and in the open garden.

The adults are greyish brown with a long snout. They can be caught by placing a sheet of paper under the plants and shaking it but

it, they can introduce virus diseases from other plants. They also produce a sticky honeydew on which moulds rapidly grow. For these reasons they need dealing with as soon as they are first seen. There are a number of chemicals that can be purchased that will deal with them or they can be patiently removed with tweezers. In the garden the presence of birds, ladybirds and lacewings help to control their numbers. Unfortunately there are some species of this pest, generally known as root aphids, that attack the roots of plants and are more difficult to detect.

There are a number of other sap-sucking insects which produce similar effects of although this might catch a few it does little to ease the problem. Below ground the grub is a creamy coloured horse-shoe of about 0.7 cm (0.3 in) in length. There was a very effective form of chemical control, but the chemical involved has become discredited and is no longer available. Currently there is no effective chemical although several make claims to be a control. Fortunately (or unfortunately perhaps, depending on your point of view) it has become an economic pest, attacking amongst, other things, strawberry crops, so some effort is now being made to control it. It will not be long before a biological control will be available. One method that quite a number of European gardeners seem to advocate for use in the open garden is to let chickens run over the infected areas but this may not be a wise practice amongst alpines. However, if the soil is friable enough it should be riddled through and all grubs removed by hand.

Moving up the scale, *caterpillars* (Fig. 22.4) can defoliate a plant and weaken it considerably. Chemicals can be used but a torch at night and a pair of tweezers is probably the most effective method of control. A search during the day amongst the leaves and down amongst the top dressing may also reveal them.

Slugs and *snails* are more of a pest and have the same tendency to strip plants of their foliage and eat through stems. Slug bait is widely available and there are new types that are not poisonous to other animals. Gravel, grit or ashes are supposed to deter them but in fact they will often wander across a top-dressed raised bed or rock garden to reach some choice plant. One of the most effective and non-chemical methods, is to hunt them at night with a torch. They can be disposed of by putting them into a jar of water containing a little washing-up liquid or, more brutally, by treading on them. Other time-honoured methods include trapping them by leaving up-turned halves of grapefruit, or something similar for them to crawl under after a night's feasting, and removing them the next day. It helps when building a rock garden to ram the earth firmly around and between rocks so that there are no ideal spots in which the slugs or snails can live.

Pets and *wild animals* can be a bit of a nuisance. There are proprietary peppers and

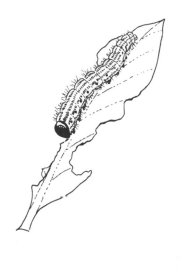

Fig. 22.4 Caterpillars, slugs and snails can all be hand picked from the plants. They are often best seen at night with the aid of a torch.

other chemicals for keeping cats and dogs at bay but their efficacy is debatable. Certain plants, such as *Nepeta* and *Micromeria*, attract cats and should be avoided if they are likely to become a nuisance. Wire netting can be used to keep these and birds away from alpine houses and frames but little can be done about the open garden unless you wish to install barricades around everything. These forms of defence can be erected around the perimeters of the garden to keep out wild pests such as rabbits and deer, which can do a lot of damage if they are allowed entry.

Moles are a constant pest in many gardens, especially those in the country. They can be trapped (with humane, non-killing traps if you so wish) or swiftly dug out of the ground when movement is detected. Smoke bombs and old fashioned ideas, such as putting brambles in their runs or planting caper spurge, unfortunately do not seem to work. One very eminent alpine gardener keeps them at bay by releasing the contents of his shot gun into a mole hill when he sees it moving. Unfortunately what ever successful method you use, more moles are bound to move in to replace the ones you have ousted and eventually the simplest method is to learn to live with the ones you have got and expend your energy more profitably elsewhere.

Disease

As with pests, disease is most likely in the cossetted atmosphere of the alpine house. Much can be done by keeping the place clean and by keeping the air circulating as rots caused by stagnant, moist air are amongst the commonest of diseases.

Diseases can be introduced on newly acquired plants or from insect carriers which arrive from a nearby infected source. Check all plants thoroughly before taking them into the alpine house or planting them in the open garden. If there is any cause for suspicion keep the plant in quarantine, away from other plants, until you are certain that it is clean.

Control of aphids and other pests that are likely to introduce virus diseases will obviously help reduce their incidence. Once this kind of disease has taken hold very little can be done and the best course of action is to burn the infected plants.

Chemicals can be used to control diseases but more and more alpine gardeners are trying to avoid them if possible, partly because of an increasing awareness of the problems associated with chemicals and partly because there are no chemicals that are safe with all plants, alpine plants being more susceptible to chemicals than other garden plants. Although the days are long gone when everything in the garden was drenched at the first sign of trouble, chemicals are still the only way effectively to combat certain complaints. The manufacturer's instructions should be rigidly adhered to and a careful watch should be kept for any adverse effects on the plants.

Fungal diseases or *rots*, particularly *botrytis*, are the commonest of diseases amongst alpine plants. Their incidence can be reduced by preventing the build-up of damp, stagnant conditions, by having maximum ventilation or by the use of fans on still days. The spores often start work on wounded areas of the plant so any broken part of the plant should be cut off cleanly. Similarly any other cut made on the plant should be clean and not ragged. Any damage, such as the result of a bad frost, should be removed as soon as possible. Prevention is all important and as well as the precautions mentioned above many growers, who are prepared to use chemicals, dust or spray all cut surfaces of a plant with a fungicide. Similarly damping off diseases, to which young seedlings are particularly prone, can be avoided by spraying with a fungicide.

Fortunately disease is not too much of a problem for alpine growers if they provide the right growing conditions but occasionally there will be outbreaks of various rots, wilts and rusts. Proprietary brands of chemicals can be used to deal with the situation or the plants can be isolated, perhaps removing the infected parts, and seeing whether they recover.

PART IV

A–Z OF ALPINE PLANTS

CHAPTER 23

Introduction to the A–Z List

The alphabetical list of alpines that follows is not fully comprehensive but still encompasses the great majority of plants grown by alpine gardeners.

Bulbs and dwarf conifers are represented by lists of genera only, for reasons that can be seen under their headings. The largest genera — particularly *Saxifraga* and *Sempervivum*, and to a lesser extent *Sedum*, *Campanula* and *Dianthus* — are restricted to those species that have significance for the appreciation of each genus as a whole. As each of these genera demands (as do the dwarf bulbs and conifers) a whole book to itself for comprehensive treatment, this was our only possible approach.

Comparatively few cultivars are mentioned, again for reasons of space, but also because new ones are added every year, old ones disappear, and it is unfortunately true that a great many should not have been distinguished by separate names in the first place. Gardeners have to use their taste and discretion when buying cultivars, but should never lose sight of the fact that among them are some of the finest of all alpines.

Some of the Latin names will inevitably give rise to disagreement. This is unavoidable, as plant naming is never static, but moves on under the influences of scientific advance and pure nomenclatural research. It is a source of profound frustration for most gardeners that this should be so, and it has to be admitted that botanists could perhaps think twice before committing us to such tongue twisters as *Chamaepericlymenum* when coining a name for a split from *Cornus*.

A prize example of change is the dreadful tangle involving the sections into which the saxifrages are divided. We believe it is necessary to let you know about these, as you will hear the words spoken among alpine gardeners and if you show alpines, they are indispensable. Alpine gardening involves the handling of botanical Latin more than almost any other kind, but it is not difficult once you realize that you have been bandying *Antirrhinum*, *Delphinium* and *Chrysanthemum* about for most of your life. Few words in botanical Latin are more difficult than these which, incidentally, are Greek.

The heights of the plants are given for when they are in flower, unless stated otherwise. Unless specified to the contrary, plants can be taken to be hardy anywhere in the British Isles and in Zones 2–8 in the United States.

CHAPTER 24

List of Alpine Plants

ACAENA (Rosaceae)

Small, mat-forming plants, resembling compact wild strawberries, but with pinnate foliage and flowers of no significance. The species have attractive foliage colour but are grown chiefly for the spiky burrs that appear in late summer and early autumn. They are invasive but ideal for paving or at the sides of paths. They must not be grown in Australia or New Zealand, where their burrs can destroy the value of wool fleeces. Propagate by division in early spring.

A. buchananii. Grey-green foliage. Makes a dense, low mat. Yellow-brown burrs. New Zealand.

A. microphylla. The leaves are silvery grey when young, becoming bronze. Tightly mat-forming. The burrs are vivid scarlet. New Zealand

A. novae-zealandiae. Quite different from other species. It is of much more lax habit and is a vigorous spreader at the top of the height range at 6 cm (2.5 in). The foliage is green and the burrs are metallic, russet-purple. New Zealand.

ACANTHOLIMON (Plumbaginaceae)

Acantholimons are spiny, hedgehog-like plants with flowers that are usually pink and surrounded by papery bracts. There are many species but very few are in cultivation. Only one, *A. glumaceum*, is capable of being grown in the open; the rest are alpine-house plants. The difficulties they present have to do with their coming from very dry, hot places. Although they experience hard winter weather, they cannot tolerate wet. Acantholimons should not be disturbed once they are established, and potting-on should be done

with care. Propagation is by seeds sown in late winter in gentle heat or by cuttings in early summer, which are not easy. Division is not recommended.

A. echinus (syn. *A. androsaceum*). A densely spiny cushion plant with clusters of pale pink flowers held clear of the foliage. The bracts are white with pink veining. For the alpine house. Early summer. Crete.

A. glumaceum. A softer, less spiny plant than most, making a thrift-like cushion with sprays of pink flowers that also betray the close relationship between this genus and *Armeria*. For cultivation in a warm spot in gritty, well-drained soil. 6 cm (2 in). Early summer. Armenia.

A. hohenackeri. A tricky plant for the alpine house with tight, blue-green, spiny cushions. This is a collector's piece that rarely flowers but is occasionally offered for sale. Caucasus.

A. venustum. The cushions are quite loose, but the leaves are very spiny and silvery grey. The clear pink flowers stand well above the foliage and have bracts of the same colour. It can be grown in a favoured, warm, extremely well-drained spot but is much better and safer in the alpine house. 18 cm (7 in). Cilician Taurus.

ACHILLEA (Compositae)

This is a large genus that includes such wild meadow flowers as the common yarrow (a dreadful weed of lawns) and is probably best known for having given rise to some fine border plants. However, the alpine members of the genus range from the fairly coarse to the tiny and choice. They all like sunny spots and seem to do best and stay most in character where the soil is on the poor side. The flowers are borne in broad, flat heads at the tops of the stems. Propagation is by division in early spring or by soft cuttings a month later.

A. ageratifolia. A fine, silver-grey plant with spoon-shaped, deeply toothed leaves in rosettes. The flowers are borne on 15 cm (6 in) stems in mid to late summer. Greece, Yugoslavia.

A. argentea. Whether this is synonymous with *A. clavennae* or whether it is a species of *Tanacetum* is a matter of great and not very interesting debate. Under either name you should be able to obtain a plant with intensely silver foliage, finely divided like filigree, and carrying tight heads of white flowers. 15 cm (6 in). Mid to late summer. Eastern Alps.

A. chrysocoma. This species is considered to include *A. aurea*, whose variety 'Grandiflora' is now to be listed as *A. chrysocoma* 'Grandiflora'. The species has bright yellow flowers and silky, grey-green, highly aromatic foliage; 'Grandiflora' has larger heads of flowers. 20 cm (8 in). Early to mid summer. Yugoslavia.

A. × lewisii 'King Edward'. An extremely long-flowering hybrid of *A. argentea*, whose soft yellow flowers are borne from late spring to early autumn.

A. tomentosa. The most widely grown of the rock garden achilleas. The foliage is soft, downy and silver-green and the flowers are rich gold. There is a cultivar, *A.t.* 'Aurea'. 25 cm (10 in). Late spring to early summer.

ACIPHYLLA (Umbelliferae)
The New Zealand 'Spaniards' are clump-forming plants with stiff, needle-pointed, dagger-like leaves. They are often omitted from lists of alpine plants and, although one would think that this was because of their danger for children, animals, and weeding gardeners, it is usually because they often fail in cultivation. They need to be grown in a paradoxical climate; one in which dry root conditions combine with a cool, moist atmosphere. In practice, very fast drainage will compensate for high rainfall and allow aciphyllas to be grown successfully in Scotland, Ireland,

Washington State and, of course, the South Island of New Zealand. Some are too tall for the rock garden, but others are ideal, given the warning implicit in the above. Propagation is sometimes possible by division in mid spring.

A. dobsonii. Less like a bundle of knives than most, this is a cushion-forming plant with rounded heads of white flowers on short stems. 10 cm (4 in). Summer.

A. monroi. This species is softer than many others, but the leaf tips are still formidable. Foliage in rosettes, each leaf having four to six leaflets. Perhaps the easiest aciphylla. 30 cm (12 in). Summer.

A. spedenii. A compact, spiny, blue-green cushion with white flowers on 20 cm (8 in) stems. For the alpine house.

ADONIS (Ranunculaceae)
A genus of plants that do not fit the narrower definition of alpines but which are often grown in rock gardens, to which they are well suited. Clumps of finely divided leaves play host to large, golden, anemone-like flowers, after first having protectively clasped the buds as the stems break through the soil after the plant's winter rest. A good, loamy soil in sun, but one that does not dry out, is best. Divide after flowering.

A. amurensis. Flowers large, golden, with a variable bronze flush on the outside. Prefers a more leafy soil in part shade. There is a double form, 'Plena'. About 23 cm (9 in). Late winter to early spring. Japan.

A. vernalis. Known as the spring pheasant's eye. An extremely fine plant with many large flowers on 30 cm (12 in) stems. Mid to late spring. European mountains.

AETHIONEMA (Cruciferae)
A genus of small sub-shrubs of neat appearance, with generously borne heads of flowers at the tips of the shoots. They are long lived in sun and a good, gritty soil. For plants that hail from the Mediterranean basin they are unusually hardy and will take severe winter weather. The species are easy to grow from seed, while named forms are easily propagated from soft cuttings taken after flowering.

A. armenum. Blue-grey foliage and pink flowers in clusters. It is mat-forming and only 10 cm (4 in) high. Early to mid summer. Armenia.

A. cordifolium. Similar to above but the flowers are very light pink. Its chief claim to notice is as a parent of 'Warley Rose' (see below). Western Asia.

A. grandiflorum. A spectacular plant in its own way when given the conditions it likes. In an old, limestone wall it will seed itself in crevices and flower prodigiously. It is short-lived, sappy and niggardly with its flowers if its soil is too rich. 30 cm (12in), but likes to hang. Late spring to mid summer. Middle East.

A. iberideum. In many ways rather iberis-like, with thinner leaves and white, fragrant flowers. It does not have the 'quality' of the other species and is generally not as long-lived. 15 cm (6 in). Early to mid summer. Turkey and Greece.

A. pulchellum. Probably only a form of *A. grandiflorum*, but it is distinct in gardens, having a more compact habit and flowers of a brighter, more solid pink. Late spring to mid summer.

A. schistosum. A variable plant which can be coarse and small flowered. It is close to *A. grandiflorum* but is not as attractive unless a notably good form turns up. Middle East.

A. 'Warley Rose'. In the front rank of rock garden plants. It is a putative hybrid between *A. cordifolium* and *A. pulchellum*, and is better than either. Its flower heads are rich carmine pink and it makes a neat, gnarled shrublet. It and 'Warley Ruber', which is slightly looser in habit and whose flowers are deep carmine red, are easy to grow and entirely rewarding. Both are about 10 cm (4 in) tall. Early to mid summer.

AJUGA (Labiatae)

The bugles are mountain plants, but hardly alpines, nor even rock garden plants in the strict sense, as they can be used to make weed-proof mats of attractive foliage almost anywhere, in sun or shade, and in the dampest or driest, most inhospitable spots. In the rock garden they are a danger to choice specimens because of their invasive habit. However they are very useful at the limits of the rock garden where the soil may become poor or difficult and where continuity of planting is not otherwise easy. Propagation is by division in spring or autumn.

A. pyramidalis. Mats of deep green leaves throw up flower stems on which the leaves become bracts that clasp the stems throughout their lengths. Towards the tops of the stems, where they subtend the flowers, they take on a purple colouring. *A. metallica* 'Crispa', in which the foliage is crimped and has a metallic sheen, is regarded as a form of this species. Flowers are usually deep violet-blue but can be pink or white. 15 cm (6 in). Mid spring to late summer. S. Europe.

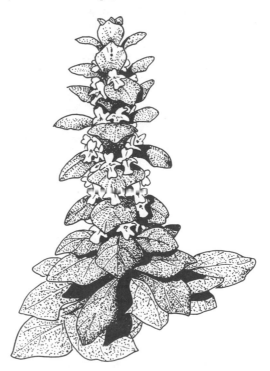

Ajuga pyramidalis

A. reptans. Similar, but a little shorter. The type has deep green leaves, but the most interesting varieties are those with coloured leaves, such as 'Atropurpurea' with purple leaves, 'Burgundy Glow' in which green is variegated with red and pink, and a form that is variously

129

called 'Multicolor', 'Tricolor', and — most frequently — 'Rainbow', whose leaves are a mixture of green, creamy yellow, purple and pink. These varieties all have flowers in some shade of blue. 13 cm (5 in). Mid spring to late summer. Most of Europe.

ALCHEMILLA (Rosaceae)

The lady's mantles are generally either too large or too invasive for the rock garden, although some are excellent for the front of the general border. A few, however, are quite miniature. The ornamental feature for which they are grown is the foliage. The rounded, lightly lobed leaves are provided with silky hairs that trap water droplets so that they sparkle like diamonds when the sun comes out after rain. Each flower is insignificant, but in the mass they make clouds of greenish yellow. Some people think the flowers a distraction from the beauty of the foliage. Propagation may be done by division in mid spring, but seeds germinate very easily.

A. alpina. The small leaves have five to seven unusually deep lobes, but otherwise is like a miniature of the widely grown *A. mollis* of the herbaceous border. Good in a semi-shaded, moist spot. Flowers in mid and late summer. Europe.

A. conjuncta. A species from the Swiss Alps that is quite widely available but more of a curiosity than an ornament.

A. ellenbeckii. This is a recent introduction and a species of different habit, as it has trailing, rooting stems. The leaves are lightly lobed and daintily neat. Typical alchemilla flowers appear in mid to late summer. Mountains of E. Africa.

ALLIUM (Liliaceae)

The vast genus to which the onions and garlics belong includes just a handful of species that are valuable alpine plants. It is as well to be highly selective, as many species that are eminently suitable for borders have in the past been included in lists of alpines. The alpines like a gritty, but not poor soil and should be planted in full sun. Seeds and division of clumps are the methods of increase.

A. amabile. A plant of vexed classification. It is currently known in some circles as *A. mairei amabile*. Others regard the pink-flowered *A. mairei* as a distinct species. It is rhizomatous, rather than a bulb, makes a delicate tuft of fine leaves, and has rich, red-purple flowers in late summer. 13 cm (5 in). China.

A. beesianum (syn. *A. sikkimense*). Another rhizomatous allium, a little taller than the previous species, with several pendent, blue flowers to each stem. A study in miniature elegance. 20 cm (8 in). Mid summer. China.

A. cyaneum. A frail-looking but perfectly tough little allium, perfect for a raised bed or trough, with clear cobalt blue flowers. 15 cm (6 in). Mid summer. China.

Allium cyaneum

A. cyathophorum farreri. A rhizomatous plant with narrow, grassy leaves and wine-red flowers. 15 cm (6 in). China.

A. flavum minus. This is the only form of the species that should be grown in the rock garden, as it is much smaller than the type. The flowers are the colour of straw. Prefers a hot, dry spot. 20 cm (8 in). Europe.

A. narcissiflorum. A beautiful plant, hardly recognizable as an 'onion', with burgundy bells in mid to late summer. Perfect for a trough and otherwise deserving of a choice place. 15 cm (6 in). Italian and French Alps.

A. oreophilum (syn. *A. oreophilum ostrowskianum*, *A. ostrowskianum*). Behind these dreadful names is a cheerful plant that will gently spread by bulbils. The umbels of flowers are rounded and large for such a small plant. 'Zwanenburg' is a selection for rich red from a species in which the colour is never less than carmine. 15 cm (6 in). Turkestan.

ALYSSUM (Cruciferae)
Alyssums are annuals or perennials and there are a few species that are sub-shrubs. They come from dry places along the whole southern European mountain chain, from the Pyrenees to the beginning of Asia. A good, well-drained soil in full sun suits them. They can be grown in the rock garden or raised bed and one or two are small enough for a trough. Propagation by half-ripe cuttings in mid to late summer.

A. alpestre. A tiny shrub for a trough or raised bed, with grey leaves and tight clusters of yellow, four-petalled flowers. Mid summer to early autumn. 5 cm (2 in). Mountains bordering the Mediterranean.

A. moellendorfianum. A Yugoslavian species, similar to *A. montanum*, with large racemes in early to mid summer. 15 cm (6 in).

A. montanum. The main species of the European Alps. It is very varied, and the foliage can be anything from silky green to greyish white, while its habit is anything from completely prostrate to a shrublet of 15 cm (6 in) in height. Early to mid summer.

A. saxatile. The common rock garden alyssum, often known as 'gold dust' because of the billowing heads of yellow flowers, is excellent on the larger rock garden as long as it is cut back after flowering, otherwise it becomes excessively woody and looks coarse. It combines well and traditionally with aubrieta. 20–23 cm (8–10 in). *A.s. citrinum* has flowers of pale lemon yellow. 'Compactum' is a most desirable dwarf form. 'Dudley Neville' has orange-tan flowers. 'Flore Pleno' is double.

A. serpyllifolium. A miniature species, possibly a form of *A. alpestre*, but distinct and even smaller.

ANACYCLUS (Compositae)
A genus of daisies from the Mediterranean region.

A. depressus (syn. *A. pyrethrum depressus*). Has finely cut, silvery-green foliage in rosettes and multi-rayed daisy flowers which are white with red reverses to the petals. A purely factual description cannot do justice to this elegant, short-stemmed treasure, as it has an indefinable immediacy to its charm. It is perfectly hardy but needs rapid drainage and a top-dressing of gravel round its collar. Late spring to late summer. 5 cm (2 in). Atlas Mountains of North Africa.

ANCHUSA (Boraginaceae)
Anchusas are usually encountered in gardens in the shape of the tall perennials which lend such a dash of true blue to the summer scene. There is one true alpine.

A. caespitosa. A mountain species that consists of a short, branched trunk, each branch of which ends in a rosette of strap-shaped, grey-green, bristly leaves, each one usually less than 5 cm (2 in) long. The whole effect is cushion-like and the gentian blue flowers, which are more like those of comfrey than of forget-me-nots, sit tightly close to it. It needs careful cultivation in an alpine house or frame but can be managed successfully in a trough or gritty raised bed. Cuttings of individual rosettes root if taken in summer but some will be lost. Early to mid spring. 15 cm (6 in). Crete.

ANDROSACE (Primulaceae)
Androsaces vary considerably, but they are all high mountain plants of exquisite grace. Some form mats of woolly rosettes on strawberry-like stolons, others neat but amorphous cushions of narrow leaves, but the aretian androsaces, some of the most ravishing of all alpines if not of all plants, make, in good conditions, perfect miniature domes of tiny, tightly packed rosettes with small, round flowers studding their surfaces. Cultivation varies and is given for each species. Stoloniferous species can be

propagated by cuttings; others by seed sown in late winter to early spring.

A. alpina (syn. *A. glacialis*). An aretian from the Alps, where it grows in lime-free moraines and moist screes. Above a cushion of green leaves, rose-pink flowers reward the few who can manage it in an alpine house. Less than 2.5 cm (1 in). Early summer.

A. carnea. This is a cushion-forming species that is quite easy to grow in a gritty, well-drained soil. Above the slender pointed leaves, flower stems, each bearing several pink flowers, rise to an average of 10 cm (4 in). Mid to late spring. Alps and Pyrenees. *A.c. alba* has white flowers. *A.c. brigantiaca* has pink or white flowers and is a larger plant, up to 15 cm (6 in) in flower. *A.c. laggeri* has flowers of bright red above very narrow leaves. *A.c. rosea* (syn. *A.c. halleri*) is an easy plant to grow. Hybrids between *A. carnea* and *A. pyrenaica* are variable but desirable plants for growing in troughs and screes.

A. chamaejasme. Rosettes of tiny, softly hairy, grey-green leaves. Spreads by stolons. Flowers white, becoming pink. 5 cm (2 in). Needs alpine house treatment or careful cultivation in a trough. Early summer. Alps.

A. ciliata. A fairly loose cushion of grey leaves in 2.5 cm (1 in) rosettes, with pink flowers held just above the foliage. Good forms have deep pink flowers. Alpine house or careful outdoor cultivation with winter protection from damp. Early summer. Pyrenees.

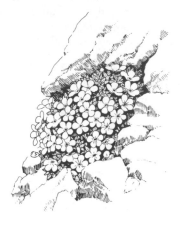

Androsace ciliata

A. cylindrica. An aretian androsace, forming tight, domed cushions of small, dark green rosettes. White flowers are borne on stems of less than 2.5 cm (1 in) and are single. Requires alpine house cultivation. Mid to late spring. Pyrenees.

A. cylindrica × hirtella. These two species hybridize readily. The progeny are very variable and only a few will be worthy of taking up alpine-house space, although occasional specimens are superb and hide their cushions with their flowers.

A. delavayi. A Chinese aretian androsace not much more than a decade in cultivation. The rosettes are soft and silky, quite large for this group of androsaces, and form cushions. The flowers are held close to the rosettes and are white, yellow-throated and have a light scent. Unlike other aretian androsaces it can be propagated by cuttings. Alpine house. Late spring. Yunnan.

A. globifera. Another species of comparatively recent introduction. It is the most woolly of the aretian androsaces, making a cushion reminiscent of some *Haastia* species. The grey-green, rosetted foliage builds up into cushions, but it is not an easy plant, even in the alpine house. Flowers are pink or white; the white-flowered forms are very difficult to grow. Propagation is by cuttings in summer. Late spring to early summer. Himalaya.

A. helvetica. One of the more difficult aretians, with damp-prone domes of tightly-packed rosettes of silky, grey leaves. The flowers are white and stemless. Alpine house. Mid to late spring. Alps.

A. hirtella. Somewhat similar to *A. cylindrica*, but the rosettes are softly downy and the rounded flowers are held tightly to the cushion. Some forms have small flowers with spaces between the petals; in others the flowers are circular and much larger. Alpine house. Mid to late spring. Pyrenees.

A. lanuginosa. Perhaps the most valuable androsace for the open garden. Long, leafy stems arise from sparse rosettes of woolly leaves and bear umbels of soft pink flowers on stems of 5 cm (2 in) or more. The plant is excellent when draping rocks from its roothold in a

Androsace lanuginosa

crevice. It is too robust for a trough. Tolerant of winter wet. Mid summer. Himalaya.

A. mathildae. An aretian species with cushions of green, glabrous rosettes and white flowers on stalks of 2.5–5 cm (1–2 in) in length. Alpine house or scree. It is not easy to keep in good condition; individual rosettes die off for no apparent reason, and the plant is short-lived. Late spring. Apennines.

A. muscoidea. Like a miniature version of *A. villosa* below, with white flowers that are said to turn pink when fertilized. *A.m. longiscapa* has mauve-pink flowers, is much more open in structure and more obviously stoloniferous. There is some work yet to be done in establishing the status of these plants. Alpine house cultivation is recommended, but very careful treatment on the scree has been successful. Himalaya, from Tibet to Nepal.

A. pyrenaica. The tightest cushions and smallest leaves of all androsaces are found in this aretian species. It makes perfect domes of clear, mid green and good forms can almost cover themselves with small, white, almost stemless flowers. It needs alpine house treatment. Even so, patches of rosettes may die off suddenly and must be removed. The most frequent cause for this is failure to remove every single seed capsule as soon as it is ripe — a precaution to be taken with all cushion androsaces to prevent rot. Mid to late spring. Pyrenees.

A. sarmentosa. There is some disagreement as to whether this species is synonymous with *A. primuloides* or a separate species. There are several forms, all making substantial rosettes of intensely woolly, overlapping leaves and having tight umbels of pink to rose-red flowers on stalks up to 10 cm (4 in) high. The most usual forms are *chumbyi*, *watkinsii*, and the neatest, *yunnanensis*. 'Galmont's Variety' should read 'Salmon's Variety'. Easy in scree. Mid to late spring. Himalaya to W. China.

A. sempervivoides. An uncharacteristically easy species, with rosettes of leathery, green leaves connected by stolons. The flowers are in short-stemmed umbels and are pink with a yellow eye that turns red. For the scree or well-drained spot in the rock garden. Mid to late spring. Western Himalaya.

A. vandellii (syn. *A. argentea*). This is not only the most beautiful androsace, but one of the choicest of all alpines. It makes tight, flattened domes of silver, and then, in good forms, hides them completely with round, white flowers that are so closely packed as to be unable fully to open. For the alpine house. It is possible to grow it out of doors and it succeeds on its side in a block of tufa (although it does not like other forms of lime), but by far the best results are obtained under glass. Mid to late spring. Alps and Pyrenees.

A. villosa. A widespread and variable species, with wooolly rosettes congregated into clusters, above which rise stems carrying umbels of white flowers. It is a popular plant, ideal for a sunny scree. *A.v. arachnoidea* (N. Yugoslavia) is neater and even more woolly. *A.v. jacquemontii* (Himalaya) is a lovely plant, more open and stoloniferous in structure, with clear pink flowers in its best forms. Late spring. Europe to Afghanistan.

ANEMONE (Ranunculaceae)

There are just a few anemones that can be thought of as alpines; others are really woodland plants in gardening terms. The rock garden anemones are easy and their flowers, made up of sepals rather than petals, are often brightly coloured. Cool positions and leafy soils suit them best. Dwarf anemones can provide flowers from late winter until the middle of summer. Propagation is by seed, which should be sown as soon as it is ripe.

A. apennina. A tuberous species with deep sky-blue flowers. There are white and pink forms. Prefers woodland conditions. Early to mid spring. 13 cm (6 in). Europe.

A. baldensis. A white-flowered species with much divided leaves. The flowers have eight to ten sepals, which are blue on the reverse. Seldom flowers well and *A. sylvestris* is preferable. 10 cm (4 in). Early to mid summer. Italy.

A. blanda. The most well-known small anemone, always offered in bulb catalogues because the root can be dried whereas those of other anemones cannot. Like *A. apennina* but with fewer sepals and the flowers are wider. Several forms in blue, rose pink and white. 8 cm (3 in). Late winter to early spring. E. Europe.

A. lesseri. Sometimes listed as *A.* × *lesseri* and cited as a hybrid of *A. sylvestris*. This is improbable, as it is an American plant and a naturally occurring hybrid with a European plant would be hard to imagine. It is easy to grow, relatively late flowering, and taller than many others. The flowers are bright pink with a dark eye. 39 cm (12 in). Early to late summer. N. America.

A. magellanica. Similar in some ways to *A. sylvestris*, but somehow contriving to look ineffective unless *A.m.* 'Major' is planted, which has larger flowers of deep cream and is quite striking. 15 cm (6 in). Late spring to early summer. Chile.

A. narcissiflora. An aristocratic plant of distinctive appearance, with cup-shaped, white flowers with soft pink reverses, several to an umbel. The foliage is soft, silky, and much divided. 30 cm (12 in). Early to mid summer. Alpine woodlands of N. hemisphere.

A. nemorosa. The wood anemone is too well known — and rightly so — to warrant detailed description. There are several easily obtainable cultivars, giving flowers in white, lavender blue, and shades of blue, sometimes with pink reverses. Early to mid spring. Europe.

A. obtusiloba. Usually grown as the cultivar 'Patula', whose flowers are soft blue. Sometimes known as the Himalayan blue buttercup. It likes full sun but must have a leafy, moisture-retentive soil. The large, solitary flowers and softly downy, palmate leaves make this a distinct and very beautiful plant. There is a white form. Flower stems spread sideways. Early to mid summer.

A. sylvestris. The European snowdrop anemone. The five sepals are broad and make a chalice-shaped flower of silky white that has a fugacious scent. Not unlike a pulsatilla in appearance and will be free flowering if its cool position is kept well drained and gritty. 20 cm (8 in). Mid to late spring. Europe and Asia.

ANEMONELLA (Ranunculaceae)

A monotypic genus from N. America.

A. thalictroides. A delicate-looking, small plant for semi-shady places with not too much competition. Its foliage is like a thalictrum, while its dainty flowers are white or, very occasionally, blush pink. 13 cm (5 in). Early to mid spring.

ANTENNARIA (Compositae)

A genus of many silvery, carpeting plants, only one of which is widely grown. Propagation is by division in spring.

A. dioica. Although a member of the daisy family, this species bears flowers with no ray florets. This means that those forms that are pink or red-flowered are the most effective. It is a modest, carpeting plant, whose main attraction is its neat, silvery foliage. It is tough and easy in a stony spot. There are several forms, of which *minima*, a much-condensed version, *rosea* and 'Nyewoods Variety', both of which have flowers in good shades of pink, are among the best. 8 cm (3 in) in flower. Late spring to early summer. N. hemisphere.

ANTHYLLIS (Leguminosae)
There are around twenty species in this genus, many of which are small, maquis-type, spiny shrubs from the Mediterranean area. Two species in particular are hardy rock garden plants, enjoying full sun and a sparse diet. Their seeds germinate readily.

A. hermanniae. A sub-shrub of 60 cm (2 ft) or more, making a tangled, spiny bush with small, silvery leaves that almost become hidden by the clusters of yellow pea flowers. Most rock garden plants under this name are rather large and the cultivar. 'Compacta', which is only half the size, should be looked for. Mid spring.

A. montana. A dwarf shrub or sub-shrub with silvery foliage and heads of pink flowers. *A.m. rubra* is a superior form with red flowers. 13 cm (5 in). Late spring to mid summer. Balkans.

APHYLLANTHES (Aphyllanthaceae)
The genus was until recently classified under Liliaceae. The species below likes a typically Mediterranean mixture of sun and a well-drained, gritty soil. Propagation is by seed.

A. monspeliensis. A rush-like plant with terminal, solitary flowers which are star-shaped, 2.5 cm (1 in) wide, and deep blue. A plant which hates disturbance. 20 cm (8 in). Mid to late summer. Mediterranean hillsides.

AQUILEGIA (Ranunculaceae)
A large genus of plants, sometimes called columbines. Many have leaves reminiscent of maidenhair ferns, and all are relatively short-lived perennials. The most attractive have flowers with five long spurs, giving them a bonnet-like appearance. Species vary from easy plants for the rock garden to tricky ones needing the alpine house. Aquilegias are highly immoral and are propagated from seed only, so it is as well to isolate the ones whose seed you wish to save.

A. alpina. Unfortunately not very 'alpine', as it is 60 cm (2 ft) tall. Best in a border. Mid to late summer. Alps.

A. bertolonii. A tiny species with large, rich slate-blue, spurred flowers. Easy in a scree. 13 cm (5 in). Late spring to early summer. Italy.

A. caerulea. Large blue and white flowers with long spurs. Often hybridizes. For the scree. N. America.

A. canadensis. Variable, sometimes short, sometimes tall, occasionally spurless, usually short-spurred. Flowers reddish to yellow and red. Easily grown; best regarded as a bit of fun. Early to late summer. N. America.

A. discolor. One of the smallest aquilegias, with cushions of foliage and large flowers that are blue with rich cream centres. Delightful in a trough. 10 cm (4 in). Mid to late summer. Spain.

A. einseliana. An easy plant, rather like *A. alpina*, but much smaller. 15–20 cm (6–8 in). Mid to late summer. Dolomites.

A. flabellata (syn *A. akitensis*). The plant almost always seen in gardens is the dwarf *A.f. pumila*, which used to be known as *A.f.* 'Nana'. It has most attractive, glaucous foliage and late blue-mauve flowers. The overall appearance is one of sturdiness and its toleration of outdoor cultivation does not belie it. 15 cm (6 in). Early summer. Japan. *A.f. pumila alba* is widely grown and usually labelled as 'Nana Alba'. *A.f. pumila kurilensis* (an unacceptable quadrinomial) has violet and cream flowers on stems on only 13 cm (5 in) and is a good alpine house plant. (N.B. This is an example of botanical nomenclature proving counter-productive. Gardeners labelling their plants *A.f.* 'Nana Alba' and *A.f.* 'Kurilensis' are advised to continue to do so, if only on the grounds that we must surely soon stop the retreat from Linnaean simplicity.)

A. glandulosa. A note of caution: only the most respected sources are to be trusted to deliver this species true. Seed should be matt-surfaced and not shiny as with all other aquilegias, and even that is not a totally reliable guide, as it is only one genetic variable; nevertheless, the true plant cannot have shiny seeds. This is one of the finest gems of the genus, with superb flowers, blue outside and white inside.

The variety *jacunda* is dwarfer and has larger flowers. 15 cm (6 in). Early summer. Altai Mountains of Central Asia.

A. jonesii. This species is one of the challenges of alpine gardening. It is tiny and each stem has one very large, short-spurred, blue flower. The foliage is minute and close to the soil surface. It grows well in the alpine house but is most reluctant to flower. However, one of us (JK) won several prizes with it, so it is possible! 8 cm (3 in). Early summer. Rocky Mountains.

A. laramiensis. The smallest aquilegia of all, with creamy white flowers. Best in the alpine house because of its size. 5 cm (2 in). Mid to late summer. Rocky Mountains.

A. nivalis. A rare beauty of the same size and bearing as *A. flabellata*, sometimes confused with compact forms of *A. glandulosa*. It has deep purple-blue flowers and protruding black stamens. Suitable for scree, trough or alpine house. 15 cm (6 in). Mid to late summer. Western Himalaya.

ARABIS (Cruciferae)
A genus consisting of a few worthwhile rock garden plants among many weeds. *A. albida* is sold in garden centres occasionally, but is invasive and commonplace. The following species are worth cultivating.

A. androsacea. A cushion plant that can take its place with some of the recognized aristocrats. The foliage is softly hairy and downy and the flowers are white, on short stems. Will grow in the scree, but can be given room in the alpine house if it is not at a premium. 5 cm (2 in). Mid to late spring. Turkey.

A. blepharophylla. A cut above your average arabis. The foliage is grey-green and the conspicuous flowers are rose pink. The best forms are almost red. Rock garden and scree. 8 cm (3 in). Mid to late spring. California.

A. bryoides. A cushiony mat of silvery hairy rosettes, neat enough for showing off in the alpine house, especially in the compact form *olympica*, and ideal for a trough. Less than 8 cm (3 in) when in flower. Late spring to late summer. Greece.

A. ferdinandi-coburgii. Almost always grown as the variegated form. It is quite unlike an arabis, and has flat rosettes of fleshy, green and cream leaves. It has white flowers 10 cm (4 in). Late spring to early summer. S. Europe.

ARCTERICA (Ericaceae)
A genus closely related to *Andromeda*, delighting in a leafy, peaty position in cool shade. It does not like lime.

A. nana. A mat-forming species, spreading in a suitable soil by underground stems, but always staying neat, like a tiny box. The urn-shaped, white, slightly fragrant flowers appear in early to mid spring. 13 cm (5 in). Sub-arctic Japan and shores of the Bering Sea.

ARCTOSTAPHYLOS (Ericaceae)
The bear berries vary from the tall, Californian *A. manzanita*, which is a shrub with beautiful, plum-coloured bark, to ground-covering, prostrate mats. All are lime haters and like a leafy, peaty soil in light shade. They may be propagated by seeds, semi-ripe cuttings, or layers.

A. alpina (syn. *Arctous alpinus*). Forms prostrate mats of reddish, rooting stems. The leaves turn brown in autumn and are held on the plant until the following spring. They have a silvery appearance. The flowers are white, pink-tinted and with dark anthers. Berries black, autumn. 8 cm (3 in). Mid spring to early summer. N. hemisphere.

A. nevadensis is similar to *A. uva-ursi* and a native of California. It is named after an Indian chief, and not the State of Nevada.

A. uva-ursi. Like a much larger version of *A. alpina*, but with truly evergreen foliage. The leaves are bright, shiny green, the flowers urn-shaped, white with a pink cast, and the berries red. It is robust and not suited to small spaces. 15 cm (6 in). Mid spring to early summer. N. Hemisphere.

ARENARIA (Caryophyllaceae)
Only a handful of the sandworts are worth considering for the rock garden. The three species described below are distinct from one another and far removed from the weedy arenarias and allied minuartias that can be a nuisance.

A. balearica. Makes a wide-spreading green film of tiny leaves on damp rock. It is pretty when growing alongside water, especially when studded with minute, pure white flowers. Late spring and early summer. Islands in the Mediterranean.

A. montana. White flowers, 20 mm ($\frac{3}{4}$ in) across, in clustered heads, make this quite a showy plant. Grey-green foliage on wiry stems. Good when draping downward from a crevice. 15 cm (6 in). Iberian Peninsula.

A. tetraquetra. Somewhat like an extremely attenuated, cushion-forming heather with flowers that are almost stemless, four-petalled, and white. For the scree, trough or alpine house. *A.t.* 'Granatensis' is even more compact and has five-petalled flowers. Early to late summer. Spain.

ARMERIA (Plumbaginaceae)
Armerias are closely tufted plants, often forming cushions of narrow, grassy leaves, with flowers — usually pink — in round, papery heads. Many have an affinity with the sea and can sometimes be found at the rims of rock pools. They like sunny, gritty places and *A. juniperifolia* is ideal for a trough. Propagation by cuttings, although old plants will be found to have rooted rosettes that can be detached.

A. juniperifolia (syn. *A. caespitosa*). A small, tight bun with flowers on very short stems. 5 cm (2 in). Late spring to early summer. Spain. *A.j.* 'Bevan's Variety' has deeper, rose pink flowers.

A. maritima. A variable plant, susceptible to habit change according to conditions and best kept in character in a poorish soil, in which case it will be about 15 cm (6 in) high when in flower. European coasts. Early summer. *A.m.* 'Alba' has white flowers. *A.m.* 'Bloodstone' has flowers of deep, blood red. *A.m.* 'Dusseldorf Pride' is rich crimson.

ARNICA (Compositae)
The alpine arnicas are plants with hairy, rosetted foliage and golden flowers that are either solitary or borne in heads. There are two, *A. alpina* and *A. montana*. Unfortunately, there is much confusion between them. Because authorities differ on almost everything about them, including their preference for or hatred of lime, it is necessary to take a position, and it is that *A. alpina* is not in general cultivation, all plants being forms of *A. montana*.

A. montana. Flowers wide, solitary, golden-yellow. Does not appear to be fussy about lime. Does not resent disturbance and can be propagated from division as well as seed. 20 cm (8 in). Late spring to early summer. Europe. (*A. alpina* hates lime and disturbance, has smaller flowers in heads, and is markedly taller.)

ASPERULA (Rubiaceae)
The woodruffs have flowers like miniature, long trumpets and make tufty mats of stems that are quite often weak and need careful handling. The leaves are heath-like and disposed in whorls of four (sometimes eight) along the stems. Cultivation requirements vary. Division makes for untidy plants, liable to rot off in patches and cuttings taken in mid spring provide the best method of propagation.

A. gussonii. A tufted species with a woody base, dark green foliage, and flowers in heads of a dozen or so, flesh pink. For sunny scree. 10 cm (4 in). Early summer. Sicily.

A. lilacaeflora caespitosa. An almost prostrate, heath-like cushion of green leaves and masses of relatively large, lilac-pink, stemless flowers. 5 cm (2 in). Early to mid summer. E. Mediterranean.

A. nitida puberula. A tiny plant, only 2.5 cm (1 in) high, with starry flowers above green foliage. Alpine house. Early summer. Greece.

A. suberosa. A frail plant, but not difficult in the alpine house. It makes a cushiony mat of fragile stems, clad in white-woolly, typically heath-shaped leaves, and has a generous crop of tubular flowers of softest pink. Groups of stems die off from time to time and should be removed. Early summer. 8 cm (3 in). Greece.

ASTER (Compositae)
A very large genus indeed, well known for Michaelmas daisies, which contains a few species that are eminently suitable for the rock

garden. They enjoy gritty soils with good drainage in full sun, but it is as well if it does not dry out. Propagation of named or especially good forms is best done by division; seed germinates well when ripe. It is doubtful if *A. farreri*, perhaps the most beautiful of all, is truly represented in cultivation.

A. alpinus. The alpine aster is a neat little plant with basal rosettes of leaves and solitary flower heads (in lay terms, flowers: in the Compositae they are compounded of many florets). They vary in size, quality and shape, and good named varieties should be sought. They are mostly 15 cm (6 in) tall. Early summer. Europe and Asia. *A.a.* 'Albus' has large, white flowers. *A.a.* 'Beechwood' is notable for very large, deep blue-purple flowers. *A.a.* 'Happy End' has large, rose pink flowers.

Aster alpinus

A. likiangensis. Possibly a miniature form of *A. alpinus* from the extreme end of its range. 8 cm (3 in). Yunnan.

A. natalensis. A mat-forming species with flowers of a good, deep blue. 15 cm (6 in). Mid to late summer. South Africa.

A. pygmaea is a woolly plant, forming low mats of hairy leaves and sometimes with the lilac flowers embedded in an outer, woolly overcoat. A rarity. 10 cm (4 in). Summer. Canadian Arctic.

ASTILBE (Saxifragaceae)
The feathery spikes of astilbes are well known to gardeners, as they are grown wherever the soil is moisture-retentive. They are strongly coloured border plants for the most part, but there are some dwarf species. A note of warning must be sounded: one or two are rapacious invaders when thoroughly suited, and this fact is virtually never mentioned in the literature. Propagation is by division.

A. chinensis. Usually offered in the compact form *A.c.* 'Pumila'. This has ferny foliage and rose-purple flowers. It must never be planted in peat beds, as it can take over completely, rendering peat blocks useless, and make rebuilding necessary within five years. 15 cm (6 in). Mid summer. China.

A. crispa. Always seen as *A.c.* 'Perkeo'. The feathery leaves are crinkled and the flowers are pink. The best 'alpine' astilbe. 8 cm (3 in). Mid summer. Japan.

A. glaberrima. Usually grown as the cultivar 'Saxatilis'. Not as thuggish as *A. chinensis*, but invasive if happy. The foliage is ferny and bronze, and the flowers pink. 15 cm (6 in). Mid to late summer. Japan.

AUBRIETA (Cruciferae)
In effect, the aubrietas we grow are all forms of one species. They may have some small degree of hybridization with others, but it is of no garden significance. Aubrietas are ideal crevice plants, making, when cut back after flowering, neat, billowing cushions, especially when allowed to grow on their sides. Very close to the sea this cutting-back is unnecessary, and they are superb salt-spray plants. Propagation is by summer cuttings, which root best with a length of old stem attached.

A. deltoidea. The true species is seldom grown, except as *A.d.* 'Variegata', for which there appear to be a number of pseudonyms. It is a neat but not very exciting plant, with variegated foliage and mauve flowers. 'Blue Beauty' is double, deep blue, and of compact growth. 'Bressingham Pink' is also double and rose pink. 'Carnival' (syn. 'Hartswood Purple') has deep violet flowers and is of vigorous habit. 'Doctor Mules' is an old variety, rich purple. 'Mrs. Rodewald' has large, rich red flowers. 'Red Carpet' is bright red. This is just a selection of well over fifty varieties that are commercially available.

AZORELLA (Umbelliferae)
Few authorities agree whether the species described belong here or in *Bolax*. Neither is notable for its flowers; each is grown for its foliage. A sunny spot in a scree suits them, and propagation is by cuttings.

A. glebaria (syn. *Bolax gummifera*). An iron-hard cushion of stony-green rosettes with tightly arranged leaves. The whole looks a little like a vegetable tortoise. Flowers greenish white but rarely borne. 15–20 cm (6–8 in). Azores

A. trifurcata. A much laxer cushion of foliage, all too often liable to collapse in the middle. The leaves are three-pointed and olive green. The flowers are in almost stemless umbels, greenish yellow. Not a scene stealer, but often appears in catalogues. 15–20 cm (6–8 in). Mid to late summer. South America.

BERBERIS (Berberidaceae)
The very large genus *Berberis* provides us with just one plant that can be said to be in character in an average rock garden. It has the great advantage among rock garden shrubs of being happy on calcareous soils. Propagation is not easy; tiny 'mallet' cuttings—a current year's shoot and a small section of the stem from which it arises—are taken after flowering.

B. × stenophylla 'Corallina Compacta'. A tiny, dense, evergreen bush with stiff, spiny leaves and orange flowers emerging from red buds. 30 cm (12 in) after several years. Mid spring.

BETULA (Betulaceae)
The birches are tough, extremely hardy trees, and the dwarf birch is no exception.

B. nana. A variable, dwarf shrub. Some forms, especially 'Glengarry' are only about 30 cm (12 in) tall, while others may be as much as 90 cm (3 ft)—still small enough for a large rock garden. They like a damp, peaty place and coolness. The small leaves turn yellow in autumn before dropping. Separate male and female catkins but both are on the same plant. Arctic and sub-Arctic.

BOYKINIA (Saxifragaceae)
This is a small genus, mainly American, of which the following species is atypical. It has twice the usual five stamens and has been transferred on that ground to *Telesonix*. Increasingly the transfer is being recognized.

B. jamesii (syn. *Telesonix jamesii*). A very rare plant, from Pike's Peak, Colorado. It is best in the alpine house, as it is slightly sticky. It also requires a poor soil but one that is lime-free, and a combination in late spring and summer of warmth above and moist but gritty coolness below. Without these conditions it will grow perfectly well but will be reluctant to flower. The kidney-shaped, toothed leaves are unique, and the racemes of cherry-red flowers are most striking in a well-grown plant. 15 cm (6 in). Early summer.

BRIGGSIA (Gesneriaceae)
Near relatives of *Ramonda* and *Haberlea*, but the one species in cultivation is much more difficult. It is, however, one of the choicest and most beautiful of alpines, as well as one of the more challenging. Propagation is by seed, which is set in cultivation on well-grown, hand-pollinated plants.

B. muscicola. The leaves, up to 10 cm (4 in) long, arise from a central point and in texture are like a superlative grade of emerald-green velvet. Tubular, light yellow blooms, similar in shape to those of a haberlea, are carried above the leaves, many on a stem. Drought kills it more readily than low temperatures, and the ideal place for it is in a cool place below the staging of the alpine house. Mid summer. Bhutan.

BRUCKENTHALIA (Ericaceae)
A genus of only one species, related to the heathers.

B. spiculifolia. A neat little plant, like a spiky-leaved but densely furnished heather. The flowers are bell-shaped and rose pink. 25 cm (10 in). Late spring to mid summer. SE Europe, Asia Minor.

CALCEOLARIA (Scrophulariaceae)
Calceolarias are southern-hemisphere plants, mainly concentrated in South America, but with outliers in New Zealand. Apart from the florists' calceolarias and the many tender species, there are some hardy plants, including one or two of the most endearing alpines. Propagate by seed or, where possible, by division.

C. biflora. A small herbaceous perennial requiring a cool, vegetable soil. The foliage takes the form of basal rosettes of downy, toothed leaves, and the yellow flowers, just under 2.5 cm (1 in) across are borne on stems of 23 cm (9 in) or so. Early to late summer. Chile.

C. darwinii. This quite astonishing plant must have alpine house or frame conditions if it is to do well, as it needs constant monitoring for aphid attack. The best preventive regime is the use of a systemic insecticide. The sticky, green leaves make a mat which would become leggy and drawn in shade and need full light to keep their character. However, light shade, such as the alpine house should have, will prevent scorching. Just above this, the flowers hang, like those basket seats hanging from chains that were so popular once. Each bloom is attached to its stem at its top, and the bulbous, pouched lower lip has a broad, horizontal, white stripe against the general light yellow, variously stippled with maroon. A cool but gritty compost is essential and it must be lime-free. Mid summer. Southern Chile.

C. fothergillii. Similar, but with much smaller flowers on considerably taller stems. It also needs alpine house treatment and is susceptible to aphids. 10 cm (4 in) if not drawn up. Late summer. Patagonia, Falklands.

One of us (JK) successfully hybridized *C. darwinii* and *C. fothergillii* in the mid-1970s. It was possibly the first time this had been done. Plants were distributed under the name *C. darwinii × fothergillii*. These varied, but were easier than *C. darwinii* and more decorative and larger flowered than *C. fothergillii*. Several forms are still in cultivation. *C.* 'Walter Shrimpton' is a selected form raised elsewhere and in the same year.

CAMPANULA (Campanulaceae)
The harebell genus is very large and contributes over one hundred species, nearly all herbaceous, to alpine gardening. There is great variation between species, both as to form and as to cultural requirements. In general, the flowers are in some shade of blue or purple and there are white forms. One species has yellow flowers. *Campanula* is confined to the northern hemisphere. Unless otherwise stated, propagation is by division in early spring.

C. allionii (syn. *C. alpestris*). A difficult plant unless frequently divided, as it apparently exhausts some essential component of the soil very quickly. It needs alpine house treatment if it is not soon to be lost. The flowers are very large for such a diminutive plant and are straightly bell-shaped. They may be anything

Calceolaria darwinii

from purple-blue to an icy steel blue or even, very rarely, pink. 5 cm (2 in). Late spring. French Alps.

C. arvatica. A tiny, mat-forming species for a trough, sink, or choice spot on the scree. The flowers are like upturned, blue stars. 5 cm (2 in). Mid summer. N. Spain.

C. aucheri. Neat foliage and large, short-stemmed chalices of deep blue. Best shown off in a dry wall or in vertical rockwork, but happy in any sunny, well-drained position. Late spring to early summer. 10 cm (4 in). Caucasus.

C. barbata. Up to twenty large, light blue, beaded bells on erect stems above flat rosettes of leaves. Said to be biennial but often behaves as a perennial. Requires good drainage and appreciates a little shade. Propagate by seed sown in late winter. 25 cm (10 in). Mid summer. Alps and Norway.

C. carpatica. In many ways *the* rock garden campanula. There are many forms of this plant, but typically it has a mat of small, heart-shaped leaves, above which large, upright, widely open cups are deep blue with a hint of purple. The flower stems are usually short. It is one of the most effective summer rock garden plants. Up to 20 cm (8 in) but usually considerably less. Late summer to early autumn. Carpathians. 'Blue Clips' has very large, blue flowers, starting in early summer. There is also a variety 'White Clips'. 'Bressingham White' flowers generously; the flowers are on the small side.

C. turbinata, which has exceptionally large flowers, is held to be a form of *C. carpatica*. The varieties 'Pallida Albescens' (a beautiful, pearly light blue) and 'Wheatley's Violet' may be found listed under that name.

C. cochlearifolia (syn. *C. pusilla*). It is impossible not to be captivated by the little, tubby, pale blue bells of this tiny plant. Its stems wander gently, making patches of minute leaves in gritty, sunny places. In the Alps, it is equally happy by the roadside or in a patch of scree. In the garden, scree, a wall, or a large trough are ideal. 8 cm (3 in). *C.c.* 'Cambridge Blue': the name speaks for itself. *C.c.* 'Miss Willmott' has darker blue flowers.

C.c. 'Miranda' is almost lost to cultivation. The flowers are like slate, smoky blue and ravishing. Those who have it (the true plant only) should distribute it as widely as possible.

The plant called 'Elizabeth Oliver', introduced to cultivation by one of us (JK) during the 1970s probably belongs here. It is a gently sprawling, double form of very light blue, good in a crevice. It first occurred in Mr Bull's garden in Nottingham and was named for his daughter. It is widely grown.

C. excisa. A choice plant from granite areas which does not like calcareous soils. It is like an exquisite harebell, distinguished by a neat puncture at the base of each petal. Treatment as for *C. allionii*. 5 cm (2 in). Mid to late summer. Simplon and Monte Rosa.

C. garganica. A species that forms mats composed of rosettes of long-stalked, small leaves and bears sprays of clear blue, starry bells. It is a good, cheery plant for the larger rock garden, looking well when hanging over rocks, but is a little too invasive for smaller scale planting. 15 cm (6 in). Late summer to mid autumn. Italy.

C. 'Halli' (syn. *C.* × *hallii*). Nobody seems to know the origin of this plant, but it is in effect a white, tufted, version of *C. cochlearifolia*. 8–10 cm (3–4 in).

C. × haylodgensis 'Flore Pleno' (*C. cochlearifolia* × *C. carpatica*). This is a stunning, dwarf campanula, never better than when decorating a vertical crevice. The wedgwood-blue flowers are of a hue found in no other alpine, and they are fully double. Some authorities believe that this is the only form of the hybrid. 5 cm (2 in). Late summer.

C. lasiocarpa. Clear blue, solitary bells above neat, rounded, toothed leaves. This is an elegant plant, deserving its required place in the alpine house. 8 cm (3 in). Mid summer. Specimens in cultivation originate from the Rocky Mountains.

C. morettiana. One of the great treasures among alpine plants, both in the wild and in cultivation. It comes from one or two ledges in the Dolomites of Northern Italy and requires a calcareous, stony, gritty compost and great care in the alpine house. It is one of the tiny band of garden plants that really must have a limy soil to do well. It makes separate, tiny tufts of grey-green leaves and relatively enormous, clear blue flowers. The white form is slightly more difficult! Propagation is by seed, which takes two years to germinate. Division is tricky, but possible as long as the compost is very stony. 2.5 cm (1 in) or less. Mid summer.

C. persicifolia planiflora. This is a recessive form of the species that is much reduced in size. Stiff, upright stems arise from rosettes of small, dark green, holly-like leaves, and bear large, light blue flowers that are dispersed on them like so many television reflector dishes. The white form, *alba*, is almost always the one seen. Seed invariably produces a return to the normal, tall form of the species. 15 cm (6 in). Mid summer.

C. piperi. One of the best campanulas for the alpine house, where it should be divided quite often and grown in pots that are never large. It runs, producing tiny rosettes of dark green, pointed leaves and really large flowers of deep blue with scarlet anthers. It requires a lime-free, very gritty compost. Hybrids of this species with *C. lasiocarpa* have been produced and are pleasant plants, easier than either parent, but still best in alpine house conditions. 8 cm (3 in). Alaska.

Campanula raineri

C. raineri. Occasionally forms of *C. carpatica* appeared under this name, but it is a distinct and outstandingly beautiful plant, requiring alpine house cultivation. The mat of leaves is only about 12 mm ($\frac{1}{2}$ in) high and becomes completely obscured by the very large, flat, open, upward-looking saucers of light saxe blue. The reason for the need for protected cultivation is that the blooms fill with water in the open and are then ruined by the sun. 8 cm (3 in). Italy.

C. tomassiniana. A non-running alpine campanula with several erect, branched, wiry stems arising from a fleshy rootstock and carrying dainty typical harebells of light, slate blue. 13 cm (5 in). Mid to late summer. Austria.

C. vidalii. This is a most atypical campanula. It is shrubby, with stiff, glossy leaves and white, waxy flowers with orange markings. The blooms are in racemes at the ends of the branches, which arise low down on the plant. It is quite tender and is best in the alpine house or in a bed in the conservatory. Propagation is by seed, which is not set by individual plants but is increasingly available commercially. 25 cm (10 in). All summer. Azores.

C. zoysii. One of the alpine gardener's best loved plants, even though it is tricky. It is something like *C. cochlearifolia*, except that the bells are pinched almost closed, flare out again, and then abruptly close down to a tiny opening. The effect is like a flight of tiny, light-blue bombs. Best in the alpine house in a pot containing lumps of tufa and a very gritty compost laden with tufa dust. It can be grown in a trough with great care, and many growers have had success with it planted directly into a tufa rock. 5 cm (2 in). Mid summer. Julian Alps and Karawanken Mountains.

There are several other campanula species offered for sale for rock gardens. Many are worth growing but some are nuisances, known better for their invasive proclivities than for their ornamental qualities. *C. portenschlagiana* is far too spreading for the rock garden; *C. poscharskyana* is entirely rampant, and *C. rapunculoides*, the creeping bellflower, is an attractive but pernicious weed.

CARDUNCELLUS (Compositae)
Thistle-like plants from the Mediterranean basin. Only one is of significant garden value.

C. rhaponticoides. The plant is wholly prostrate and consists of one to several large, flat rosettes of long, dark green leaves whose bases and mid-ribs are reddish purple. The centre of each rosette produces a rounded, stemless head of purplish blue flowers. For a sunny scree. Propagate by division in spring or root cuttings in late winter. 5 cm (2 in). Early summer. Morocco, but hardy.

CARLINA (Compositae)
It is a coincidence of alphabetical order that places this genus of stemless thistles immediately below the last. There are several (some of which do have significant stems), but one in particular has been grown in gardens for a very long time.

C. acaulis. Although the spiny, acanthus-like leaves may be up to 30 cm (12 in) long, their flatness and the stemlessness of the large, white flower heads make it a striking feature in poor soil in a large rock garden. It needs a sunny spot. Propagate by seed. 8 cm (3 in). Mid summer. Alps.

CARMICHAELIA (Leguminosae)
A curious genus of New Zealand plants that fulfil in some respects the role of brooms in that country. They are generally leafless and have green stems; occasionally a sparse furnishing of three-lobed, small leaves may occur.

C. enysii is a prostrate species, spreading its flattened, green, jointed stems over stony ground, preferably where the soil is acid. It is leafless in the adult state. The flowers are a mixture of white and purple and are borne in two- or three-flowered racemes. 8 cm (3 in). Early to late summer. S. Alps of New Zealand.

CASSIOPE (Ericaceae)
The cassiopes are at the opposite end of the size scale from the large rhododendrons, yet all are within the same plant family. They are native to Arctic and sub-Arctic regions. Whipcord stems are arranged either as tangled, but neatly-finished cushions, or rigidly upright like a green coral. The flowers are white, held close to the foliage, and bell- to urn-shaped. Cassiopes require part shade, a very peaty or at least leafy and lime-free soil, constant moisture, and coolness. With one or two exceptions they do not react well to pot culture; the best plants for exhibition are usually lifted from the open ground. Most of them flower in mid or late spring. Propagation is by removal of rooted stems, by cuttings in summer (easy in peaty, sandy compost) or the detachment of runners, as in the case of *C. wardii*.

C. fastigiata. Erect, four-angled stems with tightly adpressed leaves. Flowers quite large for a cassiope, on thread-like stems. 25 cm (10 in).

C. lycopodioides. This has the most slender branches of all and makes a cushioned mat of emerald green, scaly branchlets. It is often almost covered by the white flowers which are held close to the cushion. Too much shade prevents the short flower stems and the calyces from becoming a most attractive, russet red.

C. mertensiana. This is a dull green, partly upright shrublet of 25 cm (10 in) with white flowers near the tips of the branches. *C.m. gracilis* is very much more slender and a dainty, bright green, and neither very prostrate nor very upright. It is a most desirable plant, if a bit shy-flowering. Its botanical status is uncertain.

C. tetragona. An upright plant with four-cornered stems and open, bell-shaped flowers near their tips. 30–45 cm (12–18 in).

C. wardii. The belle of the genus, and the most difficult to grow. It is one of the few that do well in pots. It has stout, four-angled, grey green branches with the foliage tightly adpressed and large, white flowers in conspicuous groups towards the tips. The leaves have fine, white hairs, which give the plant an almost cactus-like appearance. Runners occur at its base from time to time. 25–30 cm (10–12 in). One of two or three species from Tibet.

There are several hybrids, many of which are similar to one another. The best of them are: 'Badenoch', 'Bearsden', 'Muirhead', 'Randle

Cooke', the superb, upright 'Edinburgh', and the tiny, prostrate 'Beatrice Lilley'.

CELMISIA (Compositae)
These plants of the New Zealand mountains are among the few alpine plants that are ever-green perennials. They tend to make rosettes of long, narrow, pointed semi-upright leaves, often heavily coated with hairs that give them a silver-plated appearance. They are not easy plants. In the wrong conditions they sulk and then rot away. The right conditions are best found in moist, mild climates where temperature excesses are unknown. Propagation is by seed, which usually needs to be fresh, and is often not set in cultivation.

C. bellidioides. Atypical. It is a flat, green mat of small, dark green leaves. The flowers are small, white daisies. Propagation by cuttings in summer. Likes a moist position. 5 cm (2 in). Late spring to mid summer.

C. coriacea. A typical plant has a bold, main rosette of 20–25 cm (8–10 in) leaves that are long, tapering, and highly silvered. Subsidiary rosettes are considerably smaller. Large flowers in woolly heads appear in summer on stems of 30 cm (12 in). The best forms come from Secretary Island, and their seed has greater viability than forms from the mainland.

Other species are similar to the last on the whole, but vary in size and the colour of the foliage. Several have been brought together as *Celmisia* 'Inshriach Hybrids', a cultivated strain raised at the Jack Drake Nursery in Scotland. They probably represent the best chance for non-New Zealand gardeners to succeed with this genus.

CELSIA (Scrophulariaceae)
Celsias are very closely related to verbascums (see p. 220) and hybridize readily with them. Very few of either genus are dwarf, but the ones that are, are delightful.

C. acaulis. Preferably in the alpine house, rosettes of toothed leaves give rise to clusters of mahogany buds that open to light yellow, mullein-like flowers. The flower stems are barely noticeable. 8–10 cm (3–4 in). Late spring to early or mid summer. Crete.

× CELSIOVERBASCUM (Scrophulariaceae)
Hybrids between *Celsia* and *Verbascum*. 'Golden Wings' is a rounded, small bushlet with sparse, greyish-green leaves on twiggy stems. The golden-yellow flowers are in densely furnished racemes, and flowering lasts for most of the summer. 23 cm (9 in).

CHIASTOPHYLLUM (Crassulaceae)
There is just one species in the genus. It is unusual to find hardy alpines other than *Sempervivum* and *Sedum* in this family of succulent plants.

C. oppositifolium. A crevice-loving plant, consisting of tufts of apple-green rosettes of slightly succulent leaves. The bright yellow flowers are in long, hanging racemes like open-work catkins. It enjoys sun or part shade. 15 cm (6 in). All summer. Caucasus.

CLAYTONIA (Portulacaceae)
Claytonias are relatives of lewisias and are generally not as attractive and certainly not as showy as many of them. However, one species is grown in alpine houses and frames, and is easy there as long as it is not overwatered and has a gritty compost. It may be tried in a crevice but usually disappears quite quickly. Propagate by seed.

C. nivalis (syn. *C. megarrhiza nivalis*). A small, fleshy plant with narrow leaves and heads of rich, purplish pink. 10 cm (4 in). Early summer. N. America.

CLEMATIS (Ranunculaceae)
This well-known genus of climbers would seem to be far removed from alpine gardening. However, there is one species that is undeniably alpine, occurring naturally as a tumbler over small boulders in limestone mountains in southern Europe.

C. alpina. A gentle climber, typically a clematis, but staying within the bounds of rock garden requirements as a strayer over rocks and larger, shrubby plants. The hanging flowers are powder blue in the best forms. 'Frances Rivis' is widely sold and is a robust form with darker flowers, less suitable for the purpose. Mid spring.

Clematis alpina

CODONOPSIS (Campanulaceae)
A genus of plants that can best be described as scrambling twiners. They are hardly climbers, as the tallest of them only reaches upwards some 150 cm (5 ft). There are several that are traditionally listed among rock garden plants, but most of them have such long stems that they should really be ruled out. Two species, however, are an asset to any rock garden. A cool, leafy spot suits them, especially *C. vincaeflora*. The plants are herbaceous and need protection from slugs when the new shoots are emerging in spring. Propagation is by seed.

C. clematidea. Does not twine, but its 35 cm (14 in) stems thread themselves through small shrubs. The flowers are large, very pale blue bells, beautifully marked in a deeper tone on the insides. Self-seeding. Central Asia. Mid to late summer.

C. vincaeflora. Held by some to be a sub-species of *C. convolvulacea*, a species that is far too large for alpine gardening. However, it is no more than about 35 cm (15 in) high when

scrambling in a shrub, a position in which its wide open, mid-blue flowers show up best. For a cool place. Asia. Mid summer to early autumn.

CONVOLVULUS (Convolvulaceae)
The same genus that plagues agriculture and horticulture with strangling, immensely deep-roots, also contains some great, civilized beauties. Some are tender, others are hardy but need protection from winter wet. All need fast, efficient drainage.

C. boisseri. This is held to be synonymous with *C. nitidus*. Plants under either name are similar to one another, but flower colour varies from the more common white to a pale, shell pink. The small leaves are so silkily hairy as to appear silver-plated. The plant forms a flattish cushion, which can almost disappear beneath the 2 cm (1 in) flowers. Alpine house treatment is best, with precautions being taken to avoid the plant being drawn up out of character. A poor, stony compost should be used. Propagate by summer cuttings. 8 cm (3 in). Spain. Late spring to early summer.

C. cneorum. A shrubby, completely non-invasive plant, perhaps the silkiest and most silver-leafed that can be grown out of doors. As an alpine house plant it is a failure, growing weakly and etiolated. In a very well-drained spot, particularly in a good soil liberally adulterated with tufa dust, it will grow to well over 60 cm (2 ft) across and over 30 cm (1 ft) high. The large, white flowers are flushed with pink. Hardy, even in cold winters, when the drainage is sharp. Tender when it is not. Mediterranean. Late spring to early autumn.

C. sabatius (syn. *C. mauritanicus*). The flowers of this underground creeper are among the most beautiful of any in the garden. They are wide funnels and brilliantly but softly blue. It can be grown for a short while as an alpine house plant, but soon gets out of hand. In the garden it is usually found to be tender away from the south and west coasts (but David Mowbray, of Hinckley, Leicestershire, UK, holder of the Alpine Garden Society's Gold Medal, succeeded almost too well with it in paving in a frost pocket in a cold district). It apparently needs to have its roots under rocks.

Propagate by taking very soft, new, non-flowering shoots in late spring and keep airtight until rooted. Morocco. Late spring to mid autumn.

COPROSMA (Rubiaceae)

Coprosmas are trees and shrubs from Australasia, usually quite large, often tender, but including one New Zealand alpine that is suitable for a peaty spot in the south and west.

C. petriei. This makes a mat of minute, bronzed foliage. The flowers are insignificant, but it is grown for the large, pearly, bluish, translucent berries. To obtain these a male and a female plant must be grown. These may be found under the names 'Don' and 'Lyn' respectively. Propagate by cuttings. 8 cm (3 in).

CORONILLA (Leguminosae)

Coronillas are vetch-like plants and may be annuals, perennials or shrubs. Most are on the tender side and almost all are too large for the rock garden. One, however, is ideal for a hot, sunny pocket.

C. minima. This has fresh, bluish-green, pinnate leaves with small, rounded leaflets. The sweetly fragrant flowers are bright yellow, pea-like, and borne in clusters. A dry, sunny bank in a poorish soil suits it best. It is a subshrub. 10 cm (4 in). S.W. Europe. Late spring to late summer, sometimes much longer.

CORTUSA (Primulaceae)

One species is commonly grown in the woodland fringes of the rock garden. It is usually listed as *C. matthioli*, which, if in honour of Matthioli, should be spelt with a terminal -ii. However, if the intention was to name it as 'the cortusa that is like a stock' (*Matthiola*), then the name should be *C. matthiola*.

C. matthioli. One of the quieter and most charming of the primrose relatives. It has its foliage flat to the ground, consisting of crinkled, hairy, irregularly lobed leaves. The rich, red-purple, funnel- to bell-shaped flowers are held in umbels high above the foliage. A moist, shady, leafy place suits it best. Propagation is by seed. 30 cm (12 in) or more. Mid spring to early summer. Europe and Asia.

CORYDALIS (Papaveraceae; Fumariacea)

A genus containing some highly attractive plants, one of which is among the great beauties of alpine gardening. Their place in botany is odd, as they are classified with poppies but are much more like fumitories, having narrow, tubular flowers with a protruding, terminal lower lip. Some have fibrous roots, while others arise from tubers. Propagation is by seed or division of the tuber. Division is tricky, especially with *C. cashmeriana*, and a growing point must be preserved with every division. When the tuberous species disappear in summer they have not died, but are resting. *C. cashmeriana* does not do this.

C. bulbosa. This is distinct from *C. solida*, in that its tuber is hollow instead of solid. Otherwise they are very similar, each having lobed, grey-green leaves and purple flowers. They like partly shaded, cool places and are decorative at the feet of deciduous shrubs. *C. cava* is really a white form of *C. bulbosa*. 15 cm (6 in). Europe. Late winter to early or mid spring.

C. cashmeriana. This has a small, forked tuber with a ruff of growing points around the top. The foliage is steely blue-green and divided fernily. The horizontal, narrowly tubular flowers are of an electric blue that has no peer unless among the meconopsis. It must have a leafy, peaty, well-drained but moist soil in a cool spot. There must be a total absence of lime. It is hardy, but fails for some gardeners. Possibly a soil, 95% peat and 5% sand, with no loam content at all, might help. 15 cm (6 in). Mid spring to early summer. Himalaya.

C. lutea. An easy, fibrous-rooted plant that seeds itself everywhere when happy, cropping up in tiny crevices and cracks in paving into which it would be impossible to plant. It is not a nuisance, but a ferny delight with golden-yellow flowers. 15 cm (6 in). Alps. Early spring to late autumn.

C. wilsonii. A robust, fibrous-rooted corydalis with superb foliage, more blue than green, and large, bright buttery-yellow flowers. Its fault is that it hates winter wet and is therefore destined to be confined to pots (which it also hates) unless a crevice can be found that can be covered over in winter. 23 cm (9 in). Late spring to mid summer. China.

COTONEASTER (Rosaceae)

A very large genus of berrying shrubs, among which are a few ground-hugging plants that are eminently suitable for the rock garden, paving or steps. They all have small, white stemless flowers in early summer, but it is for their berries in autumn and their habit that they are grown. They are easy in sun and fairly poor, stony soils, and may be propagated from half-ripe cuttings taken in late summer.

C. adpressus. A very dwarf, spreading shrub, making mats of tangled stems, clothed with tiny leaves. The bright red, 6 mm ($\frac{1}{2}$ in) berries are like those of holly. It is deciduous and the leaves turn bright red in autumn. China.

C. congestus. This will grip the contours of a rock or form a neat clump up to 30 cm (1 ft) high if there are no contours for it to follow. Blue-green foliage and red berries. It is evergreen. Himalaya.

C. microphyllus. This can be a little large, but *C.m. cochleatus* is prostrate and neat, while *C.m. thymifolius* is possibly the best of all the dwarf cotoneasters, with narrow, tiny, glistening leaves. Evergreen. China and Himalaya.

CRASPEDIA (Compositae)

A small New Zealand genus, a few of whose species arrive in cultivation from time to time. There seems to be a long-standing confusion between two species, in as much as they tend to be treated as if they were one, and the name of the wrong one is used.

C. uniflora. A green-leaved perennial with woolly hairs only on the margins of the leaves and on the flower stems. It is slightly coarse. Its flower head is just like a snowball on top of a stalk, and it is white, only later showing yellow, not yellow to start with as usually stated — hence its New Zealand name, woolly-head. 30 cm (12 in). Mid summer.

C. incana. This is quite different: the leaves are in definite rosettes and are covered all over with woolly hairs, giving the plant a look of *Stachys olympica* on a smaller scale. The woolly flower stems are much shorter and the flower heads show yellow much sooner. This is the plant that is often called *C. uniflora*, but it is greatly superior and a fine alpine house

plant. It must have protection from winter wet. Late summer.

CYANANTHUS (Campanulaceae)

Although related to campanulas, cyananthus look more like dainty, small-leaved periwinkles. They are highly desirable plants, requiring coolness and a peaty, moisture-retaining, but well-drained soil. They do best in climates such as those of Scotland and western Ireland. Propagation is best done by seed or by spring or summer cuttings. Division is not recommended.

C. lobatus. A prostrate plant with large (over 2.5 cm (1 in) wide) flowers in a variety of shades, from light blue or even white, down to blue-purple. Forms with near-wedgwood blue are great prizes. Mid summer to early autumn. Himalaya.

C. microphyllus. The flowers of this compact plant are clear, mid blue. The leaves are smaller than in the previous species and un-lobed. Plants grown as *C. integer* almost always belong here.

C. sherriffii. Quite a different species, this is a silvery, softly hairy plant with light blue flowers and needs alpine house conditions. It is not a lover of moisture, as it comes from dry slopes, but it still prefers coolness. The putative cross, *C. integer × sherriffii* has been made, but one needs evidence of the identity of the plant grown under the former name if it is not to be assumed to have been *C. microphyllus*.

CYATHODES (Epacridaceae)

A heath-like genus of small plants from New Zealand with whipcord stems and heather-like flowers. Most are tender, but two alpine species can be grown with great care in the rock garden, where they should be protected from severe frosts and summer drought. The alpine house or frame is probably the best environment. Propagation is by cuttings.

C. colensoi. A small, rounded, heather-like plant with tiny, adpressed leaves with conspicuously impressed veins. In most forms they are grey-green, but this is not the usual thing in the wild, where plants with reddish leaves predominate. The flowers are urn-shaped, white, and followed by attractive, conspicuous berries, which may be white, pink or crimson. 30 cm (1 ft). Mid summer.

C. empetrifolia. Equally heath-like, but prostrate, its small, white flowers are fragrant and are followed by white or red berrries. 13 cm (5 in). Mid summer.

CYCLAMEN (Primulaceae)

By choosing from the wide range of hardy cyclamen that are available, it is possible to have plants in flower for most of the year. Other species, unable to thrive in the open garden, make fine displays in the alpine house or frame. Propagation is by seed, sown as soon as it is ripe. All cyclamen require good drainage and a soil that is not sticky. Most prefer part shade and cool conditions and are often at their best at the feet of large rocks. Species recommended for the alpine house may often thrive out of doors as long as the tubers are buried deeply and there is no danger of winter waterlogging.

C. balearicum. A fragrant-flowered species for the alpine house, where it prefers shade. The leaves are pointed, toothed, and patterned with silver. Flowers white, veined pink. Balearic Isles and southern France. Mid spring.

C. cilicium. The leaves are rounded and marked with silver. The long-petalled flowers are pale pink, with deep rose-pink markings at the 'nose' — in fact the centre of the sharply reflexed flower. Turkey. Early to late autumn.

C. coum (syn. *C. orbiculatum*). The names of the putative subspecies, so-called cultivars of varying worth, and the species itself are in such a mess that it is fruitless to discuss them. What can be said is that these are the cyclamen that flower in the dead of winter, are very small and stocky, and have flowers like miniature ships' propellers. (Those with this tendency more pronounced are currently designated as *C. trochopteranthum*.) Their leaves are rounded kidney-shaped, usually very dark green, either plain or patterned with grey. They may flower with or before the leaves. They are extremely hardy, with the exception of one form from Iran. The flowers may be pink, almost red, or white. When happy these cyclamen colonize gently by seed. Mid winter to early spring. The species ranges from Eastern Europe, through Turkey, to Lebanon and beyond.

C. creticum. Small, jagged leaves with cordate bases, sharply pointed. Quite large flowers, white, flushed pink. There is a faint fragrance. Not really hardy, so best in the alpine house. Mid spring. Crete.

C. cyprium. This species has small, dark green leaves with red reverses. The flowers are white, sometimes light pink when young, and have feathered, purple stains at the bases of the petals. Not hardy enough for the open garden, so best in a frame or alpine house. Early to mid autumn.

C. hederifolium. A very easily grown and immensely long-lived plant, eventually making tubers like tea plates. It will grow in any good soil (and quite a lot of poor ones) in a partly shaded, cool place. When happy, it naturalizes itself by seeding. The ivy-shaped leaves are never the same in any two specimens and the delightful marbling of the leaves is infinite in its variation. The flowers are rose pink with a proportion of white seedlings. S. Europe. Late summer to mid autumn.

C. intaminatum. This was grown for many years as *C. cilicium alpinum*. It is very similar to that species, but even more dainty, and has white flowers with an understated veining in grey. For outdoor culture, but best supervised in a trough. Turkey. Early to mid autumn.

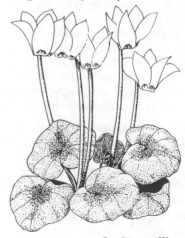

Cyclamen libanoticum

C. libanoticum. A very beautiful, large-flowered species that is too tender for the open garden but happy in the alpine house. The leaves are blue-green above, red beneath. Flowers rose pink. Lebanon. Late winter to early spring.

C. mirabile. This species is very similar to *C. cilicium* and may well turn out to be a form of it. It flowers at the same time and the flowers are similar. The foliage, though, is flushed to a varying extent with red. Turkey.

C. pseudibericum. A striking plant, unique in its colouring, which is magenta-lilac. There is a band of white at the mouth of the flower, above which is a chocolate blotch. Preferably for the alpine house, especially as the flowers are delicately fragrant. Late winter and early spring. Turkey, Asia Minor.

C. purpurascens (syn. *C. europaeum*). This cyclamen is usually misunderstood and is made to suffer drought and heat. It needs coolness and part shade and must have its tubers buried deeply, as much as 30 cm (1 ft) deep is not too far; one of the authors (JK) has found them at well over twice that depth in the eastern Alps. The flowers are sweetly scented, pale pink to rose. Mid summer to early autumn.

C. repandum. A rather neglected species, which has much to offer in shady, woodland conditions. The leaves are rather thin, plain green or slightly patterned in silver, and the flowers are carmine, elegantly shaped, and fragrant. It will naturalize around shrubs as long as it is not subject to late frosts. Mid to late spring. Mediterranean.

CYTISUS (Leguminoseae)
The brooms are easily grown shrubs, often leafless or nearly so, with green, photosynthesizing stems. There are several that are suitable for the rock garden, but care is needed in choosing them, as one or two that have repeatedly been recommended are far too large and really belong in the border. They enjoy full sun and a sandy or gravelly soil. They resent disturbance and cannot be transplanted once established. Propagation is by seed or cuttings.

C. ardoinii. A deciduous, dwarf, arching shrub with small, trifoliate, grey-green leaves and bright golden yellow, pea-shaped flowers. 20 cm (8 in). Alpes Maritimes. Mid to late spring.

C. decumbens. A prostrate, mat-forming shrublet with tiny leaves and bright golden flowers. 15 cm (6 in). Deciduous. Mediterranean. Late spring to early summer.

C. demissus. Another deciduous, mat-forming shrub. This is small enough for a trough and has trifoliate, hairy leaves and yellow flowers that are large for the size of the plant. 8 cm (3 in). Greece. Late spring to early summer.

DAPHNE (Thymelaeaceae)
Some daphnes are too large for the rock garden, but in this large genus of shrubs are many that are dwarf, beautiful in and out of flower, and scented when blooming. They can be tricky to grow; some so much so that they are not easy even in the alpine house. Cultural directions are given for each species. Propagation is also given individually.

D. arbuscula. A dwarf, dense, evergreen shrub with terminal rosettes of narrow leaves which produce large clusters of deep pink, scented flowers, often some dozens to the cluster. Rarely sets seed. Best in a trough, sink or raised bed. Propagation by summer cuttings will give about 50% strike rate. 20 cm (8 in). Czechoslovakia. Mid spring to early summer.

Daphne arbuscula

149

D. blagayana. An almost prostrate, evergreen, dwarf shrub with clusters of scented, tubular, creamy white flowers at the ends of leafy stems. It is excellent in a leafy, shady spot where the soil is rich but stony. The branches should be covered annually with a stony mixture of leafmould to encourage them to root, otherwise the plant becomes leggy and dies out. It does not set seed in cultivation. Propagate by cuttings in summer. May flower any time from early spring to early summer. S.E. Europe.

D. cneorum. Sometimes called the garland flower, this daphne can be either the crowning glory of the rock garden or a complete non-event. The key to its successful cultivation lies in burying the whole plant annually in summer so that only the leafy tips of the branches show. In this way a wide mat of foliage, 60 cm (2 ft) wide or more but only 13 cm (5 in) high, is formed which will cover itself in clusters of rose pink, deliciously scented flowers. Cuttings taken in summer are not difficult. Europe. Mid to late spring. *D.c.* 'Eximia' is more vigorous than the species and has larger flowers. *D.c* 'Variegata' has dull yellow edges to the leaves. It is not a strong-growing plant.

D. collina. A dense, evergreen, rounded shrub with leathery, oval leaves and terminal clusters of highly scented, deep-rose flowers. It will succeed in full sun but prefers a cool root run. Propagate by summer cuttings. 40 cm (16 in). Mid to late spring.

D. genkwa. A deciduous, dwarf daphne with slender branches and lateral clusters of purplish-lilac, scented flowers. The plant is silky and has small leaves. For careful cultivation in the alpine house. It is not easy and tends to be short-lived away from places with hot summers. Suggestions that it requires lime-free soil are probably erroneous; a moisture-retaining soil made stony with limestone seems to meet with most success. Propagation can be effected by late summer cuttings under mist; they must not be moved until the following spring, even if they root quickly. Root cuttings taken in mid winter are often successful as well. *D. genkwa* can also be grafted onto *D. mezereum*.

D. jasminea. There are at least two and probably three forms of this twiggy shrub, ranging from a prostrate mat to upright bushes from 20 cm (8 in) to 45 cm (18 in) in height. It needs full sun and a very gritty, well-drained soil and is best in the alpine house, as non-Mediterranean winters do not suit it. The foliage is grey-green, sparser than in many daphnes, and the sweetly scented flowers are white. In the prostrate form of the species the flowers are pinkish at first. Potting-on should be done with care, as it hates disturbance. Propagation by cuttings is tricky but perfectly possible, otherwise it may be grafted onto *D. mezereum*. Mid to late spring. Greece.

D × napolitana. Note the spelling of this species; 'neapolitana' is incorrect. It is an evergreen, dense bush with narrow leaves and pink-purple flowers in axillary and terminal clusters. Easily grown in any good rock garden soil. It is easy from late summer cuttings. 60 cm (2 ft). Late spring.

D. oleoides. A compact, dense shrub with leathery, grey-green foliage and creamy, scented flowers in terminal heads that are followed by unusual orange berries. For a well-drained soil in full sun. 45 cm (18 in). Europe and W. Asia.

D. petraea. This is one of the greatest treasures in alpine gardening. It is a prostrate or slightly domed, intensely dwarf shrub, with short, gnarled branches and tiny leaves. When well grown, which is very rare, it covers itself with clusters of flowers in rich, rose pink. The power and clean sweetness of the scent has to be experienced; it cannot be described. *D.p.* 'Grandiflora' is the form usually grown. It must have alpine house treatment, preferably in a compost well laden with limestone chippings. On its own roots from cuttings it is an invalid; plants with long lives have usually been grafted onto *D. mezereum*. About 8 cm (3 in). Cima Tombea in Italy. Mid spring to early summer.

D. retusa. An almost ball-shaped, deep green bush, with leathery leaves. Terminal clusters of rose-purple flowers are followed by red berries in some years. For a well-drained, sunny spot with a cool root run. Sow seed as soon as ripe or take half-ripe cuttings in summer which root very easily. 60 cm (2 ft). Himalaya and China. Mid to late spring.

D. tangutica. A similar but much larger species than the above, and with flatter leaves and a more open habit. China. Mid to late spring.

DELOSPERMA (Aizoaceae)
A genus into which some species, hitherto regarded as mesembryanthemums, have been placed.

D. nubigena (syn. *Mesembryanthemum* species from Basutoland). This is a most surprisingly hardy plant, which tolerates severe winter conditions, including wind, as long as it is in a crevice in a wall or other dry place. It makes cushions of bright green, succulent, evergreen leaves and has yellow, starry flowers in summer. It is markedly salt-tolerant. 2.5 cm (1 in). Summer.

DELPHINIUM (Ranunculaceae)
Alpine delphiniums are not the least like the stately border plants we know so well. Most are dwarf, with the flowers well apart from one another, some on quite long stalks. They are easily grown in full sun. Seed should be sown as soon as ripe.

D. brunonianum. This has basal rosettes of foliage and flower stems carrying very open racemes of large larkspur flowers in soft, smoky, purplish blue. 30 cm (12 in). Mid summer. Afghanistan.

D. chinense. Delicate, bright blue flowers seem to float individually in the air above neat foliage. 30 cm (12 in). Early to late summer. China.

D. muscosum. This plant is entirely different to other delphiniums in gardens. It is only about 13 cm (5 in) high and entirely covered in silky wool, including the big, blue, widely open flowers. Mid to late summer. Himalaya.

D. nudicaule. Not quite such an easy plant, this is better in the alpine house, where its flowers, brilliant in red and yellow, can be appreciated fully and where it is more likely to overwinter. There is a pure yellow form. 30 cm (12 in). N. America.

Delphinium nudicaule

DIANTHUS (Caryophyllaceae)
The pinks, carnations and sweet williams are all included in this large genus. There are a great many hybrids, and among them are some that are suitable for the rock garden environment. However, while such dwarf dianthus as 'Little Jock' and 'La Bourboule' are ideal for troughs and small rock gardens, on the whole the species appear more in keeping than most of the hybrids. Sunny places in good, gritty soils are best for dianthus. Some say that lime is essential; it is not, but the plants may be longer-lived in calcareous soils. Propagation, either by seed or cuttings, is simple.

D. alpinus. A superb, dwarf dianthus with neat mats of green (never grey-green) foliage and short stems carrying large, 2.5 cm (1 in) flowers. These may be rose pink, light pink, or

Dianthus alpinus

white, and they display a central ring of darker spots. 'Joan's Blood' is distinct, with bronzed foliage and deep, blood-red flowers with centres that are almost black. 8–10 cm (3–4 in) tall. Early to late summer. European Alps.

D. × arvernensis. A naturally occurring hybrid, possibly between *D. monspessulanus* and *D. sylvaticus*. It makes neat cushions of fine grey leaves and its flowers are rose pink. 8 cm (3 in). Mid summer. Auvergne.

D. × calalpinus. A beautiful plant, intermediate between its parents, *D. alpinus* and *D. callizonus*. 10 cm (4 in). Mid to late summer.

D. callizonus. A species that is similar to *D. alpinus*, but the flowers are even larger and have a ground colour of lavender-carmine. A central zone of rosy purple is spotted to a varying degree with white. (10 cm (4 in). Mid to late summer. Carpathians.

D. deltoides. The maiden pink is universally found seeding itself about happily in rock gardens and sometimes into nearby paths. It is not a nuisance, but a decorative species,

making low clumps of grassy foliage, over which masses of small flowers hover on wiry stems. Named forms such as 'Steriker', 'Broughty Blaze', 'Flashing Lights', and so on, have mostly become diluted with their seedlings being distributed under their names. 20 cm (8 in). Europe. Early to late summer.

D. erinaceus. Of all the dwarf dianthus, this hedgehog-like plant demands the most sun and the late winter wet. It can be reluctant to flower, but when it does, it has small, pink flowers on short stems above the tight cushion of intensely prickly leaves. 5 cm (2 in). Mid summer. Turkey.

D. glacialis. Like a smaller version of *D. alpinus*, with similarly dark green leaves. The flowers are rose pink and held on very short stems. It is said to be a lime-hater, but this is not usually borne out in practice. *D. freynii*, which has grey-green leaves may well be a form of this species, and so may the Bulgarian *D. microlepis*. All three are ideal for troughs. 5 cm (2 in). Mid to late summer. E. Alps.

D. gratianopolitanus. This name supersedes *D. caesius*. The Cheddar pink thus gives way to the Grenoble pink. Care should be exercised when choosing this plant, as it is very variable and many forms are too large or coarse for the alpine garden. The most suitable ones are pink, bearded at the bases of the petals and notched at the apices, with grey foliage and no more than 15 cm (6 in) tall. Mid to late summer. Europe.

D. monspessulanus. Worthy of inclusion because of its fine fragrance and attractively fringed petals. Pink, white or rose red. 30 cm (12 in). Alps. Mid to late summer. *D. sternbergii* is *D. m.* subsp. *sternbergii*; it is more compact and has flowers of a rich, deep, rosy red. Occurs eastward of *D. monspessulanus* in Austria and Yugoslavia.

D. myrtinervius. In effect an extremely compact *D. deltoides*, making a hard cushion of foliage and having many small, bright pink flowers on short stems. If the soil is rich it grows out of character. 10 cm (4 in). Mid to late summer. Balkans.

D. pavonius (syn. *D. neglectus*). A small plant with tufts of short, narrow, green leaves and large, matt pink flowers with characteristic buff reverses on short stems. It is said to demand lime-free soil, but this is not so. 10 cm (4 in). Early to mid summer. S. Europe.

D. subacaulis. A trough or sink plant, with dense, armeria-like cushions of stiff leaves and almost stemless, pale pink, rounded flowers. Alpes Maritimes and Pyrenees.

DIASCIA (Scrophulariaceae)
Diascias were almost unknown to gardeners until the 1970s, since when several species, most of them border plants of great value, have been introduced. There is one species and a hybrid that are suitable for the rock garden. Soft cuttings should be pinched out even before rooting takes place, otherwise they become grossly elongated.

D. cordata. A sprawling, mat-forming perennial with wiry stems, small leaves, and generously produced, nemesia-like flowers in loose heads. They are deep rose pink and each has two horn-like spurs at the back of the flower, while the front is open, hooded, and with a wide, deep lower lip. 20 cm (8 in). Early summer to early autumn. South Africa.

D. 'Ruby Field'. Raised by one of the co-authors of this book (JK) in the early 1970s. It is a deliberate hybrid between the above species and the annual (tender perennial) *D. barberae*. It is a little taller than *D. cordata* and has larger flowers that have taken on some of the salmon colouring of *D. barberae*, but the hardiness of the other parent has been retained. The plant is named for Ruby Field, who devoted her life to the care of homeless children. Early summer to mid autumn.

DICENTRA (Papaveraceae)
Most of the bleeding hearts are too large for the rock garden, but two are good alpine plants, one is a gem if it can be grown, and hybrids of it are among the most sought after plants of all. Dicentras are herbaceous perennials that grow from fleshy rootstocks.

D. cucullaria. Has the typically ferny foliage of smaller dicentras, and arching stems carrying hanging, creamy-white, locket-like flowers which give rise to the name Dutchman's breeches because of trouser-like spurs. For a cool place. 15 cm (6 in). USA. Mid to late spring.

D. eximia. A taller plant with less fine, blue green foliage and red-purple flowers with less prominent spurs. For a gritty, cool spot. 20 cm (8 in). USA.

D. peregrina. A difficult, temperamental beauty with tufts of blue-grey, tiny foliage and relatively large, pink lockets. It needs a leafy, gritty soil in a cool part of the alpine house. Dr Rokujo of Tokyo University raised a range of hybrids (Rokujo Hybrids) from *D. peregrina*. They are worth every effort to obtain and should be treated like their parent.

DIONYSIA (Primulaceae)
Dionysias are not for the beginner. They are mainly difficult alpine house cushion plants, sometimes extremely tricky to grow and only capable of being propagated by highly experienced, sensitive growers. Damp, however slight, is usually fatal; otherwise they are hardy. However, their astonishing beauty makes this all far more than just worthwhile.

Apart from *D. aretioides*, which still demands care and the alpine house, dionysias should be grown in double clay pots. The space between the inner and the outer pot should be filled with pure sand and this only should be watered. The compost in the inner pot should be extremely gritty and there should be no loam or very little present. Non-absorbent rocks should be placed under the skirt of the foliage.

Propagation may be carried out by removing the young rosettes as they develop on the parent ones. They are sometimes as little as 2 mm ($\frac{1}{16}$ in) across. They are then placed in a propagator in pure sand that has just been watered. This sand must never be watered again, even though it will take some weeks for the cuttings to root. The propagator is then placed at the foot of a north-facing wall in the open. It should be the type with ventilators in the top. These are opened slightly and pieces of slate or other small, flat stones placed on top of them. Potting-up must be done with exquisite care, as any bruising or root damage is fatal. Strike rates of 100% have been achieved with such extremely difficult species as *D. michauxii*.

There are some 40 species of dionysia. Only a few are mentioned here, and the coarser, primula-like, non-cushion-forming ones are omitted altogether.

D. aretioides. Quickly makes large, symmetrical, soft cushions of relatively large, velvety rosettes. Good forms, such as 'Paul Furse', 'Phyllis Carter' and 'Gravetye' disappear in mid to late spring under the closely packed, almost stemless, primula-like, yellow flowers. It can be grown on a lump of tufa. Mid to late spring. Iran.

D. bryoides. A difficult species, making extremely compact cushions of tiny rosettes. The flowers are stemless, long-tubed and lilac pink. Early to mid spring. Iran.

D. curviflora. This species varies in its willingness to flower. Early introductions were comparatively easy to grow but meagre with their flowers; later ones are not quite so easy but much more free-flowering. The cushion is extremely dense, smooth and firm, grey-green. The flowers are stemless, lilac-pink with a whitish yellow eye. Early to mid spring. Iran.

D. michauxii. A cushion-forming species which, although compact and tight, is very softly textured. The long-tubed, yellow flowers are large for the size of the rosettes. It detests free water; its wild haunts are on arid cliffs where none exists. It is intensely difficult and often dies after repotting. Nevertheless, fine specimens can be seen on show benches. Mid spring. Iran.

D. tapetodes. Minute rosettes, sometimes mealy, combine to form a flat cushion, almost a mat. It is very slow growing. The flowers are long-tubed and yellow. Not as difficult as some, but there are several forms in cultivation. Early to late spring. Afghanistan.

Among other dionysias in cultivation are *D. archibaldii* (flowers almost purple; occurs in the roofs of caves in Iran), *D. freitagii* (flowers violet, leaves have raised veins, Afghanistan), and *D. lamingtonii* (dense, grey cushions, yellow flowers, Iran).

DODECATHEON (Primulaceae)
A genus of plants from North America that enjoy the same conditions as the damp-loving primulas. In appearance they are something like primulas with long stems, at the tops of which are the flowers of cyclamen.

D. clevelandii. Rosettes of pale green leaves and taller than average stems bearing umbels of red-purple flowers with yellow mouths. 35 cm (14 in). Late spring–early summer.

D. dentatum has unusually shaped leaves with cordate bases and striking white flowers. 25 cm (10 in).

D. hendersonii. A neat plant with violet flowers. 30 cm (12 in).

D. meadia. The best-known dodecatheon but also probably the coarsest. With leaves up to 15 cm (6 in) long and flower stems up to 60 cm (2 ft) tall, it is not helped by having flowers that are often a jarring shade of magenta.

D. pulchellum. A much more fitting species, having neat foliage and much shorter stems that bear umbels of lilac flowers, each with a purple ring near the mouth. 'Red Wings' is a lovely shade of crimson, 30 cm (12 in) tall.

DOUGLASIA (Primulaceae)
These are North American alpines, related very closely to *Androsace*. The flowers are almost always some shade of pink, and the cushions are firm and neat, but not quite as much so as in the aretian androsaces. Propagation is by seed. The European *Vitaliana primuliflora* is the erstwhile *Douglasia vitaliana*.

D. dentata is a somewhat loose plant, making tufts of stems, rather than cushions. It is, however, only about 2.5 cm (1 in) tall. The clusters of flowers are violet-pink. Alpine house or a trough. Late spring.

D. laevigata is variable, but the best forms make tight domes of small rosettes. The flowers are in heads, almost stemless, rose-red. The average number of flowers per head varies considerably from plant to plant. For alpine house, trough, or a very well-drained place in a scree with winter protection. Mid to late summer.

D. montana is not an easy plant to grow and needs the comfort of the alpine house. Its tiny foliage makes a green mat, which becomes almost hidden by stemless flowers of light rose pink. Late spring.

DRABA (Cruciferae)
Drabas vary from weedy, insignificant plants to aristocratic denizens of the alpine house. The genus occurs in the most inhospitable places, from Spitzbergen and Greenland to the high Caucasus. Those with cushion-forming tendencies are the most desirable. Propagation is by seed. None of the species mentioned is more than 5–8 cm (2–3 in) high.

D. acaulis. A silkily hairy plant, making tight cushions of closely packed, small rosettes. The yellow flowers are in heads held closely over the foliage. A gritty, well drained compost in the alpine house. Mid spring. Cilician Taurus.

D. aizoides. Widely spread in Europe, including the British Isles. This is a species for the scree or well-drained place among rocks and consists of cushiony tufts of rosettes of bristly leaves. It has yellow flowers of a somewhat piercing shade. Mid to late spring.

D. bryoides (syn. *D. rigida bryoides*). Another densely cushiony plant, with very small, green leaves and heads of yellow flowers on short stems. The form *imbricata* is usually grown, as it is even more compact. Alpine house or frame. Mid spring. Caucasus.

D. dedeana. Yet another densely cushioned species, this time with white flowers on stems up to 5 cm (2 in) long. Scree or frame. Mid spring. Pyrenees.

D. mollissima. One of the most perfectly domed of all cushion plants, this can be grown to quite a considerable size, filling a pot 23 cm (9 in) in diameter, but it is not easy and can die off in patches. It is made up of grey-green, slightly woolly rosettes and has many heads of yellow flowers on fuse-wire stems. These must be removed in their entirety after the seed has been collected. Alpine house. Mid to late spring. Caucasus.

D. polytricha. Requires similar treatment to the last species, but is slightly easier to grow to a good size. The rosettes are larger and even more woolly but tend to die off individually. Larger flowers on wiry stems. Early to mid spring. Armenia.

DRYAS (Rosaceae)
Ground-hugging subshrubs with a northern circumpolar distribution, found from mountain heights to sea-level tundra. Dryas are reluctant to flower in good soils but give a superb display at the edges of gravel drives and other poor places. The flowers turn to follow the sun. Propagation is by half-ripe cuttings in summer or by detaching rooted stems in spring.

D. drummondii. An American species, similar to *D. octopetala* except for its yellow flowers which are never widely open and are slightly pendent. Mid to late summer.

D. octopetala. Known in Britain as mountain avens. The stems make tough mats, clothed in leaves like those of a miniature oak. Quite large, white flowers are held on upright stems. *D. o* 'Minor' is much smaller and ideal for the smallest rock garden. 15 cm (6 in). Late spring to late summer. *D.o. integrifolia* is hardly different. The name *Dryas octopetala octopetala integrifolia*, which appears in lists, is nonsense.

D. × suendermannii is a naturally occurring hybrid between the two species above. In the form usually grown, the flowers are white, yellow in bud, slightly pendent, and quite fully open.

EDRAIANTHUS (Campanulaceae)
Edraianthus and *Wahlenbergia* are genera related to *Campanula*. The chief difference between them is that the former has its flowers in clusters, while the latter has single flowers. There is considerable confusion between them. Edraianthus are plants for gritty soils in sun. Propagation is easy from cuttings taken in summer; seeds will also germinate well when available.

E. caudatus (syn. *E. dalmaticus*). Dense tufts of narrow, greyish-green leaves and flowers of a similar colouring to *E. graminifolius*, but narrower. Later flowering; mid to late summer. Yugoslavia.

E. graminifolius. A small plant, consisting of tufts of grassy, slightly bristly leaves. The dark blue, almost purple bells are held just above the foliage. The white form of this plant is rare and highly desirable. 10 cm (4 in). Late spring to mid summer. Balkans.

E. pumilio. A treasure for the scree in summer, with beautiful, small tufts of short, narrow, silvered leaves and almost stemless clusters of violet-blue flowers almost hiding the plant. 5–8 cm (2–3 in). Yugoslavia. Mid to late summer.

Edraianthus pumilio

EMPETRUM (Empetraceae)
Although this genus is not in Ericaceae, it is often thought to be. There is only one species that is at all widely grown.

E. nigrum. A small, evergreen, creeping shrub, rather heath-like, familiar to walkers on moors as the crowberry. In a moist, peaty spot it will thrive, bear its small pink flowers and, if a hermaphrodite form is found, berry. The fruit are black. 'Lucia' has golden foliage and reddish stems and is a most attractive plant all year round. 15 cm (6 in). Late spring to early summer. Northern latitudes.

EPIGAEA (Ericaceae)
An aristocratic, tricky but choice genus, of which two species are desirable and another is a pearl beyond price. Cool, peaty conditions are essential.

E. asiatica. This species is quite easy. It is a prostrate shrub with leathery leaves and racemes of scented, bell-shaped flowers, usually pink, but sometimes white. Not usually much more than 10 cm (4 in). Mid spring. Japan.

E. gaultherioides (syn. *Orphanidesia gaultherioides*). This almost exotic plant demands unfailing coolness and a good, peaty, moist, well-drained soil. It is not unlike the other species apart from its flowers, which are wide open, fully 2.5 cm (1 in) across, pale rose, and fragrant. Not fully hardy. Turkey. Early to mid spring.

E. repens. Known as the ground laurel or trailing arbutus. The leaves are shiny and quite large, and the clusters of funnel-shaped, pink or white flowers are scented. Late spring. North America.

EPILOBIUM (Anagraceae)
Alpine epilobiums have none of the noxiously invasive habits of the weeds that plague our gardens. They are easy plants, liking sun, and have the advantage of flowering late. Propagate by seed or division.

E. chlorifolium kaikourense. Perhaps once and for all the *nomen nudum*, *Epilobium kaikoense* can be dismissed and its claim to a place in the Japanese flora rebutted. This is a dwarf form of the species (but see *E. glabellum* below), which at 30 cm (12 in) tall is more than twice the height, and comes from the Kaikoura range of mountains in the Marlborough area of the South Island of New Zealand. Its flowers are trumpet-shaped, light pink, and borne on 13 cm (5 in) stems over glossy foliage. Mid summer to early autumn.

E. dodonaei. Spreads to make a wide clump of downy-leaved stems carrying large, rose pink flowers in lax racemes. Needs a gravelly or sandy, poorish soil to stay in character, otherwise it becomes coarse and lanky. 25 cm (10 in). Mid to late summer. Europe.

E. glabellum. This is not unlike *E. chlori-folium kaikourense*, but has yellowish-cream flowers. There is a form, 'Sulfureum', in which they are truly light yellow. This is a very variable species in the wild and sometimes has pink flowers. It would not be all that surprising if *E.c. kaikourense* turned out to belong here after all. 15 cm (6 in). Mid summer to early autumn. New Zealand.

ERIGERON (Compositae)

Erigerons are easily grown plants with daisy-like flowers, the ray florets of which are almost always in some shade of purple or pink (the yellow-flowered *E. aureus* is now considered to be *Haplopappus brandegeei*, see p. 165). The disc florets are always yellow. They are best in sun and a stony soil. Propagate by division in spring.

E. alpinus. Mauve flowers over hairy, grey green leaves. 15 cm (6 in). Northern Europe. Mid to late summer.

E. aurantiacus. Unusually, this has bright orange flowers. It can only be accommodated in larger rock gardens, as it is a little tall and coarse. 30 cm (12 in). Asia. Mid to late summer.

E. karvinskyanus (syn. *E. mucronatus*). Not a plant for the rock garden, but for paved areas and courtyards where there are nooks and crannies into which it can seed itself. It is a neat, dwarf plant, with a succession of pink flowers the size of the common daisy over a very long season. 10 cm (4 in). Late spring to mid autumn. North America.

ERINACEA (Leguminosae)

E. anthyllis. An intensely spiny, rigid, domed, dwarf bush with grey-green branchlets that have a few, small leaves that drop after the spring. Clusters of flowers, violet blue in the best forms, sit close to the branches. It is a fine plant, capable of being grown in a sunny scree, preferably calcareous, but generally best in the alpine house in winter and moved to an open, sunny frame in summer. Propagation is by seed when available. 25 cm (10 in). Late spring to early summer. Spain and North Africa.

ERINUS (Scrophulariaceae)

A mostly South African genus. Its one European species is grown in rock gardens, where it seeds freely. This characteristic can be put to good use by encouraging seeds to germinate in the cracks in old stone walls, buildings, etc.

E. alpinus. A tiny plant with pads of minute, toothed leaves and two-lipped flowers in rosy mauve. It flowers very freely. The best forms, which come true from seed, are 'Mrs. Chas. Boyle', pink, and the crimson 'Dr Hanele'. There is also a white form. 5 cm (2 in). Late spring to mid summer. Europe.

Erinus alpinus

ERITRICHIUM (Boraginaceae)

E. nanum. Perhaps of all alpines plants this is the ultimate challenge. It has an almost mytho-logical quality that makes it so, even though certain *Raoulia* and *Dionysia* species are even more difficult. As seen in the European Alps, particularly against the basaltic rock on the Bindelweg in the Dolomites, it is a small cushion, as if made of blue-green, scarified velvet, clinging, limpet-like to the rock. The stemless flowers, like crystalline forget-me-nots are of a blue that is uniquely, almost shockingly pure.

In cultivation a plant 2.5 cm (1 in) across is an achievement. However, its flowers are seldom stemless and never display more than a shadow of their true colour. The best method seems to be to grow it in the double pot system (*c.f. Dionysia*) in the alpine house, although Reginald Kaye grew and flowered a plant on its side in a large piece of tufa in a sink. Raising it from seed is virtually the only possible method of obtaining plants. If it flowers it will be sometime in spring.

E. howardii, E. elongatum, E. argenteum. North American analogues of *E. nanum* and showing only slight differences (for example *E. elongatum* has flower stems of 5–8 cm [2–3 in] and the other two have flowers that are slightly smaller than their European relatives). However, all three species are a little easier to grow.

ERODIUM (Geraniaceae)

Erodiums are closely related to geraniums but usually have leaves divided or lobed along the midrib, rather than palmately from a central point. The formation of the seed vessel is different, and in general erodiums are smaller plants altogether. They like sunny, gritty, warm places with good drainage. Propagate by seed or root cuttings.

E. chrysanthum. A species that is unusual in having yellow flowers and separate male and female plants. The low, neat foliage is finely divided and very silvery. 15 cm (6 in). Late spring to early summer. Greece.

E. corsicum. Softly downy, greyish, scalloped leaves and sessile, pink flowers with deeper veining look delightful in a sunny crevice or growing in a trough. Resentful of excessive winter wet. A selected rosy red form, 'Rubrum' is worth seeking out. 8 cm (3 in). Mid summer. Corsica and Sardinia.

E. guttatum. Quite a large plant in rock gardening terms, but it is worth allowing for its 60–90 cm (2–3 ft) of width. It has toothed leaves and a long-lasting mass of white flowers,

each with the two upper petals darkly and graphically blotched. 15 cm (6 in). S.W. Europe. Early summer to early autumn.

E. reichardii (syn. *E. chamaedryoides*). A perfect plant for a choice, sunny spot in a scree, trough or sink. It makes a pad of neat, small, green leaves, studded with stemless, deep rose flowers with darker veins in the more usually seen forms. Others are white with pink veins and there is a semi-double. Less than 2.5 cm (1 in). Early to late summer. Majorca.

ERYSIMUM (Cruciferae)

There are just as few wallflowers that are rock garden plants. Among the many annuals and biennials is a handful of short-lived, dwarf perennials that cheerfully take over odd chinks between rocks where nothing could be planted.

E. alpinum. A neat, dwarf wallflower with tight clusters of sulphur-yellow flowers with a pleasant scent. 'Moonlight' has flowers of a softer yellow. 15 cm (6 in). Late spring to early summer. Scandinavia.

E. cheiri. The common wallflower is represented in rock gardening by 'Harpur Crewe', a dwarf from of 25 cm (10 in) or so with sweetly scented, double flowers.

E. capitatum. Highly desirable because of its abundance of flowers, which are light gold. It has the habit of a gnarled, dwarf shrub. 25 cm (10 in). Oregon. Late spring to mid summer.

EUNOMIA (Cruciferae)

A genus of Turkish alpines, containing only two species. It is sometimes included in *Aethionema*.

E. oppositifolia. A greyish-leaved shrub with a slightly succulent appearance, more lax and inclined to flop than the aethionemas. The leaves are rounded and the heads of light pink flowers elongate as their season progresses. Not reliably hardy and often grown in a frame for that reason. Scarce. 13 cm (5 in). Mid to late summer. Turkey.

EURYOPS (Compositae)

The South African members of this genus that come from higher elevations are becoming better known in gardens. The species listed below has been recognized as a hardy rock plant for many years. It should be grown in sun and a gritty soil. Propagate by cuttings.

E. acraeus (syn. *E. evansii*). The synonym is misleading, as *E. evansii* is a totally different, taller species; however, the two are still sometimes confused in catalogues. *E. acraeus* is an intensely white-silver, domed bush, with terminal tufts of waxy, mealy, narrow leaves and bright gold daisy flowers that stand out beautifully against the foliage. Hardy in a well-drained place. Cut right back after a few years to allow suckers to take over and renew what would otherwise become straggly. 30 cm (12 in). Late spring to early summer. Drakensberg Mountains of Natal.

FRANKENIA (Frankeniaceae)
A little-known genus of heath-like plants that can be found all over the northern hemisphere, especially in warmer latitudes. A light soil and sun suits them and, usefully, they are salt-tolerant.

F. laevis. Native to Europe, including Britain. It is a neat, prostrate, carpeting plant with wiry stems and small, pink flowers. Mid to late summer.

F. thymifolia. This is a little taller, but still mat forming. It has attractive, grey foliage and countless clusters of tiny, pink flowers. 7 cm (3 in). Mid to late summer. Spain and Morocco.

FRITILLARIA (Liliaceae)
Although dwarf bulbs constitute such a large subject that their general inclusion in this book would be impractical, fritillaries are so much a part of the alpine specialist's flora that they cannot be left out. However, only a few of the smaller species are mentioned. Propagation is by seed or bulblets. All the species flower some time in the spring.

F. alburyana. Very short-stemmed and dwarf, this species, only discovered in 1966, has wide open flowers of cherry pink with slight chequering. It needs alpine house or frame culture in cool conditions with absence of wet but also freedom from drought. Turkey.

Fritillaria alburyana

F. armena. A variable, dwarf fritillary, usually with bell-shaped, slightly pendent flowers, dark plum-purple with a grey bloom, yellowish or reddish inside. Treatment as for *F. alburyana*. 15 cm (6 in). Caucasus.

F. davisii. Dwarf, with grey foliage and wide bell-shaped flowers of deep chocolate brown, chequered. Alpine house or frame. 15 cm (6 in). Greece.

F. graeca thessalica. A vigorous form of the species and the one most often seen in gardens. Wide bells, brown with a green stripe down the middle of each segment. Slightly chequered. Alpine house, perferably in a limestone compost and with a little shade. 20 cm (8 in). Greece.

F. michailowskyi. Becoming quite readily available since its introduction in 1965. Grey foliage and several flowers to a stem. They are pendent, bell-shaped, and their colouring is arresting and unique. Each flower is reddish purple with a grey bloom, and the upper third

159

is bright golden yellow. Alpine house or frame, but has also been seen successfully growing in a shallow trough. 15 cm (6 in). Turkey.

F. pudica. Perhaps the best of the more tricky, dwarf fritillaries for the inexperienced to try. It has conical, golden flowers and erect, grassy foliage. Best in the alpine house and increases rapidly. 15 cm (6 in). West coast of N. America.

F. roderickii (syn. *F. greyana*). Another American species and also introduced in the 1960s. This has two or three flowers to a stem, pendent, greenish brown, becoming white at the mouth. Alpine house. 15 cm (6 in). California.

There are many more fritillaries; some are more difficult to obtain and grow than the above, while others are plants for the open border or woodland. Those selected represent a challenge and an introduction to the immensely fascinating world of alpine bulbs.

GAULTHERIA (Ericaceae)

Gaultherias are evergreen shrubs, related to *Vaccinium* and enjoying the same peaty, acid, shady conditions. The smaller ones are ideal in the company of dwarf rhododendrons. The flowers are somewhat heather-like, urn- or bell-shaped, and are often followed by attractive berries. Propagate by means of cuttings or the removal of rooted branches.

G. adenothrix. A prostrate, tangled mat of twiggy branches and small, leathery leaves. The flowers are white with a pink tinge and are followed by comparatively large, dull red berries. 15 cm (6 in). Early summer. Japan.

G. cuneata. A ground-covering but bushy plant, rooting as it goes, with leathery leaves and white flowers and fruit. 30 cm (12 in). Early summer. China.

G. humifusa. A dwarf, creeping plant with bell-shaped flowers that are white, tinged with pink. Bright red fruits. 5 cm (2 in). Early summer. British Columbia.

G. miqueliana. A bushy plant, but with a spread three times its height. It has leathery, bright green leaves, bell-shaped, white flowers,

and white fruits with a pink tinge. 30 cm (12 in). Early to mid summer. Japan.

G. nummularioides. Another small, creeping plant, but variable. It has oval leaves, white or pink flowers, and the fruits are almost black. The forms *G.n. elliptica* and *G.n. minor* are even smaller and are sometimes available. The whole plant is hairy, not leathery. 5–10 cm (2–4 in). Early summer. Himalaya.

G. procumbens. An easily grown plant which, in peaty conditions, spreads by thrusting its branches shallowly underground, where they root. The leaves are shiny and dark green. The flowers are white with a pink flush, and the berries are bright red. 15 cm (6 in). Mid to late summer. N. America.

GENISTA (Leguminosae)

Genistas are part of the group of plants loosely referred to as brooms (others are in the genus *Cytisus*). There are several small, prostrate species that are ideal rock-garden plants. They are sometimes spiny, often leafless or nearly so, usually yellow flowered, and prefer sunny spots among rocks and good drainage. Propagation is by cuttings or seed.

G. delphinensis. A subspecies of *G. sagittalis*. It is much smaller and has its flowers in twos and threes, rather than many-flowered racemes. 5 cm (2 in). Mid to late summer. Pyrenees.

G. humifusa. In the catalogues this is probably a small, prostrate form of the dyers' greenweed, *G. tinctoria*, which is too coarse for the rock garden. It has downy branches and heads of small, yellow flowers. 13 cm (5 in). Early to late summer. Spain.

G. januensis. This is a very variable species. Some forms are prostrate; others are bushy shrubs, but all are small. The stems tend to arch, and carry single, bright yellow flowers. Said to prefer calcareous soils. 8–20 cm (3–8 in). E. Europe. Mid to late summer.

G. lydia. Not one of the smallest, but is a lovely sight in a larger rock garden or spilling its spreading branches over a wall. Short clusters of bright golden flowers. 60 cm (2 ft). Balkans. Late spring to early summer.

Iris lutescens is an American species. Despite its name – meaning yellow – both yellow and blue forms are found, often growing together in the same population.

Right: Gentians to many people epitomize mountain flora. *Gentiana aucaulis* is not always the easiest to grow but it is one of the most delightful and well worth attempting.

Below: *Linaria alpina* is one of the easiest, and yet one of the prettiest alpines to grow in the rock garden. Scatter a few seeds and it will always be with you.

Left: Dwarf narcissus are very popular with alpine growers, both in the open and under glass. This is *Narcissus triandrus*, growing in the wild.

Above: The evening primroses are a large genus with several suitable for the rock garden. The pink *Oenothera speciosa* is not an invasive plant in spite of the great sheets of it seen here in southern Texas.

Left: Individual flowers of *Oenothera speciosa* have a long and valuable season in the rock garden.

Below left: *Onosma albo-roseum* looks best tumbling over rocks or the edge of a raised bed. Its curious tubular flowers are quite distinctive.

Below: *Phlox* 'Chattahoochee' has a long flowering season and prefers a cool, humus-rich root-run to produce its best.

There are several phyllodoces suitable for the peat garden or alpine house. *P. breweri* is not one of the easiest to grow and will fare better under cover.

G. sagittalis. A prostrate, thornless, mat-forming plant with winged branches. The wings are green and narrowed at the nodes, appearing like adpressed leaves. The flowers are bright yellow and borne in dense clusters. Easy in sunny spot. 15 cm (6 in). Late spring to mid summer. Central Europe.

G. sylvestris (syn. *G. dalmatica*). A small, dense, wide bush with open spikes of yellow flowers. 15 cm (6 in). Early to mid summer. Dalmatia.

GENTIANA (Gentianaceae)

The gentians are among the great, aristocratic, classic alpine plants. They exhibit heart-stopping beauty in many different ways, but it is their flowers that attract our attention. They may be star-shaped or trumpets, and the typical colour is blue in Asia and Europe, white in New Zealand, and scarlet in the equatorial Andes. It is only possible to give a selection here.

Gentiana acaulis. This is a group name as far as garden gentians are concerned, involving two or three species and several geographical forms. The usual plant has a flat rosette of stubby leaves, above which extraordinarily large, almost stemless, vivid blue trumpets are borne. They may be more or less greenish or whitish in the throat and more or less speckled. The cultivation of this plant is not difficult, but it is found by many people to be difficult to flower. To others it presents no problem. All kinds of recipes, some sensible, others mumbo-jumbo, have been suggested to induce this gentian to flower. The best advice is to grow it in a thoroughly good, well-fed soil which is at once firm and well supplied with organic matter. 8 cm (3 in). Spring. Europe.

G. asclepiadea. This is the willow gentian and is easy to grow, but its tall habit demands a place among such plants as candelabra primulas and meconopsis. It enjoys the same damp, peaty conditions, where it will bear its groups of two or three rich blue flowers in the axils of the leaves which occur at intervals on the stems. Propagate by seed. 60 cm (2 ft). Mid summer to early autumn. E. Europe and W. Asia.

G. bavarica. A difficult, small gentian needing a pot in the alpine house but in a compost that is moist, very well drained, and consists of grit and leafmould. It is a little like *G. verna*, but the flowers are rounder. 8 cm (3 in). Mid spring, Europe.

G. bellidifolia. A New Zealand gentian with white, cup-shaped flowers and deep green, blunt leaves in rosettes. It hates disturbance and lime. Needs good, deep soil. 10 cm (4 in). Late summer.

G. brachyphylla. A high-altitude version of *G. verna* and smaller. It is also more difficult and needs alpine house treatment or careful placing in a trough. 5 cm (2 in). Europe. Early summer.

G. farreri. This is a great treasure if the true plant can be found. It is one of the Asiatic trumpet gentians, the only one that is lime-tolerant, and the only one that is difficult to propagate by division. As Asiatic gentians cross-fertilize readily, propagation by seed has tended to produce hybrids and the true form has all but disappeared. However, Joe Elliott used to grow it from seed in his English Cotswolds nursery, miles from the nearest non-limy soil and thus it stayed true. It *can* be divided and cuttings are possible. The flowers are brilliant, Cambridge blue, white in the throat. 5 cm (2 in). Early to mid autumn. Tibet.

Gentiana farreri

G. hexaphylla. Seldom seen, but is an important parent of many Asiatic hybrids. The pale blue trumpets have darker stripes on their outsides and there is a greenish tinge in the throat. Lime-free soil. Late summer. China.

G. lagodechiana see *G. septemfida*.

G. makinoi. A species making a small thicket of leafy stems, at the tops of which are speckled, slate-blue flowers, as well as in some of the leaf axils. For a lime-free, peaty place but in sun. 45 cm (18 in). Mid summer to early autumn. Japan.

G. pneumonanthe. The European marsh gentian still grows wild on wet heaths in the south of England. In cultivation it is more robust. In a leafy, cool spot it has a single, blue flower in every leaf axil along each stem. 30 cm (12 in). Mid to late summer.

G. saxosa. Like a small version of *G. bellidifolia*. Its white flowers are veined with greenish brown. If it is kept on the dry side in winter it is, like other New Zealand gentians, quite hardy, but a wet soil makes it far less so. For a deep trough or a rich scree, in sun. 5 cm (2 in). Mid summer to early autumn.

G. scarlatina. Very occasionally, Andean gentians come fleetingly into cultivation. They are mentioned here because of their red or yellow colouring — among others are *GG. scarlatinostriata, chrysotaenia* and *incurva*. The closest relatives are the gentians of New Zealand.

G. septemfida. This is the 'everyman's' gentian. It is easy to grow in almost any decent soil in full sun. It is a leafy plant with erect stems and terminal and axillary clusters of variable flowers. In good forms they are deep blue. Propagate by seed or cuttings. 25 cm (10 in). Mid to late summer. Caucasus.

G. sino-ornata. This is the archetypal Asiatic gentian. By this term is meant not all gentians from Asia, but those with trailing, wiry, herbaceous stems and small, very narrow leaves in basal rosettes and set along the stems. In this species the stems root where they touch the ground and the large trumpets, whose bases lie on the soil, are deep, rich, royal blue with indigo and green tones occurring in longitudinal zones. It requires a peaty, lime-free, moist soil. Given that, it will tolerate a good deal of sun. A parent of many hybrids. 'Brin Form' will scramble into dwarf shrubs. 8 cm (3 in). China. Early to mid autumn; sometimes a week or so longer.

G. verna. This is the spring star gentian. It makes groups of rosettes of fresh, green, stumpy, pointed leaves and bears stemless, starry flowers of an intense, pure blue. It is not difficult in a stony scree or a trough as long as the drainage is good. Propagation is by seed. It is a difficult procedure; the seedlings have to be potted when they are minute and root damage is usually fatal. 8 cm (3 in). Europe (including locations in England and Ireland). Mid to late spring. *G.v. angulosa* is a slightly larger and sturdier plant and is the one usually seen in gardens. It comes from the Caucasus.

Asiatic Hybrid Gentians. Apart from *G. sino-ornata*, most Asiatic gentians grown in gardens are hybrids. There are many of them, and with few exceptions they are superb plants. They can be propagated with ease in early spring if they are lifted and the crowns gently separated, each with a 'thong' of roots. Among the best are 'Caroli', 'Devonhall', 'Drake's Strain', 'Fasta Highlands', 'Glendevon', 'Inverleith', 'Kidbroke Seedling', 'Kingfisher' and 'Susan Jane'.

GERANIUM (Geraniaceae)

The geraniums are mainly hardy plants, completely distinct from *Pelargonium* (in which the zonal 'geraniums' belong) and include the cranesbills. It is a large genus; many species are border plants, but the smaller species are important to the rock gardener. Propagation is in some cases by division; some species may be grown from seed, which must be harvested with care, as it is catapulted a long way from the parent plants, and others growing from undivided rootstocks may be propagated from root cuttings. A good soil in sun or part shade is all they require.

G. argenteum. This lovely species is not often grown nowadays. Its foliage is much divided and silkily silver, while the pink flowers, veined with darker pink, are held on short stems. It is an admirable plant for a scree. 10 cm (4 in). Spring. Europe.

G. cinereum. Another small geranium with deeply cut leaves, but in this case they are grey-green. The flowers are in shades of pink, always veined with a deeper colour, and there is a white form. 15 cm (6 in). Early to mid summer. Pyrenees.

Geranium cinereum

G. dalmaticum. A mat-forming species, adept at insinuating its strong, stubby stems among rocks. It has green, lobed foliage and a long series of flowers in rich, sugar pink. The white form is excellent. Prostrate. Late spring and early summer. Yugoslavia.

G. farreri (syn. *G. napuligerum*). Although this species will grow in a well-drained scree or trough, a home in the alpine house should be found if possible. Its low clumps of kidney-shaped, grey-green leaves give rise to short-stemmed flowers of great beauty. They are soft pink, made dramatic by black anthers. It is susceptible to wet. Seed is sparingly set and should be watched for carefully, as the plant cannot be divided. 10 cm (4 in). Early to mid summer. China, Yunnan Province.

G. sanguineum. A species that occurs throughout much of Europe, including Britain. It is variable in colour, from shades of magenta to light pink. On Walney Island, part of Barrow-in-Furness, in north-west England, a form with pink flowers, heavily veined in carmine, is found. This is *G.s. lancastriense*, a very fine rock plant indeed and an example of how 'alpines' may be natives of places at sea level. 15 cm (6 in). Early summer to early autumn.

G. subcaulescens. This is thought by some authorities to be a form of *G. cinereum*. It has green leaves, not so deeply divided, and carmine flowers with a black eye. If this classification is right, *G.* 'Ballerina', a plant with deep lilac flowers with dark purple veining, is not a hybrid, but a form of *G. cinereum*. Be that as it may, all this group of geraniums are highly desirable rock garden plants.

GEUM (Rosaceae)

Geums are attractive herbaceous perennials. A few are small and elegant enough for the rock garden. They are easily grown in most kinds of garden soils, although one or two species can be tricky.

G. × borisii. Nature's attempt to tame the fractious *G. reptans* by allowing it to cross with a coarser species in the wild has given us a clump-forming, easy, showy plant with bright orange flowers. It is sometimes referred to as *G.* 'Borisii'. 30 cm (12 in). Early to late summer.

G. montanum. A well-behaved plant, making leafy clumps and with masses of golden-yellow flowers well over 2.5 cm (1 in) across. Easily grown in sun. 15 cm (6 in). Early to mid summer. European Alps.

G. reptans. A frustrating plant, needing a lime-free very stony soil but highly likely to die at a moment's notice. It is totally intolerant of drought, although it seems to need sun (in the wild it never strays onto south-facing slopes, however). It seeks to make colonies by means of its strawberry-like runners, but hardly succeeds in cultivation. 13 cm (5 in). European Alps.

G. × rhaeticum. Has larger flowers up to 4 cm (1.5 in) wide and brilliant orange colouring like *G. reptans*, but allied to the ease of cultivation of *G. montanum*.

GLOBULARIA (Globulariaceae)

The globularias are mostly cushion or mat-forming plants, more or less woody, with dark green leaves and small, rounded heads of flowers like blue pompons (they are occasionally white). They range from plants for the scree to small treasures for the alpine house or frame. All of them like dryish, sunny positions. Propagation is by seed or division.

G. cordifolia. The best known of the genus, making ground-hugging mats of notched leaves and blue heads of flowers. 8 cm (3 in). Late spring to early summer. Europe.

G. incanescens. Easily distinguishable by its blue-grey leaves and small, violet-blue flower heads. Cushion-forming and probably best in the alpine house or frame. 5 cm (2 in). Late spring to mid summer. Italy.

G. meridionalis (syn. *G. bellidifolia*). Grey-blue flower heads over prostrate mats of un-notched leaves; otherwise similar to but slightly larger than *G. cordifolia* and, like it, happy on the scree. 10 cm (4 in). Late spring to mid summer. Europe.

G. repens. Like a dense, compact, almost miniature form of *G. cordifolia*. The foliage is minute, and the flowers are like tiny, furry, blue buttons. Best in the alpine house or frame. 2.5 cm (1 in). Western Alps and Pyrenees.

GYPSOPHILA (Caryophyllaceae)

This is a large genus for one which is so little represented in gardens. The reason for this is that most species are not particularly attractive. Apart from the well-known border plants, however, there are one or two quite surprising alpines.

G. aretioides. The most usually seen form of this is *G.a. caucasica*. It is an iron-hard cushion — more of a pad — of minute rosettes of tiny, shiny leaves. It is reluctant to flower, but once in many years may practically cover

itself with small, stemless, white flowers like miniature dianthus. Caucasus.

G. cerastioides. An altogether looser plant, with tufts or lax cushions of grey-green leaves and sprays of white flowers with pink veins. There is a form, only half the height of the type, that has its flowers veined with purple. 10 cm (4 in). Late spring to late summer. Himalaya.

G. repens. Not unlike a miniature form of the border gypsophilas. The branched flower stems fly off in all directions and make a little cloud of white or pink flowers. The best forms are 'Rosea' (a good pink), 'Dorothy Teacher', which has a long flowering period and a more compact habit, and 'Dubia', with bronzed foliage instead of the bluish grey of the other forms. 10 cm (4 in). Early summer to early autumn. Europe.

HAASTIA (Compositae)

Cushion plants from New Zealand that, with some raoulias come under the vernacular heading of 'vegetable sheep'.

H. pulvinaris. A successfully grown plant will probably be a cushion of not more than 5 cm (2 in) across. It is made up of extremely woolly, ochre-coloured rosettes and is seldom seen to flower in cultivation. Double-pot cultivation in the alpine house gives the best chance of success but it dies if subject to drought.

HABERLEA (Gesneriaceae)

Haberleas are related to ramondas and like to grow on their sides in north-facing crevices with a constant supply of moisture and in an organic soil. Propagation is by division or seed.

H. rhodopensis. Makes rosettes of hairy-leathery, bright olive green, toothed leaves. The flowers are pale lilac and somewhat primula-like, with gold in the throat, held in umbels. *H. ferdinandi-coburgii* is increasingly recognized as a form of the species with larger, more open flowers. 'Virginale' is white. 23 cm (9 in). Mid spring to early summer. Balkans.

HACQUETIA (Umbelliferae)

There is only one species in the genus.

H. epipactis. Appears above ground as golden-yellow flowers surrounded by apple-green bracts. They are followed by the three-lobed, glossy foliage. Choose a peaty, moist, shady spot. Valuable for its very early flowering. Divide when dormant or propagate from seed. 15 cm (6 in). Late winter to early spring. Eastern Alps.

HAPLOPAPPUS (Compositae)
A very large genus in the huge daisy family. Only two species (one of which is only recently transferred from *Erigeron*) are grown as rock plants.

H. brandegeei (syn. *Erigeron aureus*). It is not guaranteed that this name is taxonomically or etymologically correct. A tiny plant, excellent in the corner of a trough, which keeps on producing its bright yellow daisies for many weeks. 5 cm (2 in). Spring and summer. Western N. America.

H. coronopifolius. There seem to be two or more forms of this plant, varying from 15 to 30 cm (6–12 in) in height and with flowers of varying sizes up to 2.5 cm (1 in) across. It is like a shrubby, golden daisy with dark green, leathery leaves. N. America. Early to late summer.

HEBE (Scrophulariaceae)
Hebes are New Zealand plants with flowers much like veronicas in spikes. The leaves are either adpressed to the stems (whipcord hebes) or deployed in imbricated ranks along the stems. The alpine hebes are in effect reduced versions of the larger ones. They can be grown in any part of the rock garden, and will accept shade, although they are better in sun. Propagation by cuttings is simple.

H. buchananii. Makes a bun-shaped dome of congested branches and tiny, dark green leaves. The flowers are white, but not freely produced. *H.b.* 'Minor' is even smaller. 30 cm (12 in). Early to mid summer.

H. 'Carl Teschner'. A fairly stiff, procumbent plant, with dark green leaves on blue-black stems and freely produced spikes of violet blue flowers with white throats. 20 cm (8 in). Early to mid summer.

H. epacridea. A small, prostrate, whipcord hebe, looking somewhat like a conifer until it produces its clusters of white, fragrant flowers. 30 cm (12 in). Mid summer.

H. pinguifolia 'Pagei'. This is the cultivar of this species which is almost always grown. It makes a gently domed mass of prostrate stems, with blue-grey leaves and dense spikes of white flowers. 25 cm (10 in). Late spring to late summer.

HELIANTHEMUM (Cistaceae)
Helianthemums are the rock roses that make such attractive pools of bright colour on the summer rock garden. They are related to *Cistus* and *Halimium* and have the same delight in a sunny position in poorish soil. In the main they are prostrate shrubs. They should be cut back hard after the first, long flush of flowering, so that they may grow more compactly, live longer, and probably flower again. Propagation is by summer cuttings. Almost all the ones grown are cultivars of *H. nummularium*, and the following list is a representative one. The flowers are single unless otherwise indicated.

Helianthemum

'Alice Howarth': semi-double, mulberry-crimson

'Ben Fhada': yellow

'Ben Heckla': copper

'Ben Mhor': brownish orange

'Cerise Queen': cerise; double

'Henfield Brilliant': brick red, grey foliage

'Kathleen Druce': warm gold, double

'Mrs Earle': clear red, double

'Orange Surprise': rich orange, double

'Raspberry Ripple': double, mixed streaks of red and cream

'The Bride': white

'Wisley Pink': soft pink, yellow eye, vigorous

'Wisley Primrose': soft yellow, very vigorous

HELICHRYSUM (Compositae)

A very large genus of plants with a great variety of form. Among them are a few that are hardy rock garden plants.

H. bellidioides. A creeping, mat-forming plant with cobwebby, trailing stems and heads of white flowers. It is hardy, although it has a reputation for tenderness. Propagate by division. Mid to late summer. New Zealand.

H. coralloides. One of the most remarkable of all alpines. Its woolly stems, made lizard-scaly with adpressed leaves, assemble to appear just like a branched, upright, grey-green coral. Very rarely it flowers, with yellow buttons at the branch ends. Previously, it was always given alpine house treatment, but is perfectly hardy in a trough. It hates drought. Propagate by taking whole, small branchlets as cuttings. 15–20 cm (6–8 in). New Zealand.

H. frigidum. This species makes tufted mats of silvery foliage and bears papery, white, ever-lasting flowers. It is best in the alpine house but can be grown in a trough if protected from winter wet. Propagate by division. 8 cm (3 in). A long period in summer. Corsica.

H. milfordiae. One of the most remarkable of alpines. It makes broad cushions of symmetrical, silver, woolly rosettes, on which sit flower buds striped in white and crimson like old-fashioned mint humbugs. These open to silvery-white everlasting flowers when the sun shines and close again when it goes in or at dusk. It is hardy and stands winter on a tufa boulder, but otherwise needs protection from wet. Propagate by division. 5 cm (2 in). A long period in summer. South Africa.

H. selago. Another plant of the persuasion of *H. coralloides*, but much more slender, giving it a heath-like, rather than a coral-like appearance. Occasionally bears its yellow flowers. Propagate as *H. coralloides*. 15 cm (6 in). New Zealand.

HEPATICA (Ranunculaceae)

Hepaticas are related to anemones but are quickly distinguishable from them. The flowers are made up of coloured sepals with leafy bracts beneath. From resting buds, wiry flowering stems unfurl early in the year and are followed by the leaves, which are silvery-hairy when young. The leaves are kidney-shaped and soon turn dull green. The flowers are single and the usual colour is blue or mauve. They enjoy a leafy, cool place in part shade. Large clumps may be divided while dormant; seed must be gathered while still green and be sown straight away.

H. acutiloba. An American species which is like *H. nobilis*, but smaller.

H. × media 'Ballardii'. This resulted from a cross between *H. nobilis* and *H. transsilvanica*. It is the best hepatica, with very large, perfectly round flowers of clear blue without (as is sometimes maintained) any hint of mauve.

H. nobilis (syn. *H. triloba*). The best known species. It is native to much of the northern hemisphere and appears in several forms. The leaves are deep green and kidney-shaped and the flowers are up to 2.5 cm (1 in) across, six- to nine-petalled, and may be a shade of blue, white, pink, or even (in Scandinavia) red. Mid to late spring, sometimes earlier.

H. transsilvanica. Similar to *H. nobilis* but is significantly larger. The flowers are shades of blue-mauve, occasionally pink.

Hepatica transsilvanica

HIPPOCREPIS (Leguminosae)
A genus of mainly Mediterranean shrubs and perennials.

H. comosa. A perennial with a woody base, known as the horseshoe vetch. It is offered for sale, but only the cultivar 'E. R. Janes' is worth cultivating on the rock garden. This is a compact form with lemon yellow flowers on fairly prostrate branches. 20 cm (8 in). Late spring to early summer. Much of Europe.

HORMINIUM (Labiatae)
H. pyrenaicum. This is the only species. Its relationship to sage can be seen in the violet-blue flowers, which are borne in spikes over rosettes of rough, leathery leaves. White and pink forms are known. 30 cm (12 in). Early to late summer. Pyrenees.

HOUSTONIA (Rubiaceae)
There are several houstonias, but only one is in cultivation to any extent.

H. caerulea. A dainty, mat-forming, ground-covering plant, ideal for shady, woody places. The species usually has blue flowers, but the form usually seen in gardens, 'Fred Millard', has darker flowers with a hint of purple. 8 cm (3 in). All summer. N. America.

HUTCHINSIA (Cruciferae)
H. alpina. This is the only species. It is not a spectacular plant, but seeds itself about in a scree in a pleasant way. It is a tiny plant with ferny foliage and dense clusters of white, four-petalled flowers. 5 cm (2 in). Late spring to mid summer. Europe.

HYPERICUM (Hypericaceae)
Hypericums range from dwarf, sometimes prostrate plants to medium-sized shrubs. The flowers are usually yellow and have five broad petals surrounding a central, conspicuous boss of stamens of the same colour as the corolla. The rock garden species are sun lovers and most of them enjoy any good, well-drained soil. One or two are not reliably hardy. Propagation by soft cuttings.

H. aegypticum. A dwarf, evergreen shrub which requires the protection of the alpine house, as it is not entirely hardy. It makes a rounded mound of tiny, grey green leaves, which the stems carrying solitary, yellow flowers just above the foliage. 25 cm (10 in). Late spring to early summer. W. Asia.

H. balearicum. Hardy in mild areas; otherwise it should have protection. It is a dwarf shrub with leathery leaves that are unusual in being warty. The flowers are quite large and golden yellow. 30 cm (12 in). Late spring to mid summer. Balearic Islands.

H. coris. Although this small plant has been grown for many years, it is not often seen, possibly because it is only just hardy and thus frequently lost in the open. It should be kept going by cuttings and grown in a well-drained, sunny scree. It has heath-like stems and foliage and terminal, light yellow flowers. 15 cm (6 in). Early to mid summer. S. Europe.

H. cuneatum. A tangled mat of brittle, reddish stems and small leaves with dark markings supporting clusters of small, red-budded, yellow flowers. Once again, a species that is on the tender side. 8 cm (3 in). Mid spring to mid summer. Asia Minor.

H. empetrifolium oliganthum. A prostrate, heath-like plant with a wealth of yellow flowers if it can be maintained in a warm, sunny position. Slightly tender. Early to late summer. W. Asia.

H. olympicum. Probably the best of the rock garden hypericums. It is perfectly hardy. A mass of upright stems fan slightly outwards from a woody base, and each bears one or more very large, rich yellow flowers. The buds are spirally veined in orange-pink. *H.o.* 'Citrinum' is superior, with flowers of cool lemon yellow. *H. polyphyllum*, as one has known it, has smaller, more slender leaves, ash-green, and is more elegant. However, botanists now place it in *H. olympicum*. 25 cm (10 in). Late spring to mid summer. W. Asia.

H. reptans. Prostrate, with trailing stems and small leaves that turn red in autumn. The flowers, emerging from red buds, are bright yellow and very large — up to 5 cm (2 in) across. It is at its best trailing over rocks. Early to mid summer. Sikkim.

HYPSELA (Campanulaceae)
A genus of small, creeping plants from the southern hemisphere that enjoys cool, peaty soils in cool places. Propagation is by division, but they can become a little invasive.

H. reniformis. Has bright green, kidney-shaped leaves and makes a tight carpet, just above which are the nearly stemless, pale pink, lipped flowers with darker markings. Something like a tiny lobelia. A white form is known as 'Greencourt White'. All summer. Chile.

IBERIS (Cruciferae)
Iberis are annuals (candytuft) or perennials. The alpine ones are mostly evergreen subshrubs or at least woody based. They are sun-loving, easy plants for the open rock garden or for walls. The flowers have two petals longer than the other two. Propagation is by soft cuttings.

I. gibraltarica. The apices of the dark, green, narrow leaves of this species should be toothed. Untoothed leaves indicate that the specimen is not true, and is a form of *I. sempervirens*. It should be a smallish subshrub with flat heads of white flowers with a slight pinkish or purplish tinge. 23 cm (9 in). Gibraltar, Morocco. Late spring to mid summer.

I. saxatilis. A dwarf subshrub with foliage like that of a tiny yew and flat heads of white flowers. 10 cm (4 in). Mid spring to early summer. S. Europe.

I. semperflorens and **I. sempervirens**. These two species appear to have become inextricably confused and plants appear under either name quite indiscriminately. However, it is the cultivars that are grown, so they may be designated simply as *Iberis* 'Snowflake', 'Little Gem', and 'Pygmaea'. All are very similar and are dwarf and dark-leaved. Strictly speaking, flat flower heads denote *I. semperflorens* and tight racemes (more cylindrical) are indicative of the other species, but these are hardly plants for academic debate. Flowering takes place between mid spring and early summer.

Iberis semperflorens

INULA (Compositae)

Inulas are mostly large perennials with big, coarse leaves and large, golden flowers, grown mainly in shady, moist borders. However, there are two species that are grown by alpine gardeners.

I. acaulis. Consists of flat rosettes of toothed, hairy leaves, on which sit large, golden daisies 2.5 cm (1 in) or more across. For a scree or gritty soil. Mid summer. Asia Minor.

I. ensifolia. Taller, with heads of yellow daisies. It prefers a moister, slightly shady spot. 25 cm (10 in). Mid to late summer. S. Europe.

IRIS (Iridaceae)

Apart from the smaller bulbous irises, which no rock garden should be without, there are several dwarf species that are ideally suited to the rock garden. Most of them are truly rhizomatous, while a few have masses of fibrous roots; their propagation by division in either case. Pacific coast irises should be divided and transplanted immediately after flowering.

I. bracteata. Each bracted stem bears two yellow flowers, veined with purple, over leathery, shiny leaves. 23 cm (9 in). Spring. N. America.

I. chamaeiris (syn. *I. lutescens*). Should not be confused with *I. pumila*; it is taller and keeps its leaves most of the winter. However, it is very variable but characterized by stiffly upright leaves and very large flowers for the size of the plant. They may be in shades of white, yellow, blue or purple. 'Jackanapes' and 'Campbellii' are the best known named forms; the latter has extra large flowers of very deep blue. 13–25 cm (5–10 in). Mid to late spring. S. Europe.

I. cristata. Has a short season of flower but is grown because of its great beauty. In a cool but gritty, sheltered place it makes a tangled mat of small rhizomes from which arise pairs of flowers on wiry stems. They are pale mauve with yellow-gold throats, and the falls have conspicuous white throats. The rare white form is to be treasured. 15 cm (6 in). Late spring. N. America.

I. innominata, tenax and **douglasii**. These and possibly other species from California and Oregon, comprise the Pacific Coast irises. They are mostly in shades of mauve, with heavy, dark veining; they have grassy foliage in dense clumps, and are about 25–30 cm (10–12 in) tall. *I. innominata* in particular tends towards forms with buff and subdued gold tones. These mix with the mauve in some hybrids to give a surprisingly satisfying colour range. The plants require a peaty, leafy, lime-free soil (unusual for irises) and can take full sun in a constantly moist place, needing part shade if it is likely to become at all dry. They must be divided only immediately after flowering finishes. The 'Broadleigh' series of hybrids (Broadleigh 'Ann', 'Florence', 'Lavinia', etc.) are excellent plants. Late spring to early summer.

I. lacustris. Regarded as a species in its own right but for garden purposes this is a compact form of *I. cristata*. Great Lakes of N. America.

I. mellita (syn. *I. suaveolens*). A tiny flag iris with smoky brown flowers veined with reddish purple. A form with red edges to the leaves is called 'Rubromarginata'. 8 cm (3 in). Mid to late spring. S. Europe.

I. pumila. In effect, a miniature flag iris with flowers that are almost stemless, making them seem very large. The range of colours is similar to that of *I. chamaeiris*. The iris known as *I. attica* belongs here, and is a Greek variant with soft yellow flowers, veined with brown. 10 cm (4 in). Mid spring. Balkans.

ISOPYRUM (Ranunculaceae)

I. thalictroides. Increasingly uncommon in cultivation for some reason. Until recently it was the only species grown and may still be so. It may be thought of as a delicate plant with grey-green leaves, something like a thalictrum with small, white, anemone-like flowers. For a cool, moist position in part shade. 15 cm (6 in). Early to late spring. Europe.

JANKAEA (Gesneriaceae)

J. heldreichii. This is the only species. It is closely related to *Ramonda* and *Haberlea* and has ramonda-like rosettes of foliage that are

169

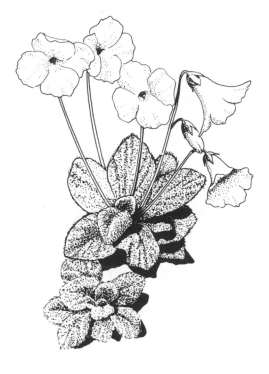

Jankaea heldreichii

heavily felted with silky hairs. The flowers are several to a stalk, open bell-shaped, and pale violet-pink. It inhabits shady crevices on Mount Olympus, Greece, where it may be seen by standing on the back of a donkey! In cultivation the best bet for this hater of winter wet is a pot kept under the alpine house bench, in which the plant is wedged between pieces of rock in a leafy compost. 8 cm (3 in). Mid to late spring.

JASIONE (Campanulaceae)
The sheepsbits and sheepsbit scabious are very similar to *Scabiosa* species, even though they belong to the campanula family. Their crowded heads of blue flowers are superficially similar. They are easily grown in sunny positions and attract butterflies. Propagate by seed.

J. heldreichii. Confusingly, as it coincidentally follows *Jankaea* alphabetically, its synonym is *J. jankae*. It is an erect plant with low tufts of narrow, hairy leaves and clean, branching stems carrying fine flower heads of clear, pure blue. 25 cm (10 in). Early to late summer. Balkans.

J. laevis (syn. *J. perennis*). This is the sheepsbit scabious. It has unbranched stems and is a little invasive. The flowers are not quite true blue, but 'Blue Light', a selected form, comes close. 20 cm (8 in). Mid to late summer. Europe.

JASMINUM (Oleaceae)
Of all the jasmines, there is just one dwarf shrub that is suitable for the alpine gardener. Propagation is by cuttings.

J. parkeri. A small, gnarled bush with tiny, three-lobed foliage and yellow jasmine flowers close to the branches. It makes a delightful specimen in the alpine house where, although it is often grown in troughs and screes, its slight tenderness is best catered for. 30 cm (12 in). Early summer. N.W. India.

JEFFERSONIA (Berberidaceae)
One of the genera that demonstrate the strange and extremely close relationship between the floras of eastern Asia and eastern N. America. There are only two species; one from Northern China and the other from N. America. They are propagated from seed.

J. diphylla (syn. *Plagiorhegma diphylla*). Wiry leaf stalks arise from a central stock and end in sharply two-lobed leaves. The flowers are large at 2.5 cm (1 in) across and white. Humus-rich soil and light shade. 20 cm (8 in). Early spring. Tennessee.

J. dubia (syn. *Plagiorhegma dubia*). The flowers of this species are rounded, over 2.5 cm (1 in) wide, and clear, soft, hepatica-blue. They appear before the leaves, which are metallic purple at first, unfolding to be kidney-shaped, glaucous, and with a delicate flush of reddish-violet, eventually green. Hardy, but best in the alpine house for display. 10 cm (4 in). Early to mid spring. North-east China.

Jeffersonia dubia

JOVIBARA (Crassulaceae)

Until quite recently the jovibarbas were included in *Sempervivum*. The differences are mainly of botanical interest, but the flowers are different, having six broad petals rather than ten narrow ones, making the blooms bell-shaped, rather than spikily starry. They all make fleshy, sessile rosettes, increasing by offsets, with the flowers on fleshy, scaly stems. They grow anywhere in sun, even in the poorest places.

J. allionii, arenaria, arenaria, and **hirta**. All similar, having globose rosettes whose offsets are like tiny, scaly marbles that can easily roll away from the parents. *J. heuffellii* has flatter, more open rosettes that increase by dividing after the manner of cells. There is a great degree of variation in leaf colour, from red-tipped to cream, and a whole host of varieties, especially cultivars and forms of *J. heuffellii glabra* and *J.h. patens*, can be found in catalogues. They are, one suspects, of greatest interest to specialists in the two related genera.

Flowering mainly occurs from mid summer to early autumn, and the centré of population is south-east Europe.

KALMIA (Ericaceae)

A genus of North American evergreen shrubs with flowers that are shaped like cookie cutters. They are usually pink, but can be red.

K. microphylla. The two latest revisions of the genus accord this specific status; hitherto it has been regarded as a naturally occurring variety of *K. polifolia*. It is a truly dwarf shrub with small leaves and heads of flowers on wiry stems. These are pink and saucer-shaped but for the glandular pouches that create a pentagonal shape. For a lime-free, peaty soil in part shade. Propagate by cuttings. 15 cm (6 in). Mid spring.

Kalmia microphylla

KALMIOPSIS (Ericaceae)

K. leachiana. This is the only species. It is one of the most beautiful of all alpine shrubs, growing to be a dwarf, rounded, evergreen bush with small, dark green leaves and racemes of flowers that are kalmia-like but more bell-shaped. Their colour is rich pink and they are

171

large for the size of the shrub. 'Le Piniec' and 'Umpqua Valley Form' are selections from the wild; 'Glendoick' arose in cultivation. It enjoys a peaty, lime-free, slightly gritty soil and shade at the hottest part of the day. Propagate by cuttings or seed. Grows slowly to 30 cm (12 in). N.W. America.

× KALMIOTHAMNUS (Ericaceae)

Bigeneric hybrids between *Kalmia* and *Rhodothamnus*. At the time of writing, no full collective hybrid name had been published for this cross. However, three different forms were available from the raisers, who described them as being compact bushes with plentiful pink flowers and ideal for the peat garden.

KELSEYA (Rosaceae)

K. uniflora. This is the only species in the genus. It is now extremely rare in the wild and is seldom seen in cultivation. It is possibly the dwarfest shrub of all, and at its largest is a silky, grey-green, domed cushion about 25 cm (10 in) wide — usually much smaller in cultivation. Occasionally it will flower, studding itself with white, hawthorn-like flowers, flushed with pink. Not easy, and definitely for the alpine house. Declining in the wild; alpine gardeners are its long-term hope for survival. Big Horn Mountains, Wyoming.

LEIOPHYLLUM (Ericaceae)

L. buxifolium. A neat, dense, evergreen shrub in its best forms. The stems are dusky red and the foliage small and box-like. The flowers, in terminal clusters, are pink, becoming white. Care should be taken when choosing this plant, as it can grow to 60 cm (2 ft) or more and it is those forms of only 30 cm (12 in) that should be sought, preferably from cuttings of known plants. For a peaty, cool place. Late spring to early summer. N. America.

LEONTOPODIUM (Compositae)

This is the well-known edelweiss.

L. alpinum. The typical edelweiss from the Alps of Europe is a variable plant, coarse and leggy at worst, neat and fascinating at best, unwilling to keep in character in lowland gardens. The grey-green, whitely hairy leaves

are not as well known as the heavily white-felted flower heads and their attendant bracts. It is hardy on the rock garden but always seems to look dirty. If *L.a. nivale* from the Apennines can be obtained, it is worth a place in the alpine house, where its clean whiteness and large heads on short stems can be admired. 5–20 cm (2–8 in). Late spring to early summer.

L. haplophylloides. Much more slender, not as striking, but has a lemon aroma. It is rare. Mid to late summer. Himalaya.

LEPIDIUM (Cruciferae)

L. nanum. A species that forms extremely close, hard cushions of tiny, green leaves in the wild. Its flowers are inconspicuous but it is one of the legendary alpines because of its highly developed cushion habit, its remote habitat, and the difficulty that is met with in growing it at all, let alone keeping it in character. As seedlings, there is little hint of the subsequent character of the plants. For the alpine house. The Great Basin of North America. (See Davidson, R. *et al.* The Great Lepidium Hunt: *Bull. Amer. Rock Gard. Soc.,* **32** (1).)

LEPTOSPERMUM (Myrtaceae)

The myrtle family is ill represented in alpine gardening. This is not surprising, as it tends to be a family of tender, woody genera from the southern hemisphere, some of which, like *Eucalyptus* and *Callistemon* come very close to hardiness. *Leptospermum* is such a genus, but it has one or two dwarf members. They are not fully hardy and require winter protection, lime-free soils, and sun. Propagate from cuttings.

L. humifusum Almost entirely hardy, but not quite. It is a low, spreading shrub with small, leathery leaves and groups of white flowers, each with five separated, rounded petals. 23 cm (9 in). Late spring to early summer. Tasmania.

L. scoparium. The species itself is quite a large, variable shrub with small, dark green leaves. The 'Nanum' group is a rapidly increasing set of cultivars. They are very small, dense, often gnarled shrubs with flowers the same size as their larger relatives. They are winter hardy in very mild places only. The cultivar 'Nicholsii' ('Nicholsii Nanum') has been in cultivation for a long time; new names like 'Huia', 'Kiwi', 'Kotuku', and 'Red Falls' are worth investigating. 'Red Damask', an astonishingly beautiful double, is too large for the rock garden but should be obtained at all costs for the conservatory. Late spring to early summer, but very likely later. New Zealand.

LEUCOGYNES (Compositae)

The two species that are grown in alpine gardens are said to be the New Zealand equivalents of edelweiss. This is a somewhat strained comparison, as it is their intensely silvery foliage which makes them so attractive. They are best in the alpine house but will grow in a peaty, leafy soil with plenty of grit and in a cool place that is not too shaded.

L. grandiceps. Makes a tiny thicket of woody stems, thickly furnished with leaves that are so silkily hairy as to be silvered. The flower clusters are yellow and held among woolly bracts at the ends of the branches. 15 cm (6 in).

L. leontopodium. Taller and more slender. 18 cm (7 in).

LEWISIA (Portulacaceae)

Lewisias are among the most showy of alpine plants and also the most challenging. The problem they set is not necessarily how to coddle them in protected cultivation, but how to persuade them to be at their best, which, for the evergreen species, is in a crevice in a retaining wall or between rocks. Some species are herbaceous, making annual growth from a perennial rootstock, but most have rosettes of persistent leaves and spectacular, branched inflorescences of brightly coloured flowers. They do not tolerate wet around their necks, but for all that some can be grown on the flat as long as their foliage is lying on impermeable rock, such as slate. They are superb in the alpine house, particularly forms of *L. tweedii*, which not a success in the open. They are all from North America and like a rich, gritty soil. They are said to dislike lime, but this is perhaps true only in the case of *L. tweedii*. However, they are not easy to please in very calcareous soils, such as chalk. Propagation is by seed.

L. brachycalyx. Herbaceous with a thick, carrot-like rootstock. The foliage is blue-green, fleshy and flat, forming a rosette, in the centre of which the flowers, which are large — up to 5 cm (2 in) wide — and white, flushed with pink, are produced on short stems. Not an easy species. Mid to late spring.

L. columbiana. Has small, flat rosettes of neat, strap-shaped leaves. The flowers, quite small, are carried in panicles and are magenta-pink. In 'Rosea' they are more of a warm, deep pink, and *L.c. wallowensis* has white, pink-veined blooms. 25 cm (10 in). Late spring to early summer.

L. congdonii. This is a collector's plant in that it is not a great beauty. It is herbaceous and has flaccid, flat leaves and unbranched stems with magenta-pink flowers. 20 cm (8 in). Late spring to early summer.

L. cotyledon. Under this name are grown the great majority of lewisias. Because propagation is by seed and lewisias hybridize readily, such species as *L. howellii*, *L. heckneri* and the natural variants of *L. cotyledon* itself have effectively become subsumed into a large hybrid swarm of cultivation. The rosettes of fleshy leaves, broadest just below the apex, which is often furnished with a downcurved hook, support multi-branched stems which carry round flowers of good size in rose, salmon, orange, soft yellow and white, with or without various forms of striping. Many forms have attractivly undulated leaf margins. 30 cm (12 in). Late spring to early summer.

L. nevadensis. Unusual in being summer-deciduous, which means that extra care must be taken with its watering regime. The white flowers are borne singly to a stem and nestle among the short, linear leaves. 8 cm (3 in). Mid to late spring.

L. oppositifolia. Similarly summer-dormant. It has taller stems, each with up to four white or light pink flowers. 20 cm (8 in). Mid to late spring.

L. pygmaea. Similar to *L. nevadensis* but has up to three flowers which may be white or shades of pink. Late spring to early summer.

173

L. rediviva. Like the other species that are deciduous in summer, requires treatment in the alpine house so that watering may be controlled. The leaves die away just as the plant flowers and reappear later in the year. The flowers are thus made the more conspicuous and are very large — over 5 cm (2 in) across — and usually blush pink. Flower stems 5 cm (2 in). Early to mid summer.

Lewisia rediviva

L. tweedyi. Probably the most beautiful lewisia of all. The leaves are large and fleshy and the flowering stems, of the same length as the leaves, bear blooms 5 cm (2 in) in a delicious range of shades of peach, soft rose and apricot. 15 cm (6 in). Mid to late spring.

LIBERTIA (Iridaceae)
L. sessiliflora caerulescens. A great rarity, often described as 'legendary', probably because it is so seldom grown or seen in the wild. However, seeds arriving in Britain from the Andes via New Zealand in 1974 gave rise to 15 cm (6 in) plants with iris-like leaves and large, sky-blue, open, six-pointed stars hanging on slim pedicels and nodding in every slight current of air. It is hardy even when young. Summer.

LINARIA (Scrophulariaceae)
A large genus, among which are some desirable alpines. One or two that are sometimes listed, such as *L. maroccana*, are omitted here as they are little more than annuals. Linarias are familiar from their two-lipped, horned, toadflax flowers.

L. alpina. A short-lived perennial that keeps itself going in the rock garden by seeding. It is never a nuisance. It has grey-blue foliage and dense clusters of purple and orange flowers. It can be encouraged to grow in a wall. 13 cm (5 in). Late spring to early autumn. Europe.

L. supina. Taller, more permanent, but still with a talent for seeding. Its flowers are usually yellow, but reddish purple and even maroon forms occur. 20 cm (8 in). Early summer to early autumn. S.W. Europe.

L. tristis. A richer-coloured version of *L. alpina* from the Iberian peninsula, tending towards yellow with a greater or lesser degree of purple markings. The most outstanding form is one from Djebel Toubkal, in Morocco, which was named 'Toubkal', but which is now regarded as representative of *L.t. lurida*. It is sturdier than the type, the foliage is blue rather than grey, and the flowers have a ground colour of lavender-gold, deeply veined and blotched with purple. Best in the alpine house. 15 cm (6 in). Early to late summer.

LINNAEA (Caprifoliaceae)
There is only one species.

L. borealis. The twin flower of northern woodlands. It makes a dainty but tangled mat of stems, with small, round leaves and dangling bells of blush pink on slender, upright stems. The flowers are lightly scented. It needs a leafy, well-drained, cool soil and dislikes drought. 5 cm (2 in). Late spring to early summer. *L.b. americana* is the form found in N. America; it is a little larger in all its parts and has flowers of a deeper pink.

LINUM (Linaceae)
The genus that includes the true flax. Linums are perennials, sometimes with a woody base, and tend to have several, centrally arising stems with conspicuous flowers in blue, yellow

or pink. They are mostly easy plants. Propagation is by seed or cuttings, which should be taken at the peak of summer from non-flowering shoots.

L. arboreum. A shrubby plant with grey-green leaves and clusters of large, golden-yellow flowers. 20 cm (8 in). Early to late summer. Greece and Turkey.

L. 'Gemmell's Hybrid'. Far more often grown than its parent, above. It is more compact and leafy, and is a very floriferous plant indeed, with a summer-long succession of large, glossily golden flowers. Though welcome, this makes propagation of large numbers of plants difficult, as it is not easy to find non-flowering shoots.

L. flavum. Needs to be in the alpine house, as it is not entirely hardy. It is a small, woody plant, which has a tendency to cover itself with clusters of golden-yellow flowers. 30 cm (12 in). Summer. E. Europe.

L. suffruticosum salsaloides nanum. Another unacceptable quadrinomal refers to a delightful, mat-forming, heath-like plant with pearly white flowers on short stems. Summer. S.W. Europe.

LITHODORA (Boraginaceae)
L. diffusa (syn. *Lithospermum diffusum*). An evergreen mat of woody stems clad in bristly, narrow, dark green leaves. The flowers that cover it are stemless and rich gentian blue. 'Heavenly Blue' should have larger, lighter blue flowers, while those of 'Grace Ward' should be even larger. However, the two seem to have become completely mixed and are seldom found true to type. 'Cambridge Blue' is easier to tell apart, and there is a white form. The plants require a peaty, lime-free soil in full sun. If the site is too wet, yellowing of the foliage occurs with runting of the flowers. Propagate by cuttings taken at the end of July in the northern hemisphere; the end of January in the southern. The date is fairly critical, but even so success can be had at other times in good years; in bad years no cuttings will strike at all. This seems to have something to do with hormone levels in the plants. Late spring to early or mid summer. S. Europe.

L. oleifolia. A subshrub with tufted stems bearing hairy, dull green leaves and sky blue flowers that open from pink buds. Not a lime hater. 20 cm (8 in). Early to mid summer. Pyrenees.

L. rosmarinifolia. A dwarf, dark green bush with clusters of beautiful, rich blue flowers. Not fully hardy and best in a crevice in full sun or the alpine house. 20 cm (8 in). Early to mid summer. Greece.

L. zahnii. Evergreen, dwarf and bushy, grey-leaved, and has clusters of white flowers with flushes and blurred stripes of blue. Needs a hot, dry place. Not fully hardy. 20 cm (8 in). Summer. Greece.

LOBELIA (Campanulaceae)
Lobelias vary from the well-known bedding annuals to the statuesque *L. tupa*, a waterside plant over 1.8 m (6 ft) tall. One is suitable for a moist soil and is valued for its late flowering.

L. syphylitica 'Nana'. This is a dwarf form of *L. syphylitica* only 20 cm (8 in) high. The flowers are large, pale blue, lipped, and borne singly in the axils of the leaves. Early to mid autumn. Eastern USA.

LOISELEURIA (Ericaceae)
L. procumbens. This is the only species. Known as the creeping azalea, it is northern circumpolar. In the wild it is usually on non-calcareous rocks, but it can be found in peaty pockets above limestone. In cultivation it requires the same conditions as dwarf rhododendrons, where it will, if happy, produce its small pink, bell-shaped flowers close to its mat of tiny leaves. Early to late summer.

LEUTKIA (Rosaceae)
L. pectinata. This is the only species. It is a mat-forming plant with white flowers very similar to those of a spiraea and the leaves similar to those of a mossy saxifrage. It prefers a crevice where its roots can keep cool under rocks. Early to late summer. N. America.

LUPINUS (Leguminosae)
A very large genus of annuals and perennials, including the well known Russell lupin of

borders. There are a few small, highly ornamental species for alpine gardeners. Propagate by seed.

L. lyallii. A miniature with silver filigree foliage and short flower stems bearing clusters of bright blue flowers. It is quite long lived in the alpine house in a gritty, leafy, lime-free soil. 10 cm (4 in). Early to late summer. N. America.

L. ornatus. Taller and has racemes of intensely blue flowers above silkily hairy, silver foliage. It will grow in the open in a leafy, gritty, lime-free soil and sun. 30 cm (12 in). Late spring to early summer. California.

LYCHNIS (Caryophyllaceae)
This genus includes the campions and catchflys but is small, containing only about a dozen species in all. It is related to *Dianthus* and *Silene* and has their shape of flower. Cultivation is easy in a good soil and sun.

L. alpina (syn. *Viscaria alpina*). Dense heads of pale, pinkish-purple heads of flowers above leafy tufts of dark green foliage. There is a good pink, 'Rosea', and a white form. 10 cm (4 in). Late spring to mid summer. Europe.

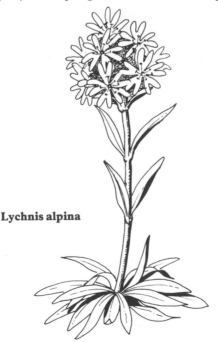

Lychnis alpina

L. flos-jovis. A variable plant, the shorter-stemmed forms of which should be sought. The basal foliage is heavily felted in white hairs and the stems carry many-flowered heads of a somewhat strident magenta. There are good pink forms, however, such as 'Hort's Variety'. A white form exists. 20–30 cm (8–12 in). Early to mid summer. Europe.

L. × haageana. A hybrid with bronzed leaves and showy heads of flowers. The colour is usually orange-scarlet and the petals are slashed and lobed somewhat after the manner of ragged robin. 20–30 cm (8–12 in). Early to mid summer.

MARGYRICARPUS (Rosaceae)
M. pinnatus. This is the only species in general cultivation. It is a dwarf, woody plant with pinnate, spine-tipped leaves and inconspicuous, greenish flowers. It is grown for its masses of pure white berries, which persist for many weeks. 30 cm (12 in). Early summer. Andes of Chile.

MAZUS (Scrophulariceae)
Mimulus-like perennials from the Asia and Australasia. They are easily cultivated in well-drained soil in sun and are not moisture lovers. Propagate by cuttings.

M. pumilio. Makes spreading mats of dark green foliage with blue-white, yellow-centred flowers on 5 cm (2 in) stems. Mid to late summer. Australia and New Zealand.

M. reptans. A perennial, making a tight mat of foliage with large, purple flowers with white and yellow markings. For the scree or alpine house. 5 cm (2 in). Early to late summer. Himalaya.

MECONOPSIS (Papaveraceae)
On the whole, meconopsis are not rock garden plants, but belong in the peaty, moist wild garden. However, alpine gardeners love growing the plants that live in such places, including candelabra primulas, which are the perfect accompaniment to meconopsis, and they have to be included in any list of alpines. They are poppy-like plants, best in cool places and best of all in the cooler, moister areas, where the intense blue tones that many of them

have remain pure and where the plants themselves thrive better. They are Asiatic with the one exception of the yellow-flowered *M. cambrica*.

M. bella. The most tantalizing of all, as it is rare in cultivation and difficult to grow. It has been likened to a blue version of *Papaver alpinum*, and has four-petalled, bowl-shaped, clear blue flowers on short stems above ferny foliage. It probably needs a pot of peaty, very gritty soil in a shady part of the alpine house. 13 cm (5 in). Early summer. Nepal, Bhutan.

M. betonicifolia. The best known of all meconopsis, the Himalayan blue poppy, is far from being a rock plant. However, it is not possible to mention the genus and leave it out. It is tall, graceful, and requires a shady, peaty soil with no lime. The flowers are pure blue in moist, cool climates; shot with mauve in drier, warmer ones. Other meconopsis of this persuasion include *M. grandis* and the hybrids *M.* × *sarsonii* and *M.* × *sheldonii*. The last named consists of forms which are outstandingly superior in the genus. Propagation of hybrids is by division; of species, by seed which may be stored for spring sowing.

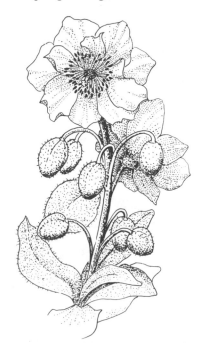

Meconopsis betonicifolia

M. cambrica. The Welsh poppy is a yellow-flowered meconopsis that is native to western Europe. The dainty four-petalled flowers arise from fernily lobed foliage. It is an easy plant once it takes to a site, seeding itself sometimes with vigour. There is also an orange form, *M.c. aurantiaca*, and both the yellow and orange Welsh poppies can occur as doubles. Whereas other meconopsis are lime haters, this species has a degree of lime tolerance. 30 cm (12 in). Early to late summer.

M. horridula. Suitable for the shady parts of the larger rock garden. It is bristly with spiny hairs. It is monocarpic but if it is kept going annually from seed it is possible to have specimens flowering every year. The flowers in the best forms are a beautiful blue, but can be purplish and there are white forms. It is described by various authorities as anything from 45 cm (18 in) to 90 cm (3 ft). In fact, specimens of 23 cm (9 in) are not uncommon and seed from the shortest forms should be selected for immediate sowing. Early to mid summer. Himalaya.

M. quintuplinervia. The best species for the rock garden. It is soundly perennial and in a cool, peaty place will produce solitary flowers of slaty blue on slender stems. Propagation can be by division or by seed which must be sown as soon as ripe. 30 cm (12 in). Early to mid summer. China.

MENTHA (Labiatae)
Only one species among the mints qualifies for inclusion.

M. requienii. A delightful, tiny, closely mat-forming plant with minute leaves and clusters of very small lilac flowers held tightly above the leaves. Its foliage is strongly aromatic, smelling refreshingly of peppermint. For paving, cracks in rocks, or edging, but allow it some shade as it dislikes dryness and too much sun. Early to mid summer. Corsica, Sardinia.

MENZIESIA (Ericaceae)
Shrubs from North America and eastern Asia with tiered branches and typically ericaceous, bell- or urn-shaped flowers.

M. ciliicalyx. This is the species most usually grown by alpine gardeners, as it is a dwarf shrub of neat habit. It is not unlike a compressed enkianthus, having the same tendency to whorled foliage and terminal, hanging clusters of flowers, which shade from greenish to pink. *M.c. purpurea* has crimson, white-bloomed flowers. About 60 cm (2 ft), but there is a still dwarfer form. Late spring to early summer. Japan.

MICROMERIA (Labiatae)
Thyme-like, aromatic plants from hot, dry places. They are not reliably hardy, but are neat perennials or subshrubs, valuable for their late flowering. For gritty soils or the scree. Propagation by seed or cuttings.

M. corsica. A small, lavender-scented subshrub with a profusion of small, lavender-pink flowers over grey foliage. The long-standing name is invalid and should in future be referred to as *Acinos corsicus*. 13 cm (5 in). Mid to late summer. Corsica and Sardinis.

M. microphylla. A twiggy, much branched, aromatic shrublet with small, dark grey-green leaves and purple-pink flowers. 23 cm (9 in). Late summer to early autumn. Corsica, Sicily.

MIMULUS (Scrophulariaceae)
The monkey flowers — also known as musks – are bright, almost flamboyant, clump-forming plants with bright green foliage and large, snapdragon-like, two-lipped flowers in a summery range of gold, red and orange. They enjoy cool, moist spots; the wetter they are, the more sun they can take. Seed or cuttings provide methods of propagation.

sp. Mac&W 5257. Plants from seed collected by MacPhail and Watson. (One of us (JK) had the seed in 1975 as C & W 5257, i.e. Cheese and Watson.) The most widely grown is *M.* 'Andean Nymph', and this has come to be, for the time being, the name by which the species is known. 'Andean Nymph' itself is pale cream, marked with strawberry pink and 10–15 cm (4–6 in) tall. There are other forms, such as 'Andean Pink', which has large, pink flowers and is taller at 25 cm (10 in). Late spring to early autumn. Andes.

M. cupreus. An Andean species of tufted habit, with yellow flowers that turn copper as they age. It has given rise to several cultivars, including 'Bee's Dazzler', bright crimson, 'Red Emperor', and the widely grown 'Whitecroft Scarlet'. They range from 10–15 cm (4–6 in) and flower in summer.

M. guttatus. A North American species, naturalized in ditches in northern Europe. It is too tall for the rock garden, but several of its forms and hybrids with other species are excellent, such as 'A. T. Johnson', with large, yellow flowers with red flecks; 'Highland Red', crimson, 10 cm (4 in); and the little 'Inshriach Crimson', which is only 8 cm (3 in) high .

MINUARTIA (Caryophyllaceae)
Minuartias are sandworts, closely related to arenarias and saginas and often confused with them.

M. stellata. Makes hard, pad-like cushions of tightly packed rosettes of small, narrow leaves. The tiny, white, starry flowers, usually solitary, are held just above the foliage. Less than 2.5 cm (1 in). Late spring to early summer. Balkans.

M. verna. A slightly domed, firm cushion of needle-like leaves with white, five-petalled flowers on wiry stems. They are purple in the throat. For a trough or scree. 5 cm (2 in). Late spring to mid summer. Balkans.

MITCHELLA (Rubiaceae)
There are two species; only one is in general cultivation.

M. repens. Partridge berry. An entirely prostrate shrublet with glossy green leaves and daphne-like, stemless flowers, pink with a red flush. Conspicuous red berries. For a peaty, shady place or a pan in the alpine house. Early to mid summer. N. America.

MOLTKIA (Boraginaceae)
Shrubby or herbaceous plants, closely related to *Lithospermum*. They are happy in any well drained soil and do not mind lime — in fact they may prefer it. Propagation is by summer cuttings.

M. × intermedia (syn. *Lithospermum × intermedium*). A hybrid between *M. petraea* and *M. suffruticosa*. It is a subshrub with hairy, greyish green leaves and spreading croziers of bright blue, tubular to funnel-shaped flowers. 25 cm (10 in). Early summer.

M. petraea. A dense, somewhat twiggy, dwarf shrub with grey-hairy leaves and brilliant blue, narrowly funnel-shaped flowers opening from pink buds. 25 cm (10 in). Early summer. Greece.

MONARDELLA (Labiatae)
The alpine monardellas are miniature bergamots from North America. They like sheltered, sunny spots with a gritty, well-drained soil.

M. macrantha. A tufted plant that spreads gently, making a mass of roots. The oval leaves are tinted with red except in white flowered forms. The flower heads consist of narrow, lipped, scarlet tubes in tight heads, surrounded by pinkish purple bracts. 20 cm (8 in). Mid to late summer. California.

M. villosa. Not as spectacular with smaller flowers in shades from purple to red. A selected form, 'Sheltonii', is sometimes offered. 25 cm (10 in).

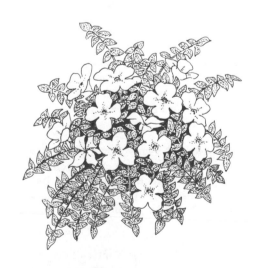

Morisia monanthos

MORISIA (Cruciferae)
M. monanthos. This is the only species. It makes flat rosettes of deep green, much cut leaves, just above which are the relatively large, four-petalled, rich yellow flowers. It is long-flowering and highly decorative in a trough, scree or pot, but needs a poor soil in order to retain its character and length of life. Propagate by root cuttings. 5 cm (2 in). Mid spring to mid summer. Corscia and Sardinia.

MYOSOTIS (Boraginaceae)
The forget-me-nots are mostly weedy, short-lived and prone to mildew, but a few are among the finest gems of alpine gardening. The New Zealand species, like the gentians from that country, are almost all white. Propagation is by seed.

M. alpestris. Short-lived, but well worth growing for its typically blue, forget-me-not flowers on neat, tufted plants. It prefers a damp soil but in a sunny position. The larger leaved form, 'Ruth Fischer', which has larger flowers on shorter stems, is usually grown. 20 cm (8 in). Early to mid summer. European mountains. *M.a. rupicola* is a 5 cm (2 in) dwarf for a trough.

M. australis. In effect a hairy, upright forget-me-not with yellow flowers. Wild forms are sometimes white, 20 cm (8 in). Early to mid summer. New Zealand.

M. azorica. Occasionally in cultivation. It is safest in the alpine house, as it is not entirely hardy. It has very large, deep blue flowers that open from violet-purple buds. 20 cm (8 in). Summer. Azores, Canaries.

M. colensoi. A creeping perennial with prostrate stems, neat, downy, grey-green foliage, and large, usually single, white flowers in the leaf axils. Mid spring to early summer. Canterbury, New Zealand.

M. explanata. An upright, tufted plant with terminal clusters of white flowers over softly downy foliage. 15 cm (6 in). Late spring to early summer. Arthur's Pass, New Zealand.

MYRTEOLA (Myrtaceae)
A dozen dwarf myrtles have been separated from *Myrtus* into their own genus.

M. nummularia (syn. *Myrtus nummularia*). Quite unlike the usual idea of a myrtle. This is a prostrate mat of tiny, oval leaves on tangled, reddish stems. It is aromatic and enjoys moist, peaty situations in sheltered gardens away from the coldest areas. It has small, white, stemless flowers and conspicuous pink berries. Often grown in a pot in the alpine house. Self-rooted stems may be detached and treated as cuttings. Late spring. Falklands and Straits of Magellan.

NIEREMBERGIA (Solanaceae)
There are two species in this genus that are grown in rock gardens. Although they are members of the potato family, the flowers are more campanula-like. They thrive in sunny places where there is no danger of drought. Propagation is by seed or division.

N. caerulea. The flowers of this small, bushy plant are blue-mauve and hardly caerulean. However, they are large for the size of the plant and have a long season. It is hardy only in mild areas. 15 cm (6 in). Early summer to early autumn. Argentina.

N. repens (syn. *N. rivularis*). Not bushy, but creeping and rooting as it goes, with even larger flowers of pearly white. It is hardier than the previous species and highly ornamental, especially in paving. 5 cm (2 in). Mid to late summer. Argentina, Chile.

NOTOTHLASPI (Cruciferae)
N. rosulatum. The penwiper plant is one of the two species in the genus. It is rarely seen, but is a 'classic' alpine. It forms an imbricated, flat rosette of leaves, serrate or dentate, pointed, and covered with white hairs. From it arises a stout, short flower stalk which carries a dense head of surprisingly large, creamy white, highly fragrant, four-petalled flowers. It is monocarpic and seeds from New Zealand are not always easy to germinate. Growing it is not that difficult in the alpine house in a very gritty, stony compost, but getting it to flower well is a triumph. 10 cm (4 in). Early to mid summer. Marlborough to South Canterbury, New Zealand.

Notothlaspi rosulatum

OENOTHERA (Onagraceae)
The evening primroses vary from tall perennials to plants that are almost entirely sessile. They are almost all yellow flowered, with large, cup-shaped blooms. They are easily grown in sunny, well-drained positions. Propagation is by seed or root cuttings.

O. acaulis. Has dandelion-like leaves, prostrate branches, and white flowers as much as 8 cm (3 in) across that turn pink as they age. *O.a. aurea* has yellow flowers. Mid summer to early autumn. Chile.

O. caespitosa. A nearly stemless species, with large, white flowers, 9 cm (3½ in) across over rosettes of spatulate leaves. The blooms become suffused with pink as they age and are fragrant. 10 cm (4 in). Mid to late summer. N. America.

O. fruticosa. A variable plant, suitable only in its shorter forms. It has large, deep yellow flowers. Plants from 15–30 cm (6–12 in) only. Mid summer to early autumn. N. America.

O missouriensis. Has flowers that are almost too large for the rock garden. They are 15 cm (6 in) across and very beautiful. The stems are trailing. Mid summer to early autumn. N. America.

O. pumila (syn. *O. perennis*). The flowers in this species are unusually small but are congregated into spikes. It is in many ways the best for the rock garden as it is not too overpowering. 15 cm (6 in). Mid summer to early autumn. N. America.

O. speciosa. A pink-flowered species with relatively modest flowers that are about 3 cm (just over 1 in) across. Most plants belong to the variety *childsii*. 20 cm (8 in). Mid to late summer. N. America.

OMPHALODES (Boraginaceae)
Plants with a similarity to forget-me-nots but with larger, more conspicuous flowers and a general preference for cool, shady positions, although some are sun lovers. Propagation by seed, division or cuttings.

O. cappadocica. An easily grown, rhizomatous perennial with mats of long, heart-shaped leaves and sprays of intensely blue flowers. It prefers a leafy, cool position. 15 cm (6 in). Mid to late spring. Caucasus.

O. luciliae. From tufts of blue-grey leaves arise sprays of large flowers of a unique, opalescent, light sky blue. The plant requires a gritty soil in sun, but shade in the hottest part of the day and it dislikes drought. For these reasons it is often given the intensive supervision of the alpine house, but is hardy. It is said to need lime, but this is doubtful. 15 cm (6 in). Early to mid summer. Greece.

O. verna. The blue-eyed Mary of the European Alps is delightful in a shady, peaty, leafy spot, where it spreads by runners and may almost become invasive. Its small flowers are pure, deep blue. 15 cm (6 in). Late winter to mid spring.

OMPHALOGRAMMA (Primulaceae)
A genus of plants very closely related to primulas and differing from them botanically in only minor ways. For gardeners, however, they represent great refinement, with their large, often sumptuously coloured flowers contrasting with short stems and small leaves. In some ways they resemble miniature gloxinias. After flowering, the stems lengthen and the leaves enlarge. They are difficult to grow but become easier in cool, humid climates such as those of Scotland. They resent an excess of winter wet, however, and are best in a well-drained but leafy spot in part shade. Propagate by seed or by dividing established clumps — essential to ensure continued flowering.

O. elegans. One of the easier species. Its flowers are very large and richly bluish purple, appearing before the leaves. 8–10 cm (3–4 in) at flowering; taller later. Summer. Tibet.

O. vinciflorum. The easiest species (but still not exactly child's play). It is variable, with some forms flowering while the stem is quite short, but the usual being about 15 cm (6 in) in height. It flowers after the oval, hairy leaves have developed and blooms are large and violet. Summer. W. China.

ONONIS (Leguminosae)
The species that are grown by alpine gardeners are lovers of sun and stony places and represent a genus centred on the Mediterranean but with outliers elsewhere, including Britain. Propagate by seed or cuttings.

O. cristata (syn. *O. cenisia*). A tricky plant, best in a pot in the alpine house but it has a long tap-root and is intolerant of disturbance. It makes a low mat of tough stems with small, trifoliate leaves and solitary, pink, delicately veined pea-flowers in profusion. 8 cm (3 in). Early summer to early autumn. French Alps.

O. fruticosa. A compact, dwarf shrub with flowers in two shades of rose-pink. For a place on a sunny scree. 30 cm (12 in). Early to late summer. Pyrenees.

O. natrix. A subshrub for the driest, stoniest, poorest places, which encourage it to keep in character and not become leggy and soft. It is then a bushy plant with many yellow flowers with red-streaked standard petals. 30 cm (12 in). Late spring to late summer. Central and S. Europe.

181

O. rotundifolia. This is the most beautiful of the ononis, making a rounded bush with small, round leaves and a long succession of large, pea-shaped flowers in rose pink, the standards being streaked with red. They are borne in axillary clusters of two or three. 30 cm (12 in). Late spring to late summer. Central and S. Europe.

ONOSMA (Boraginaceae)
Onosmas are on the coarse side. Some are not worthy of cultivation, but others are quite fascinating in a hairy sort of way. They enjoy hot, dry positions in gritty soils. Propagate by seed or cuttings.

O. albopilosum. A hater of winter wet and is worth growing in the alpine house. Its leaves are a downy grey and its flowers, several to a cluster, are tubular- to trumpet-shaped, 2.5 cm (1 in) long, white, flushed with rose pink. 20 cm (8 in). Summer. Asia Minor.

O. alboroseum. Often taken to include the former species but is currently regarded as separate. The leaves are more silvery and hairy and the white flowers age to a deep rose pink.

O. tauricum. Includes plants grown as *O. echioides*, although the species are distinct. Both have croziers of hanging, yellow flowers, but *O. echioides* is a coarse plant, whereas *O. tauricum* is neat tucked into a crevice between rocks in a hot, sunny position. Its flowers are fragrant. 20 cm (8 in). Summer. Asia Minor.

OPHIOPOGON (Liliaceae)
O. planiscapus. Almost always grown as the variety *nigrescens*. It looks very much like a small, tufted grass with leaves that are almost black. It bears racemes of small, white bells that turn bluish as they mature. Black berries follow. It is easily grown in any good soil, not necessarily in the alpine garden. 8 cm (3 in). Late summer to early autumn. Japan.

ORIGANUM (Labiatae)
This is the genus to which the majorams (origano) belong. Most of them are too coarse for the rock garden, although the golden majoram makes a fine edging for a border. These aromatic plants require sun and a well-drained soil.

O. amanum. A small, wiry, tufted plant with apple green leaves and large, two-lipped flowers of rose pink, subtended by light pink, greenish-tinted bracts. For a sunny, hot crevice, scree, or a pot in the alpine house. 10 cm (4 in). Mid to late summer. Turkey.

O. dictamnus. The Dittany of Crete that seventeenth-century army surgeons used to carry as routine because of its efficacy in treating wounds. It is not hardy, but deserves a place in the alpine house because of its neat, domed appearance, softly felted, rounded leaves and terminal heads of pink flowers enclosed in greenish pink bracts that are so large as to give a hop-like effect. 20 cm (8 in). Early summer to early autumn.

O. laevigatum. Hardy and robust, although quite small. It makes a neat mat of dark green leaves that are not hairy, above which rise wiry stems of 25 cm (10 in) which arch so as not to rise more than 15 cm (6 in) or so. The branched sprays of reddish purple are extremely elegant and long-lasting and the plant is easily grown. Late summer to mid autumn. Turkey.

OURISIA (Scrophulariaceae)
Ourisias are plants that enjoy peaty, moist places. They thrive in the wet as long as it is not stagnant. They shrink from the sun and require shade, even if the soil is moist. They are not patient with lime. Ourisias are found in South America, as well as in Australia and New Zealand.

O. caespitosa. A small, tightly mat-forming species, with grey-green, notched leaves and slender, wiry stems bearing clusters of white flowers. The variety *O.c. gracilis*, which is even neater, is the only usually grown. 10 cm (4 in). Late spring to early summer. New Zealand.

O. coccinea. Has many wiry flowering stems rising well clear of fresh green mats of foliage, carrying tubular flowers of brilliant scarlet, reminiscent of narrow-bloomed penstemons. 25 cm (10 in). Late spring to autumn. Chile.

O. 'Loch Ewe'. A hybrid between *O. coccinea* and *O. macrophylla*. It has mats of green foliage and sprays of delicate pink flowers. 30 cm (12 in). Summer.

O. macrocarpa. Coarse by comparison, with large, flashy, light green leaves; the flowers are large too, pure white, and up to eight in a head. 45 cm (18 in). Summer. New Zealand.

O. macrophylla. Also somewhat coarse in the leaf, but its stems are shorter and the white flowers are most generously produced in showy heads. Good ground cover for a moist, peaty corner. 25 cm (10 in). Summer. New Zealand.

O. 'Snowflake'. A putative hybrid between *O. caespitosa and O. macrocarpa*. It covers itself with large, shining white flowers in summer. 20 cm (8 in).

Ourisia 'Snowflake'

O. suaveolens. A high alpine cushion plant, with rosettes of short, overlapping, dark green leaves and rose-pink flowers, fading to shell pink. They are five-petalled, and each petal has a deep terminal notch. The effect is similar to a dionysia or primula. 2.5–5 cm (1–2 in). Argentina.

OXALIS (Oxalidaceae)

Oxalis count among their number some of the most infuriating weeds and some of the most

enchanting alpines. Too many of the former have been introduced as garden plants and great care should be taken over any new oxalis. The late Roy Elliott described some of them as having 'the reproductive proclivity of frog-spawn'. The following need hold no such terrors.

O. acetosella. This is the wood sorrel of European woodlands. It is charming, especially when grown, as it usually is, in the form *O.a.rosea*, which has pink flowers instead of white. The trifoliate leaves spread on runners, and the plant is not for the rock garden, but for a cool spot among trees. 5 cm (2 in). Early to mid spring.

O. adenophylla. A fine plant that keeps to itself, making a neat clump of bulbs, heavily coated in fibre. The leaves are grey-green and made up of a dozen or so folded leaflets so that they look like ruffs, or half-open parasols. The flowers are round and silky pink, paler at the centres. 10 cm (4 in). Mid to late spring. Chile.

O. enneaphylla. This is perhaps the gem of the genus. The root is a short, branched, non-invasive rhizome, from which thread-like stalks support tiny, round, ruff-like leaves, each with nine leaflets. The flowers are large for the size of the plant, roundly cup-shaped and pearly white. 5 cm (2 in). Late spring to mid summer. Falklands and Patagonia. *O.e. rosea* has flowers of a beautiful, deep rose pink. *O.e. minutifolia* is an even smaller plant, ideal for a trough, with large, pink flowers. *O.e. rubra* is almost as small as the last named and has flowers of the deepest pink. The tiny leaves are suffused with maroon at the edges.

O. laciniata. One of the finest alpines. The thready leaf stalks carry daintily folded leaves like minute catherine wheels, and the large flowers are of the deepest, royal purple. For a choice spot in a trough. 5 cm (2 in). Early summer. Patagonia.

O. magellanica. This is enjoying renewed popularity. It is completely prostrate and has white flowers just above the foliage. For a cool, woodland spot. South America.

O. oregana. This is for all purposes a pink, North American version of *O. acetosella*.

Oxalis laciniata

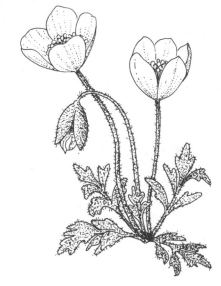

Papaver alpinum

O. deppei, chrysantha, articulata, obtusa and *depressa* are all recommended from time to time, but we suggest caution in introducing them to the alpine garden.

PAPAVER (Papaveraceae)
A few poppies are delightful in the rock garden. Propagation is by seed.

P. alpinum. This is not really a species but an aggregate of many species. This is not to denigrate it, as the short-lived plants are dainty and charming. They have finely divided, grey-green foliage, slender flower stems, and cup-shaped flowers in pink, white, orange and yellow. They succeed anywhere in sun where the soil is well drained. 15 cm (6 in). Early summer and for weeks thereafter. Alps and Pyrenees.

P. miyabeanum. This unfortunate plant has been catalogued under all sorts of wrong names, notably "Papaver tok-wokii" and "Papaver tattywackii". The author of the name, Tatewaki, appears in abbreviated form (Tatew) after the name of the plant, which is in honour of another botanist, Miyabe. Both are

Japanese. This is a delightful alpine poppy with creamy yellow flowers. 15 cm (6 in). Summer. Japan.

PARAHEBE (Scrophulariaceae)
The parahebes have been separated off from the hebes — New Zealand shrubby veronicas — which in turn were removed from *Veronica*. They are all from New Zealand and like a sunny position away from frosty winds. Their flowers are in racemes and are similar to those of speedwells. Propagate by cuttings.

P. × bidwillii. Makes a very small, neat shrub with rounded leaves and heads of flowers that are white, veined with pink. 20 cm (8 in). Summer.

P. catarractae. A more erect, but still small shrub, with white flowers with crimson eyes. A blue-flowered hebe is sometimes offered incorrectly under this name. 20 cm (8 in). Late summer to mid autumn.

P. lyallii. A semi-prostrate, humpy, small shrub with leathery leaves and white flowers veined with pink. A parent of *P. × bidwillii*. 20 cm (8 in). Late summer to early autumn.

PARAQUILEGIA (Ranunculaceae)
This is one of the genera that sets a problem for alpine gardeners; most are all too keen to solve it. The plants need the shelter of the alpine house generally, but in climates like those of Scotland, they enjoy the combination of coolness and high humidity, while relishing the freshness that comes from not needing to be shaded. Their size and need for perfect drainage makes a trough their ideal station.

P. anemonoides (syn. *P. grandiflora*). Rue-like foliage grows close to the ground with large, bowl-shaped flowers in a delicate, luminous shade of mauve blue. They have, with some justification, been described as 'diaphanous'. 10–15 cm (4–6 in). Mid to late spring. Himalaya to W. China.

Paraquilegia anemonoides

P. microphylla. Has even smaller, more intricately cut leaves and smaller, white flowers. 10 cm (4 in). Mid to late spring. Himalaya.

PARNASSIA (Parnassiaceae; Saxifragaceae)
Parnassias are little-known plants for peaty, cool places, preferring damp, even wet soils.

They have bright green leaves that are slightly succulent, and five-petalled flowers, each petal having an associated staminode (petaloid stamen). Nearly all are white. Propagate by division, or by seed which should be sown as soon as it is ripe. The species are remarkably similar to one another.

P. fimbriata. The fringed, white flowers sometimes exceed 2.5 cm (1 in) in width. 15–30 cm (6–12 in). Mid to late summer. N. America.

P. nubicola. The white flowers are large and closely approach 2.5 cm (1 in) in width. Heart-shaped basal leaves. 15–25 cm (6–10 in). Late summer to early autumn. Himalaya.

P. palustris. The white flowers, beautifully veined with green, are usually a little more than half the size of the two species above. It is a native of Europe, including Britain (grass of Parnassus), but is not easy to grow. 10–20 cm (4–8 in). Mid summer to early autumn.

PAROCHETUS (Leguminosae)
P. communis. At present this is the only species. It is found in the Himalaya and mountains of East Africa, but the East African form will constitute another in the near future. The Himalayan form is known as the shamrock pea, which describes it very well. Its trifoliate leaves with brown markings are not unlike some clovers and the vivid blue flowers on short, upright stems, are as large as those of cultivated peas. It is a beautiful plant, rooting as it goes, but only marginally hardy. It should be given a sheltered place and some degree of protection in severe weather. 8 cm (3 in). Mid autumn to late winter.

PARONYCHIA (Illecebraceae; Caryophyllaceae)
A genus of mat-forming plants, rather thyme-like, with conspicuous, papery bracts that hide the clusters of insignificant flowers and give the plants a silvery appearance. They come from Mediterranean areas and like a hot, dry position.

P. argentea and **P. capitata**. Virtually identical species. They make neat mats, hidden for a long period in summer by the bracts.

PENSTEMON (Scrophulariceae)

To attempt accurately to list penstemons is to tempt fate, as their nomenclature is in a parlous condition. They may be tall herbaceous perennials or have woody bases and long, straight non-woody stems, or dwarf, even mat-forming shrubs. These last are the most suitable for the alpine garden and include subshrubs. The flowers are always more or less tubular and two-lipped. They require hot, sunny positions and if the soil is fairly poor they can live in excess of a decade; otherwise they are short-lived. There is only one species in the whole genus that does not come from North America or Mexico. Propagation is by summer cuttings.

P. davidsonii. A variable species. Under the species name are grown contour-hugging, dwarf, gnarled shrubs with short flower stems carrying racemes of large flowers in the lavender-pink to ruby red range. 10–15 cm (4–6 in). Early to mid summer. *P.* 'Six Hills' is a fine, vigorous hybrid of the above with pink flowers. *P.d. menziesii* is variable but generally more erect, with sprays of lavender-pink to purple flowers. 20 cm (8 in). *P.d. menziesii* 'Microphyllus' is smaller but has flowers of large size for the plant. 10 cm (4 in).

P. heterophyllus. A woody-based plant with quite tall stems and long, lanceolate stems. For the alpine garden the form 'True Blue', which is less than 30 cm (12 in) tall, should be chosen. Its flowers are clear, azure blue and very beautiful. Mid to late summer.

P. hirsutus pygmaeus. A fine little plant with reddish leaves, rather like an erect thyme. The relatively showy flowers of lilac pink are produced in large quantities. 15 cm (6 in). Early to mid summer.

P. newberry. A tight, mat-forming shrub with leathery leaves and many-flowered, compact racemes of bright, purplish red. 23–30 cm (9–12 in). Mid summer. *P.n. humilior* is the plant for many years known as *P. roezlii*. There is no 'true *Penstemon roezlii*' — a phrase often heard among alpine gardeners who might one day turn out to have been right. It is similar to the above but neater and has bright, clear, cherry-red flowers.

P. pinifolius. An entirely distinct species. It is a neat subshrub with bright green leaves like short pine needles all along the branches, giving a distinctly feathery look to the plant. The flowers are vivid scarlet and narrowly tubular, more reminiscent of *Zauschneria* than *Penstemon*. 20 cm (8 in). Late summer.

Penstemon pinifolius

P. procerus tolmiei. A most unusual member of the genus, forming domed mats of neat foliage and bearing rounded heads of red-purple flowers. For the scree or a sunny position in gritty soil. 13 cm (5 in). All summer.

P. rupicola. Very similar to *P. newberryi humilior*, but is quite prostrate and has few-flowered racemes of rose-carmine flowers. Late spring to early summer.

P. scouleri. This species is currently taken by some authorities to be *P. fruticosus scouleri*. It is a variable plant with flower colour from a fair red, through lilac, to white and is large-flowered and floriferous. 23–30 cm (9–12 in). Mid summer.

PENTACHONDRA (Epicradaceae)

P. pumila. A tiny, congested shrub with small, glossy, bronzed leaves. The white, tubular flowers are followed by red berries. It requires shade, moisture, and a lime-free soil. Propagate by cuttings in early summer. New Zealand.

PEREZIA (Compositae)

A genus of plants with daisy-like flowers. Most come from Peru, but one species from the Falklands and Tierra del Fuego sometimes appears in cultivation.

P. recurvata. A stiffly-branched plant with short, down-curved, linear leaves. If a free-flowering form can be raised which has the pure, deep blue of the best forms, it would be a welcome return of a plant that is best kept going from cuttings taken every year. It is hardy, but dies off as if homesick. 10 cm (4 in). Summer.

PERNETTYA (Ericaceae)

Evergreen, shrubs, grown for their berries rather than for their flowers. The popular *P. mucronata* is too large for the rock and alpine garden, but the following species are prostrate shrublets, ideal for spaces between dwarf rhododendrons and other plants that need the same peaty, part-shade, moist conditions.

P. nana. A spreading, low subshrub, making a triangle of wiry branches with tiny leaves, solitary white flowers and small red berries. 10 cm (4 in). New Zealand.

P. prostrata. This is in cultivation in two forms, *P.p. purpurea* and *P.p. pentlandii*. They have small, leathery, shiny leaves, flowers like a small lily-of-the-valley in summer, and pink to red fruits in autumn. Chile.

P. pumila. A prostrate, spreading, soft-branched shrublet with larger, pink or white fruits. Falklands and Tierra del Fuego.

P. tasmanica. The gem among the small pernettyas. It makes cushioned mats that become conspicuously studded with large red fruits in autumn. There is a white-berried form. 2 in (5 cm). Tasmania.

PERSICARIA (Polygonaceae)

This genus is one of the fractions of the erstwhile *Polygonum*, which is now divided into *Persicaria*, *Fallopia* and *Polygonum*, with most of the weeds left behind in the old genus, which used to include border plants such as the bistort, as well as the two alpine garden species.

P. affinis (syn. *Polygonum affine*). A fibrous woody, prostrate plant with long leaves sheathing the reddish stems. The branches curve towards the ends, thrusting upwards the conspicuous spikes of tiny rose-red flowers. 23 cm (9 in). Late summer to early autumn. Himalaya. The named forms 'Donald Lowndes', 'Dimity' and 'Darjeeling Red', especially the last, have red, rather than rusty coloured flowers.

P. vacciniifolia (syn. *Polygonum vacciniifolium*). Altogether more slender, forming neat mats of branches that upturn sharply to hold upright the long, slim spikes of bright red flowers. These turn a pretty brown in autumn and are worth leaving on the plant. 15 cm (6 in). Early to mid autumn. Himalaya.

PETROCALLIS (Cruciferae)

P. pyrenaica. At its best, this sole representative of the genus in cultivation is very beautiful indeed; grown badly it is worthless. It makes a moss-like pad of foliage which, in the wild and in a well-grown specimen, becomes entirely covered in heads of small flowers that are pink with a hint of lilac. The more easterly forms, particularly that from the Hoch Obir in Austria, are clear, soft pink. The flowers are scented. Best in a pan in the alpine house or frame in a stony compost. Propagate by seed or by treating branches as late summer cuttings. Less than 5 cm (2 in). Late spring. Pyrenees to Kawawanken.

PETROCOPTIS (Caryophyllaceae)

A genus of one or two species, related to *Lychnis* and found in the Pyrenees. It should be noted by nurserymen that the specific epithet *lagascae* refers to a species in this genus and not in *Petrocallis*. For a sunny place on the rock garden.

P. glaucifolia (syn. *P. lagascae*, *Lychnis lagascae*). Tufted, blue-grey foliage and campion-like, carmine-pink flowers with a white eye. 15 cm (6 in). Early summer.

P. pyrenaica. Similar to the above, but with greener leaves and flowers of soft pink, sometimes white. 15 cm (6 in). Early summer.

PETROCOSMEA (Gesneraceae)
Only one species of this ramonda-like genus is in cultivation. It requires alpine house treatment, preferably in a shady corner, with a top dressing of non-absorbent stone. Propagate by seed. Division is possible, but daunting. *P. nervosa*, with blue flowers and *P. parryorum*, violet, are only occasionally seen.

P. kerrii. This has foliage like a ramonda, but more velvety, and flowers that are more bell-shaped. They are two-lipped, white, with yellow centres. The plant is of arresting beauty, but is difficult. 10 cm (4 in). China. Summer.

PETROPHYTUM (Rosaceae)
A genus of plants from North America, cushion-forming, alpine versions of *Spiraea*, requiring crevice planting or very quick drainage and a gritty soil. Three species are found in alpine gardens and are summer-flowering.

P. caespitosum. Silkily hairy, small-leaved cushions bear dense, fluffy racemes of minute, white flowers.

P. cinerascens. Similar, but the foliage is much less silky and a matt, grey-green.

P. hendersonii. Has dark bronze-green cushions and short spires of flowers immediately above the foliage.

PHACELIA (Hydrophyllaceae)
Phacelias are North American plants and are mostly annuals and biennials, including some good border plants. One species, however, is a classic alpine. It is thought to be biennial or naturally short-lived but is in fact a perennial that is difficult to grow.

P. sericea. Consists of rosettes of silver-silky, lobed leaves, from which rise stems bearing long, dense racemes of blue-purple, bell-shaped flowers with protruding stamens. It is a lovely plant but needs a very gritty soil, similar to that given to aretian androsaces, and protection from winter damp, preferably in the alpine house. Propagation is by seed. 15 cm (6 in). Late spring.

PHILESIA (Liliaceae)

P. magellanica (syn. *P. buxifolia*). This is the only species in the genus. It is a small, much-branched shrub with narrow, leathery, dark green leaves and superbly conspicuous, bright crimson-rose flowers, 5 cm (2 in) long, in ones or twos at the ends of the branches. They are tubular and very large for such a small shrub. It prefers a moist, well-drained, peaty, leafy, lime-free soil in part shade. It is hardy in mild areas and in shelter. Propagate by division or by lifting and detaching suckers. 30 cm (12 in). Early summer. Chile.

PHLOX (Polemoniaceae)
Phloxes are Northern American plants with one unimportant exception. They are annuals, border perennials, or mat-forming rock plants. Of the later, a dozen or so species are in cultivation, but hundreds of cultivars exist. With occasional exceptions they are happy in a well-drained soil in sun and can be easily propagated by soft cuttings taken as the last flowers fade.

P. adsurgens. Rather more upright than most rock garden phloxes. It has slender stems and quite large, pink or white flowers but few to head. 15–20 cm (6–8 in). Late spring to early summer. California and Oregon.

P. bifida. Makes prostrate mats, above which are flowers of quite large size in white or lavender. 20 cm (8 in). Mid to late spring. E. North America.

P. borealis. A tight cushion of tiny, prickly foliage, studded with light lilac flowers. For a choice place in a raised bed or trough. Rare. 2.5 cm (1 in). Mid to late spring.

P. caespitosa. This is even tighter than *P. borealis*, making a neat mat with stemless, white or pale blue flowers. it benefits from being grown in a frame or the alpine house. Late spring. W. North America.

P. 'Chattahoochee'. Probably a hybrid of *P. divaricata*. It is not mat-forming, but makes a loose, lightly leafy tangle of stems, 30 cm (12 in) long (but the plant is less than two-thirds this height), and loose heads of deep violet flowers with a pink-purple eye appear in late spring.

P. douglasii. This neat species makes tight, prickly mats and has rounded, mauve flowers. The round flowers and general habit are transmitted to its many cultivars, of which a selection follows. They are excellent plants for the scree, crevices, raised beds and troughs. Most are from 5–10 cm (2–4 in) and flower in late spring.

'Apple Blossom': showy, lilac pink
'Apollo': compact, rich violet
'Boothman's Variety': large, circular flowers, clear mauve with dark centre
'Crackerjack': compact, brilliant crimson red, long flowering
'Eva': lavender-pink with a crimson eye
'Iceberg': compact, white flowers tinged with blue
'Lilac Cloud': vigorous, lilac
'Red Admiral': crimson red, free flowering

P. 'Kelly's Eye'. A seedling of *P. borealis*, possibly hybridized by chance with *P. subulata* 'Samson', that occurred spontaneously in the garden of one of the authors of this book. It is a very neat plant, making a tight mat of small, prickly leaves, and bearing such masses of flowers that the foliage becomes hidden. They are white at first with a discreet carmine eye, becoming gently flushed with carmine-pink as they age. A fellow nurseryman coined the name, though the assertion that it refers to a bloodshot condition is, of course, without foundation! Mid to late spring.

P. kelseyi. This is almost always seen in gardens in the form of the cultivar 'Rosette', which is a dwarf cushion of slightly succulent leaves and clusters of deep violet-pink flowers on 5 cm (2 in) stems.

P. nana ensifolia. This represents a whole group, or style of phlox, to which the names *P. mesoleuca* and *P. triovulata* have been applied from time to time. There are several phlox of the *nana* type in the wild, but the one usually seen in cultivation — almost always as an alpine house specimen — consists of long shoots springing from a central point and from underground, each tough, wiry and prostrate, though the whole is tangled, and furnished sparsely with long, linear leaves. The terminal flowers are on 2.5 cm (1 in) stems and are very large indeed. Their colour is a rich, solid rose-pink with a white eye. It needs a lime-free compost. Root cuttings are the preferred method of increase. Late spring to early summer. Texas.

Phlox nana ensifolia

P. x procumbens. Represented by the cultivar 'Millstream'. It has leafy, procumbent stems and large, mauve-pink flowers with a central red eye, surrounded by a white ring.

P. stolonifera. Until recently considered synonymous with *P. procumbens* but the former is now thought of as a distinct species and the latter as a hybrid of it. The species typically has procumbent, leafy stems in mats while

189

erect stems of 15 cm (6 in) or so carry the flower heads. The colours are in the lavender-violet-purple range, often with a flare or diffuse stripe of carmine. 'Ariane', 'Blue Ridge' and 'Pink Ridge' are the most usual cultivars. 20 cm (8 in). Mid to late spring. Eastern N. America.

P. × rugellii. A gentle plant for part shade, where it produces many blue-violet flowers with orange centres. The foliage is an attractive olive-green, forming a mat of narrow leaves. 8 cm (3 in). Summer. Western N. America.

P. subulata. A highly variable species that virtually never appears in gardens as such, but almost always as cultivars. It varies in size from the small-leaved, neat mats of *P.s. brittonii* to the coarse, rather ugly sprawl of forms like 'Temiskaming'. These are highly valued rock garden plants, flowering for a long period in mid to late spring, and the following is a small selection from the forty-odd that are available.

> *P.s. brittonii* 'Rosea' is one of the smallest phloxes, with tiny leaves making the branches individually distinguishable, and jewel-like, pink flowers. For a scree, raised bed or trough.
> *P.s.* 'Beauty of Ronsdorf' has lilac flowers. 8 cm (3 in).
> 'G. F. Wilson' is clear blue. 10 cm (4 in).
> 'Margery' is bright rose pink. 10 cm (4 in).
> 'Sampson' has large deep rose pink flowers. 10 cm (4 in).
> 'Scarlet Flame' is vigorous, carmine-scarlet. 15 cm (6 in).
> 'Temiskaming' is strong and vigorous, on the coarse side, magenta. 15 cm (6 in).
> 'Vivid' is dwarf and has deep pink flowers. Its constitution is weak, but it has a unique refinement and beauty.

PHUOPSIS (Rubiaceae)

P. stylosa. This is the only species. It is hardly an alpine, but is grown in rock gardens as ground cover. It is not unattractive, having upright stems clad in whorls of small leaves and ending in flat heads of pink, tubular flowers. It may become invasive in small rock gardens when given an open, sunny position, but can be contained. Propagation is by division. 25 cm (10 in). Late spring to early summer. Caucasus.

× PHYLLIOPSIS (Ericaceae)

A bigeneric hybrid between *Phyllodoce* and *Kalmiopsis*. It requires a peaty, lime-free soil in part shade.

× P. hillieri 'Coppelia'. This resulted from hybridization between *Kalmiopsis leachiana* and *Phyllodoce empetriformis*. It is similar to the plant below but more vigorous and has an abundance of lavender-pink flowers. Mid to late spring.

× P. hillieri 'Pinocchio'. A hybrid between *Kalmiopsis leachiana* and *Phyllodoce breweri*. It has proved itself to be a first-class dwarf shrub, bearing masses of deep, pink, rounded flowers for a long period from mid spring into early summer. 25 cm (10 in).

PHYLLODOCE (Ericaceae)

Phyllodoces are beautiful, very small, prostrate or tufted shrubs with a northerly circumpolar distribution. They have small, linear, under-rolled leaves crowding the branches and resemble refined heaths with nodding, urn-shaped flowers in terminal or subterminal clusters. They need peaty, leafy, lime-free soils in part shade.

P. aleutica. A compact, carpeting species with creamy or pale yellow, pitcher-shaped flowers. 23 cm (9 in). Late spring to early summer. Aleutian Island, Alaska, Japan, *P.a. glanduliflora* is more erect and has urn-shaped flowers of pale yellow, tinged green. *P.* 'Flora Stack' is probably a hybrid with *P. caerulea*, but has large, pure white flowers.

P. breweri. A more lax species from high altitudes in California with spreading branches and elongated, terminal custers of bright purplish pink flowers that are more widely open than in other species. It is not an easy plant and may be better in a shady part of the alpine house. 30 cm (12 in). Late spring.

P. caerulea. About the same height and grows with a mixture of procumbent and ascending branches. The flowers are purple and not blue as the name would suggest. Northern areas of Europe, N. America and Asia.

P. empetriformis. An easy-going species, soon making a well-furnished, tufted, small shrub with erect stems. When really well-suited it is capable of making quite wide mats. The flowers are clustered at the tops of the branches and are red-purple to rose pink. 25 cm (10 in). Mid to late spring. Western N. America.

P. × intermedia. A hybrid between *P. empetriformis* and *P. aleutica glanduliflora*. It is vigorous and easy, making wide mats and flowering generously. 25 cm (10 in). *P.×i.* 'Drummondii' has masses of crimson-purple flowers in late spring. *P.×i.* 'Fred Stoker' is similar, just as good, but with lighter coloured flowers.

P. nipponica. This is the smallest species. It is an erect shrublet with neat foliage, white-felted underneath, and the flowers are white, nodding, and in terminal clusters. 20 cm (8 in). Late spring to early summer. Japan.

× PHYLLOTHAMNUS (Ericaceae)
A bigeneric hybrid between *Phyllodoce* and *Rhodothamnus*.

×P. erectus. A hybrid between *Phyllodoce empetriformis* and *Rhodothamnus chamaecistus*. It is a most attractive plant, taller than most phyllodoces but, like them, crowded with linear leaves. The flowers are neither urn- nor bell-shaped, but fashioned like funnels and bright rose pink. It likes the same conditions as phyllodoces.

PHYSOPLEXIS (Campanulaceae)

P. comosa (syn. *Phyteuma comosum*) This is one of the classic alpines. It dies away completely in winter, sending up its little, jagged leaves in spring. In summer the flowers appear on stems of 2.5–5 cm (1–2 in) and take the form of clusters of wine-bottle-shaped blooms in cream and blue, tipped with black. It is safest in the alpine house but will grow happily for years in a crevice in a trough as long as slugs do not invade. It is one of the few plants that seems to have a genuine preference for limestone. 8 cm (3 in). Summer. Dolomites.

PHYTEUMA (Campanulaceae)
Most phyteumas are flowers of the hay meadows in the European Alps, but one or two are true alpines from high elevations. In general they are campanula-like perennials, but the flowers are closed at the tips and have protruding stamens. Another difference is that they are arranged in scabious-like heads.

P. globulariifolium. This species is from higher altitudes. It is a small, tufted plant with spoon-shaped leaves and short stems bearing heads of three to seven deep blue flowers. 5 cm (2 in). Mid summer to early autumn.

P. hedraianthifolium. Also a plant of the high mountains. Its leaves are much longer, grassy and toothed and beneath the flower head are several needle-shaped bracts. The flower heads are dark, violet-blue. 15 cm (6 in). Mid to late summer.

P. hemisphaericum. Similar to the previous species, but the leaves are untoothed, the bracts are oval and shorter, and the flowers are lighter blue. 10–15 cm (4–6 in). Early to late summer.

P. scheuchzeri. A taller plant with relatively small heads of deep blue flowers subtended by long, slender bracts. Blue-green, toothed leaves. 30 cm (12 in). Late spring to late summer.

PIMELIA (Thymelaeaceae)
A genus of small, twiggy, daphne-like shrubs from Australasia, of which one or two from New Zealand are grown by alpine gardeners. They are marginally hardy and require lime-free soils. They are probably best in the alpine-house or frame.

P. prostrata. Now considered to include *P. coarctata*, which should be treated as a more compact form of the species. It is a flat mat of tangled stems, with tiny, grey foliage and terminal heads of small, fragrant, white, daphne-like flowers. 5–8 cm (2–3 in). Late spring.

PLATYCODON (Campanulaceae)
Platycodons are really plants for the border. They are similar to campanulas but are balloon-like in the bud and finally larger

flowered. One species has forms that are excellent rock garden plants.

P. grandilorus. A perennial with blue-grey foliage and upright, slender stems that bear large, solitary, shallowly bell-shaped flowers up to 5 cm (2 in) across. They do not open fully until they are completely formed. 30 cm (12 in). Mid to late summer. Japan and China. *P.g. mariesii* is about 20 cm (8 in) tall, with deep purple flowers. There is a pink form and also a white. *P.g.* 'Apoyama' is superior, with a height of only 10 cm (4 in) and purplish blue flowers that are even larger. The white form is 'Apoyama Alba'.

PLEIONE (Orchidaceae)

Pleiones are hardy terrestrial orchids. They grow from pseudobulbs that renew themselves annually and gradually multiply, either by developing new, full sized ones in the year or by producing tiny, offset pseudobulbs many times smaller than the main ones. The flowers form in early spring, often before the leaves, and are something like those of cymbidiums, but have no stem, the lowest part of the flower forming a short, stem-like tube.

Flower colour may be anything from deep purple to white or light, golden yellow, almost always with strong markings in the tube and flushed tones on the five wing petals.

Pleiones should be grown in the alpine house or frame, in shallow pans of leafy soil that is never allowed to become dry once watering starts in the late winter. The pseudobulbs should be planted so that only one quarter of their height is in the soil, and if a layer of fine moss is used as a top dressing, this should be included as soil. They should be allowed to become completely dry as the foliage turns brown and falls in autumn and then may be left alone or, a little later, when the roots have shrivelled, they can be lifted from the compost and stored as bulbs in a frost-free drawer or airy box. Pleiones are about 5–8 cm (2–3 in) high when in flower and come from China and the Himalayan Chain.

Pleione nomenclature and descriptions
This is the only occasion involving a departure from the format of this part of the book, and it is imposed by the state of naming and classification of pleiones, which is a long-term source of scientific disagreement, fuelled by exciting material reintroduced from the wild. It is necessary to take all the alpine pleiones together in order to come to some understanding of the state of affairs at the time of writing.

To an extent, the genus has been reorganized into Groups under the umbrella of *P. bulbocoides*. This eliminates the following species: *P. formosana, limprichtii, pricei, henryi* and *delavayi*. Some of the lost species names appear in the Group names, e.g. *P. bulbocodioides* Formosana Group, Limprichtii Group, and Pricei Group.

The following species remain: *P. forrestii, hookeriana, humilis, maculata* and *speciosa. P. speciosa* used to be called *P. pogonioides*. Of these, the yellow-flowered *P. forrestii* is of great importance as, since its reintroduction in 1981 by the Sino-British Expedition to the Cang-Shan, it has been used for hybridizing with others to produce some cultivars of exquisite beauty.

P. bulbocodioides. Cultivars in the Formosana Group include 'Alba', 'Blush of Dawn', 'Clare', 'Iris', 'Lilac Beauty', 'Oriental Jewel', 'Oriental Splendour', 'Polar Star' and 'Snow White', in the Limprichtii Group, 'Primrose Peach', and in the Pricei Group', 'Yunnan'.

The influence of *P. forrestii* is most marked in the 'Shantung' series of hybrids.

POLYGALA (Polygalaceae)

Polygalas are the plants commonly known as milkworts, which can be annual, perennial, or even shrubby. Their distinctive flowers have a central tube and two conspicuous wings.

P. calcarea. A low, clump-forming plant with flowering stems arising from basal rosettes of spoon-shaped leaves. The flowers are small but plentifully produced and brilliant blue. It is a short-lived perennial, slightly more permanent in a limy soil. 8 cm (3 in). Late spring to early summer. Downlands in Europe.

The Californian *P. suffrutescens* is a distinctive shrubby primula, shown here growing in a well-drained crevice probably containing some humus.

Above: Primula is a large genus with many plants for the alpine gardener, some easy, some posing a definite challenge. *Primula hirsuta* is not too difficult if given winter protection.

Right: The genus *Ranunculus* produces some weeds but also some beautiful flowers, none more so than *R. amplexicaulis*.

Far right: *Ranunculus gramineus* has yellow flowers more typical of the genus but is not invasive as are some of its relatives. An easy but very effective rock garden plant.

Above: All rock gardens should include some shrubs and the willows provide a good selection. *Salix reticulata* is a ground hugging species with intriguing, upright catkins.

Right: Soldanellas are amongst the daintiest of alpines. They will do well if you keep the slugs at bay. This is *Soldanella alpina* growing in the Dolomites.

Far left: *Sternbergia lutea* is an autumn flowering bulb which will thrive in a sunny, well-drained position.

Left: Trilliums are splendid for the peat bed or woodland garden. *Trillium grandiflorum* would be a delightful one to start with. Although slow it is easy to grow.

Below: Late summer flowering rock garden plants are at a premium. *Teucrium pyrenaicum* is one such plant and is not at all difficult to grow.

Right: *Viola calcarata* has a long flowering season and a variety of colours exist. Although short lived it is easy to grow from seed.

Below: *Zauschneria californica* is a very welcome sight flowering in late summer and continuing well into the autumn. It is easy to grow in a sunny position in well-drained soil.

P. chamaebuxus. A dwarf, compact shrub never more than 15 cm (6 in) high. It has lanceolate, leathery, olive-green leaves and pairs of large flowers with bright yellow tubes and red-maroon wings. The colour is variable but constant in a given population in the wild; flowers may be all yellow or brownish orange, but the variety *P. purpurea*, sometimes listed as *grandiflora* is the plant to choose. Alps to Carpathians. Mid spring to early summer.

P. vayredae. Has narrower leaves and a less robust habit. The wings are a more conspicuously and brilliant red-purple. 10 cm (4 in). Mid to late spring. Pyrenees.

POLYGONATUM (Liliaceae)
Polygonatums are commonly called Solomon's seals.

P. hookeri. A true miniature, whose flowers show their colour as they break through the soil. They are rose-purple in bud, becoming warm, mauve-pink. The stems then lengthen, displaying the flowers beautifully. For a trough or raised bed. 10 cm (4 in). Late spring. Sikkim to West China.

POTENTILLA (Rosaceae)
A large genus of herbaceous and shrubby plants with five-petalled flowers, the petals more or less separated to show the calyx below.

P. aurea. A creeping, much-branched perennial, making mats of five-lobed, silky leaves. The flowers are a deep golden yellow, sometimes orange in the centre. There is a double form. 5 cm (2 in). Early summer to early autumn. Europe.

P. brauniana. A small, tufted, woody species with trifoliate leaves that are slightly hairy. The flowers are small and yellow. 8 cm (3 in). Early to late summer. Pyrenees and Alps.

P. crantzii. Similar to the above, but more tufted and upright. The leaves are not silky. Yellow flowers with broad petals. 155 cm (6 in). Mid summer to early autumn. N. America, Asia and Europe.

P. eriocarpa. A shrubby plant, easy to grow, with woody stems in spreading mats. The foliage is deeply lobed, almost palmate and grey-green. The flowers are 2.5 cm (1 in) across and pure, light yellow. 5 cm (2 in). Early summer to early autumn. Himalaya.

P. nitida. A highly variable plant in the wild, with some forms showing the reluctance to flower that is sometimes encountered in cultivation. Selected forms, however, flower well in tight crevices in limestone rock. Typically, it makes pad-like cushions of silky, three-lobed leaves. The flowers are stemless, rose-pink to rose-red, and large for the size of the plant. At its best it is one of the great alpine classics. 5 cm (2 in) or less. Early to mid summer. Alps and Apennines. *P.n.* 'Lissadell' has rose-pink flowers and intensely silvery foliage. Like the following variety, it flowers best if its stems are in actual contact with rock, and this is best achieved in a tight crevice. *P.n.* 'Rubra' is similar, but has extra large flowers of rich rose-red. Similar forms occur above the Sella Pass in the Dolomites of Italy.

P. x tonguei. A hybrid, whose parentage is thought to be *P. aurea* × *P. nepalensis*. Its small stature recalls the former, while the flowers, apricot with crimson centres, recall the cultivar 'Roxana' of the latter. 20 cm (8 in). Early summer to early autumn.

PRATIA (Campanulaceae)
Pratias are creeping perennials that root as they go. They have rounded, small, slightly succulent leaves and flowers that are lobelia-like but also bear resemblance to violets. The flowers are followed by colourful berries. They like moist, leafy, partly shaded places.

P. angulata. This is said by some to be distinct from a species known as *P. treadwellii*, and by others to have a superior cultivar, *P.* 'Treadwellii'. In fact, the latter is the more likely, as the species is variable in the wild in New Zealand and the name as a specific epithet does not seem to occur in the literature. It forms mats with pale green, almost perfectly rounded leaves and stemless, white flowers, streaked with purple. The berries are purple. 5 cm (2 in). Mid spring. *P.a.* 'Ohau', named after a New Zealand lake, has large, white flowers and red fruits. *P.a.* 'Jack's Pass' has red-purple berries.

P. pedunculata. This is more vigorous with oval leaves. The mauve-pink flowers are not stemless, but have slender stalks about 2.5 cm (1 in) long. It is inclined to be invasive, particularly in the moist, peaty places it likes best. *P.p.* 'County Park' has purple-blue flowers that verge on being stemless. *P.p.* 'Tom Stone' is less than 2.5 cm (1 in) high and has pale blue flowers. Both are relatively non-invasive.

PRIMULA (Primulaceae)

Primulas are found right round the northern hemisphere but for a discontinuity occurring in and near to Iran. For alpine gardeners it is a very large genus with much to interest them, including the tall species in the Candelabra section.

Primula is divided into many sections and most of them contain plants for alpine and rock gardeners. It is beyond the scope of this book to define them, but where it is important horticulturally the section is given, so that reference can be made to other works. The most important distinction for gardeners is that between European and Asiatic primulas, with American species making a small, third group.

Propagation of all primulas is by seed or division. Unless otherwise mentioned, it may be taken as being simple. Seed should never be covered with compost but just gently pressed into the surface.

EUROPEAN PRIMULAS

In general, European primulas have short stems and upward-looking flowers. They are lovers of moist soils, but they must be gritty, leafily organic and well drained. They enjoy dappled, broken shade but will tolerate sun if they have shade during the hotter parts of the day. Places in the rock garden in the shelter and part shade of rocks are ideal. Not all of them fall within this generalization, however.

P. allionii. A moderately difficult primula for the alpine house. It makes cushions of 2.5 cm (1 in) rosettes of grey-green, short, blunt leaves, more or less wavy, which are stickily glandular. The foliage must never become wet, and any spillage or splashing of soil onto the leaves must be avoided, as it can never be completely removed. The flowers are stemless and large for the size of the plant, hiding the foliage in good forms. They vary from white, through light, apple-blossom pink to a magenta red. Propagation is by careful teasing out of the crowns. They are fragile where the leaves meet the roots and any becoming detached without roots will root readily as cuttings. 5 cm (2 in). Early to mid spring. Maritime Alps. There are several named forms, from the white 'Avalanche' to the rich, rose red of 'Crowsley Variety'.

P. amoena. A primrose-like plant with branched heads like a polyanthus. The flowers are violet or mauve-violet, with a yellow eye. Forms of it are often listed as *P. altaica*, and it is likely soon to be subsumed into the species *P. elatior*, which includes the oxlip. 15 cm (6 in). Late winter to early spring. Caucasus.

P. auricula. The species is variable, but the flowers are always clear yellow and held in umbels. They are usually heavily powdered with a white farina, which is often concentrated into an eye-ring. The foliage consists of flat rosettes of smooth leaves.

There are a few wild and many garden forms and even more hybrids, all of which might be termed auriculas. The word has, however, come to be applied narrowly to two main kinds of primula hybrids; show, border and garden. Show auriculas, with their heavy dressings of farina and formally-zoned flowers are inappropriate for outdoor cultivation, let alone for the alpine garden, but alpine auriculas have enough of their wild ancestry evident to make them sit well among rocks. The best known are probably the old 'Yellow Dusty Miller' and 'Red Dusty Miller'. There are a great many of them, and a choice should be made when they are in flower. Other hybrids of *P. auricula* are described elsewhere.

P. 'Beatrice Wooster'. A superb hybrid of *P. allionii*, probably with a form of *P. marginata*. The flowers are stemless, large, and apple-blossom pink with a white eye, and the foliage is not very sticky. Early to mid spring.

P. x berninae. This is a hybrid of *P. hirsuta × P. latifolia*. It has heads of fine, purple flowers. The dwarf form, 'Windrush', is slightly more red. Early to mid spring.

P. ✕ bilekii. This has been merged with *P. ✕ forsteri*, both being considered to be hybrids between the same parents. It forms a flat cushion of curved, toothed, distinctive leaves and has large, sessile flowers of deep rose pink. Less than 5 cm (2 in). Mid spring.

P. clusiana. Umbels of up to four magenta flowers with a white eye. Tricky to place because of its colour, but a beautiful plant with unusually large flowers. Late spring to early summer. Alps.

P. 'Dianne'. This has the hybrid *P. ✕ forsteri* as a parent and is not unlike it, although its foliage is more bold. Its flowers are very large, magenta and held on short stems.

P. farinosa. The bird's eye primrose is present in all of Europe apart from Greece and Ireland. The greyish leaves are white-mealy beneath, the short scapes are covered in white meal, and the many-flowered umbels are clear pink to lavender-pink, with a yellow eye. It is not a long-lived plant, but is beautiful when given the sun, grittiness, humus and moisture that it needs. 10 cm (4 in). Early to mid spring.

P. ✕ fosteri (c.f. *P. bileckii*). This is *P. minima* ✕ *P. hirsuta*. It is similar to *P. minima*, but with glossier leaves, and it has large, short-stemmed, bright pink flowers with a white eye. Less than 5 cm (2 in).

P. frondosa. For all purposes a larger, more long-lived version of *P. farinosa*. Early to mid spring. Balkans.

P. ✕ Garryarde is a *nomen nudum*. It refers to a group of polyanthus of distinctive appearance, most of which are now hard to find. One, however, is widely grown. It should be referred to as *P. 'Guinevere'* but has for almost all its life been called *P. ✕* Garryarde 'Guinevere', which is on at least two counts impermissible. However, it is a lovely plant, with deeply bronzed, crinkled leaves, reddish-bronze stems, and heads of delicately soft pink flowers. Other forms are, or were, in a range of lavenders and lilacs. 20 cm (8 in). Spring.

P. glutinosa. Difficult to grow and detests lime, unlike most European primulas. Its sticky foliage demands a frame or alpine house, where it may be persuaded to produce its true blue flowers. 8 cm (3 in). Late spring.

P. hirsuta (syn. *P. rubra*). A variable plant, with wide, slightly sticky, toothed leaves and heads of flowers that can be anything from mauve to a good red with a white eye. It is a plant of high altitudes that may need protection in wet winters. There is a white form. Mid to late spring. Europe.

Primula hirsuta

P. juliae. Distinct in appearance, having creeping, woody stems and very neat, dark green leaves. The flowers are on very short stems, solitary, and deep, vivid red-purple with a white eye. It is a lovely plant in its own right but probably less well known than its offspring with its relative, the primrose, *P.* 'Juliana' and *P.* 'Wanda'. It enjoys moisture. Early to mid spring. Causasus. 5 cm (2 in).

P. marginata. Best grown in a frame or alpine house, even though it is perfectly hardy. The reason for this is the farina, which is distributed in highly attractive patterns on the leaves, particularly at the markedly toothed edges. The flowers, in shades of mauve-blue to clear blue, are perfectly matched to the foliage. There are several named forms and some hybrids. Among the best are 'Linda Pope', 'Marven', 'Clear's Variety' and 'Caerulea'.

P. minima. A tiny plant, often badly grown because it is not realized that it flowers in the wild at high altitude in close turf that is soaking wet as the snows melt. Any hint of drought is enough to set it severely back and discourage subsequent flowering. The 2.5 cm (1 in) wide flowers are enormous for the size of the plant and the pink petals are so deeply notched as to be Y-shaped. For a trough or raised bed. Less than 5 cm (2 in). Mid to late spring. Dolomites.

P. x pubescens. The name covers many putative crossings between a handful of species, of which the most certain are *P. auricula* and *P. hirsuta*. They have little in common apart from broad, smooth leaves, sometimes mealy at the edges. Most are 10–15 cm (4–6 in) and flower in mid to late spring. Among the many cultivars are 'Bewerley White', 'Boothman's Variety' (bright crimson), 'Faldonside' (dusky crimson), 'Freedom' (deep lilac), 'Mrs. J.H. Wilson' (deep violet) and 'Rufus' (brick red).

P. scotica. A gem but not an easy one. It is like a miniature version of *P. farinosa*, with short scapes and umbels of deep, clear purple flowers with a white eye. It needs gritty but humus-laden soil in a cool but not sunless position, preferably in a trough or raised bed. 5 cm (2 in). Late spring. Northern Scotland.

P. warshenewskyana. Pronounced 'var-shen-ev-ski-ana', this is a minute primula and one of the very few that spreads by stolons. Its clumps of foliage are tiny, and its rose-pink flowers are bright and conspicuous, particularly in the peaty, moist soil it demands. Although it is from Turkestan and Pakistan, and therefore Asiatic, it has all the hallmarks of a bridge between the two great divisions of *Primula*. Less than 2.5 cm (1 in). Early to mid spring.

ASIATIC PRIMULAS
There is a great variety among Asiatic primulas and they display many kinds of growth and habit. In general, they are lovers of moisture, sometimes even wetness, and enjoy more peaty soils than their European counterparts. The moister the situation, the more sun they can take, but they do better in cool, humid climates and welcome the less strong sun of northern latitudes. Propagation is by seed or division.

P. alpicola. Sikkimensis section. Tall stems bear one or sometimes two umbels of funnel-shaped flowers. The most common colour is yellow, but white and purple forms occur (*P.a. alba* and *violacea*). Scented, as are other members of this section. 30–60 cm (1–2 ft). Late spring to early summer. Tibet.

P. aurantiaca. Candelabra section. One of the smaller of its section, with two to six whorls of bright orange-red flowers. Valuable as a source of this colour when hybrids form. 23 cm (9 in). Mid summer. Yunnan.

P. aureata. Petiolaris section. A ravishing beauty among primulas, but difficult to grow. It spends the winter as a resting bud (when moisture causes rotting) and is best in the alpine house. The leaves are flat and mealy, and from their rosettes arise clusters of light, creamy yellow flowers with deep, yolk-yellow to orange centres. The whole plant is only 8 cm (3 in) tall. Early to mid spring. Nepal.

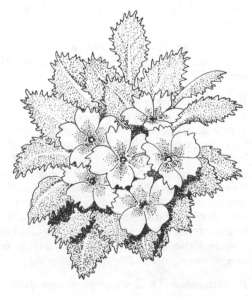

Primula aureata

P. bhutanica (syn. *P. whitei*). Petiolaris section. Typically petiolarid, it has a winter-resting bud and rosettes of flat leaves with the flower scape very short. The flowers are ice blue. Alpine house. 8 cm (3 in). Early to mid spring. E. Himalaya.

P. bracteosa. Petiolaris section. Perhaps the easiest of the section and less inclined to complete winter rest. The leaves are mealy and toothed, and the flower scape, which bears a many-flowered cluster of lilac-pink, lengthens as flowering progresses. The bracts that form may be pegged down and will root. 10 cm (4 in). Mid spring. Bhutan.

P. bulleyana. Candelabra section. Whorls of yellow flowers on tall flower stems. It is late flowering and imparts its colouring to many good mixture strains, such as 'Inshriach Hybrids' and others, in which shades of orange, red, purple and yellow arise from seed. It is happier than most in less cool places. 60 cm (2 ft). Early to mid summer. China.

P. capitata. Capitatae section. The whole plant is farinose and the flower heads in blue-purple are crowded and congested with the flowers looking sideways. *P.c. mooreana* is larger in all its parts. On average 25 cm (10 in). Mid to late summer. Himalaya.

P. chionantha. Nivales section. Rosettes of upright leaves, powdered beneath with yellow farina, give rise to stems with up to four whorls of nodding, scented, white flowers. Moist conditions. 30 cm (12 in). Late spring. China.

P. chungensis. Candelabra section. A coarse plant, valuable mainly for the orange tones of its flowers. Almost 90 cm (3 ft). Late spring to early autumn. Himalaya and China.

P. clarkei. Farinosae section. A miniature among Asiatic primulas, whose rose-pink flowers appear before the small, toothed leaves in short umbels or singly. It has a reputation for shy-flowering and difficulty, but grew well for one of us (JK) in deep shade and pure peat, where it flowered prolifically for several years. 5 cm (2 in) or less. Late winter to mid spring. Kashmir. P. 'Peter Klein' is a superb little hybrid between *P. clarkei* and, it is said, *P. rosea*. It is easy in peat and part shade.

P. cockburniana. The smallest member of the Candelabra section, with two to three whorls per stem of small, brilliant orange flowers. Renew annually from seed. 15 cm (6 in). Late spring to early summer. China.

P. denticulata. Denticulata section. This is the well-known drumstick primula. Planted in ones and twos, this plant is boring and common and is much better seen in drifts between rocks in moist places. The spherical heads of flowers are usually mauve to purple, with pink shades and white, but some fine reds such as 'Inshriach Carmine' can also be obtained. 25 cm (10 in). Early to late spring. Himalaya.

P. edgeworthii. Petiolaris section. The foliage of this exquisitely beautiful primula is wavy and mealy, and the flower scapes, hardly rising above it, consist of umbels of cool, pale mauve flowers with a yellow eye surrounded by a white eye ring. The consistency of the petals has been compared to fine kid. The sensitivity of the resting bud demands alpine house treatment. 8 cm (3 in). Mid winter to mid spring. Himalaya.

P. forrestii. Bullatae section. This is an anomalous species among Asiatic primulas in that it prefers a dry, rocky site. It grows as a woody rhizome that likes to cling to the rock surface. This gives rise to tufts of bullate, leathery leaves and short scapes bearing one-sides umbels of rich yellow flowers with an orange eye. It is best in the alpine house. Seed is occasionally set in cultivation and germinates readily if left uncovered. 15–23 cm (6–9 in). Late spring to early summer. China.

P. gracilipes. Petiolaris section. One of the easier members of its section, succeeding outdoors in a moist, peaty place, particularly in cooler climates. Elsewhere it is not difficult in the alpine house. The plant forms a neat dome, with pale pink to magenta flowers over neat foliage. 8 cm (3 in). Mid to late spring. Sikkim.

P. helodoxa. Candelabra section. A yellow-flowered, tall primula with up to six whorls of flowers on stems that are anything from 60–90 cm (2–3 ft) or more. For a boggy spot. Early to mid spring. China.

P. 'Inverewe'. One of the finest candelabra primulas ever raised. It has several 45 cm (18 in) stems, each furnished with several whorls of vivid orange-scarlet flowers. 'Rowallane' is similar, with more rounded flowers of a clean red.

P. ioessa. Sikkimensis section. A neat, attractive primula with elegant stems and umbels of up to 8 drooping, cup-shaped flowers. This species is usually available as mixed forms or hybrids in pink, lavender or cream. There is a scent of apricots. 25 cm (10 in). Late spring to early summer. Tibet.

P. japonica. Candelabra section. This is the most popular of the candelabras, but in many ways it is disappointing. While it is easy to grow, its habit is stiff and coarse, and it often fails to produce more than one or two whorls of flowers. The colours, too, are strident, but it is of great value as an ingredient in hybrid mixes of candelabra primulas. The forms most usually seen are 'Miller's Crimson' (in fact a dark magenta) and 'Postford White'. Usually about 35 cm (14 in). Late spring to mid summer. Japan.

P. nutans (syn. P. flaccida). Soldanelloidae section. A very beautiful, but short-lived primula, which luckily is prolific with its seed. The basal rosettes of leaves are fairly upright, and the scapes bear umbels of pendant flowers a surprising 2.5 cm (1 in) across. They are blue-violet. 23 cm (9 in). Early summer. China.

P. pulverulenta. Candelabra section. This is in many ways the best of the candelabra primulas. It is easy-going and happy in all kinds of cool temperate climates and grows in sun or shade as long as the soil is rich and moist. It is long-lived and seeds when suited. The whorls of flowers are soft rose-red. 60–90 cm (2–3 ft). *P.p.* 'Bartley Strain' produces a high proportion of plants with clear, shell pink flowers, unique among candelabra primulas. Red-flowered seedlings should be discarded.

P. reidii williamsii. Soldanelloideae section. Few plants can match this primula for beauty. The leaves are velvety and silky, and the flowers appear large on their short scape, semi-pendent in neat umbels, and bell-shaped. The colour is a pale, ethereal blue, shading to white. Delicately fragrant. It disappears down to pinhead buds for the winter, when it must be kept almost entirely dry. Alpine house. 15 cm (6 in). Late spring. Himalaya.

P. rosea. Farinoseae section. An easy species for a moist spot, with carmine-rose flowers appearing before the leaves have developed. The scape is 15 cm (6 in) high at flowering and then lengthens as the leaves extend to their eventual 20 cm (8 in). 'Micia Visser de Geer' is a good form with deeper coloured flowers.

P. secundiflora. Sikkimensis section. This looks like a deeply claret-coloured *P. sikkimensis*, but it is a lover of woodland conditions, rather than a bog. 45 cm (18 in). Early summer. China and Tibet.

P. sieboldii. Cortusoides section. This is a neglected primula that deserves a return to popularity. It has velvety, wavy-edged leaves and short stems, each with one or two very large, fringed flowers. It is easily grown in any good peaty or leafy soil that does not dry out. There are several seed strains, including 'Dancing Ladies' (mostly white, some pink), 'Manakoora' (blues and whites suffused with blue) and 'Pago-Pago' (reds and pinks). All are reliably hardy. 23 cm (in). Late spring to early summer. Japan.

P. sikkimensis. Sikkimensis section. The pinnacle of elegance among primulas. Slim foliage and slender stems bearing one or two whorls of pendent, fragrant, widely funnel-shaped, soft yellow flowers. Loves a boggy place or stream bank to colonize. 45–60 cm (18–24 in). Late spring to early summer. Himalaya.

P. sonchifolia. Petiolares section. From a resting bud like a green farmyard egg emerges a large, rounded umbel with up to 20 large flowers on short stalks. The colour is always some shade of blue — anything from light ice-blue to deep blue-purple with a red eye. It needs alpine house conditions, as the base of the winter bud easily rots if damp. 10 cm (4 in) at flowering; a little taller later. Late winter to early spring. China and Tibet.

P. vialii. Muscarioides section. A unique primula, with rosettes of erect leaves and straight stems bearing pyramids of flowers, some opened and some not, in the manner of a red-hot poker. The open flowers are lavender-violet and the unopened buds at the top are bright crimson. Perennial when well suited, but often disappears for no apparent reason. 45 cm (18 in). Early to mid summer. China.

AMERICAN PRIMULAS

P. ellisiae. A moisture-loving species whose need for perfect drainage makes it a plant for the alpine house. It is not tall, and its scape bears umbels or rose-mauve flowers with a yellow eye. 20 cm (8 in). Late spring to early summer. New Mexico.

P. parryi. Not an easy plant away from the wild. It has long, narrow leaves and flat, magenta-purple flowers that are not often evident in cultivation. 35 cm (14 in). Late spring to early summer. Colorado.

P. rusbyi. Similar to *P. ellisiae* and may be a form of it. The flowers incline more towards brick-red.

P. suffrutescens. A completely distinct primula, in that it is shrubby. The branches are almost prostrate and the leaves, which tend to be near the tips, leaving the stems bare and brown, are short, curved and toothed at the ends. The flowers are deep rose with a yellow throat. For a gritty, peaty soil, not in too much shade; or the alpine house or frame. 10 cm (4 in). Early to mid summer. California.

PRUNELLA (Labiatae)
Cultivated prunellas should not be confused with the British native self-heal, *P. vulgaris*, which is a weed, invasive by both spreading and self-seeding.

P. grandiflora. Far better behaved, making tufted mats of deep green leaves. The purple or blue-purple flowers are borne in dense heads. Colour forms, such as 'Pink Loveliness' and 'White Loveliness' are sometimes listed as *P. × webbiana*. 15 cm (6 in). Early summer to early autumn. Europe.

PRUNUS (Rosaceae)
Among the cherries, plum and almonds are a handful of small shrubs suitable for the rock garden.

P. prostrata. A tiny, twiggy shrub with small leaves and small, pink, almond-like flowers. It likes a well-drained soil and sun and is small enough for a trough or raised bed. 30 cm (12 in). Early to mid spring. E. Mediterranean.

P. tenella. A very variable shrub. The specimens to look out for are those that are ultimately not much more than 30 cm (12 in) tall—many others attain three times the height. They will invade a small area by means of suckers, but that is a small price to pay for a delightful thicket of branches, each one clad with small, bright pink flowers. Early to mid spring. Russia.

PTERIDOPHYLLUM (Papaveraceae)
P. racemosum. The only species grown. It has dainty rosettes of fern-like leaves and sprays of small, white, four-petalled flowers. It enjoys cool, part-shaded, leafy conditions. 15 cm (6 in). Late spring to early summer. Japan.

PTEROCEPHALUS (Dipsacaceae)
A genus of scabious-like plants that enjoy hot, dry positions reminiscent of their native Mediterranean habitat.

P. perennis. (syn. *P. parnassii*). The only species grown. It is a plant of short stature, with heads of pinkish mauve flowers arranged as in a scabious. It is easily grown in a rock garden or scree. Propagate by seed or division. 8 cm (3 in). Early to late summer. Greece.

PTILOTRICHUM (Cruciferae)
A small genus of Mediterranean subshrubs, related to *Alyssum* and preferring hot, dry, gritty positions.

P. spinosum. A small, spiny bush consisting of a tangle of twigs. The sparse, tiny leaves are grey and the short racemes of alyssum-like flowers are white. *P.s. roseum* is variable, and the best, rich pink form is a fine little plant. 20 cm (8 in). Early to mid summer.

PULSATILLA (Ranunculaceae)

Pulsatillas are beautiful plants, closely related to anemones. They have ferny, feathery foliage and large flowers, less open than anemones, made of sepals; there are no petals. They enjoy gritty, gravelly soils and benefit if gravel is applied as a top-dressing, as it prevents disfiguring soil-splash. The soil should, however, be well endowed with humus. Sunny places suit them best. Propagate by seed, sowing it as soon as it is ripe.

P. alpina. This great beauty has finely-divided foliage and large flowers of glistening white; the sepals have a flush of purple on the reverses. The central boss of golden stamens adds to the impact of the plant. It is not always free-flowering in cultivation and is slow to reach maturity from seed. 23 cm (9 in). Late spring. Limestone mountains in Europe. *P.a. apiifolia* (syn. *P. sulphurea*, *P.a. sulphurea*) is similar, but the flowers, often 5 cm (2 in) across, are pure, deep yellow. It is found on acid rocks, or in peaty deposits over dolomite.

P. caucasica. An altogether smaller species, with flowers ranging from an acid, greenish yellow to pale pink. 20 cm (8 in). Late spring. Caucasus.

P. halleri. Similar to garden forms of *P. vulgaris* (see that species also) but more hairy. The flowers are large and deep, silky purple. E. Europe. 'Budapest', when true, has extra large flowers of an extremely light, eggshell blue.

P. pratensis and *P. albana*. One and the same plant; pinnate foliage and very dark purple flowers. Balkans and S. Russia.

P. rubra. Similar to garden forms of *P. vulgaris* (see that species also), but the flowers are in shades of deep to rusty red.

P. vernalis. The most beautiful of all pulsatillas, with intensely divided, hairy leaves and short stems, each bearing a single large, white, chalice-shaped bloom, the outside of which may be faintly blushed with pink. In bud, the overall silky effect is at its height, with the blue-flushed calyces and stem leaves being furnished with silky hairs. It is best grown unsullied by weather in a frame or alpine house. 13 cm (5 in). Mid to late spring. Europe.

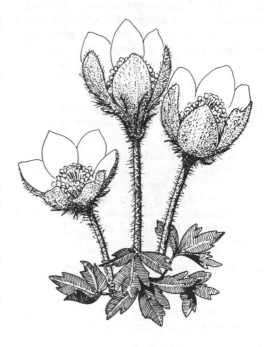

Pulsatilla vernalis

P. vulgaris. The Pasque flower of English downland, where it looks more like a purple crocus than anything to do with the cultivated forms. That these are mostly hybrids with or between other European species can hardly be in doubt, and *P. halleri*, *P. rubra* and others are probably involved in the make-up of plants under this name. They are generally robust plants, up to 25 cm (10 in) tall, with several stems arising from finely-cut foliage, each carrying a large flower which may be anything from white through shades of red or mauve to purple. Mid to late spring.

PYGMAEA (Scrophulariceae)

New Zealand high alpine cushion plants, now in the process of becoming *Chionohebe*. One species in particular has a good hold in cultivation.

P. pulvinaris. A velvety, mossy, grey-green cushion plant as close and dense as an aretian androsace. When happy, its surface becomes studded with bluish white, veronica-like flowers of small size. It was thought that alpine house treatment was essential, but it will grow for years in a shaded trough, where it can never suffer from drought. Late spring to early summer. Mountains of New Zealand, from Nelson to Canterbury.

PYROLA (Pyrolaceae)

The wintergreens are often listed fairly comprehensively, with many of the twenty or so species being recommended. In fact, few are obtainable and all are tricky to grow. In woodland conditions where they will not be disturbed, they are beautiful in an understated way.

P. rotundifolia. A good, evergreen perennial for a leafy, cool place. The leaves are almost round and have long stalks. The scented, white flowers are in racemes some 5 cm (2 in) long on 15 cm (6 in) stems. Late spring to mid summer. Europe and N. America.

P. uniflora (syn. *Moneses uniflora*). A beautiful plant with single, nodding, scented, white flowers of a waxy texture, held clear of the nearly round leaves. It is not easy to establish and needs a firm, but leafy soil and little fluctuation in moisture. 13 cm (5 in). Summer. Europe and N. America.

RAMONDA (Gesneraceae)

Ramondas are temperate, alpine relatives (though fairly distant) of African violets, and the similarity can be seen in the flowers and the very dark green, hairy leaves which are, however, characteristically rugose (corrugated and wrinkled). They are found in the Pyrenees (*R. myconi*) and also in the Balkans (the other two species of the genus). They should be grown in shade, preferably on their sides, and once established they will remain for many years, enduring droughts that curl their leaves, but preferring an occasional soaking. North-facing crevices are ideal. Propagate by seed, sown very thinly.

R. myconi. Makes large rosettes, up to 25 cm (10 in) across, of rough leaves with coppery hairs underneath. The flowers are flat, five-petalled, and rich mauve, with a central pyramid of stamens calling to mind the flowers of a potato. 15 cm (6 in). Mid to late spring. There are white, blue and pink forms.

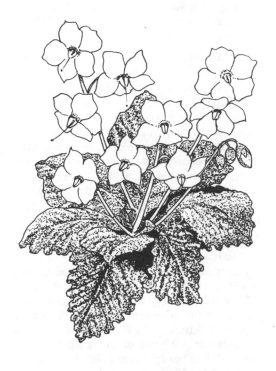

Ramonda myconi

R. nathaliae. A neater plant, with glossier, lighter green leaves with hairs along the margins. The flowers are not flat, but more bell-shaped. The typical colour is purple-blue and there is a white form. 10 cm (4 in). Mid to late spring. Balkans.

R. serbica. Has even more bell-shaped flowers which are easily distinguishable from the other two species by the stamens, which are purple instead of yellow. 10 cm (4 in). Mid to late spring. Balkans.

RANUNCULUS (Ranunculaceae)

Mountain buttercups, which lack the coarseness of their lowland counterparts but often have flowers that are even larger, are usually quite easy to grow. Others, though, are difficult and need special treatment. However, common to all is a need for gritty, well drained soil and a constant supply of summer moisture. Propagation is by seed, which must be sown as soon as it is ripe.

R. amplexicaulis. Has slender, entire leaves and large white flowers. 15 cm (6 in). Mid to late spring. Pyrenees.

R. asiaticus. The most striking of all the buttercups and looks much more like a poppy. It has lobed basal foliage and wiry stems, each of which bears several flowers that are frequently over 5 cm (2 in) wide. They may be yellow or white, but the most sought-after colour forms are cherry-red. They all have conspicuously contrasting black anthers. It is best in the alpine house, as its tuberous root demands dryness from the time the foliage dies down to the first signs of its reappearance. 30 cm (12 in). Early to mid summer. E. Mediterranean).

R. calandrinioides. Another poppy-like ranunculus. This species has grey foliage and flowers up to 5 cm (2 in) across. The colour is pale, water-colour pink and the stamens are yellow. It dies down in summer, the leaves appear in autumn, and it flowers in winter, a fact that makes it better off in the alpine house, although it is hardy. 15 cm (6 in). Early to late winter. Atlas Mountains of Morocco.

R. glacialis. A difficult species, requiring a moist but very gritty compost in the alpine house in summer; dry in winter. Its leaves are rounded, lobed, small and fleshy, and the flowers, on short stems, are white, but become rose pink. It should have a lime-free compost. 10 cm (4 in). Mid spring to mid summer. Glacial moraines in Europe.

R. gramineus. A more usual type of buttercup as far as the flowers go, but with narrow, unlobed, grass-like leaves. It is variable, but generally becomes taller as it ages. Young plants may be suitable for a trough, but the scree is the best place for it. 15–25 cm (6–10 in). Summer. Europe.

R. parnassifolius. Also variable, this can be a fine plant, with rosettes of heart-shaped leaves and white flowers up to 2.5 cm (1 in) across that turn rose pink as they age, but forms with hardly any petals at all can turn up, so the plant should be seen in flower if it is being purchased. It requires a sunny, gritty place free from drought. 10 cm (4 in). Mid to late spring. Alps and Pyrenees.

R. pyrenaeus. Not wholly unlike *R. gramineus* in its foliage, apart from being grey-green. The flowers are white with yellow stamens. Flower size is variable, but in good forms they may be 2.5 cm (1 in) wide. Not easy, but possible in a gritty, sunny but moist scree. 18 cm (7 in). Mid to late spring. Alps and Pyrenees.

R. seguieri. A smaller, easier, edition of *R. glacialis* and its counterpart from limestone formations. Its foliage is greyer and slightly hairy and the flowers remain pure white rather than age to pink. It is much more likely to flower in cultivation than *R. glacialis* and can be successfully grown in a well-drained scree. 8 cm (3 in). Early to mid summer. Europe.

RANZANIA (Berberidaceae)

R. japonica. This is the only species. It flowers before the leaves develop, sending up stems bearing nodding, saucer-shaped, six-petalled flowers of smoky mauve-blue. The leaves develop in whorls on the same stems. It should have a place in peat, leafmould and part shade, or in a leafy mixture in the alpine house. Although it is hardy, it is also rare, but is occasionally available commercially. 20 cm (8 in). Late spring. Japan.

RAOULIA (Compositae)

This quite extraordinary genus from Australia and New Zealand consists of the scabweeds and the vegetable sheep. The former are flat, thin mats of foliage that is often silver; the appropriately named latter make domed masses of tightly packed, woolly rosettes that appear at a distance like so many sheep on the mountain side. In general, the scabweeds are easily grown, while the vegetable sheep present one of the greatest of all challenges (c.f. *Haastia*, p.164). Propagation is by division for the mat-forming species, by seed for the vegetable sheep.

SCABWEEDS

R. australis. Makes a film of tiny, silvery-hairy leaves that develops patches of yellow in when it flowers. For a sunny, fine-textured scree. All summer. New Zealand. (The epithet *australis* means 'southern').

R. glabra. Slightly larger than the above. The distinct rosettes, together making up a wide mat, are green, and the flowers, more significant in this species, are starry and white. Scree. Summer. New Zealand.

R. haastii. Similar, but its green, undulating mat turns rich bronze in winter. The white flowers are like tiny 'everlastings'. Scree. Late summer. New Zealand.

R. hookeri. The best species for gardens, as it is larger and intensely silver, making highly attractive mats either on the scree or in the alpine house. Late summer, but often does not flower. New Zealand.

VEGETABLE SHEEP

Raoulia eximia, mammillaris, rubra and **buchananii**. Plants that, in the wild, gradually build up to make massive cushions of wool. Internally, they consist of moist masses of branches, which terminate at the surface in woolly rosettes that are often silvery-white. They demonstrate the ultimate in adaptation to rapidly changing, harsh, mountain weather conditions.

The most silvery are *R. mammillaris* and *eximia*, and they are the most frequently attempted of the vegetable sheep. Although plants the size of two sheep occur in New Zealand, one as big as a mouse is a fine achievement in cultivation.

Watering is critical. Too much, and the plant rots and dies; too little and it gradually changes from silver or bronze to bone-white or straw-coloured, both indicating that the plant is dead. Alpine house cultivation is essential. Flowering in cultivation, apart from being a non-event, is extremely rare.

RAOULIA × LEUCOGYNES (Compositae)

Raoulia hectori × Leucogynes grandiceps. An intensely silver plant that makes almost flat cushions of small, tightly-packed leaves. It tends to go out of character when grown under glass and is happiest in a peaty soil and part shade. However, if the alpine house environment is sufficiently light and airy, it can be kept reasonably compact but needs a lot of water to maintain its shape. Found wild in New Zealand.

RHODODENDRON (Ericaceae)

Dwarf rhododendrons are an integral part of the flora of the mountains of much of the world and are an important and extremely beautiful ingredient of alpine gardening. Those with limy soils can grow them in raised beds and troughs containing prepared soil and, contrary to received opinion, they will not suffer in the least from being watered with hard water as long as they are also subject to rain. As far as sun and shade for the genus as a whole go, the best rule of thumb is that the smaller the leaf, the more sun the plant will take. This means that almost all dwarf rhododendrons will grow in a good deal of sun as long as the soil is moist, but should have shade during the hottest part of the day in more southerly latitudes.

The number of dwarf rhododendrons available is now quite vast and growing rapidly as new cultivars, many of them truly wonderful plants, appear each year. It is simply not possible to list them here in any sort of a meaningful, let alone comprehensive way. Therefore, the following is a descriptive list of the main dwarf species that are not only beautiful and appropriate in their own right but have, in most cases, played their part in giving rise to the hundreds of cultivars that grace our gardens. It portrays, too, the great variety that exists among these plants. All are hardy unless otherwise stated.

R. anthopogon. An upright species with clusters of small, white or pink-tinged flowers. 60 cm (2 ft). Late spring to early summer. Himalaya and Tibet. *R.a. hypenanthum* 'Annapurna' has yellow flowers.

R. calostrotum. In its best forms this is a tight, compact, bushy plant with crimson-purple flowers well over 2.5 cm (1 in) wide. 60 cm (2 ft). Late spring. Himalaya and China. *R.c. calciphilum* has smaller leaves and pink flowers. *R.c.* 'Gigha' has aromatic foliage and large, rosy red flowers.

R. campylogynum. A dainty gem with long-stalked, thimble-like bells in shades of cream, pink or purple. 15–60 cm (6 in–2 ft). Himalaya and China. *R.c.* 'Salmon Pink' is compact at 30 cm (1 ft). *R.c. cremastum* 'Bodnant Red' is true red, 60 cm (2 ft). *R.c. myrtilloides* is only 15 cm (6 in), pink.

R. camtschaticum. A very hardy, unusual species. It is deciduous and has mahogany, peeling bark. It does not appreciate heat and does better in the north. Usually two bursts of flower, reddish purple and wide open. There are very rare red, pink and white forms. 20 cm (8 in). Late spring to early summer and often again later. North Asia, also occurring in N.W. America.

Rhododendron camtschaticum

R. forrestii. This is usually offered in the form *R.f. repens*, a more compact plant which flowers more readily than the pure species. It is stiffly branched, with oval, dark green leaf reverses. The flowers are large, waxy and a beautiful blood red. Protect from late frosts. 10 cm (4 in). Mid to late spring. China and Tibet.

R. haematodes. Has leaves with woolly reverses and flowers of glowing scarlet. Very hardy. 90 cm (3 ft). Late spring to early summer. China.

R. hanceanum. Not one of the best in itself, although attractive enough. The oval leaves accompany clusters of creamy-white flowers. However, other forms of it are excellent. 30 cm (12 in). Late spring to early summer. China. *R.h. nanum* is a superb dwarf plant that

disappears beneath bright yellow flowers. 20 cm (8 in). *R.h.* 'Canton Consul' has bronze growths of the current year.

R. impeditum. Variable in size, but at its best is very dwarf, dense, and generous with flowers in the mauve to blue-purple range. 35–45 cm (14–18 in). Late spring. China.

R. keiskii. Has large, yellow flowers and lanceolate leaves. The young foliage is chocolate-bronze and remains so for most of the year. 30 cm (12 in). Mid to late spring. Japan. *R.k.* 'Yaku Fairy' is prostrate and extremely free with its creamy-yellow flowers.

R. keleticum is an easily grown, compact plant with attractive foliage and wide, flat flowers 2.5 cm (1 in) across, deep purple with red speckles. 30 cm (12 in). Late spring to early summer. China and Tibet. *R.k. radicans* (syn. *R. radicans*) is the dwarfest rhododendron of all, with quite large, purple flowers over mats of tiny foliage barely 2.5 cm (1 in) high.

R. lepidostylum. One of the few that is more of a foliage plant than one grown for its flowers. The leaves are steel blue, furnished with rows of bristles, and overlapping so as to make a solid mass of colour. The flowers are yellow. 45 cm (18 in). Early summer. China.

R. lowndesii and **R. ludlowii**. Magnificent little plants with large, flat, yellow flowers. Neither is easy, but each is a parent of several hybrids, all of which are in the first rank of dwarf rhododendrons. They are anything from 30–90 cm (1–3 ft) and are in a variety of colours, not always in the yellow range. Some are themselves parents of further hybrids of first-class quality.

R. pemakoense. Needs a little protection against late frosts, as the flowers may be lost. It is otherwise an easily grown, cheekily beautiful, dwarf shrub with large, pale pink flowers that completely hide it. 30 cm (1 ft). Early to mid spring. China and Tibet.

R. sargentianum. A very dwarf plant with tiny leaves and clusters of daphne-like, yellow flowers. 30 cm (1 ft). Late spring. China. *R.s.* 'Whitebait' is larger, a little later-flowering, and has larger, creamy-white flowers. 60 cm (2 ft).

RHODOTHAMNUS (Ericaceae)

R. chamaecistus. Thought to be the only species until the discovery in 1962 of *R. sessilifolius* in Anatolia, 1500 miles away from its most easterly station. Other than that, its closest relative is *Kalmiopsis leachiana*, from the north-west of North America. It is a tiny shrub with a wiry, twiggy structure and very small, oval leaves. The flowers are very large for such a small shrub — up to 2.5 cm (1 in) wide, bowl-shaped, and a clear, soft pink. Although found over limestone in nature, it should be given a peaty soil. It should be shaded during the hottest part of the day, but otherwise in sun. The soil must never become dry. As a lover of short, moist turf it is not that easy to accommodate, but it succeeds well when planting among Asiatic gentians. Unlike most ericaceous plants it bitterly resents attempts to move it. Once established, however, it is reliable and long-lived. Propagate by cuttings in late summer or seed, which ripens very quickly. 15 cm (6 in). Dolomites and Austria.

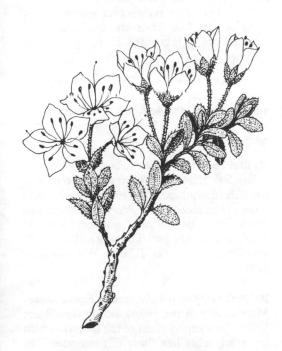

Rhodothamnus chamaecistus

RIBES (Grossulariacae)

The genus of the currants and gooseberries, the former without spines at the leaf joints, the latter armed with them. There is one species small enough for the larger rock garden.

R. laurifolium. An unarmed shrub, grown chiefly for its very early flowering. It is not a spectacular beauty and it is as well to obtain a male plant, as the flowers will be larger and the inflorescences longer. Typically they are greenish yellow and borne in dense racemes 5 cm (2 in) long. It is easily grown and needs no pruning apart from removal of very old wood. 90 cm (3 ft). Later winter to early spring. China.

RICOTIA (Cruciferae)

R. davisiana. A rarity with a tenuous hold on cultivation because of its short life. It is attractive in a pan in the alpine house, where its grey, fleshy, trefoil leaves and rounded heads of quite large, pink flowers can be seen at their best. Propagate by seed. 10 cm (4 in). Mid to late spring. Turkey.

ROMANZOFFIA (Hydrophyllaceae)

There are only four species in this genus, two of which are in cultivation. They resemble meadow saxifrages and enjoy the same moist, cool, leafy conditions. Propagation is division or seed.

R. californica and *R. sitchensis*. These appear in lists as separate species but are synonymous, with the former name taking precedence. They refer to a tufted plant with kidney-shaped leaves and branched sprays of five-petalled, white flowers held well above the foliage. It looks very much like *Saxifraga granulata*. 15 cm (6 in). Mid spring. N.W. America.

R. unalaschkensis. Considerably smaller and its flowers usually have mauve markings. It is ideal for a shaded trough or raised bed. 5 cm (2 in). Mid spring. Aleutians and Alaska.

ROSCOEA (Zingiberaceae)

The ginger family is scarcely represented among alpines, but the genus includes some dwarf, hardy plants with spectacular, if short-lived flowers. If the rhizomes are planted 15 cm

(6 in) deep in a friable, vegetable soil, upright leaves will emerge, eventually to sheath the stems, each of which bears, singly or in clusters, large flowers whose hooded and lipped structure lends them an exotic, orchid-like appearance. Propagation by division.

R. alpina. The most dwarf and has solitary, purplish pink flowers on very short stems. 15 cm (6 in). Mid to late summer. China and Himalaya.

R. cautleoides. Possibly the most beautiful species. It has spikes of soft, yellow flowers and is the easiest and most reliable species to grow in cooler climates. 30 cm (12 in). Early to mid summer. China.

R. humeana. A dramatic species when displaying its large, violet-purple flowers before the leaves develop. 30 cm (12 in) but only 20 cm (8 in) at flowering and before the stems attain their full length. Early to mid summer. China.

R. purpurea. Quite tall, often exceeding 30 cm (12 in) and is probably more suited to the front of a border. It is often described as 'handsome', and the word suits its stature and large, purple flowers in clusters of two to four. Early to late summer. Himalaya.

ROSMARINUS (Labiatae)
Rosemaries are aromatic shrubs, mostly too large for a rock garden. However, one species is dwarf and prostrate and looks superb when draping hot, sunny rocks.

R. lavandulaceus. A doubtful name, applied to what has been thought of as a prostrate form of the common rosemary, *R. officialis*. The plant is flat, about 90 cm (3 ft) wide, and has the expected leathery, green leaves and pale violet flowers. Not reliably hardy. Late spring. Mediterranean.

ROSULARIA (Crassulaceae)
Sempervivum-like plants with rosettes of succulent leaves. Many are not entirely hardy and are best managed in the alpine house or in a gritty compost in a sunny, sheltered place. Propagate by seed or division.

R. chrysantha (syn. *R. pallida*). Has rosettes of green leaves, softly hairy at the edges. The flowers, in an erect raceme, are cream, reasonably large, and bell-shaped. 15 cm (6 in). Mid to late summer. Turkey.

R. platyphylla. Slightly wider leaves and white flowers, but is otherwise similar. Mid summer. Altai Mountains.

R. sedoides (syn. *Sempervivella alba*). Has small, bright green rosettes, tinged with crimson, that build up into tight cushions and white flowers. It is hardy. 15 cm (6 in). Early autumn. Himalaya.

R. sempervivum. Has flat rosettes and pink flowers. 15 cm (6 in). Summer.

RUBUS (Rosaceae)
The genus of the brambles, raspberries, loganberries, etc. There are three species that are grown as alpines, but they should not have too rich a diet, otherwise they may become invasive.

R. arcticus. The Arctic bramble makes a thicket of creeping stems but without prickles. It has bright, rosy red flowers almost 2.5 cm (1 in) across. The fruits are small, dark red 'blackberries'. 15 cm (6 in). Early to mid summer.

R. chamaemorus. The cloudberry of northern Europe. It has much the same habit and height as the last, but the flowers are smaller and white. The berries are orange and edible. Early to mid summer.

R. illecebrosus. The strawberry-raspberry. It is less frail than the two previous species and has attractive foliage with red tints that become more pronounced as autumn approaches. The fruits are large and mulberry-like in appearance and colour. They are edible but not very exciting. 30 cm (12 in). Mid summer. Japan.

RUPICAPNOS (Papaveraceae; Fumariaceae)
Membership of the poppy family should not lead to false expectations of the flowers, which are much more like those of fumitories than poppies, as they are narrow, tubular and lipped.

R. africana. A most attractive plant, but short-lived and susceptible to winter wet. The leaves are grey and ferny, and the flowers are basically white, more or less tinted with pink. Best in the alpine house. Propagate by seed, which needs care in its collection. 15 cm (6 in). Mid to late summer. N. Africa.

SALIX (Salicaceae)

There are several dwarf willows that are not only suitable for the rock garden but also contribute substantially to its overall character and appearance. With age they become gnarled and ancient-looking and disburse an air of permanence and maturity. Plants are male and female; males should be obtained, as their catkins are longer and more beautiful than those of the females, especially when they turn golden with pollen. All are perfectly hardy and can readily be increased from cuttings. None of them relishes dryness. All are spring-flowering.

S. arbuscula. Usually supplied by nurseries in dwarf forms that will reach eventual heights of little more than 60 cm (2 ft). It has deep green leaves that are grey-blue beneath and long, grey catkins, becoming yellow. Europe.

S. × boydii. A hybrid, found just once by William Brack Boyd in Perthshire in the 1880s and never found again. He took two cuttings, one of which was later given to Miss Logan Home of the Edrom Nurseries, and it was from these plants that all others have derived. It is extremely slow-growing and gnarled like a venerable bonsai. The leaves are bullate and ash grey. A specimen, given to one of us (JK) by the late Stuart Boothman, complete with its trough, was 38 cm (15 in) high and 30 years old but had been used as a stock plant for cuttings. Annual top-dressings helped it to attain 45 cm (18 in) during the ensuing 12 years. The original Logan Home specimen was 90 cm (3 ft) tall in 1980, approaching its centenary.

S. helvetica. Relatively large and sometimes reaches 1.5 m (5 ft), but is usually much less. It is a bushy shrub with leaves that are glossy green above but felted with white beneath. The catkins are silvery, becoming gold and are borne as the leaves unfold. Late spring to early summer. Alps.

S. herbacea. In nature this willow inhabits the tundra, and hides its branches underground with only its foliage above. In a soft, moist soil it will do the same in cultivation, making an intriguing little carpet of small, green leaves. Bright yellow catkins. Northern Europe and Asia.

S. lanata. The woolly willow is perhaps a trifle tall at 90 cm (3 ft) but that should not exclude it, as its habit is entirely consistent with a mountain species and the white, silky wool that covers the wide, oval leaves and extends to the branchlets is very beautiful indeed. Catkins appear before the leaves. Europe.

S. lapponum. Something like the above, but downy rather than woolly leaves and silvery catkins. Northern Europe.

S. myrsinites. The variety *S.m. jacquinii* is almost always listed, but has been renamed *S. alpina*. It is a prostrate, twiggy bush with unusual red catkins. Less than 30 cm (12 in). Europe.

S. reticulata. An entirely prostrate, slow-growing, contour-hugging shrub, with leathery, net-veined leaves that are covered in a silver plating of well-groomed, flat hairs. Later, they fall away to reveal the green beneath. Upright catkins. Europe and W. Asia.

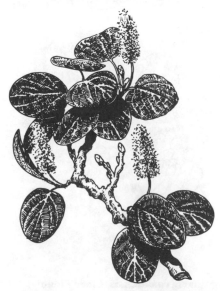

Salix reticulata

S. retusa. A little too widely spreading, but see the following.

S. serpyllifolia. (syn. *S. retusa serpyllifolia*). This delightful dwarf now has specific status. It is a rock-hugging miniature version, with minute leaves and gnarled, twisting branches. Small catkins. Europe.

SANGUINARIA (Papaveraceae)

S. canadensis. The only species in the genus shows itself above ground for a remarkably short time, dying away shortly after flowering and not reappearing until the following spring. The leaves are grey green and lightly lobed. The flowers are solitary, anemone-like, and well over 2.5 cm (1 in) across. They are among the purest white flowers in all gardening but are fugacious. The completely double form *S.c.* 'Flore Pleno' is easier to grow, and its flowers last considerably longer. For a peaty soil with no lime but a little sand. Propagate by careful division in late summer, but mark their position in spring. 10–15 cm (4–6 in). Mid spring. N. America.

Sanguinaria canadensis 'Flore Pleno'

SAPONARIA (Caryophyllaceae)

The soapworts are easily grown plants for any position in sun. They are closely related to *Lychnis*.

S. caespitosa. Forms dense cushions or tufts of linear leaves and has tight sprays of bright pink, five-petalled flowers. The petals are rounded and not notched. 13 cm (5 in). Mid to late summer. Pyrenees.

S. ocymoides. This is to summer what aubretia is to spring, making similar cushions of hairy leaves and similarly covering itself with flowers if a good form is grown in a soil that is not too rich. The flowers are reddish pink and there is a white form. 15 cm (6 in). S. Europe. All summer.

S. × olivana. An excellent garden plant, easily grown, and very free-flowering. It is a hybrid of *S. pumilio*, which is not at all easy. Its flowers are fully 2.5 cm (1 in) across, bright pink and borne all over the cushion. Most of the summer.

S. pumilio. Difficult and rather unsatisfactory. Although it is a very small plant with large flowers of brilliant rose pink, it is shy-flowering and when it does so tends to bloom round the edges of the cushion. It also hates lime. The best way to grow it is to plant it in a poor scree and leave it alone for several years until its deep root system provides the constant conditions it needs. 5 cm (2 in). Late summer to early autumn. Austria and Italy.

SARCOCAPNOS (Papaveraceae)

Sarcocapnos, *Rupicapnos* and *Corydalis* share the fumitory shape of flower that is so unexpected in the poppy family. The plants in this genus are very much like *Rupicapnos* and are best in the alpine house.

S. enneaphylla. Forms a loose tuft of ferny, grey-green foliage and sprays of light yellow flowers with purple markings. It is short-lived but sets abundant seed. 13 cm (5 in). Early to mid summer. Spain and N. Africa.

SATUREIA (SATUREJA)
(Labiatae)

S. montana. The only species in general cultivation; others have now been included in it. It is a small, wiry, aromatic shrub with deep mauve flowers in tight whorls. It is very much like a shrubby thyme. It requires a sunny, well-drained position. The usual form seen in gardens is *S.m.* 'Pygmaea', which is only 15 cm (6 in) high. Early to mid summer. Mediterranean.

SAXIFRAGA (Saxifragaceae)

This is a huge genus, made all the larger for gardening purposes by the great numbers of cultivars. It is, with *Campanula*, *Primula*, *Dianthus* and to a certain extent *Rhododendron*, one of the backbone genera of alpine gardening. It would be impossible to give a full account of them without writing a separate book, so what follows is a guide to the genus, which, it is hoped, will lead on to further reading.

The plants are so diverse in their forms and habits that it is impossible to generalize about them. All they have in common is the flower structure that defines them as belonging to the same genus. However, it can be said that most species are perennial mountain plants of small stature and a tendency towards compact growth.

Because of its size and diversity the genus has been divided into sections. It is also undergoing considerable revision as the years go by. We have decided to list the plants in their sections, so that those with most in common are grouped together. However, we have left out several sections altogether, as they are of little interest to alpine gardeners apart from specialists in saxifrages.

It might well be thought that the classification could only possibly be of interest to such specialists. However, it is essential once alpine gardening advances beyond the beginner stage. It is just unfortunate that so much complicated Latin is associated with such simple, beautiful plants. The sections included here are as follows. A typical species is mentioned for each:

Section Gymnopera – was Robertsoniana (*S. umbrosa*)

Section Trachyphyllioides – was Dactyloides (*S. moschata*)

Section Aizoonia – was Euaizoonia (*S. paniculata*)

Section Porophyllum – was Kabschia, then Kabschia and Engleria. Englaria was separated as Tetrameridium but is now merged back into Porophyllum. (*S. burseriana* as a typical 'kabs-chia'; *S. grisebachii* as an 'engleria')

Section Porphyrion (*S. oppositifolia*)

Section Diptera (*S. fortunei*)

SECTION GYMNOPERA
Plants typified by *S. umbrosa* and its hybrid, the London pride. Cabbagy rosettes of evergreen, leathery, spoon-shaped leaves, reproducing by runners. Tall flower stems with white or pink flowers.

S. cuneifolia. Like a miniature form of *S.* × *urbium* (q.v.). It forms a pleasant carpet in partly shaded places and has panicles of starry, white flowers. 20 cm (8 in). Late spring to mid summer. Central and S. Europe.

S. × geum. A hybrid of *S. umbrosa*, covering the ground in shady places. It has sprays of white flowers, spotted to a greater or lesser extent with pink. 25 cm (10 in). Early to mid summer. Pyrenees.

S. spathularis. Makes mats of somewhat open rosettes of spoon-shaped leaves. The flowers are white but marked with minute, red speckles. Rare in gardens but an attractive weed in JK's garden in S.W. Ireland, where, along with Spain and Portugal, it is native. 25 cm (10 in). Early to mid summer.

S. umbrosa. Forms dense mats of rosettes. The leaves are oval and regularly wavy-edged, leathery and spoon-shaped. The flowers are in generous sprays, white or pink, spotted with red. Early to late summer. Pyrenees.

S. × urbium. This is a hybrid of *S. umbrosa* × *S. spathularis*. Known as London pride, it is a strong, easily grown plant for places in part shade. The flowers are white, spotted with red. 30 cm (12 in). Late spring to early summer. *S. × u.* 'Clarence Elliott' is only half the size.

SECTION TRACHYPHYLLIOIDES

The mossy saxifrages consist of cushions of rosettes with leaves that are wider towards their ends and terminate in multiple notches. They are sometimes sticky with glands. The flowers are white, pink or red and occasionally light yellow. Most mossy saxifrages grown in gardens are hybrids. They flower in spring or the earliest part of summer and typically make soft, green cushions with flowers in shades of pink and red, sometimes white. Most of those listed in catalogues are worth growing, but all share a tendency to burn in full sun.

S. cebennensis. Makes tightly domed cushions of grey-green, very sticky cushions. The flowers are white and quite large. A very attractive species, best in the alpine house, as its sticky foliage soon becomes dirty outside. 20 cm (8 in). Late spring. Cevennes.

S. demnatensis. Even stickier and also requires alpine house treatment. It has pale, aromatic leaves and sprays of up to ten white, green-veined flowers. 13 cm (5 in). Late spring to early summer. Atlas Mountains.

S. moschata. A species making domed cushions of soft, green leaves that end in three short lobes. The flower stems carry up to seven cream flowers that are sometimes tinged with red. For a sunny position. 10 cm (4 in). Late spring to early summer. Europe. *S.m.* 'Cloth of Gold' is slower growing and has golden foliage with no hint of green. It needs a shady position.

SECTION AIZOONIA

These are the silver saxifrages. They make cushions or clumps of stiff, flat rosettes, in which the leaves are to varying degrees encrusted with silvery lime deposits. The flowering rosettes, from the centres of which arise the sturdy, usually curved flowering stems, die after flowering, but the plant fills itself in as new rosettes are formed. The flowers are usually white, often with pink or red spots. Silver saxifrages will grow happily in sun or a little shade and are most effective on their sides in crevices. They enjoy limy soils but grow perfectly well on acid ones.

S. callosa. A typical member of the section, with blue-green, heavily limed, 5 cm (2 in) leaves. The arching stems carry many-flowered sprays of white. There are a handful of varieties. 30 cm (12 in). Early to mid summer. Italy.

S. cochlearis. Smaller and more clump-forming. The leaves are notably long and spoon-shaped, up to 2.5 cm (1 in), and heavily lime-encrusted. The flowers are white on 20 cm (8 in) stems. Late spring to early summer. S.W. Alps. *S.c.* 'Major' is larger and probably a hybrid with *S. callosa. S.c.* 'Minor' is very much smaller, making a rounded, neat cushion suitable for a trough.

Saxifraga × arco-valleyi

S. cotyledon. Anomalous in that it dislikes lime in the soil and secretes very little from its leaves. Its rosettes are up to 15 cm (6 in) across and the flower stem, bearing many white flowers, is up to 90 cm (3 ft) long. Dramatic in a crevice. Early to late summer. Alps. *S.c.*

'Southside Seedling', which has flowers heavily speckled with rose red, is a highly desirable plant.

S. cotyledon × S. longifolia 'Tumbling Waters'. The most spectacular of all. Its rosette takes several years to become 15 cm (6 in) wide, heavily silvered, and composed of a great many narrow leaves. When the rosette flowers it produces a 90 cm (3 ft) plume bearing countless white flowers in a broad panicle. The rosette dies after flowering but produces side rosettes that must be cut off and treated as cuttings, otherwise the whole plant dies. Best displayed in a vertical crevice. Early summer.

SECTION POROPHYLLUM

The botanists have with some justification combined the old Kabschia and Engleria sections to form this new one. Plants from the two divisions readily hybridize and some species approach one another in physical characteristics across the man-made divide.

However, there is an overall difference to the eye in the cases of most of these saxifrages. Kabschias tend to make bun-shaped cushions of rosettes of short, needle-like leaves, more or less lime-pitted. Englerias generally have larger rosettes of slightly wider leaves and are visually somewhere between the silver saxifrages and the kabschias. Although it is unscientific and probably logically unsound, we are retaining the distinction to the extent of placing a very unofficial K or E alongside the plant names, as we believe that this will provide the most help for gardeners.

This is a very large section indeed and only a small, representative selection is given here. It includes several hybrids, chiefly because they are good garden plants and often preferable in that respect to the species. All flower between early and late spring.

S. × apiculata (K). The most robust of all, making wide, undulating, cushiony mats of prickly, green needles. The primrose-yellow flowers are in sprays. This hybrid is unusual in taking full sun all day without burning.

S. × arco-valleyi (K). For some arcane reason now called 'Ophelia', this has hard buns of crowded rosettes and almost stemless, pink flowers.

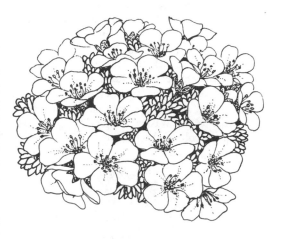

Saxifraga cochlearis

S. × borisii (K). Has hard rosettes of pointed, blue-grey leaves and 8 cm (3 in) reddish stems bearing lemon-yellow flowers.

S. burseriana (K) (probably correctly *burserana*). Perhaps the loveliest of the species. It makes dense, hard, prickly cushions of blue-grey leaves and has large, round, white flowers, solitary on 5 cm (2 in) reddish stems. *S.b.* 'Brookside' has flowers 2.5 cm (1 in) wide. *S.b.* 'His Majesty' has large, pink-tinted flowers. *S.b.* 'Sulphurea' has soft yellow flowers. *S.b. minor* is a condensed form with large, white flowers, which exists in the wild on one mountain in southern Austria.

S. 'Cranbourne' (K). The best deep pink flowered 'kabschia'. Its cushions are hard, slow growing and made up of flat rosettes so that they are not prickly. The flowers are large, almost stemless, and deep rose pink.

S. 'Faldonside' (K). Slow growing, prickly, high-domed, and has large, almost stemless, yellow flowers.

S. grisebachii (E). Has loose clumps of wide, flat rosettes of spoon-shaped leaves, heavily silvered with lime. The flower stems are crozier-shaped and furnished with red-purple, green-tipped stems leaves and the whole is covered with red glandular hairs. The pink flowers are semi-hidden in the purple calyces and form a cluster at the head of the crozier. It is a good plant for a raised bed but is often best appreciated in the alpine house. 15 cm (6 in). Balkans. *S.g.* 'Wisley Variety' is a robust, brilliantly coloured selection.

Saxifraga grisebachii

S. 'Jenkinsae' (K). Probably the best pale pink 'kabschia'. It is very free-flowering, with stemless blooms over tight rosettes. 'Irvingii' is smaller and not as easily kept.

S. lilacina (K). An anomalous member of the section, as it is the only species that dislikes lime. Its rosettes are small and flat and it makes a tight cushion with almost stemless, lilac-pink flowers. It is the parent of most pink- and red-flowered hybrids. It is not easy to grow satisfactorily. Himalaya.

S. mariae-theresae (K × E). A hybrid between *S. burseriana* and *S. grisebachii*. It has rosettes of short, pointed, grey leaves and small, pink flowers in short sprays. 10 cm (4 in).

S. media (E). The silvery rosettes, spoon-shaped leaves with abrupt points, leafy, glandular stems with small, pink, pendent flowers almost hidden in the calyces, make this a typical example of what was thought of as an engleria saxifrage. 13 cm (5 in). Pyrenees.

S. porophylla (E). Gives its name to the section; it is similar to *S. grisebachii*, but considerably smaller. A very fine form, *S.p. thessalica* now appears to be a distinct species, *S. sempervivum*. 15 cm (6 in). Italy.

S. strbrnyi (E). Has handsome rosettes of silvery leaves and good, branched sprays of pink flowers amid purple calyces. 10 cm (4 in). Bulgaria.

S. wendelboi (K). A comparatively recent introduction. It has dense cushions, not unlike those of *S. burseriana* and white flowers in threes or fours. The calyces are purple. It is early flowering and best in the alpine house or frame, although it is hardy. It is unusual in coming from Iran.

PORPHYRION SECTION

S. oppositifolia. This species forms prostrate mats of stems, clothed in opposite pairs of very small, triangular, deep green leaves. The stems interlace to form cushions. The main and lateral shoots produce almost stemless, solitary flowers anything from deep, rosy purple through the usual mauve-pink to a very fine, clear red. The best forms have large, rounded flowers, while poor ones have short, pointed petals. There are white forms but they are seldom satisfactory. The plant is unequal to full sun and prefers a partly shaded position — dappled shade is best. In too much shade, however, it flowers and grows poorly. It should have a damp but well-drained soil that never dries out. 2.5 cm (1 in). Early summer. Widely distributed in the northern hemisphere. *S.o.* 'Ruth Draper' has large, rosy-red flowers. *S.o. latina* has purple flowers of good size, reliably produced.

S. retusa. Like a miniature version of *S. oppositifolia*, but instead of solitary flowers it has clusters of up to five ruby red flowers. They are not as rounded and are smaller. It is not difficult in a soil well provided with humus and a lightly shaded spot in a trough or raised bed. 2.5 cm (1 in). Mid to late spring. Pyrenees and Alps.

DIPTERA SECTION
Plants that do not form cushions, but which have rounded leaves on long stalks. The flowers have petals of uneven size.

S. fortunei. Usually grown as 'Wada's Form' these days, as its ruby-purple leaves are such an improved foil for the white flowers when compared to the usual brownish upper sides and red lower surfaces of most other forms. They are seven-lobed, glossy, and long-stalked. The flowers have the five petals of saxifrages, but the lowest two are more than three times the length of the other three. Prefers a shady, peaty place. 35 cm (14 in) or more. Early to mid autumn. Japan.

SCABIOSA (Dipsacaceae)

The scabiouses, both annual and perennial, include many good garden plants. One or two are eminently suitable for the rock garden.

S. columbaria. A downland species, often reaching over 60 cm (2 ft) in height. However, mountain forms are much shorter and have summer-long displays of blue-purple flower heads in sunny positions on the rock garden. They usually incorporate 'Nana' in the name and may be found listed as *S. alpina nana*. 15 cm (6 in). Early summer to early autumn. Europe.

S. graminifolia. Has beautifully silver-plated leaves and heads of lavender-pink flowers. 20 cm (8 in). Mid summer to early autumn. S. Europe.

SEDUM (Crassulaceae)

Sedums are succulent plants that vary from large denizens of the herbaceous border to some of the tiniest alpines. They are almost all easily grown in the poorest soils and often spread by sowing their leaves, which root where they fall. The flowers are usually small, five-petalled and starry. There are a great many species and it is a genus that has been divided by botanists into sections. However, we have decided to treat the genus alphabetically and, once more, our selection is necessarily only representative.

S. acre. This is the common stonecrop. It is far from a plant to be despised, as it will grow where nothing else will, on no soil at all, and will cheerfully put out its golden flowers all summer long. 2.5 cm (1 in). Northern hemisphere except America.

S. album. Has slightly larger, cylindrical, succulent leaves. They are shiny and green, tinged with red. The red stalks carry sprays of white flowers. 'Murale Coral Carpet' is less invasive and its leaves and flowers are pink. 13 cm (5 in). All summer. Europe.

S. dasyphyllum. Has small, egg-shaped leaves of a lovely mixture of grey, light green, and bluish mauve-pink. The flowers are pale pink. 5 cm (2 in). All summer. Europe.

S. humifusum. Has creeping shoots covered with tiny, green leaves that become red as they age. The yellow flowers are unusual for the genus, as they are solitary. This is not a very easy plant, as it must be kept dry in winter but strangely enough requires a lot of water in summer. It is also slightly tender and the best place for it is the alpine house or a frame. 5 cm (2 in). Mid spring to early summer. Mexico.

S. lydium. A red-tinted, mat-forming mass of rooting stems with cylindrical leaves and white flowers. 5 cm (2 in). Early to mid summer. Turkey.

S. middendorffianum. Makes twiggy, tufted mats with dull green, spatulate, partly toothed, flat leaves. The flowers are yellow and borne in flat heads. The flowering stem dies and remains brown, while new shoots appear at the base of the plant in autumn.

S. oreganum. A species with spatulate leaves (often found in American sedums), arranged in rosettes. They tend to be tinged with red. The flowers are yellow and formed into flat heads. 8 cm (3 in). Mid to late summer.

S. spathulifolium. An American species making neat mounds of soft, fleshy, spathulate leaves on brittle, waxy stems. The whole plant is covered in a white bloom, and this is most marked in the form 'Capa Blanca', in which the foliage is smaller and entirely white. 'Purpureum' has purple leaves with a bloomy finish. The flowers are yellow and borne in a handsome head, 8 cm (3 in) across. 13 cm (5 in). Summer. California and Oregon.

S. spurium. An extremely easily grown plant that will succeed anywhere, even under trees. It makes tangled mats of shoots clad in opposite pairs of flat, slightly toothed leaves and has white or pink flowers. 'Schorbusser Blut' (scorpion's blood) is said to be a form of it, but needs a hot, dry place. It is red-purple and has red flowers. 10 cm (4 in). Summer. Caucasus.

SEMIAQUILEGIA (Ranunculaceae)

A genus of plants similar to *Aquilegia* but with spurless flowers.

S. ecalcarata (syn. *A. adoxioides*). A neat perennial with ferny foliage and many-flowered sprays of purple-brown flowers. A pretty plant for the space. Propagate by seed. 30 cm (12 in). Late spring to early summer. China.

SEMPERVIVUM (Crassulaceae)

The houseleek genus is not all that large, botanically speaking, as it contains only about 25 species. However, many of them occur in several geographic forms and there are a large number of cultivars. There is little to choose between many of them. Some, indeed, are almost indistinguishable one from the other, and it is perfectly possible for nursery catalogues to differ about which plant takes which label.

They are all plants with rosettes of fleshy, pointed leaves, usually producing offsets like strawberry runners. The typical flower is a ten-pointed star, forming part of a flat, fairly congested head atop a fleshy stem. The flowering rosettes die after flowering.

Sempervivums will grow just about anywhere — on roofs, rocks, and even on the outsides of troughs if given a start with a smear of manure. Propagation is simply done by cutting off individual rosettes and placing them where they are to grow. At the time of writing there were approximately 500 sempervivums available to gardeners — always assuming that the names referred to distinct varieties. Those mentioned below are a drop in the ocean but demonstrate the chief characteristics of the genus and show the extent of variation that occurs.

S. arachnoideum. A very variable species. Plants may have rosettes as much as 2.5 cm (1 in) across down to little more than a quarter of that size. What they have in common is a spider's web of white hairs covering the rosettes; in some smaller forms this is most conspicuous. The rosettes are green with pink leaf-tips, and may be flat-topped globes, as in the larger forms or perfect little balls in the smallest ones. The rosettes always congregate to form tight mats. The flowers are pink. Summer. Alps and Apennines.

S. tectorum. This species is taken out of alphabetical order as it represents the opposite end of the sempervivum scale from *S. arachnoideum*. The rosettes are open and quite flat, not globular, and can be well over 8 cm (3 in) across. The leaves are very succulent, green or blue-green and tipped with blackish or brownish purple. Occasionally, as in 'Triste' (was this originally 'Trieste'?) the leaves are uniformly mahogany-brown. The flowers, deep pink, are borne on 30 cm (12 in) stems. Mid summer to early autumn. Central and S. Europe.

S. calcaratum. A hybrid of *S. tectorum* with blue-green leaves tipped with crimson, and purple flowers.

S. ciliosum. A variable species, seemingly with a different form on every mountain. The rosettes are always globular and quite small. The leaves are incurved and usually light green, sometimes so covered with hairs as to appear white. Forms with red or purple leaves also occur, of which the most deeply coloured — also one of the smallest — is *S.c. galicium* 'Mali Hat Form'. Yellow flowers on short stems. Mid to late summer. Bulgaria.

S. dolomiticum. Has small, semiglobular rosettes with the leaves turning upwards to point vertically. The leaves are light green, with tips and edges red-brown to bright red. The flowers are a rich carmine pink. Mid summer to early autumn. Eastern Alps.

S. grandiflorum. Has quite large rosettes of dull green with brown tips. The leaves are covered with almost invisible, sticky hairs and the plant has an aroma that makes some people think of resin and others of billy goats. The flowers are yellow and each petal has a purple spot at the base, a characteristic that is passed on to many hybrids bred from this species. Summer. Alps.

S. kindingeri, pittonii and ruthenicum. All similar, but with yellow flowers, and all three have much in common with *S. grandiflorum*.

S. kosaninii. A species with large rosettes up to or more than 8 cm (3 in) across. The leaves are very succulent and purple-tipped and the flowers are red on 20 cm (8 in) stems. Mid summer to early autumn. Macedonia and Greece.

S. montanum. A parent of many hybrids and crosses readily with several other species. The rosettes are relatively small (usually less than 2.5 cm (1 in) across), dark green, hairy, and with a resinous/goaty aroma. The flowers are violet-purple. The plant is prolific with its offsets. Early summer to early autumn. Central and S. Europe.

SENECIO (Compositae)

Senecios include some of the most dangerous agricultural weeds, some of the most undistinguished of all plants, and some of the best. Among their 2000 species or so, just one is an outstanding alpine.

S. incanus carniolicus. A perennial with small tufts of rosettes of deeply lobed leaves. They are so densely covered with adpressed hairs as to appear almost white. The flowers, in rather small heads, are rich gold. It is a choice plant, for a position in a hot, sunny scree. 10 cm (4 in). Mid to late summer. Alps and Apennines.

SHORTIA (Diapensiaceae)

Sortias are among the most sought-after and most beautiful of alpines. They are plants for cool, moist, peaty places and are small and low growing, with polished, leathery, evergreen leaves that are suffused with deep red, particularly in winter. The flowers are soldanella-like but considerably larger and pink or white. They must have a lime-free soil. Propagate by seed or very careful division.

S. galacifolia. Widely bell-shaped flowers and long-stalked, glossy, rounded leaves with undulate edges, becoming bronze-tinted in autumn. The flowers are white, pink-tinged and funnel-shaped. 13 cm (5 in). Mid to late spring. USA.

S. soldanelloides (syn. *Schizocodon soldanelloides*). Has shiny leaves that are more conspicuously toothed than in the following species. The foliage turns dark red in autumn and winter but is green at other times. The flowers are not solitary but are borne in racemes, usually not less than four and seldom more than six. They are deep rose pink, deeply fringed and more narrowly bell-shaped. There are forms with smaller stature, larger leaves, and there are two with white flowers. 15 cm (6 in). Mid to late spring. Japan.

Shortia soldanelloides

S. uniflora. A sturdy little plant with heart-shaped, dentate leaves. The flower stems bear solitary, wide-open, light pink bells, slightly fringed, with a slight perfume. The foliage is red-tinged all year round. 13 cm (5 in). Early to mid spring. Japan. *S.u. grandiflora* has flowers between 2.5 and 5 cm (1–2 in) wide with deeper pink flowers and a more noticeable fragrance.

SILENE (Caryophyllaceae)

Silenes are mostly meadow plants, including campions, ragged robins and catchflies, but also include some alpines. They have five-petalled, somewhat dianthus-like flowers and generally prefer a well-drained, gritty soil in a sunny position. Propagate by seed.

S. acaulis. This is one of the tightest cushions among alpines, making domed mats of bright green. The stemless, pink flowers stud the cushions in the wild, but are less generously produced in cultivation. A poor scree soil is the best means of encouraging flowering. *S.a. pedunculata* has stalked flowers that are more freely produced. There is a white form. Early to mid summer. Europe.

S. alpestris. A tufted plant that rambles and tumbles over rocks. It has sprays of smallish, white flowers. *S.a.* 'Flore Pleno' has fully double flowers. 25 cm (10 in). Early to late summer. E. Alps.

S. elizabethae. Has lanceolate, glossy leaves and very large flowers like rose-purple ragged robins. Often recommended for the alpine house, it is perfectly happy on a well-drained, sunny scree. 15 cm (6 in). Early to late summer. Italy.

S. hookeri. A difficult plant of great beauty, needing to be grown in the alpine house in lime-free soil and kept dry in winter. Its flowers are enormous for the size of the plant, fully 5 cm (2 in) wide, light pink, and with deeply lobed petals. 8 cm (3 in). Late spring to mid summer. California.

S. kieskii minor. A small, tufted plant making cushions of soft, deep green leaves with short-stemmed heads of pink flowers. 8 cm (3 in). Mid to late summer. Japan.

S. schafta. A variable plant making wide, tufted mats of dark green foliage and sprays of magenta-pink flowers. It is easily grown and valuable for its late flowering but its colour makes it difficult to place. 15 cm (6 in). Mid summer to mid autumn. Caucasus.

SISYRINCHIUM (Iridaceae)

Sisyrinchiums are plants with iris-like foliage and starry flowers, native to the American continents and islands. They range from tall border plants to small ones for the rock garden. It should be noted, however, that propagation may not be necessary, as some are adept at sowing themselves. Others require more care.

S. angustifolium. Makes tufts of grassy leaves and has pure blue, starry flowers. 20 cm (8 in). Mid summer to early autumn. N. America.

S. bermudianum. Similar but has flowers of deeper blue, almost purple, and slightly coarser growth. 23 cm (9 in). Early summer to early autumn. Bermuda, and a true native of wet meadows in western Ireland.

S. brachypus. Has fans of leaves like a tiny bearded iris and bright yellow flowers. Beautiful, but it can be a nuisance. 10 cm (4 in). Early to late summer. N. America.

S. douglasii. An entirely different species with narrow, rush-like leaves and pairs of satiny purple flowers. It is a plant for a choice position, which should be carefully marked, as it dies down after flowering and is then easily damaged by mistake. Propagation is best done by seed, as plants are often lost when division is attempted. 20–25 cm (8–10 in). Late summer. N. America.

S. filifolium. Superficially like the last species, but is more elegant and slender. Its pendent flowers are delicate, silky white, faintly and intricately veined with wine-purple. 20 cm (8 in). Early summer. Falklands.

SOLDANELLA (Primulaceae)

Soldanellas are among the most daintily attractive of European alpines. Typically they have small, round to kidney-shaped leaves on long stalks that build up into cushions like overlapping scales. The flowers are held well clear of the foliage and end in downturned, fringed bells like little hats. They are usually in some shade of blue. They often flower through the fringes of snowfields in very wet conditions and fare best in peaty, leafy, moist soil in part, but not too much, shade. Propagate by division, or by seed if available.

S. alpina. Grows well enough in cultivation but is reluctant to flower. When it does, its purple-blue bells perfectly match its dark green, round, rather leathery leaves. 10 cm (4 in). Early to late spring. Europe.

S. carpatica. More vigorous than the foregoing and flowers reliably, with deeply fringed, purple-blue flowers. The leaves are purple beneath. There is a white form. 15 cm (6 in). Mid to late spring. Carpathians.

S. minima. A tiny species with minute, round leaves on long stalks. The narrow, fringed bells are solitary and usually pale violet. There is a white form. On limestone formations in the wild, but lime is not necessary in cultivation. 5 cm (2 in). Early to mid spring. E. Alps.

S. montana. A vigorous soldanella. It has kidney-shaped, deep green leaves and flowers profusely, with many upright stems, each with a cluster of up to ten blue, fringed, widely bell- to funnel-shaped flowers. 15 cm (6 in). Mid spring. Alpine woodland in Europe.

S. pusilla. Slightly larger than *S. minima* and has solitary flowers of a unique, straight-sided bell shape with slight fringing. Pale violet. Flowers most readily in a pot in the alpine house.

S. villosa. The most vigorous species with finely hairy leaf stalks and flower stems. It is easily grown and flowers readily, with heads of blue-purple flowers. 25 cm (10 in). Late spring. Pyrenees.

SORBUS (Rosaceae)

S. reducta. A miniature mountain ash. There appear to be two forms in cultivation, one making a sturdy, gnarled bush, the other a small thicket of stems arising at ground level. Both have pinnate leaves, white flowers in summer and bright red berries in autumn. It is very slow growing. The bush form is the more desirable. Propagate by seed, but remove the seeds from the berries first, as it is surprising how many people sow the whole berry and have to wait a long time for germination. About 20 cm (8 in). China.

SYNTHYRIS (Scrophulariaceae)

This North American genus is closely related to the European *Wulfenia* and has similar two-lipped, tubular flowers in shades of violet-blue or blue. Some species have green leaves and can be grown out of doors; others have woolly or silky leaves and are difficult, but beautiful. Divide the green-leafed species, but propagate the others by seed.

S. lanuginosa pinnatifida. Has pinnate, silver leaves and spikes of tubular flowers of clear blue. It is a lovely subject for the alpine house, where it can be kept from winter wet and not subjected to the disturbance that it hates. Gritty compost. 20 cm (8 in). Mid to late spring. Washington State, USA.

S. missurica. The leaves are lobed, leathery and dark green and the flowers are in spikes of violet-blue. Scree. 23 cm (9 in). Spring. The name was originally a mistake; the plant comes from Washington, south to California and east to Idaho, nowhere near the Missouri, which rises in Montana.

S. reniformis. Comes from a similar area and also has green leaves. They are kidney-shaped and bluntly toothed. The flowers are purplish blue on short stems. 15 cm (6 in). Early to mid spring.

TANAKAEA (Saxifragaceae)

T. radicans. This is the only species. It has the appearance of a small, white-flowered astilbe. Its foliage arises from running, woody rhizomes and the leaves are rounded and deep green. It prefers a sandy, peaty, lime-free soil in part shade. Division. 15 cm (6 in). Late spring to early summer. China and Japan.

TELESONIX (Saxifragaceae)

Boykinia jamesii (q.v.) is becoming relegated to the synonym of *Telesonix jamesii*, which now constitutes a new, monotypic genus.

TEUCRIUM (Labiatae)

A genus of shrubby plants for the most part, with aromatic foliage and unusual flowers whose labiate shape is changed by the absence of the upper lip. They are plants of the Mediterranean basin, preferring hot, dry positions in full sun. Propagate by seed or cuttings.

T. ackermanii. A subshrub forming a mat of grey-green foliage with heads of crimson-violet. 13 cm (5 in). Late summer. Turkey.

T. aroanum. A tiny shrub with tangled branches, small, hairy leaves, and heads of grey-purple flowers. 10 cm (4 in). Late summer. Greece.

T. chamaedrys. A subshrub with glossy, dark green, oak-like leaves and small heads of pink flowers. It needs a poor soil, otherwise it becomes too large. However, *T.c.* 'Nanum' is considerably smaller at less than 15 cm (6 in) tall. Early summer to early autumn.

T. pyrenaicum. Makes mats of rounded, woolly leaves and has larger flowers than in other species. They are cream or lavender or a mixture of both. 10 cm (4 in). Early to late summer. Pyrenees.

T. subspinosum. Another of the spiny, dwarf, aromatic shrubs that cats love to use for scratching themselves. It is a dense bush with tiny, crinkled, grey leaves and bright pink flowers, but you may have to remove the cat fur in order to see them. For the hottest, grittiest part of the rock garden. 15 cm (6 in). Late summer. W. Asia.

THALICTRUM (Ranunculaceae)

The meadow rues are generally too tall for the rock garden and some of them are first-class border plants. The alpine species are genuine miniatures, however, and share with their larger cousins the finely cut foliage and the airy, open sprays of many small flowers. Propagate by seed or division.

T. kiusianum. The most attractive species; it spreads gently, but never too much and has pretty, grey, slightly bronzed foliage. The little flowers, made conspicuous by their numbers, are pink-purple. 13 cm (5 in). Early to mid summer. Japan.

THLASPI (Cruciferae)

Mostly weedy annuals, but one species is a beautiful alpine.

T. rotundifolium. Has fairly undistinguished clumps of small leaves, but it becomes transformed into a glorious cushion of soft, daphne-pink at flowering time, when it becomes covered in small flowers with a scent of honey. In the wild it is a wonderful sight, and this can be emulated with careful cultivation in the alpine house. Propagate by seed or cuttings. 8 cm (3 in). Late spring to early summer. Alps and Apennines.

Thlaspi rotundifolium

THYMUS (Labiatae)

The thymes are well known as aromatic plants, many of them used in cookery. The mat-forming kinds are ideal for planting in paving, as they do not mind in the least being walked on, and the pressure of feet releases their aromas.

T. caespititius. Makes small clumps of neat foliage and has heads of purplish flowers. 5 cm (2 in). Late summer. Spain and Azores.

T. cilicicus. A shrubby species, not mat-forming, neither is it notably aromatic. However its four-angled, closely leaf-clad stems and round heads of pink flowers make it an attractive and unusual dwarf shrub. 15 cm (6 in). Mid to late summer. Turkey.

T. × citriodorus. A beautiful thyme, more of a shrub than a mat, with strongly lemon-scented foliage and small heads of lilac flowers. There are many forms, particularly variegated ones, in which green and gold or green and silver combine effectively. 'Aureus', 'Silver Queen' and 'Doone Valley' (which is probably of different parentage) are among the best of these thymes. 15–25 cm (6–10 in).

T. membranaceus. A bushy, twiggy, dwarf shrub with tiny leaves. It is distinct in that its small, purple flowers are enclosed in large, conspicuous, papery bracts that are white but become slightly flushed with purplish pink as they age. Slightly tender and intolerant of winter wet, so best in the alpine house. 25 cm (10 in). Early to late summer. Spain.

T. serpyllum. The European wild thyme is a mat-forming plant with minute leaves and small heads of flowers anywhere from light pink to purple and crimson. There are many garden forms. Mid spring to mid summer.

TRACHELIUM (Campanulaceae)

A late-flowering genus from the Mediterranean, best in the alpine house.

T. asperuloides. Masses of tiny, stalkless leaves go to make up a dense, soft cushion. Short stems arise from this, bearing heads of small, lilac-blue flowers. It detests overhead wet but is delightful in a pan. The flower stems should be trimmed off after flowering to avoid rot spreading to the foliage. 5 cm (2 in). Late summer to early autumn. Banks of the river Styx, Greece.

TRILLIUM (Liliaceae; Trilliaceae)

Of the 30 or so species of trilliums, almost all are in cultivation. This is not surprising, as they are beautiful plants. All the parts — leaf lobes, petals, etc. — are in threes and the petals are usually large and conspicuous. They are woodland plants, enjoying moist, peaty, leafy soils in part shade and all are from North America. The fleshy stems arise from a rhizome and gradually increase in numbers. The easier and most ornamental trilliums are listed here. Propagate by seed or division.

T. cernuum. Has bold foliage and small, white, downward-looking flowers on tall stems. 45 cm (18 in). Mid to late spring.

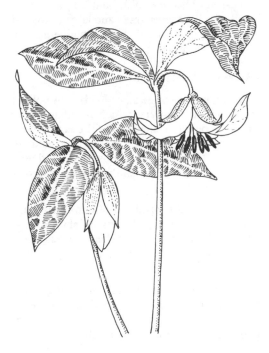

Trillium cernuum

T. erectum. Has deep green, mottled leaves and has red-purple petals with brownish sepals. Known as the red trillium. 30 cm (12 in). Late spring.

T. grandiflorum. The wake robin of North-East American woodland (the British wake robin is *Arum maculatum*). It has broad, bold leaves and large, over 5 cm (2 in) across, semipendent flowers of lustrous white, becoming pink-flushed as they age. 30 cm (12 in). Mid to late spring.

T. luteum. Green leaves mottled with brown and upright flowers of lemon yellow with a slight scent. 20 cm (8 in). Late spring to early summer.

T. nivale. The dwarf white trillium. A small, early flowering plant with white, almost stalkless flowers. Early to mid spring. 15 cm (6 in).

T. rivale. Even smaller, with pink and white flowers. Best in the alpine house or a frame. 10 cm (4 in). Mid spring.

T. sessile. Has beautiful, bold leaves, usually marbled with deeper green and large flowers of chocolate-purple whose petals stand erect and stalkless. 25 cm (10 in). Early to mid spring.

TROLLIUS (Ranunculaceae)

The globe flowers are so called because of the shape of their flowers, which is enhanced by the calyx being petaloid and of the same colour as the petals. In some species there are petaloid stamens. They like moist soils in sun and tend to be short-lived in shade. Propagate by seed or division.

T. acaulis. Has lobed, buttercup-like foliage and rounded, golden flowers on short stems. When fully open they lose their globose shape and become flat. 15 cm (6 in). Early to mid summer. Himalaya.

T. pumilus. Similar but can be distinguished by its leaves, which are divided into five, each fifth being again divided into three. 20 cm (8 in). Early to mid summer. China.

TROPAEOLUM (Tropaeolaceae)

The genus of the nasturtiums includes a species of great beauty for the rock garden.

T. polyphyllum. A curious plant, growing from a rootstock that, once planted, is difficult to find again. From it arise trailing stems between 30 and 45 cm (12–18 in) long, bearing deeply lobed, grey leaves. Later, they become wide plumes of brilliant yellow, small nasturtium flowers. It needs a sunny position and a deep, well-drained, nutritious soil and is at its best when planted high to trail over rocks. It is a rarity but one which, almost

unbelievably, can become an embarrassment when well suited. Early to mid summer. Chile and Argentina.

VACCINIUM (Ericaceae)

Vacciniums are acid-loving shrubs, mainly of moorland, that enjoy peaty soils and cool conditions but not complete shade. There are evergreen and deciduous species and they have racemes of small, bell-shaped flowers. The fruit is a berry and the vaccinium family includes bilberry, cranberry (British and American), whortleberry, cowberry and blueberry. Propagation by seed or cuttings.

V. delavayi. A compact evergreen with small, glossy green leaves, sometimes with a red flush. The flowers are white, cream or pink, held in terminal clusters and the fruits are black-purple. Tender except for mild areas. 90 cm (3 ft). Late spring to early summer. China.

V. nummularia. Another species of marginal hardiness, but worth trying, as it is a lovely plant. It is an evergreen, compact bush of small size, whose little, leathery leaves become hidden by masses of pink, pendent, urn-shaped flowers in dense clusters. 30 cm (12 in). Mid to late spring. Sikkim, Bhutan.

V. ocycoccos. The British (and European) cranberry. It has long, creeping, wiry stems with small, white-backed, evergreen leaves. The flowers are reflexed like tiny, pink cyclamen. The berries are red and edible. Late spring to mid summer.

V. praestans. A prostrate, deciduous shrub that forms low carpets. The flowers are white or reddish, bell-shaped, and the berries are edible, sweet, and red. 10 cm (4 in). Late spring to early summer. Japan.

VERBASCUM (Scrophulariceae)

A genus closely related to and hybridizing with *Celsia*. There are a great many species, including the tall perennials and biennials of the border. Just a few species are dwarf enough for the rock garden and they are first-rate alpines. Propagate by cuttings.

V. dumulosum. A rounded bush with grey, softly hairy, rounded leaves and short racemes of clear yellow flowers. 30 cm (12 in). Early summer. Asia Minor.

V. spinosum. A small, twiggy shrub with each branch ending in a spine. The leaves are grey and lanceolate, not rounded, and the mullein flowers are clear yellow. 30 cm (12 in). Early to mid summer. Crete.

V. 'Letitia'. A hybrid between the two, observed and propagated at Kew. It needs a warm position such as a raised bed and is beautiful in the alpine house. It is a dense, twiggy shrub with small, grey, lobed leaves and many racemes of primrose-yellow flowers fully 2.5 cm (1 in) across. 20 cm (8 in). All summer.

VERONICA (Scrophulariaceae)

The large speedwell genus contains many beautiful, easy-going sun-loving alpines.

V. bombycina. A fine alpine house plant, making loose cushions of slender stems with small leaves, the whole closely felted with white. The flowers are electric-blue veronicas. It needs a very gritty soil, careful watering in the growing season, and dryness in winter. Propagate by cuttings in pure sand. 5 cm (2 in). Late summer. Lebanon.

V. fruticans. Mat-forming, with terminal sprays of deep blue flowers with a reddish eye. 8 cm (3 in). All summer. Europe.

V. gentianoides. The specific epithet refers to the clumps of leaves, which are similar to those of *Gentiana acaulis*. From these arise stems carrying many pale blue flowers. 25 cm (10 in). Early summer. Caucasus. There is a dwarfer form ('Nana'), a white ('Alba') and a variegated variety ('Vareigata').

V. prostrata. A very easy rock garden plant with many sprays of blue flowers over mats of deep green leaves. Among the many forms are *V.p. rosea*, 'Blue Sheen', 'Spode Blue', 'Alba', and 'Mrs. Holt,' which is another pink.

VIOLA (Violaceae)

The genus *Viola* covers violets, violas, pansies and violettas. Alpine gardeners are chiefly concerned with species, but some of the less highly developed, smaller pansies have their place as well. A typical flower has large back petals, with smaller ones making up the lip and wings. Unless otherwise stated, the plants can be grown in a sunny spot on the rock garden. Propagate by seed, or by cuttings of named varieties.

V. beckwithii. Has neat tufts of leaves and flowers with velvety violet back petals, the rest of the flower creamy. 8 cm (3 in). Summer. N. America.

V. calcarata. A miniature, long-spurred pansy. It is a small, compact grower with flowers in many colours from light blue to deep purple and including yellow and parti-coloured forms. It is short lived but easily grown and raised from seed. 10 cm (4 in). A very long season, from mid spring to mid autumn. Central and S. Europe. *V.c. zoysii* is even more compact and has large, pure, rich yellow flowers on short stems. It is liable to scorch and to yellowing in dry conditions, but in the alpine house it makes a superb show. 8 cm (3 in). Much of the summer. Eastern and Julian Alps.

V. cazorlensis. A rare shrubby viola with small, narrow leaves and long-spurred, narrow-petalled flowers of rich rose pink. It is a difficult but exquisitely beautiful plant that should be grown in the alpine house. Spain.

V. cenisia. Similar to *V. calcarata* but more elegant. The flowers are lavender, long-spurred and beautifully veined. Not an easy plant and best cared for in the alpine house. 8 cm (3 in). All summer. Alps.

V. cornuta. The horned pansy is native to the Pyrenees and is widely grown in many forms. Typically the flowers are lilac or violet, but the range in gardens is wide. The best cultivar for rock gardens is *V.c.* 'Minor', which has clear blue flowers on 8 cm (3 in) stems from mid summer to autumn.

V. delphinantha. Another shrubby viola with woody, gnarled stems, narrow leaves, and deep pink flowers on long, erect stalks. It is not at all easy and is best in a crevice between tufa rocks in a pot in the alpine house. 10 cm (4 in). Early to mid summer. Greece.

V. eizanensis. Has unusually dissected leaves and rounded, purple flowers with a tubby, short spur. For a gritty soil. 10 cm (4 in). Mid spring. Japan.

V. jooii. Small, wide leaves and rounded, pale violet, short-stemmed flowers in profusion. 5 cm (2 in). Late spring to late summer. Carpathians.

V. lutea. The European mountain pansy. It is short-spurred and extremely variable in colour; in spite of its name forms occur in white and even purple. It is easy and makes itself permanent by self-sowing. 15 cm (6 in). Early summer to early autumn.

V. pedata. Has palmate leaves and large flowers on short stems. The colour varies, some forms having dark violet back petals and lighter lip and wings, while others are self-coloured violet or even pink. It is not easy and is best in a leafy compost in a shaded part of the alpine house.

V. saxatilis aetiolica. A small-flowered pansy with spreading stems and masses of yellow flowers. 13 cm (5 in). E. Mediterranean. Early spring to early autumn.

VITALIANA (Primulaceae)

There is only one species, split off from *Douglasia*.

V. primuliflora (syn. *Douglasia vitaliana*). This makes a neat clump of silvery green, needle-like foliage in narrow, elongated rosettes. The stemless, solitary flowers are bright yellow, long-tubed and primula-like, but never quite fully open. The form *V.p. praetutiana* is considerably more free flowering and more open than the type, which is niggardly even in the wild. For a crevice between rocks in sun. Propagate by removing rooted stems. 5 cm (2 in). Mid to late spring. Alps.

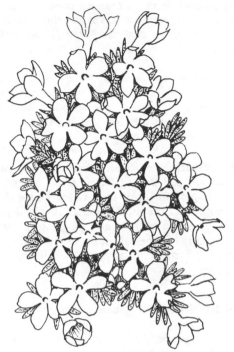

Vitaliana primuliflora

WAHLENBERGIA (Campanulaceae)

A genus of plants closely related to *Edraianthus*, but with solitary, rather than clustered flowers. Best propagated from cuttings.

W. dinarica. A dense mat of silvery, narrow leaves and solitary, large, violet purple bells on short stems. For scree or gritty soil in sun. 8 cm (3 in). Mid summer. Balkans.

W. hederacea. A creeping, dainty perennial with slender stems bearing pendent, pointed-petalled bells of pale blue. Needs a peaty, leafy soil and a cool position but not in too much shade. 8 cm (3 in). Mid to late summer. Europe.

W. serpyllifolia. Has neat mats of grassy, linear foliage. In the usually grown 'Major' form, the cushions become virtually covered with very large, upturned bells of deep, striking, purple-blue. For scree or gritty, well drained soil. 5 cm (2 in). Early to mid summer. Balkans.

WULFENIA (Scrophulariaceae)

W. carinthiaca. The aristocrat of a fairly coarse genus. It makes flat rosettes of smooth, slightly wavy leaves from underground rhizomes and bears racemes of violet-blue, tubular flowers. It needs a moist but well drained position. 25 cm (10 in). Early to late summer. Balkans.

ZAUSCHNERIA (Onagraceae)

A genus of subshrubs from California and Mexico with brilliant scarlet, tubular flowers. They are slightly tender but survive most winters except in the coldest areas. Their late flowering allows their strong colouring to shine without clashing, but care should still be exercised.

Z. californica. Known as the Californian fuchsia. It is a sparsely-branched subshrub with small but long, willow-like leaves and terminal clusters of tubular flowers 2.5 cm (1 in) or more long. 30 cm (12 in). Late summer to mid autumn. There is a move afoot to transfer this genus to *Epilobium*, with this species becoming *E. canum*. *Sic transeunt genera plantarum*.

CHAPTER 25

Dwarf Bulbs

The gardening definition of an alpine is at variance with the botanical one. Alpine gardeners consider that an alpine is a plant that looks 'right' on a rock garden, while botanically an alpine is a plant whose natural habitat is between the tree line and the permanent snow line.

As far as dwarf bulbs go, the alpine gardener has extended his 'definition' to include plants that are appropriate for the bulb frame and other means of cultivation described in this book. What this means in practical terms is that there is such a huge range of bulbs suitable for 'alpine' gardening that only the sketchiest approach is possible here.

You would be ill-served by a species-by-species listing and descriptions as it would have to be as long as the gazeteer part of this book. Anything less would be of no value at all and could be misleading.

Accordingly, the following is a list of genera only. The ones included are those containing species of interest to growers of alpines and rock gardeners. In recent years there have been a number of books written by our leading experts on dwarf bulbs, and you should refer to them for further information.

Those marked * require cool greenhouse treatment in the UK and similar climates. Genera marked ** are dealt with in some detail in the main body of the book.

Albuca	*Hyacinthus*	
Allium	*Hypoxis*	
*Anemone**	*Ipheion*	
Anioganthus	*Iris* (in part)	
Arisarum	*Ixia*	
Arum	*Leucojum*	
*Babiana**	*Merendera*	
Brodiaea	*Moraea**	
Bulbocodium	*Muscari*	
Calochortus	*Muscarimia*	
Caloscordium	*Narcissus*	
Chionodoxa	*Ornithogalum*	
Chionoscilla	*Oxalis***	
Colchicum	*Pinellia*	
*Conanthera**	*Pseudomuscari*	
*Cooperia**	*Puschkinia*	
Crocus	*Rhodohypoxis*	
*Cyanella**	*Romulea*	
*Cyclamen***	*Roscoea***	
*Eleutherine**	*Scilla*	
Eranthis	*Sparaxis*	
Erythronium	*Sternbergia*	
*Ferraria**	*Synnotia*	
*Fritillaria***	*Syringodea**	
Galanthus	*Tecophilaea*	
*Habranthus**	*Tigridia*	
*Herbertia**	*Triteleia*	
Hermodactylus	*Tulipa*	
Hyacinthella	*Zephyranthes*	

CHAPTER 26

Dwarf Conifers

For much the same reasons as in the case of dwarf bulbs it is not possible to give any sort of descriptive listing of dwarf conifers. There are so many that they demand in effect a complete book of their own.

Furthermore, it is paradoxically one of the fastest moving fields of ornamental horticulture, and the preferred cultivars (and most dwarf conifers are cultivars) of one decade tend to be eclipsed by new ones the next. For example, early in the 1970s there were about 170 cultivars of *Chamaecyparis* alone in commercial cultivation. Today it is well over 300 and rising. Approximately 60% of these—and it is very approximate—are 'dwarf' or 'slow growing'.

A telling example of this is the 'Ellwoodii' group of cultivars of *Chamaecyparis lawsoniana*. Twenty years ago, nurseries were able to offer 'Ellwoodii', 'Ellwood's Gold' and 'Ellwood's White'. Today you can obtain those three plus (all prefixed by 'Ellwood's') 'Empire', 'Glauca', 'Nymph', 'Pillar', 'Pygmy', 'Silver', and 'Variegata'—a total of 10 cultivars.

What constitutes a 'dwarf' conifer is, too, a matter of interpretation. Do you restrict yourself to those that grow to a size of 90 × 150 cm (3 × 5 ft) in thirty years, or do you include those that reach that size in ten or much less? In fact, taking the former definition, which is not that restrictive, there are very large numbers of plants available. Taking all 'dwarf' and 'slow-growing' conifers into account is to attempt to describe a body of plants well beyond the scope of this book. Then, too, proportion must be taken into account. Alpine conifers can be quite tall in the wild, with heights of several metres being widely encountered where alpine plants grow. On the rock gardens of Wisley and Kew, large specimens are in proportion, whereas in the rock garden in a small home garden, only a handful of the smallest should be considered.

Therefore, the following is a list of the genera in which dwarf and slow-growing conifers are found, and you should refer from it to books specializing in the subject or, probably more effectively, to the catalogues of the responsible nurseries dealing in these plants.

Abies
Calocedrus
Cedrus
Cephalotaxus
Chamaecyparis
   lawsoniana
C. *nootkatensis*
C. *obtusa*
C. *pisifera*
C. *thyoides*
Cryptomeria
Cupressus
Juniperus

Microcachrys
Picea
Pinus
Podocarpus
Pseudotsuga
Sequoia
Sequoiadendron
Taxus
Thuja occidentalis
T. *orientalis*
T. *plicata*
Thujopsis
Tsuga

CHAPTER 27

Dwarf Shrubs

Several genera of alpines (*Cassiope* is a good example) consist wholly or in part of plants that are technically shrubs because their stems are entirely woody and do not have soft portions that are annually renewed. To gardeners, though, they do not qualify. This has to do with the perfectly reasonable but botanically untenable view that a dwarf shrub should look like a dwarf version of a shrub. There is nothing, for instance, that looks remotely like a large cassiope, unless it is a cactus from the Sonora Desert, in whose mighty image *C. wardii* might have been mischievously cast.

The following shrubby genera include plants that alpine gardeners (and show judges) recognize as dwarf shrubs:

Arcterica
Berberis
Betula
Convolvulus cneorum
Cotoneaster
Cyathodes
Cytisus
Daphne
Erinacea
Gaultheria
Genista
Helianthemum
Jasminum
Kalmia
Kalmiopsis
× Kalmiothamnus

Leptospermum
Menziesia
Penstemon
Pernettya
Prunus
× Phylliopsis
Phyllodoce
× Phyllothamnus
Rhododendron
Rhodothamnus
Rubus
Salix
Sorbus
Thymus cilicicus
T. membranaceus
Vaccinium

CHAPTER 28
Plants for Specific Places

Plants for peat beds

Arcterica
Arctostaphylos
Betula nana
 'Glengarry'
Bruckenthalia
Cassiope
Cortusa
Corydalis cashmeriana
Cyananthus
Dodecatheon
Empetrum
Epigaea
Gaultheria
Gentiana (Asiatic)
Haberlea
Hacquetia
Hepatica
Hypsela
Kalmia
Kalmiopsis
× Kalmiothamnus
Leiophyllum
Loiseluria

Meconopsis
Menziesia
Mitchella
Omphalogramma
Ourisia
Pentachondra
Pernettya
× Phylliopsis
Phyllodoce
× Phyllothamnus
Primula
Ramonda
Ranzania
Rhododendron
Rhodothamnus
Salix
Sanguinaria
Saxifraga fortunei
Shortia
Soldanella
Tanakaea
Trillium
Vaccinium

Plants for tufa

Androsace (except
 aretians)
Armeria juniperifolia
Asperula lilacaeflora
 caespitosa
A. nitida puberula
Campanula
 morettiana
C. zoysii
Dianthus (dwarf)
Dionysia aretioides
Draba
Ericacea
Eritrichium
Helichrysum
 milfordiae

Petrocallis pyrenaica
Petrophytum
Phacelia sericea
Phlox (small)
Physoplexis comosa
Potentilla nitida
Primula allionii
P. forrestii
Ramonda (in shade)
Raoulia australis
R. hookeri
Saxifraga (many)
Silene acaulis
Veronica bombycina
Viola cazorlensis
V. delphinantha
Vitaliana primuliflora

Plants for troughs and sinks

Acantholimon
 glumaceum
Aethionema 'Warley
 Rose'
Allium narcissiflorum
A. cyaneum
Alyssum alpestre
Anacyclus depressus
Anchusa caespitosa
Androsace (a few)
Aquilegia beckwithii
A. bertolonii
A. discolor
Arabis bryoides
Armeria juniperifolia
Asperula gussonii
A. lilacaeflora
 caespitosa
Aster pygmaea
Betula nana
 'Glengarry'
Campanula arvatica
C. cochlearifolia and
 similar
C. tomassiniana
Cassiope
Celsia acaulis
Cytisus demissus
Daphne arbuscula
Dianthus (many)
Douglasia dentata
D. laevigata
Draba
Edraianthus pumilio
Erinacea
Fritillaria (a few)
Erodium reichardii
Genista delphinensis
Gentiana
 brachyphylla
G. saxosa

G. verna
Globularia repens
Haplopappus
 brandegeei
Helichrysum
 coralloides
H. frigidum
H. milfordiae
H. selago
Iris mellita
Jasminum parkeri
Jovibarba
Lewisia
Loiseluria procumbens
Mentha requienii
Morisia
Oxalis
Paraquilegia
Petrocallis
Petrophytum
Phlox (small)
Physoplexis comosa
Polygonatum hookeri
Potentilla nitida
Primula (a few)
Pygmaea
Raoulia (scabweeds)
Salix boydii
Saponaria × olivana
Saxifraga (most)
Sedum spathulifolium
Sempervivum
Silene acaulis
Soldanella
Sorbus reducta
Thalictrum kiusianum
Thlaspi rotundifolium
Viola
Vitaliana

Plants for the alpine house

Acantholimon
Androsace
Aquilegia jonesii
A. laramiensis
Asperula nitida
  puberula
A. suberosa
Boykinia jamesii
Briggsia muscicola
Calceolaria darwinii
C. fothergillii
Campanula allionii
C. excisa
C. lasiocarpa
C. morettiana
C. piperi
C. raineri
C. vidalii
C. zoysii
Cassiope wardii
Celsia acaulis
Convolvulus sabatius
Craspedia incana
Cyananthus sherriffii
Cyathodes
Cyclamen (several)

Daphne jasminea
D. petraea
Delphinium nudicaule
D. muscosum
Dicentra peregrina
  (and hybrids)
Dionysia
Douglasia
Draba
Erinacea
Eritrichium
Fritillaria
Gentiana bavarica
G. brachyphylla
Globularia repens
Gypsophila repens
G. aretioides
Haastia
Helichrysum
  coralloides
H. milfordiae
H. selago
Jankaea
Kelseya
Leontopodium
  alpinum nivale

Lepidium nanum
Leptospermum
Leucogynes
Lewisia
Linaria tristis
Lupinus lyallii
Mitchella
Myosotis azorica
Myrteola nummularia
Notothlaspi rosulatum
Onosma albopilosum
Paraquilegia
Petrocallis
Phacelia sericea
Phlox nana ensifolia
Physoplexis comosa
Pimelia
Pleione
Primula (American)
Primula (Petiolaris
  section)
P. allionii (and
  hybrids)
P. forrestii
P. reidii-williamsii
Pulsatilla vernalis

Ramonda
Ranunculus asiaticus
R. calandrinioides
R. glacialis
Raoulia (vegetable
  sheep)
R. × Leucogynes
Rhodothamnus
Ricotia
Rupicapnos
Saponaria pumilio
Sarcocapnos
Saxifraga (many)
Silene acaulis
S. hookeri
Synthyris lanuginosa
  pinnatifida
Thlaspi rotundifolium
Trachelium
  asperuloides
Verbascum
Veronica bombycina
Viola cazorlensis
V. delphinantha
V. pedata

APPENDICES: GOING FURTHER

Appendix I
Joining Societies

Many gardeners are solitary people preferring the company of themselves and their plants to any other. On the other hand many more enjoy meeting other like-minded people and for them talking about plants is almost as enjoyable as growing them. One way of meeting people is by joining a society.

Alpine garden societies thrive in many parts of the world. Many work on two levels: national and local. The main national society provides the overall structure with the central services such as magazines, seed exchanges, national shows, organized tours to the mountains and conferences to exchange information. The local groups are much more intimate affairs with members meeting perhaps once a month to listen to lectures, have plant sales, visit gardens, organize local shows, exchange plants and just chat.

The personal contacts that one makes through the societies are invaluable. One can learn a tremendous amount from other people's experiences as well as swapping ideas and plants. Magazines and lectures provide another invaluable source of information and keep one's interest alive during winter evenings particularly when there are few practical things to do. Conferences also provide a wealth of information as well as giving members the chance to meet others from further afield. One of the big benefits of most societies is that they provide a seed exchange which enables members to acquire seed of plants that they would otherwise be unable to obtain. Shows are not just for those who like to show off their prowess; they are also a wonderful opportunity to see a wide range of plants, many rare and all well-grown.

The opportunity to meet other gardeners is one that should not be missed but even for those who live far away from other gardeners or have an aversion to meeting people the societies still have a lot to offer as their magazines and seed exchanges alone are worth the subscription.

Alpine Garden Society (W.J. Simpson) AGS Centre, Avon Bank, Pershore WR10 3JP

Alpine Garden Club of British Columbia (Graeme Bain) 3510 West 22nd Avenue, Vancouver, British Columbia V6S 1J3, Canada

North American Rock Garden Society (Jacques Mommens) PO Box 67, Milwood, New York 10546, USA

New Zealand Alpine Garden Society PO Box 2984, Christchurch, New Zealand

Scottish Rock Garden Club PO Box 14063, Edinburgh EH10 4YE

As well as the main alpine gardening societies there are a number of specialist ones covering one or more genera of plants. These are obviously smaller societies than the main ones but are none the less very active, providing many facilities. Examples include:

American Iris Society (Jeanne Clay Park) 8426 Vinevalley Drive, Sun Valley, California 91352, USA

American Primrose, Primula and Auricula Society (Addaline Robinson) 41801 South West Burgasky Road, Gaston, Oregon 97119, USA

British Iris Society (Mrs E. M. Wise) 197 The Parkway, Iver Heath, Iver, Buckinghamshire SL0 0RQ

Cyclamen Society (Vic Aspland) 27 Osmaston Road, Norton, Stourbridge, West Midlands DY8 2AL

RHS Lily Group (Michael Upward) Wilton Cottage, Eckington, Pershore, Worcestershire WR10 3NB

Saxifrage Society (Adrian Young) 7 Alpha Court, Hockliffe Road, Leighton Buzzard, Bedfordshire LU7 8JW

Appendix II
Going to the mountains

One of the great attractions of alpine gardening is that so many of the plants that are grown in the garden can also be seen in the wild. Apart from the sheer pleasure of being in the mountains, much can be learnt that will help the gardener from seeing a plant in its natural habitat.

There are several ways of going to the mountains. A trip can be made alone or with friends, where all the arrangements are made by the travellers. Many alpine societies organize trips to various parts of the world with the sole intention of searching out plants. They are organized and led by people interested and knowledgeable in the subject and the members of the party are there because of their interest, so the *raison d'être* of the trip is to see and talk about mountain flowers. Increasingly, there are a number of tour companies who run excursions to the mountains to look at plants. Although organized by non-plantsmen, they are often led by a famous plantsman or botanist. The groups can be more mixed than the society parties and the itineraries may take in other things as well as plants, such as birdwatching or looking at buildings and other aspects of the country's heritage.

Some of the organized trips are quite strenuous with several days trekking and primitive conditions. However, a large range of ages make the journey, and the societies and tour companies will advise on the suitability of the trip.

When considering where to go a good starting point is Lionel Bacon's *Mountain Flower Holidays in Europe* (Alpine Garden Society Publications), which goes into all the mountain ranges in Europe in detail. The magazines of the various societies carry travelogues of other alpine growers' experiences in mountains all over the world. Details of the more formal trips can be obtained from Alpine Garden Society Tours and from the various tour companies that advertise regularly in many of the garden magazines.

Whether the trips are organized by tour companies or by the gardener himself, travelling in the mountains is dangerous. All sensible precautions for personal safety should be carried out. Never venture far away from a car or camp witout taking extra clothes, water, food and a torch. Always wear sensible footwear and carry waterproof clothing. Hats are sensible wear both for keeping the heat in and the sun out.

Leave plants and flowers where they are for others to enjoy. Never attempt to collect plants to take home; the chances are they will die before you get them there and they are probably already available, often in better forms, from a nursery. There are already enough pressures on plants in the wild without adding to them. Photographs are a good and more permanent way of recording what you find.

Appendix III
Building a Library

Many gardeners scorn the use of books, particularly modern books which are full of pictures and empty of facts. However, in alpine gardening it helps to build up a basic library of books, not so much about techniques as about the flowers themselves.

There are several books written for alpine gardeners which are entirely about plants, a good example being Will Ingwersen's *Manual of Alpine Plants* or Chris Grey-Wilson's *Manual of Alpine and Rock Garden Plants.* These cover the majority of plants that are commonly in cultivation, giving a description of the plant and its cultural needs. New plants and seeds are constantly being introduced from the wild and these are the ones that are difficult to find information about (and it can be critical whether a plant grows in sun or shade, acid or limey conditions, moist or free-draining soil, etc.). Many alpine gardeners try to collect floras of the various countries where alpines grow. These can be expensive but to the serious grower they can be worth their weight in gold. Examples of these would include Polunin and Stainton's *Flowers of the Himalaya* or Polunin's *Flowers of Greece and the Balkans.*

Another category of books worth investing in are monographs on individual genera or groups of plants. Examples of these would include John Blanchard's *Narcissus*, Brian Mathew's *The Crocus*, *The Iris* or *Hellebores* or the same author's various general books on bulbs.

Another extremely good source of information about plants are the magazines put out by various alpine societies. Do not throw them away once they have been read; hold on to them because you will find that in the long run they are more useful as retrospective sources of information than they are as current reading matter.

Books, especially specialist books, are expensive. There are a number of specialist second-hand booksellers that advertise in the gardening press who may well be able to produce copies at a cheaper rate than buying new. One way round the problem of the expense of book buying is to start a book fund and grow extra plants to sell specifically for that purpose. Books for a basic library are listed below.

General reading

Bacon, L. *Mountain Flower Holidays*. AGS Publications, 1979.

Elliott, R. *Alpine Gardening.* AGS Publications, 1988.

Ingwersen, W. *Alpine and Rock Garden Plants.* Dent, 1983.

Stearn, W. T. *Botanical Latin*. David & Charles, 1983.

Techniques

Bird, R. *A Guide to Rock Gardening*. Christopher Helm, 1990.

Buczacki, S. and Harris, R. *Collins Guide to the Pests, Diseases and Disorders of Garden Plants.* Collins, 1981.

Dryden, K. *Alpines in Pots*. AGS Publications, 1988.

Elliott, J. *Alpines in Sinks and Troughs*. AGS Publications, 1974.

Heath, R. H. *Collectors Alpines*. Collingridge, 1981.

Hills, L. D. *The Propagation of Alpines*. Faber & Faber, 1950.

Hulme, J. K. *Propagation of Alpine Plants*. AGS Publications, 1982.

Rolfe, R. *The Alpine House*. Christopher Helm, 1990.

Manuals

Farrer, R. *The English Rock Garden*. Nelson, 1919.

Grey-Wilson, C. *Manual of Alpine and Rock Garden Plants*. Christopher Helm, 1989.

Griffith, A. N. *Collins Guide to Alpines and Rock Garden Plants*. Collins, 1973.

Ingwersen, W. *Manual of Alpine Plants*. Ingwersen, 1978.

Plants

Blanchard, J. *The Narcissus*. AGS Publications, 1990.

Brickell, C. D. and Mathew, B. *Daphne*. AGS Publications, 1976.

Cribb, P. and Butterfield, I. *The Genus Pleione*. Christopher Helm, 1988.

Green, R. *Asiatic Primulas*. AGS Publications, 1976.

Grey-Wilson, C. *The Genus Cyclamen*. Christopher Helm, 1988.

Grey-Wilson, C. *The Genus Dionysia*. AGS Publications, 1989.

Horny, R. *et al. Porophyllum Saxifrages*. Byam-Grounds, 1986.

Mathew, B. *The Crocus*. Batsford, 1982.

Mathew, B. *The Genus Lewisia*. Christopher Helm, 1989.

Mathew, B. *Hellebores*. AGS Publications, 1989.

Mathew, B. *The Iris*. Batsford, 1981.

Smith, G. F. *et al. Primulas of Europe and America*. AGS Publications, 1984.

Smith, G. F. and Lowe, D. B. *Androsaces*. AGS Publications, 1977.

Webb, D. A. and Gornall, R. J. *Saxifrages of Europe*. Christopher Helm, 1989.

Yeo, P. *Hardy Geraniums*. Christopher Helm, 1985.

Individual countries

Grey-Wilson, C. *The Alpine Flowers of Britain and Europe*. Collins, 1979.

Huxley, A. and Taylor, W. *Flowers of Greece*. Chatto & Windus, 1977.

Huxley, A. *Mountain Flowers of Europe*. Blandford, 1986.

Mark, A. F. and Adams, N. M. *New Zealand Alpine Plants*. Reed Methuen, 1979.

Ohwi, J. *Flora of Japan*. Smithsonian Institution, 1983.

Polunin, O. *Flowers of Greece and the Balkans*. Oxford University Press, 1980.

Polunin, O. and Huxley, A. *Flowers of the Mediterranean*. Chatto & Windus, 1978.

Polunin, O. and Smythies, B. E. *Flowers of South West Europe*. Oxford University Press, 1973.

Polunin, O. and Stainton, A. *Flowers of the Himalaya*. Oxford University Press, 1984 (plus supplement 1988).

Tutin, T. G. *et al. Flora Europaea*. 5 vols. Cambridge University Press, 1964.

Index